Lecture Notes in Computer Science

Vol. 1: GI-Gesellschaft für Informatik e.V. 3. Jahrestagung, Hamburg, 8.–10. Oktober 1973. Herausgegeben im Auftrag der Gesellschaft für Informatik von W. Brauer. XI, 508 Seiten. 1973. DM 32,–

Vol. 2: GI-Gesellschaft für Informatik e.V. 1. Fachtagung über Automatentheorie und Formale Sprachen, Bonn, 9.–12. Juli 1973. Herausgegeben im Auftrag der Gesellschaft für Informatik von K.-H. Böhling und K. Indermark. VII, 322 Seiten. 1973. DM 26,–

Vol. 3: 5th Conference on Optimization Techniques, Part I. (Series: I.F.I.P. TC7 Optimization Conferences.) Edited by R. Conti and A. Ruberti. XIII, 565 pages. 1973. DM 38,–

Vol. 4: 5th Conference on Optimization Techniques, Part II. (Series: I.F.I.P. TC7 Optimization Conferences.) Edited by R. Conti and A. Ruberti. XIII, 389 pages. 1973. DM 28,–

Vol. 5: International Symposium on Theoretical Programming. Edited by A. Ershov and V. A. Nepomniaschy. VI, 407 pages. 1974. DM 30,–

Vol. 6: B. T. Smith, J. M. Boyle, B. S. Garbow, Y. Ikebe, V. C. Klema, and C. B. Moler, Matrix Eigensystem Routines – EISPACK Guide. X, 387 pages. 1974. DM 28,–

Vol. 7: 3. Fachtagung über Programmiersprachen, Kiel, 5.–7. März 1974. Herausgegeben von B. Schlender und W. Frielinghaus. VI, 225 Seiten. 1974. DM 20,–

Vol. 8: GI-NTG Fachtagung über Struktur und Betrieb von Rechensystemen, Braunschweig, 20.–22. März 1974. Herausgegeben im Auftrag der GI und der NTG von H.-O. Leilich. VI, 340 Seiten. 1974. DM 26,–

Vol. 9: GI-BIFOA Internationale Fachtagung: Informationszentren in Wirtschaft und Verwaltung. Köln, 17./18. Sept. 1973. Herausgegeben im Auftrag der GI und dem BIFOA von P. Schmitz. VI, 259 Seiten. 1974. DM 22,–

Vol. 10: Computing Methods in Applied Sciences and Engineering, Part 1. International Symposium, Versailles, December 17–21, 1973. Edited by R. Glowinski and J. L. Lions. X, 497 pages. 1974. DM 34,–

Vol. 11: Computing Methods in Applied Sciences and Engineering, Part 2. International Symposium, Versailles, December 17–21, 1973. Edited by R. Glowinski and J. L. Lions. X, 434 pages. 1974. DM 30,–

Vol. 12: GFK-GI-GMR Fachtagung Prozessrechner 1974. Karlsruhe, 10.–11. Juni 1974. Herausgegeben von G. Krüger und R. Friehmelt. XI, 620 Seiten. 1974. DM 42,–

Vol. 13: Rechnerstrukturen und Betriebsprogrammierung, Erlangen, 1970. (GI-Gesellschaft für Informatik e.V.) Herausgegeben von W. Händler und P. P. Spies. VII, 333 Seiten. 1974. DM 30,–

Vol. 14: Automata, Languages and Programming – 2nd Colloquium, University of Saarbrücken, July 29–August 2, 1974. Edited by J. Loeckx. VIII, 611 pages. 1974. DM 48,–

Vol. 15: L Systems. Edited by A. Salomaa and G. Rozenberg. VI, 338 pages. 1974. DM 30,–

Lecture Notes in Computer Science

Edited by G. Goos and J. Hartmanis

15

L Systems

Edited by Grzegorz Rozenberg and Arto Salomaa

Springer-Verlag
Berlin · Heidelberg · New York 1974

Prof. Dr. Rozenberg
Mathematisch Instituut
Rijksuniversiteit te Utrecht
Utrecht/Holland

Prof. Dr. A. Salomaa
Institute of Mathematics
University of Aarhus
Dept. of Computer Science
Ny Munkegade
8000 Aarhus/Denmark

Library of Congress Cataloging in Publication Data

Main entry under title:

L systems.

(Lecture notes in computer science, 15)
Most of the papers were presented at a conference in Aarhus, Denmark, Jan. 14-25, 1974.
Bibliography: p.
1. L systems. I. Rozenberg, Grzegorz, 1934- ed.
II. Salomaa, Arto, ed. III. Series.
QH491.L2 574'.028'5424 74-16417

AMS Subject Classifications (1970): 68A30, 92A05, 68A25, 94A30, 02F10
CR Subject Classifications (1974): 5.22, 5.23

ISBN 3-540-06867-8 Springer-Verlag Berlin · Heidelberg · New York
ISBN 0-387-06867-8 Springer-Verlag New York · Heidelberg · Berlin

Offsetdruck: Julius Beltz, Hemsbach/Bergstr.

PREFACE

Since the introduction of developmental languages in 1968 by A. Lindenmayer ("Mathematical models for cellular interactions in development", Parts I and II, Journal of Theoret.Biology, 1968, v.18, 280-315), this field, now commonly referred to as the study of L systems, has been very active. The number of people interested in this area has become larger and larger, and the yearly growth in the number of papers has so far been exponential. One reason for this widespread interest seems to be that this field is able to attract people with quite different backgrounds. For instance, automata and formal language theorists, like the present editors, have found in L systems an interesting and fruitful alternative to the ordinary Chomsky type of grammars.

From the biological point of view, L systems have provided a useful theoretical framework within which the nature of cellular behaviour in development can be discussed, computed and compared. Their study has also provided a number of biologically interesting results.

From the mathematical point of view, L systems have opened a new dimension in formal language theory. Its novelty is reflected in both new types of problems and new techniques for solving them.

For a survey of biological aspects of the theory the reader is referred to the contribution by A. Lindenmayer to the book "Developmental systems and languages" by G.T. Herman and G. Rozenberg (North Holland Publ. Company, 1974). The first paper in the present volume serves as a survey of the mathematical theory of L systems. It is hoped that the remaining ones give an idea of the current research. In this sense the above mentioned book and this volume should complement each other: the first being more tutorial and the second more research oriented.

The division of papers into sections is not intended to be too conclusive. It just provides a division line which might help the reader. As far as referencing is concerned, a common bibliography is provided at the end of the volume. The reference numbers in the individual papers refer to this bibliography.

Most of the papers in this volume were presented at a conference in Aarhus, January 14-25, 1974. The conference was the third in a series of Open House meetings arranged by the Computer

Science Department of the University of Aarhus. The topics of the first two meetings in 1972 and 1973 were: "unusual automata theory" (proceedings available from the department) and "semantics of programming languages" (no proceedings). This time the topic was L systems, and most of the people active in this area were present.

The editors express their gratitude to all the participants, as well as to Statens Naturvidenskabelige Forskningsrad in Denmark for financial support

UTRECHT, May 1974

Grzegorz Rozenberg   Arto Salomaa

CONTENTS

A SURVEY OF MATHEMATICAL THEORY OF L SYSTEMS

THEORY OF L SYSTEMS:

FROM THE POINT OF VIEW OF FORMAL LANGUAGE THEORY

by

G. Rozenberg

Institute of Mathematics, Utrecht University, Utrecht - De Uithof, Holland
and
Department of Mathematics, University of Antwerp. UIA, Wilrijk, Belgium

CONTENTS

0. INTRODUCTION

The theory of L systems originated from the work of Lindenmayer [59,60]. The original aim of this theory was to provide mathematical models for the development of simple filamentous organisms. At the beginning L systems were defined as linear arrays of finite automata, later however they were reformulated into the more suitable framework of grammar-like constructs. From then on, the theory of L systems was developed essentially as a branch of formal language theory. In fact it constitutes today one of the most vigorously investigated areas of formal language theory.

In this paper we survey the mathematical theory of L systems. As to the biological aspects of the theory we refer the reader to an excellent paper by Lindenmayer ("Developmental systems and languages in their biological context" a contribution to the book Herman and Rozenberg [45]).

This paper is organized in such a way that it discusses several typical problem areas and the results obtained therein. The results quoted here may not always be the most important ones but they are quite representative for the direction of research in this theory. It is rather unfortunate that we have no space here to discuss the basic techniques for solving problems in this theory, but information about these can be found in the listed references. As the most complete source of readings on L systems the book Herman and Rozenberg [45] is recommended to the reader.

In this paper we assume the reader to be familiar with basic formal language theory, e.q. with the scope of the book "Formal Languages and their relation to automata" by J. Hopcroft and J. Ullman, Addison-Wesley, 1969. We shall also freely use standard formal language notation and terminology. (Perhaps the only unusual term used in this paper is "coding" which means a letter-to-letter homomorphism).

We also want to remark that this survey is of informal character, meaning that quite often concepts are introduced in a not entirely rigorous manner, and results are presented in a descriptive way rather than in a form of very precise mathematical statements. This was dictated by both the limited size of the paper and by the profile of its experted reader. We hope that this does not decrease the usefulness of this paper.

Finally, I would like to state that this survey is by no means exhaustive and the selection of topics and results presented reflects my personal point of view.

1. L SCHEMES AND L SYSTEMS

In this section we give definitions and examples of basic objects (the so called L schemes and L systems) to be discussed in this paper. We start with the most general class, the so called TIL schemes and TIL systems. (They were introduced in K.P. Lee and G. Rozenberg "TIL systems and languages" [submitted for publication]). TIL systems are intended to model the development of multicellular filamentous organisms in the case when an interaction can take place among the cells and the environment can be subject to changes.

Definition 1.1. Let $k,l \in N$. An L scheme with tables and with $< k,l >$ interactions (abbreviated $T < k,l > L$ scheme) is a construct $S = < \Sigma, \mathcal{P}, g >$ where Σ is a finite nonempty set (the alphabet of S), g is a symbol which is not in Σ (the masker of S), $\mathcal{P}$ is a finite nonempty set, each dement P of which (called a table of S) is a finite nonempty relation satisfying the following:

$$P \subseteq \bigcup_{\substack{i,j,m,n \geqslant 0 \\ i+j = k \\ m+n = l}} \{g^i\}\Sigma^j \times \Sigma \times \Sigma^m\{g^n\} \times \Sigma^*$$

and for every $< \alpha, a, \beta >$ in $\bigcup_{\substack{i,j,m,n \geqslant 0 \\ i+j = k \\ m+n = l}} \{g^i\}\Sigma^j \times \Sigma \times \Sigma^m\{g^n\}$ there exists a γ in Σ^* such that $< \alpha, a, \beta, \gamma > \in P$.

(Each element of P is called a production).

Definition 1.2. Let $S = < \Sigma, \mathcal{P}, g >$ be a $T < k,l > L$ scheme. We say that S is:

1) an L scheme with $< k,l >$ interactions (abbreviated $< k,l > L$ scheme) if $\# \mathcal{P} = 1$.

2) an L scheme with tables and without interactions (abbreviated TOL scheme) if $k = l = 0$.

3) an L scheme without interactions (abbreviated OL scheme) if both $\# \mathcal{P} = 1$ and $k = l = 0$.

Definition 1.3. A construct $S = < \Sigma, \mathcal{P}, g >$ is called a TIL scheme (IL scheme) if, for some $k,l \in N$, S is a $T < k,l > L$ scheme ($< k,l > L$ scheme).

Definition 1.4. Let $S = < \Sigma, \mathcal{P}, g >$ be a $T < k,l > L$ scheme. Let $x = a_1 \dots a_n \in \Sigma^*$, with $a_1, \dots, a_n \in \Sigma$, and let $y \in \Sigma^*$. We say that x directly derives y in S (denoted as $x \underset{S}{\Longrightarrow} y$) if $y = \gamma_1 \dots \gamma_n$ for some $\gamma_1, \dots, \gamma_n$ in Σ^* such that, there exists a table P in Σ and for every i in $\{1,\dots,n\}$ P contains a production of the form $< \alpha_i, a_i, \beta_i, \gamma_i >$ where α_i is the prefix of $g^k a_1 \dots a_{i-1}$ of length k and β_i is the suffix of $a_{i+1} \dots a_n g^l$ of length l. The transitive and reflexive closure of the relation $\underset{S}{\Longrightarrow}$ is denoted as $\overset{*}{\underset{S}{\Longrightarrow}}$ (when $x \overset{*}{\underset{S}{\Longrightarrow}} y$ then we say that x derives y in S).

Definition 1.5. A TIL system (IL system) is an ordered pair $G = < S, \omega >$ where S is a TIL scheme (an IL scheme) and ω is a word over the alphabet of S. The scheme S is called the underlying scheme of G and is denoted as S(G). G is called a $T < k,l > L$ system (a $< k,l > L$ system, a T0L system, a 0L system) if S(G) is a $T < k,l > L$ scheme (a $< k,l > L$ scheme, a T0L scheme, a 0L scheme).

IL systems in restricted form originated from Lindenmayer [59,60]; in the form they are discussed here they were introduced in Rozenberg [86,87]. T0L systems were introduced in Rozenberg [81] and 0L systems were introduced in Lindenmayer [61] and Rozenberg and Doucet [91].

Definition 1.6. Let $G = < S, \omega >$ be a TIL system. Let $x,y \in \Sigma^*$. We say that x directly derives y in G, denoted as $x \underset{G}{\Longrightarrow} y$ (x derives y in G denoted as $x \overset{*}{\underset{G}{\Longrightarrow}} y$) if $x \underset{S}{\Longrightarrow} y$ ($x \overset{*}{\underset{S}{\Longrightarrow}} y$).

Notation. It is customary to omit the marker g from the specification of a T0L system. If S is an IL or a 0L scheme (system) such that $\#\mathcal{P} = 1$, say $\mathcal{P} = \{P\}$, then in the specification of S we put P rather than $\{P\}$. Also to avoid cumbersome notation in specifying a TIL system G we simply extend the n-tuple specifying S(G) to an (n+1)-tuple where the last element is the axiom of G. (In this sense we write, e.g., $G = < \Sigma, \mathcal{P}, g, \omega >$ rather than $G = \ll \Sigma, \mathcal{P}, g >, \omega >$). In specifying productions in a table of a given TIL systems one often omits those which clearly cannot be used in any rewriting process which starts with the axiom of the system. If $< \alpha, a, \beta, \gamma >$ is a production in a TIL scheme (system) then it is usually written in the form $< \alpha, a, \beta > \rightarrow \gamma$ (where $< \alpha, a, \beta >$ is called its left-hand side and γ is called its right-hand side). When the productions of a TOL scheme (system) are being specified, then we write $a \to \gamma$ rather than $< \Lambda, a, \Lambda > \to \gamma$.

Example 1.1. Let $\Sigma = \{a,b\}$, $P_1 = \{< g,a,\Lambda > \to a^3, < a,a,\Lambda > \to a, < a,b,\Lambda > \to b^2, < b,b,\Lambda > \to b^2, < b,a,\Lambda > \to a\}$, $P_2 = \{< g,a,\Lambda > \to a^4, < a,a,\Lambda > \to a, < a,b,\Lambda > \to b^3, < b,b,\Lambda > \to b^3, < b,a,\Lambda > \to a\}$ and $\omega = a^5 b^6 a$. Then $G = < \Sigma, \{P_1, P_2\}, g, \omega >$ is a $T < 1,0 > L$ system.

Example 1.2. Let $\Sigma = \{a,b\}$, $P = \{< a,a,\Lambda > \to a^2, < b,a,\Lambda > \to a^2, < g,a,\Lambda > \to a, < a,b,\Lambda > \to b^2, < b,b,\Lambda > \to b^2, < g,b,\Lambda > \to b^2, < g,b,\Lambda > \to ab^2\}$ and $\omega = ba$. Then $G = < \Sigma, P, g, \omega >$ is a $< 1,0 > L$ system.

Example 1.3. Let $\Sigma = \{a,b\}$, $P_1 = \{a \to a^2, b \to b^2\}$, $P_2 = \{a \to a^3, b \to b^3\}$ and $\omega = ab$. Then $G = < \Sigma, \{P_1, P_2\}, \omega >$ is a TOL system.

Example 1.4. Let $\Sigma = \{A, \bar{A}, a, B, \bar{B}, b, C, \bar{C}, c, F\}$, $P = \{A \to A\bar{A}, A \to a, B \to B\bar{B}, B \to b, C \to C\bar{C}, C \to c, \bar{A} \to \bar{A}, \bar{A} \to a, \bar{B} \to \bar{B}, \bar{B} \to b, \bar{C} \to \bar{C}, \bar{C} \to c, a \to F, b \to F, c \to F, F \to F\}$ and $\omega = ABC$. Then $G = < \Sigma, P, \omega >$ is a OL system.

2. SQUEEZING LANGUAGES OUT OF L SYSTEMS

There are several ways that one can associate the language with a given word-generating device. In this section we shall discuss several ways of defining languages by L systems.

2.1. Exhaustive approach.

Given an L system G (with alphabet Σ and axiom ω) it is most natural to define its language, denoted L(G), as the set of all words (axiom included) that can be derived from ω in G; hence $L(G) = \{x \in \Sigma^* : \omega \overset{*}{\underset{G}{\Rightarrow}} x\}$.

Example 2.1.1. The language of a $T < 1,0 > L$ system G from Example 1.1 is $\{a^{2n+3m} b^{2^n 3^m} a : n,m \geq 1\}$. The language of a TOL system from Example 1.3 is $\{a^{2^n 3^m} b^{2^n 3^m} : n,m \geq 0\}$.

The languages obtained in this way from OL, TOL, TIL and IL systems are called OL, TOL, TIL and IL languages respectively. (Their classes will be denoted by $\mathcal{L}(OL)$, $\mathcal{L}(TOL)$, $\mathcal{L}(TIL)$ and $\mathcal{L}(IL)$ respectively). For $k,l \geq 0$, a $< k,l > L$ language (a $T < k,l > L$ language) is a language generated by a $< k,l > L$ system (a $T < k,l > L$ system).

One may notice here two major differences in generating languages by

0L and IL systems on the one hand and context-free and type 0 grammars on the other. 0L and IL systems do not use nonterminal symbols while context-free and type-0 grammars use them. Rewriting in 0L and IL systems is absolutely parallel (all occurrences of all letters in a word are rewritten in a single derivation step) while rewriting in context-free and type-0 grammars is absolutely sequential (only one occurrence of one symbol is rewritten in a single derivation step).

2.2. Using nonterminals to define languages.

The standard step in formal language theory to define the language of a generating system is to consider not the set of all words generated by it but only those which are over some distinguished (usually called terminal) alphabet. In this way one gets the division of the alphabet of a given system into the set of terminal and nonterminal (sometimes also called auxiliary) symbols. In the case of L systems such an approach gives rise to the following classes of systems.

Definition 2.2.1. An *extended 0L*, (*T0L*, *IL*, *TIL*) *system*, abbreviated E0L (ET0L, EIL, ETIL) system, is a pair $G = \langle H, \Delta \rangle$, where H is a 0L (T0L, IL, TIL) system and Δ is an alphabet (called the *target alphabet of G*).

Definition 2.2.2. The *language* of an E0L (ET0L, EIL, ETIL) system $G = \langle H, \Delta \rangle$, denoted as L(G), is defined by $L(G) = L(H) \cap \Delta^*$.

An E0L (ET0L, EIL, ETIL) system $G = \langle H, \Delta \rangle$ is usually specified as $\langle \Sigma, P, \omega, \Delta \rangle$ ($\langle \Sigma, \mathcal{P}, \omega, \Delta \rangle$, $\langle \Sigma, P, g, \omega, \Delta \rangle$, $\langle \Sigma, \mathcal{P}, g, \omega, \Delta \rangle$) where $\langle \Sigma, P, \omega \rangle$($\langle \Sigma, \mathcal{P}, \omega \rangle$, $\langle \Sigma, P, g, \omega \rangle$, $\langle \Sigma, \mathcal{P}, g, \omega \rangle$) is the specification of H itself.

Example 2.2.1. Let $G = \langle \Sigma, P, \omega, \Delta \rangle$, where Σ, P, ω are specified as in Example 1.4 and $\Delta = \{a,b\}$. Then $L(G) = \{a^n b^n c^n : n \geq 1\}$.

If K is the language of an E0L (ET0L, EIL, ETIL) system, then it is called an *E0L* (*ET0L*, *EIL*, *ETIL*) language. The classes of E0L languages, ET0L languages, EIL languages and ETIL languages are denoted by $\mathcal{L}$(E0L), $\mathcal{L}$(ET0L), $\mathcal{L}$(EIL) and $\mathcal{L}$(ETIL) respectively.

E0L systems and languages are discussed in Herman [35]; ET0L systems and languages were introduced in Rozenberg [89]; EIL systems and languages are discussed e.g. in van Dalen [12] and Rozenberg [86,87]; ETIL systems and languages were introduced in "TIL systems and languages" by

K.P. Lee and G. Rozenberg.

It is very instructive at this point to notice that, as far as generation of languages is concerned, the difference between E0L and EIL systems on one hand and context-free and type-0 grammars on the other hand is the absolutely parallel fashion of rewriting in E0L and EIL systems and the absolutely sequential fashion of rewriting in context-free and type-0 grammars.

2.3. Using codings to define languages.

When we make observations of a particular organism and want to describe it by strings of symbols, we first associate a symbol to each particular cell. This is done by dividing cells into a number of types and associating the same symbol to all the cells of the same type. It is possible that the development of the organism can be described by a developmental system, but the actual system describing it uses a finer subdivision into types that we could observe. This is often experimentally unavoidable. In this case, the set of strings generated by a given developmental system is a coding of the "real" language of the organism which the given developmental system describes. Considering codings for defining languages of L systems gives rise to the following classes of systems.

Definition 2.3.1. A 0L (T0L, IL, TIL) system with coding, abbreviated C0L (CT0L, CIL, CTIL) system, is a pair $G = \langle H,h \rangle$, where H is a 0L (T0L, IL, TIL) system and h is a coding.

Definition 2.3.2. The language of a C0L (CT0L, CIL, CTIL) system $G = \langle H,h \rangle$, denoted as L(G), is defined by $L(G) = h(L(H))$.

Example 2.3.1. Let $H = \langle \{a,b\},\{a \to a^2, b \to b\}, ba \rangle$ and h be a coding from {a,b} into {a,b} such that $h(a) = h(b) = a$. Then $L(\langle H,h \rangle) = \{a^{2^{n+1}} : n \geq 0\}$.

If K is the language of a C0L (CT0L, CIL, CTIL) system, then it is called a C0L (CT0L, CIL, CTIL) language. The classes of C0L, CT0L, CIL and CTIL languages are denoted by $\mathcal{L}$(C0L), $\mathcal{L}$CT0L), $\mathcal{L}$(CIL) and $\mathcal{L}$(CTIL) respectively.

Using codings to define languages of various classes of L systems was considered, e.g., in Culik and Opatrny [10], Ehrenfeucht and

Rozenberg [20,25,27] and Nielsen, Rozenberg, Salomaa, Skyum [71,72].

2.4. Adult languages of L systems.

An interesting way of defining languages by L systems was proposed by A. Walker (see [47] and [118]). Based on biological considerations concerning problems of regulation in organisms, one defines the adult language of an L system G, denoted as A(G), to be the set of all these words from L(G) which derive (in G) themselves and only themselves. Thus we can talk about adult 0L languages, adult T0L languages, adult IL languages and adult TIL languages (their families are denoted by symbols $\mathcal{L}_A(0L)$, $\mathcal{L}_A(T0L)$, $\mathcal{L}_A(IL)$ and $\mathcal{L}_A(TIL)$ respectively).

Example 2.4.1. Let $G = \langle \Sigma, P, \omega \rangle$ be a 0L system such that $\Sigma = \{a,b\}$, $P = \{a \to \Lambda, a \to ab, b \to b\}$ and $\omega = a$. Then $A(G) = \{b^n : n \geqslant 0\}$.

In the sequel we shall use the term L language to refer to any one of the types of language introduced in this section.

2.5. Comparing the language generating power of various mechanisms for defining L languages.

Once several classes of language generating devices are introduced one is interested in comparing their language generating power. This is one of the most natural and most traditional topics investigated in formal language theory. In the case of L systems we have, for example, the following results.

Theorem 2.5.1. (see, e.g., Herman and Rozenberg [45]).

1) For X in {0L, T0L, IL, TIL}, $\mathcal{L}(X) \subsetneq \mathcal{L}(EX)$.
2) For X in {0L, T0L, IL, TIL}, $\mathcal{L}(X) \subsetneq \mathcal{L}(CX)$.
3) $\mathcal{L}(0L)$ is incomparable but not disjoint with $\mathcal{L}_A(0L)$.

Theorem 2.5.2. (Ehrenfeucht and Rozenberg [20,27], Herman and Walker [(47]).

1) $\mathcal{L}(E0L) = \mathcal{L}(C0L)$ and $\mathcal{L}(ET0L) = \mathcal{L}(CT0L)$.
2) $\mathcal{L}_A(0L) \subsetneq \mathcal{L}(E0L)$.

3. FITTING CLASSES OF L LANGUAGES INTO KNOWN FORMAL LANGUAGE THEORETIC FRAMEWORK

The usual way of understanding the language generating power of a class of generative systems is by comparing them with the now classical Chomsky hierarchy. (One reason for this is that the Chomsky hierarchy is probably the most intensively studied in formal language theory.) In the area of L languages we have, for example, the following result. (In what follows $\mathcal{L}$(RE) denotes the class of recursively enumerable languages, $\mathcal{L}$(CS) denotes the class consisting of every L such that either L or L-{Λ} is a context-sensitive language, and $\mathcal{L}$(CF) denotes the class of context-free languages.)

Theorem 3.1. (van Dalen [12], Rozenberg [89], Herman [35]).
$\mathcal{L}(EIL) = \mathcal{L}(RE)$, $\mathcal{L}(ET0L) \subsetneq \mathcal{L}(CS)$ and $\mathcal{L}(CF) \subsetneq \mathcal{L}(E0L)$.

Note that this theorem compares classes of systems all of which use nonterminals for defining languages. Thus the only real difference (from the language generation point of view) between (the classes of) EIL, ET0L and E0L systems on the one hand and (the classes of) type-0, context-sensitive and context-free grammars respectively on the other hand is the parallel versus sequential way of rewriting strings. In this sense the above results tell us something about the role of parallel rewriting in generating languages by grammar-like devices. In the same direction we have another group of results of which the following two are quite representative.

Theorem 3.2. (Lindenmayer [61], Rozenberg and Doucet [91]).
A language is context-free if and only if it is the language of an E0L system $< \Sigma, P, \omega, \Delta >$ such that, for each a in Δ, the production $a \rightarrow a$ is in P.

Theorem 3.3. (Herman and Walker [47]).
A language is context-free if and only if it is the adult language of a 0L system.

As far as fitting some classes of L languages into the known formal language theoretic framework is concerned, results more detailed than those of Theorem 3.1 are available. For example we have the following results. Let $\mathcal{L}$(IND) denote the class of indexed languages (see A. Aho "Indexed grammars - An extension of context-free grammars" J. of the ACM. 15 (1968), 647-671) and let $\mathcal{L}$(PROG) denote the class of Λ-free programmed languages (see D. Rosenkrantz "Programmed grammars and classes of formal languages" J. of the ACM. 16 (1969), 107-131).

<u>Theorem 3.4.</u> (Culik [7] and Rozenberg [89]).
$\mathcal{L}(\mathrm{ETOL}) \subsetneq \mathcal{L}(\mathrm{IND})$ and $\mathcal{L}(\mathrm{ETOL}) \subsetneq \mathcal{L}(\mathrm{PROG})$.

Results like these can be helpful for getting either new properties or nice proofs of known properties of some classes of L languages. For example, the family $\mathcal{L}(\mathrm{IND})$ possesses quite strong decidability properties which are then directly applicable to the class of ETOL languages. An example will be considered in section 8.

4. OTHER CHARACTERIZATIONS OF CLASSES OF L LANGUAGES WITHIN THE FRAMEWORK OF FORMAL LANGUAGE THEORY

A classical step toward achieving a mathematical characterization of a class of languages is to investigate its closure properties with respect to a number of operations. There is even a trend in formal language theory, called the AFL theory (see S. Ginsburg, S. Greibach and J. Hopcroft "Studies in Abstract Families of Languages", Memoirs of the AMS, 87, (1969)) which takes this as a basic step towards characterizing classes of languages. The next two results display the behaviour of some of the families of L languages with respect to the basic operations considered in AFL theory. There are essentially two reasons for considering these operations. One reason is that in this way we may better contrast various families of L languages with traditional families of languages. The other reason is that we still know very little about what set of operations would be natural for families of L languages. (In what follows the symbols $\cup, \cdot, *, \mathrm{hom}, \mathrm{hom}^{-1}, \cap_R$ denote the operations of union, product, Kleene's closure, homomorphism, inverse homomorphism and intersection with a regular language respectively.)

<u>Theorem 4.1.</u> (Rozenberg and Doucet [91], Rozenberg [81], Rozenberg [86], Rozenberg and Lee "TIL systems and languages")
None of the families of OL, TOL, IL, TIL languages is closed with respect to any of the following operations: $\cup, \cdot, *, \mathrm{hom}, \mathrm{hom}^{-1}, \cap_R$.

<u>Theorem 4.2.</u> (Rozenberg [89], van Dalen [2], Herman [35])
The families of ETOL and EIL languages are closed with respect to all of the operations $\cup, \cdot, *, \mathrm{hom}, \mathrm{hom}^{-1}, \cap_R$. The family of EOL languages is closed with respect to the operations $\cup, \cdot, *, \mathrm{hom}$ and $\cap_R$ but it is not closed with respect to the hom^{-1} operation.

When we contrast the above two results with each other we see the role of nonterminals in defining languages of L systems. On the other hand contrasting the second result with the corresponding results for the classes of context-free and context-sensitive languages enables us to learn more about the nature of parallel rewriting in language generating systems.

In formal language theory, when a class of generative devices for defining languages is given, one often looks for a class of acceptors (recognition devices) which would yield the same family of languages. Such a step usually provides us with a better insight into the structure of the given family of languages and (sometimes) it provides us with additional tools for proving theorems about the given family of languages.

Several machine models for L systems are already available, see Culik and Opatrny [9], van Leeuwen [55], Rozenberg [90], Savitch [108]. (Of these, the most general models are those presented by Savitch).

As an example, we discuss now the notion of a pre-set pushdown automaton introduced in van Leeuwen [55]. Roughly speaking a pre-set pushdown automaton is like an ordinary pushdown automaton, except that at the very beginning of a computation a certain location on the pushdown store of the automaton is assigned as the maximum location to which the store may grow during the computation. Such a distinguished location is used in such a way that when the automaton has reached it then it switches to a different transition function. When a pre-set pushdown automaton is constructed in such a way that there is a fixed bound on the length of a local computation (meaning a computation that the pointer does not move) then we call it a <u>locally finite pre-set pushdown</u> automaton. We say that a pre-set pushdown automaton has a <u>finite return property</u> if there is a fixed bound on the number of recursions that can occur from a location.

<u>Theorem 4.3.</u> (van Leeuwen [55,56], Christensen [6])
The family of languages accepted by pre-set pushdown automata contains properly the family of E0L languages and is properly contained in the family of ET0L languages.

<u>Theorem 4.4.</u> (van Leeuwen [55])
The family of languages accepted by locally finite pre-set pushdown automata with the finite return property equals the family of E0L languages.

5. SQUEEZING SEQUENCES OUT OF L SYSTEMS.

From a biological point of view the time-order of development is at least as interesting as the unordered set of morphological patterns which may develop. This leads to investigation of sequences of words rather than unordered sets of words (languages), which is a novel point in formal language theory. It turned out that investigation of sequences (of words) gives rise to a non-trivial and interesting mathematical theory (see, e.g., Herman and Rozenberg [45], Paz [74], Paz and Salomaa [75], Rozenberg [82], Szilard [111], Vitanyi [116]).

The most natural way to talk about word sequences in the context of L systems is to consider such L systems which (starting with the axiom) yield the unique next word for a given one. We define now one such class of such L systems.

Definition 5.1. An IL system $G = \langle \Sigma, P, g, \omega \rangle$ is called deterministic (abbreviated DIL system) if whenever $\langle \alpha, a, \beta, \gamma_1 \rangle$ and $\langle \alpha, a, \beta, \gamma_2 \rangle$ are in P then $\gamma_1 = \gamma_2$.

Note that a 0L system is a particular instance of an IL system. Hence we shall talk about D0L systems. The most natural way to define sequences by DIL systems is to take the exhaustive approach, which simply means to include in the sequence of a DIL system the set of all words that the system generates (and in the order that these words are generated).

Definition 5.2. Let $G = \langle \Sigma, P, g, \omega \rangle$ be a DIL system. The sequence of G, denoted as E(G), is defined by $E(G) = \omega_0, \omega_1, \ldots$ where $\omega_0 = \omega$ and for $i \geq 1$, $\omega_{i-1} \underset{G}{\Longrightarrow} \omega_i$.

Example 5.1. Let $G = \langle \Sigma, P, g, \omega \rangle$ be a DIL system such that $\Sigma = \{a,b\}$, $\omega = baba^2$ and $P = \{\langle g,b,\Lambda \rangle \to ba, \langle a,b,\Lambda \rangle \to ba^2, \langle a,a,\Lambda \rangle \to a, \langle b,a,\Lambda \rangle \to a\}$. Then $E(G) = baba^2, ba^2ba^4, \ldots, ba^kba^{2k}, \ldots$.

Definition 5.3. Let s be a sequence of words. It is called a DIL sequence (D0L sequence) if there exists a DIL system (D0L system) G such that s = E(G).

Obviously as in the case of L languages (see section 2) one can apply various mechanisms of squeezing sequences out of DIL systems. Thus, in the obvious sense, we can talk about EDIL and ED0L sequences (when using nonterminals for defining sequences) or about CDIL and CD0L sequences (when using codings for defining sequences). Comparing the sequence generative power of these different mechanisms for sequence definition, we have, for example, the following result.

Theorem 5.1. (Nielsen, Rozenberg, Salomaa, Skyum [71,72])
The family of DOL sequences is strictly included in the family of EDOL sequences, which in turn is strictly included in the family of CDOL sequences.

In the sequel we shall use the term L sequence to refer to any kind of a sequence discussed in this section.

6. GROWTH FUNCTIONS; AN EXAMPLE OF RESEARCH ON (CLASSES OF)L SEQUENCES

As an example of an investigation of properties of L sequences and their classes we will discuss the so called growth functions. It happens quite often(in both mathematical and biological considerations) that one is interested only in the lengths of the words generated by an L system. When the system G under a consideration is deterministic then, in this way, one obtains a function assigning to each positive integer n the length of the n'th word in the sequence of G. This function is called the growth function of G. The theory of growth functions of deterministic L systems is one of the very vigorously (and succesfully) investigated areas of L system theory (see, e.g., Doucet [15], Paz and Salomaa [75], Salomaa [98], Vitanyi [116]). It also lends itself to the application of quite powerful mathematical tools (such as difference equations and formal power series).

Definition 6.1. Let G be a DIL system with $E(G) = \omega_0, \omega_1, \ldots$. The growth function of G, denoted as f_G, is a function from nonnegative integers into nonnegative integers such that $f_G(n) = |\omega_n|$.

Example 6.1. Let $G = \langle \{a,b\}, \{a \to b, b \to ab\}, a \rangle$ be a DOL system. Then $f_G(n)$ is the n'th element of the Fibonacci sequence 1,1,2,3,5,... .

Example 6.2. Let $G = \langle \{a,b,c,d\}, \{a \to abd^6, b \to bcd^{11}, c \to cd^6, d \to d\}, a \rangle$ be a DOL system. Then $f_G(n) = (n+1)^3$.

Directly from the definition of an L system we have the following result.

Theorem 6.1.
The growth function of a DIL system G such that L(G) is infinite is at most exponential and at least logarithmic.

The following are typical examples of problems concerning growth

functions.
Analysis problem: Given a DIL system, determine its growth function.
Synthesis problem: Given a function f from nonnegative integers into nonnegative integers, determine if possible a system G belonging to a given class of systems (say, DOL systems) such that $f = f_G$.
Growth equivalence problem: Given two DIL systems, determine whether their growth functions are the same.

In the following there are some typical results about growth functions.

Theorem 5.2. (Paz and Salomaa [75])
If G is a DOL system then f_G is exponential, polynomial or a combination of these.

Theorem 5.3. (Paz and Salomaa [75])
If f is a function from the nonnegative integers into the nonnegative integers such that
(i) For every n there exists an m such that
$f(m) = f(m+1) = \dots = f(m+n)$, and
(ii) $\lim_{t\to\infty} f(t) = \infty$,
then f is not the growth function of a DOL system.

7. STRUCTURAL CONSTRAINTS ON L SYSTEMS

One of the possible ways of investigating the structure of any language (or sequence) generating device is to put particular restrictions directly on the definition of its various components and then to investigate the effect of these restrictions on the language generating power. Theorem 2.5.1 represents a result in this direction (it says for example that removing nonterminals from ETIL, EIL, ETOL or EOL systems decreases the language generating power of these classes of systems). Now we indicate some other results among the same line.

The first of these results investigates the role of erasing productions in generating languages (sequences) by the class of EOL (EDOL) systems. (A production $\langle \alpha, a, \beta \rangle \to \gamma$ is called an erasing production if $\gamma = \Lambda$).

Theorem 7.1. (Herman [39])
A language K is an EOL language if and only if there exists an EOL system G which does not contain erasing productions such that $K - \{\Lambda\} = L(G)$.

<u>Theorem 7.2.</u>
There exists an EDOL sequence which does not contain Λ, and which cannot be generated by an EDOL system without erasing productions.

Our next result discusses the need of "two-sided context" (more intuitively: "two-sided communication") in IL systems.

<u>Theorem 7.3.</u> (Rozenberg [86])
There exists a language K such that K is a $< 1,1 >$ L language and for no $m \geq 0$ is K an $< m,0 >$ L language or a $< 0,m >$ L language.

Our last sample result in this line says that for the class of IL systems with two-sided context it is the amount of context available and not its distribution that matters as far as the language generating power is concerned.

<u>Theorem 7.4.</u> (Rozenberg [86])
A language is an $< m,n >$ L language for some $m,n \geq 1$ if and only if it is a $< 1,m+n-1 >$ L language. For each $m \geq 1$ there exists a $< 1,m+1 >$ L Language which is not a $< 1,m >$ L language.

8. DECISION PROBLEMS

Considering decision problems for language generating devices is a customary research topic in formal language theory. It helps to understand the "effectiveness" of various classes of language generating devices, explores the possibilities of changing one way of describing a language into another one, and, in connection with this, it may be a guide line for a choice of one rather than another class of specifications of languages. (For example it is quite often the case that when a membership problem for a given class of language defining devices turns out to be undicidable, one looks for a subclass for which this problem would be decidable). Various decision problems are also considered in the theory of L systems. In addition to more or less traditional problems considered usually in formal language theory new problems concerning sequences are also considered.

Some results concerning decision problems are obtained as direct corollaries of theorems fitting different classes of L languages into known hierarchies of languages. For example, as an application of Theorem 3.4 we have the following result.

<u>Theorem 8.1.</u>
Membership, emptiness and finiteness problems are decidable in the class of ETOL systems.

The following result by Blattner (for different solutions see also Salomaa [99] and Rozenberg [84]) solved a problem which was open for some time.

Theorem 8.2. (Blattner [6])
The language equivalence problem is not decidable in the class of 0L systems.

The corresponding problem for the class of D0L systems is one of the most intriguing and the longest open problems in the theory of L systems. Some results are however available about subclasses of the class of D0L systems.

Theorem 8.3. (Ehrenfeucht and Rozenberg)
If G_1, G_2 are D0L systems such that f_{G_1} and f_{G_2} are bounded by a polynomial (which is decidable) then it is decidable whether they generate the same language (sequence).

The following result points out "undecidability" of various extensions of the class of 0L systems. (In what follows an F0L system denotes a system which is like a 0L system, except that it has a finite number of axioms rather than a single one).

Theorem 8.4. (Rozenberg)
It is undecidable whether an arbitrary IL (C0L, E0L, F0L) system generates a 0L language.

For L sequences we have for example the following results.

Theorem 8.5. (Paz and Salomaa [75] , Vitanyi [115])
The growth equivalence problem is decidable in the class of D0L systems but it is not decidable in the class of DIL systems.

Theorem 8.6. (Salomaa [98] , Vitanyi [115,116])
Given an arbitrary D0L system G it is decidable whether f_G can be bounded by a polynomial. This problem is not decidable if G is an arbitrary DIL system.

Theorem 8.7. (Nielsen [70])
The language equivalence problem for D0L systems is decidable if and only if the sequence equivalence problem for D0L systems is decidable.

Theorem 8.8. (Ehrenfeucht, Lee and Rozenberg)
If G_1, G_2 are two arbitrary D0L systems and x is a word then it is decidable whether x occurs as a subword the same number of times in the

corresponding words of sequences generated by G_1 and G_2.

9. GLOBAL VERSUS LOCAL BEHAVIOUR OF L SYSTEMS

The topic discussed in this chapter, global versus local behaviour of L systems, is undoubtedly one of the most important in the theory of L systems. Roughly speaking, a global property of an L system is a property which can be expressed independently of the system itself (for example a property expressed in terms of its language or sequence). On the other hand a local property of an L system is a property of its set of productions (for example a property of the "graph" of productions of a given system). In a sense the whole theory of L systems emerged from an effort to explain on the local (cellular) level global properties of development.

As an example of research in this direction we discuss the so called locally catenative L systems and sequences (see Rozenberg and Lindenmayer [95]). Locally catenative L sequences are examples of L sequences in which the words themselves carry in some sense the history of their development.

Definition 9.1. An infinite sequence of words $\tau_0, \tau_1, \dots$ is called locally catentative if there exist positive integers $m, n, i_1, \dots, i_n$ with $n \geqslant 2$ such that for each $j \geqslant m$ we have $\tau_j = \tau_{j-i_1}\tau_{j-i_2}\dots\tau_{j-i_n}$.

Definition 9.2. A DIL (or a DOL) system G is called locally catenative if E(G) is locally catenative.

Very little is known about locally catenative DIL sequences. For locally catenative DOL sequences some interesting results are available. Our first result presents a property of a DOL sequence which is equivalent to the locally catenative property.

Let G be a DOL system such that $E(G) = \omega_0, \omega_1, \dots$ is a doubly infinite sequence, meaning that the set of different words occurring in E(G) is infinite. We say that E(G) is covered by one of its words if there exist $k \geqslant 0$ and $j \geqslant k+2$ and a sequence s of occurrences of ω_k in (some of the) strings $\omega_{k+1}, \omega_{k+2}, \dots, \omega_{j-1}$ such that ω_j is the catenation of the sequence of its subwords derived from respective elements of s.

Theorem 9.1. (Rozenberg and Lindenmayer [95])
A DOL system G is locally catenative if and only if E(G) is covered by one of its words.

Our next theorem presents the result of an attempt to find a "structural" property of the set of productions of a DOL system such that its sequence is locally catenative. First we need some more notation and terminology.

If $G = \langle \Sigma, P, \omega \rangle$ is a DOL system then the graph of G is the directed graph whose nodes are elements of Σ and for which a directed edge leads from the node a to the node b if and only if $a \to \alpha b \beta$ is in P for some words α, β over Σ.

Theorem 9.2. (Rozenberg and Lindenmayer [95])
Let $G = \langle \Sigma, P, \omega \rangle$ be a DOL system without erasing productions such that both E(G) and L(G) are infinite, ω is in Σ and each letter from Σ occurs in a word in E(G). If there exists σ in Σ such that $\omega \overset{*}{\underset{G}{\Longrightarrow}} \sigma$ and each cycle in the graph of G goes through the node σ then E(G) is locally catenative.

We may note that neither of the above results is true in the case of DIL sequences (systems).

10. DETERMINISTIC VERSUS NONDETERMINISTIC BEHAVIOUR OF L SYSTEMS

An L system is called deterministic if, roughly speaking, after one of its tables has been chosen, each word can be rewritten in exactly one way. Investigation of the role the deterministic restriction plays in L systems is an important and quite extensively studied topic in the theory of L systems (see, e.g., Doucet [14], Ehrenfeucht and Rozenberg [17], Lee and Rozenberg [52], Nielsen [70], Paz and Salomaa [75], Rozenberg [82], Salomaa [98], Szilard [111]). First of all, some biologists claim that only deterministic behaviour should be studied. Secondly, studying deterministic L systems, especially when opposed to general (undeterministic) L systems, allows us to better understand the structure of L systems. Finally, the notion of determinism studied in this theory differs from the usual one studied in formal language theory. One may say that they are dual to each other: "deterministic" in L systems means a deterministic process of generating strings, "deterministic" in the sense used in formal language theory means a deterministic process of parsing. Contrasting these notions may help us to understand some of the basic phenomena of formal language theory.

Definition 10.1. A TIL system $G = \langle \Sigma, \mathcal{P}, g, \omega \rangle$ is called deterministic (abbreviated DTIL system) if for each table P of $\mathcal{P}$ if $\langle \alpha, a, \beta \rangle \to \gamma_1$ and $\langle \alpha, a, \beta \rangle \to \gamma_2$ are in P then $\gamma_1 = \gamma_2$.

A TOL system is a special instance of a TIL system hence we talk about DTOL systems.

As an example of a research towards understanding deterministic restriction in L systems we shall discuss deterministic T0L systems.

It is not difficult to construct examples of languages which can be generated by a T0L system but cannot be generated by a DT0L system. One would like however to find a nontrivial (and hopefully interesting) property which would be inherent to the class of deterministic T0L languages. It turns out that observing the sets of all subwords generated by DT0L systems provides us with such a property. In fact the ability to generate an arbitrary number of subwords of an arbitrary length is a property of a T0L system which disappears when the deterministic restriction is introduced. More precisely, we have the following result. (In what follows $\pi_k(L)$ denotes the number of subwords of length k that occur in the words of L).

<u>Theorem 10.1.</u> (Ehrenfeucht and Rozenberg [17])
Let Σ be a finite alphabet such that $\#\Sigma = n \geqslant 2$. If L is a language generated by a DT0L system, $L \subseteq \Sigma^*$, then $\lim_{k\to\infty} \frac{\pi_k(L)}{n^k} = 0$.

Various ramifications of this result are discussed in Ehrenfeucht, Lee and Rozenberg [18].

11. L TRANSFORMATIONS

An L system consists of an L scheme and of a fixed word (the axiom). An L scheme by itself represents a transformation (a mapping) from Σ^+ into Σ^* (where Σ is the alphabet of the L scheme). From the mathematical point of view, it is the most natural to consider such transformations. This obviously may help to understand the nature of L systems. Although not much is known in this direction yet, some results about T0L transformations are already available (see Ginsburg and Rozenberg [31]).

Let a T0L scheme $G = \langle \Sigma, \mathcal{P} \rangle$ be given. (Note that each table P of $\mathcal{P}$ is in fact a finite substitution, or a homomorphism in the case that $\mathcal{P}$ satisfies a deterministic restriction). The basic situation under examination consists of being given two of the following three sets: a set L_1 of (start) words over Σ, a set L_2 of (target) words over Σ, and a (control) set $\mathcal{C}$ of finite sequences of applications of tables from $\mathcal{P}$. The problem is to ascertain information about the remaining set. (Note that we can consider a sequence of elements from $\mathcal{P}$ either as a word over $\mathcal{P}^*$, called a control word, or a mapping from Σ^* into Σ^*. We shall do both in the sequel but this should not lead to confusion). The following are examples of known results concerning this problem.

Theorem 11.1. (Ginsburg and Rozenberg [31])
If L_2 is a regular language, and L_1 an arbitrary language then the set $\mathcal{C}$ of control words leading from L_1 to L_2 is regular.

Theorem 11.2. (Ginsburg and Rozenberg [31])
If L_2 is a regular language and $\mathcal{C}$ is an arbitrary set of control words then the set of all words mapped into L_2 by $\mathcal{C}$ is regular.

Theorem 11.3. (Ginsburg and Rozenberg [31])
If L_1 is a regular language and $\mathcal{C}$ is a regular set of control words then the set of all words obtained from the words of L_1 by applying mappings from $\mathcal{C}$ is an ETOL language. Moreover each ETOL language can be obtained in this fashion.

Also the following is quite an interesting result.
Theorem 11.4. (Ginsburg and Rozenberg [31])
There is no TOL scheme $S = \langle \Sigma, \mathcal{P} \rangle$ such that $\mathcal{P}^*$ is the set of all finite nonempty substitutions on Σ^*. There is no TOL scheme $S = \langle \Sigma, \mathcal{P} \rangle$ such that $\mathcal{P}^*$ is the set of all homomorphisms on Σ^*.

We may also mention here the following result concerning "adult L transformations". Roughly speaking the adult language of an IL scheme G with an alphabet Σ is the set of all those strings over Σ^* which are transformed by G into themselves and only themselves.
Theorem 11.5.
There are regular languages which are not adult languages of IL schemes.

12. GETTING DOWN TO PROPERTIES OF SINGLE L LANGUAGES OR SINGLE L SEQUENCES

Undoubtedly, one of the aims of the theory of L systems is to understand the structure of a single L language or a single L sequence. Although some results in this direction are already available (see, e.g., Ehrenfeucht and Rozenberg [19,22,24] and Rozenberg [82]), in my personal opinion, there is not enough work done on this (rather difficult) topic.

Here are two samples of already available results.

Let Σ be a finite alphabet and B a non-empty subset of Σ. If x is a word over Σ then $\#_B(x)$ denotes the number of occurrences of elements from B in x. Let K be a language over Σ and let $I_{K,B} = \{n : \#_B(w) = n$ for some w in K$\}$. We say that B is numerically dispersed in K if $I_{K,B}$

is infinite and for every positive integer k there exists a positive integer n_k such that for every u_1, u_2 in $I_{K,B}$ such that $u_1 > u_2 > n_k$ we have $u_1 - u_2 > k$. We say that B is clustered in K if $I_{K,B}$ is infinite and there exist positive integers k_1, k_2, both larger than 1, such that for every w in L if $\#_B(w) \geq k_1$ then w contains at least two occurrences of symbols from B which are distant less than k_2.

Theorem 12.1. (Ehrenfeucht and Rozenberg [24])
Let K be an EOL language over an alphabet Σ and let B be a nonempty subset of Σ. If B is numerically dispersed in K, then B is clustered in K.

Results like the above one are very useful for proving that some languages are not in a particular class. This is often a difficult task. For example as a direct corollary of Theorem 12.1 we have that the language $\{w \text{ in } \{0,1\}^* : \#_{\{0\}}(w) \text{ is a power of } 2\}$ is not an EOL language. (The direct combinatorial proof of this fact in Herman [35] is very tedious.)

For DOL sequences we have the following result. (In what follows if x is a word and k a positive integer then $Pref_k(x)$ denotes either x itself if $k \geq |x|$ or the word consisting of the first k letters of x if $k < |x|$. Similarly $Suf_k(x)$ denotes either x itself if $k \geq |x|$ or the word consisting of the last k letters of x if $k < |x|$).

Theorem 12.2. (Rozenberg [82])
For every DOL system G such that $E(G) = \omega_0, \omega_1, \ldots$ is infinite there exists a constant C_G such that for every integer k the sequence $Pref_k(\omega_0), Pref_k(\omega_1), \ldots$ (respectively $Suf_k(\omega_0), Suf_k(\omega_1), \ldots$) is ultimately periodic with period C_G.

The above result is not true for DIL sequences; the corresponding sequences of prefixes (or suffixes) are not necessarily ultimately periodic.

It should be clear that Theorem 12.2 can provide elegant proofs that some sequences are not DOL sequences.

13. GENERALIZING L SYSTEMS IDEAS; TOWARDS A UNIFORM FRAMEWORK

As in every mathematical theory, also in the (mathematical) theory of L systems one hopes to generalize various particular results and concepts and get a unifying framework for the theory. One still has to wait for such a uniform framework for the theory of L systems, however partial results are already available.

It was already noticed in early papers on L systems (see, e.g., Rozenberg [81]) that the underlying operation is that of the iterated substitution. This operation was quite intensively studied in formal language theory, however in the theory of L systems it occurs in somewhat modified way (one has a finite number of finite substitutions, tables, and then performs all their possible "iterative" compositions). This point of view was taken by J. van Leeuwen and A. Salomaa and (as a rather straightforward generalization of the notion of an ETOL system) they introduced the so called K-iteration grammars (van Leeuwen [57], Salomaa [103]).

For a language family K, a K-substitution is a mapping σ from some alphabet V into K. The mapping is extended to languages in the usual way. A <u>K-iteration grammar</u> is a construct $G = \langle V_N, V_T, S, U \rangle$ where V_N, V_T are disjoint alphabet (of nonterminals and terminals), $S \in (V_N \cup V_T)^*$ (the axiom) and $U = \{\sigma_1, \ldots, \sigma_n\}$ is a finite set of K-substitutions defined on $(V_N \cup V_T)$ with the property that, for each i and each a in $(V_N \cup V_T)$, $\sigma_i(a)$ is a language over $(V_N \cup V_T)$. The language generated by such a grammar is defined by

$$L(G) = \bigcup \sigma_{i_k} \ldots \sigma_{i_1}(S) \cap V_T^*,$$

where the union is taken over all integers $k \geq 1$ and over all k-tuples $(i_1, \ldots, i_k)$ with $1 \leq i_j \leq n$. The family of languages generated by K-iteration grammars is denoted by $K_{\underline{iter}}$. For $t \geq 1$, we denote by $K_{iter}^{(t)}$ the subfamily of K_{iter}, consisting of languages generated by such grammars where U consists of at most t elements.

<u>Example 13.1.</u> If we denote the family of all finite languages by F, then it is clear that $F_{iter}^{(1)} = \mathcal{L}(EOL)$ and $F_{iter} = \mathcal{L}(ETOL)$.

The families of K-iterated languages can be related to Abstract Families of Languages (AFL's) as follows.

<u>Theorem 13.2.</u> (van Leeuwen [57], Salomaa [103])
If the family K contains all regular languages and is closed under finite substitution and intersection with regular languages then both K_{iter} and $K_{iter}^{(t)}$ are full AFL's.

The notion of a K-iteration grammar was extended to the case of context-sensitive substitutions by D. Wood in "A note on Lindenmayer systems, spectra and equivalence" McMaster University, Comp. Sc. Techn. Dep. No. 74/1. Some results are also available about possibly extending a few basic properties of the families of L systems (or L languages) to the case of families of K-iteration grammars (or languages) (see, e.g., Salomaa [103] and the above mentioned paper by Wood).

14. CONCLUSIONS

We would like to conclude this paper with two remarks.

(1) In the first five years of its existence the mathematical theory of L systems has become each year fruitful and popular. This is exemplified by exponential growth of the number of papers produced (per year), and a linear (with a decent coefficient) growth of both the number of results and the number of people joining the area.

(2) It may have already occurred to the reader (and it is certainly clear to the author of this paper) that both formal language theory and the theory of L systems have benefited by the existence of the other.

ACKNOWLEDGEMENT

The author is indebted to A. Lindenmayer and A. Salomaa for their useful comments on the first version of this paper.

A MODEL FOR THE GROWTH AND FLOWERING OF ASTER NOVAE-ANGLIAE ON THE BASIS OF TABLE < 1,0 > L-SYSTEMS

D. FRIJTERS and A. LINDENMAYER

Theoretical Biology Group
University of Utrecht
Heidelberglaan 2
Utrecht, The Netherlands

Summary

L-systems (1, 2, 3)* were introduced by one of us in order to model morphogenetic processes in growing multicellular filamentous organisms. We will show here, how a computer model of the growth and flowering of *Aster novae-angliae* could be built using a particular L-system.

Introduction

Champagnat (4) and Nozeran, Bancilhon and Neville (5) classified various internal correlations in the morphogenesis in higher plants: They argue that often there is evidence of internal correlations which involve the whole plant and of correlations which involve parts of the plant such as organs, regions or even one tissue. Internal correlations with respect to pattern formation in growth and flowering of higher plants are interesting, because of the relationships between position and time of flowering and flower development.

---

*Since our references are mostly to biological papers, we deviate from the format used in this book and we list our references at the end of this article.

There seems to be enormous diversity in the inflorescences and inflorescence formation in higher plants. Within a plant species, however, the pattern of the inflorescence and its development are quite constant and show great similarity to the patterns of related species as has been shown by Troll (6) and Weberling (7). Several theories and models have been put forward to explain the evolution of inflorescences, cf. Maresquelle (8, 9, 10, 11), Stauffer (12) and Sell (13). Champagnat (4) and Nozeran, Bancilhon and Neville (5) held gradients responsible for the pattern-formation in their plants. Maresquelle and Sell (14) also assumed gradients which in their opinion controlled the descending inflorescences in higher plants (these are inflorescences where flowering proceeds from the top down). Sell (15, 16) and Jauffret (17) also gathered experimental data about correlations between growth and flowering. However, the question how growth and flowering in plants are correlated is still open. This is mainly due to the fact, that no suitable representation and calculation devices are available to work out the consequences of different theoretical correlation mechanisms. Most correlations were supposed to depend on gradients. These gradients are supposedly formed by diffusion and/or active transport. For the calculation of their effects differential equations must be solved. Because the plant is also growing, the equations cannot be solved analytically, but by step-by-step approximations. L-systems can be used to obtain approximate solutions. In this case, all states of a growing filament are simultaneously replaced by new states at discrete time steps, according to certain transition rules (as for example growth and division rules). Furthermore, L-systems have been defined so that computer programs can be based on them, cf. Baker and Herman (18, 19, 20). They are suitable for representing and quantifying correlations in growing systems as long as these systems can be treated as simple or branching filaments.

In personal communication Sell advised us on the suitability of Aster as a subject for an inflorescence development model. This genus belongs to a large family (Compositae) that makes it convenient to compare it with other plants. Aster novae-angliae, a species of Aster, reaches a height of about one meter. Its pattern of growth and flowering is quite complex. It can form up to 30 side-branches on any one branch. It shows apices which turn into flowers and apices which stay vegetative. It produces hundreds of easily countable and classifyable flowers. Branches in various parts of the plant exhibit easily recognizable patterns of growth. Flowering is presumably triggered by an environmental signal (short days). Fully developed flowers appear first midway along the plant and susequently appear above and below this point (ascending and descending flowering sequence). Aster forms its organs at the apices of its shoots. Growth in length only takes place in a zone just under the apex, growth in girth might take place anywhere.

We had to formulate first the minimum requirements for a meaningful model. A number of characteristics of Aster are not relevant to our purpose. Therefore, we decided to disregard phyllotaxis and shape and size of leaves. We regarded as essential to the model: (1) the number and order of branches, and their positions, (2) the positions and time order of the appearance of floral buds, and their development, and (3) the lengths of all internodes. We insisted that the computer model should show the same features in these respects as the actual plant.

Characteristics of Aster novae-angliae

The features of Aster novae-angliae, limited to those which were under consideration in the computer model, were as follows.

Figures 1 and 2 (all figures which are shown have been drawn by computer, as will be described later) show a diagrammatic representation of a plant of Aster novae-angliae growing in a garden in Huis ter Heide, The Netherlands, on 7 Sept. 1973. The internodes on the main branch (the 0-order branch), and the branches of the main axis and their "flowers" have been indicated (Aster plants have compound inflorescences typical of Compositae, where the smallest inflorescence units are the so called "heads". These we shall refer to as individual "flowers"). The internodes seem to decrease gradually in length from base to apex. The 15 lower internodes bear no branches (leaves are not shown in these figures). The first order branches increase suddenly in length as function of their position on the main axis (from base up) and decrease gradually after that. The plant does not seem to posess either purely descending or

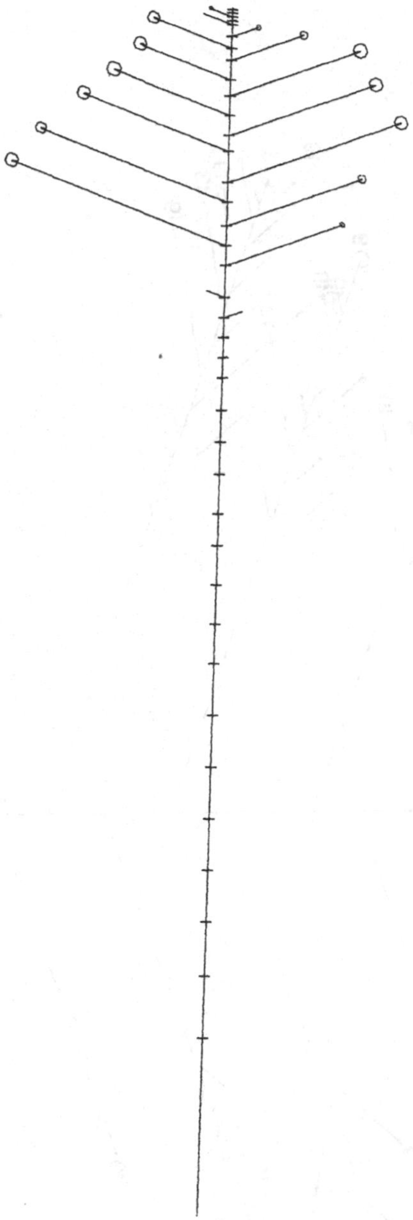

Fig. 1. Diagram of a plant of Aster novae-angliae on 7 Sept. 1973. The main axis with its internodes, its side branches, and the apically born flowers (heads). The symbols denote the flowers, the size of the symbols show the state of their development.

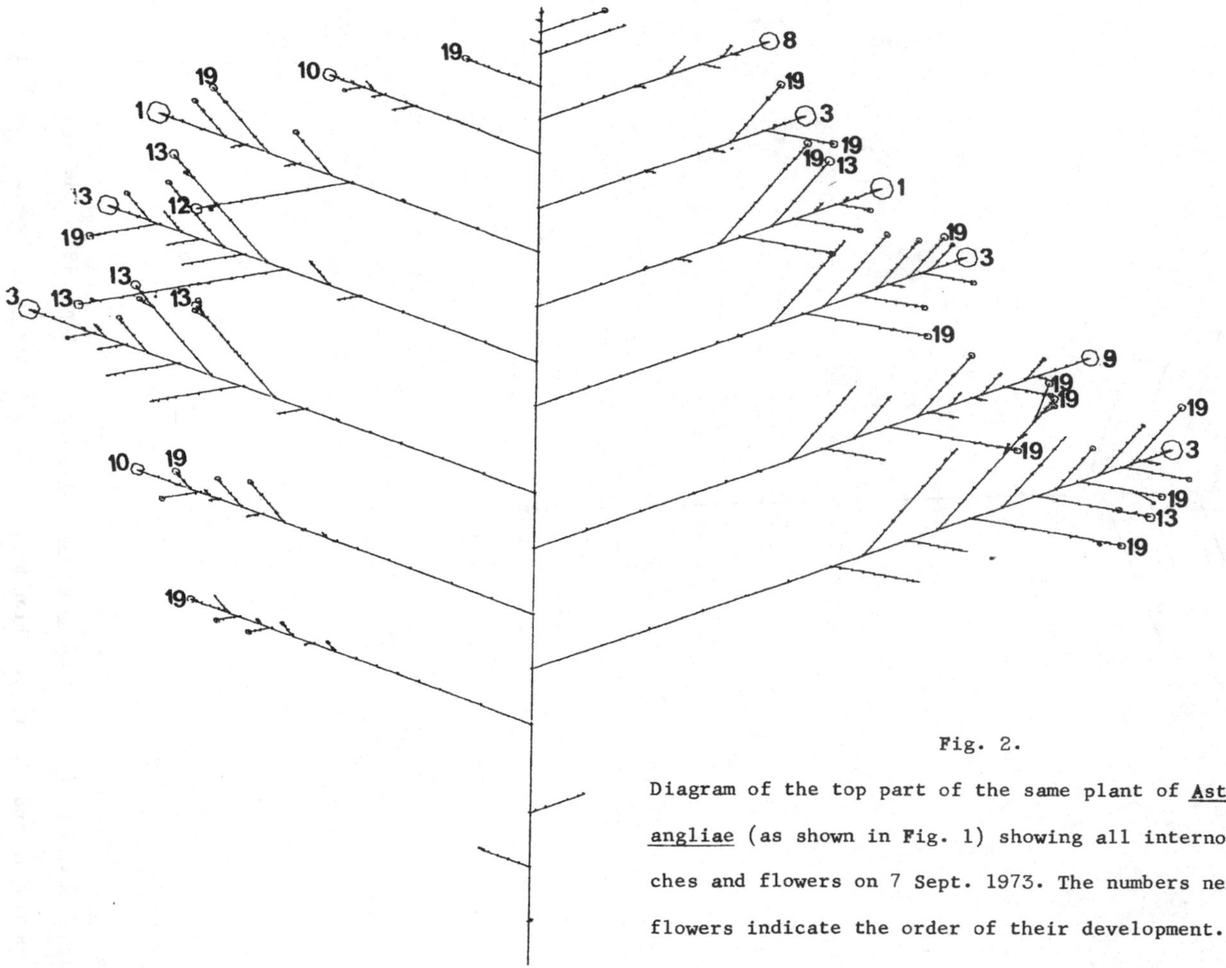

Fig. 2.

Diagram of the top part of the same plant of <u>Aster novae-angliae</u> (as shown in Fig. 1) showing all internodes, branches and flowers on 7 Sept. 1973. The numbers next to the flowers indicate the order of their development.

purely ascending order of flowering, the most developed flowers are found on the branches positioned midway along the main axis.

Figure 2 is an enlarged detail of the top part of Fig. 1. Here, all internodes and flowers, and to some extent the order of development of the flowers, have been indicated. As on the 0-order branch, it can be seen that the internodes of the higher order branches decrease in length gradually from base to apex. The lower placed branches on any branch, have shorter internodes than their mother branch above the branching point, the higher placed branches have internode lengths equal to their mother branch above the branching point.

The first order branches seem to be able to grow faster than the 0-order branch: starting with the longest first order branch, they show about twice as many internodes as the corresponding parts of the 0-order branch above the branching points. This phenomenon appeared to be repeated in the higher order branches. The 0-order branch had 15 branchless internodes, the higher order branches showed always less branchless internodes, frequently exactly 3, while the branches nearest to the base often had the highest number of branchless internodes and the ones nearest to the top the lowest. In total numbers this plant had on that date: 25 first order branches, 125 second order branches, 200 third order branches, 10 fourth order branches and no fifth order branches. Other plants frequently show more branches, as well as fifth and even sixth order branches.

The flowering order which consists of flower development starting midway along the first order branches, was also encountered in the higher order branches. However, the topmost flower of a certain branch was nearly always further developed than the flowers of the side branches of that branch. We noticed that the larger a plant had grown or the longer a particular branch had become, the less developed was the apex of that plant or branch as compared to some of the flowers on its side-branches. In our plant this was visible in the complete absence of a flower at the top of the main axis.

On 26 Sept. 1973, we observed again the same plant represented in Figs. 1 and 2. We

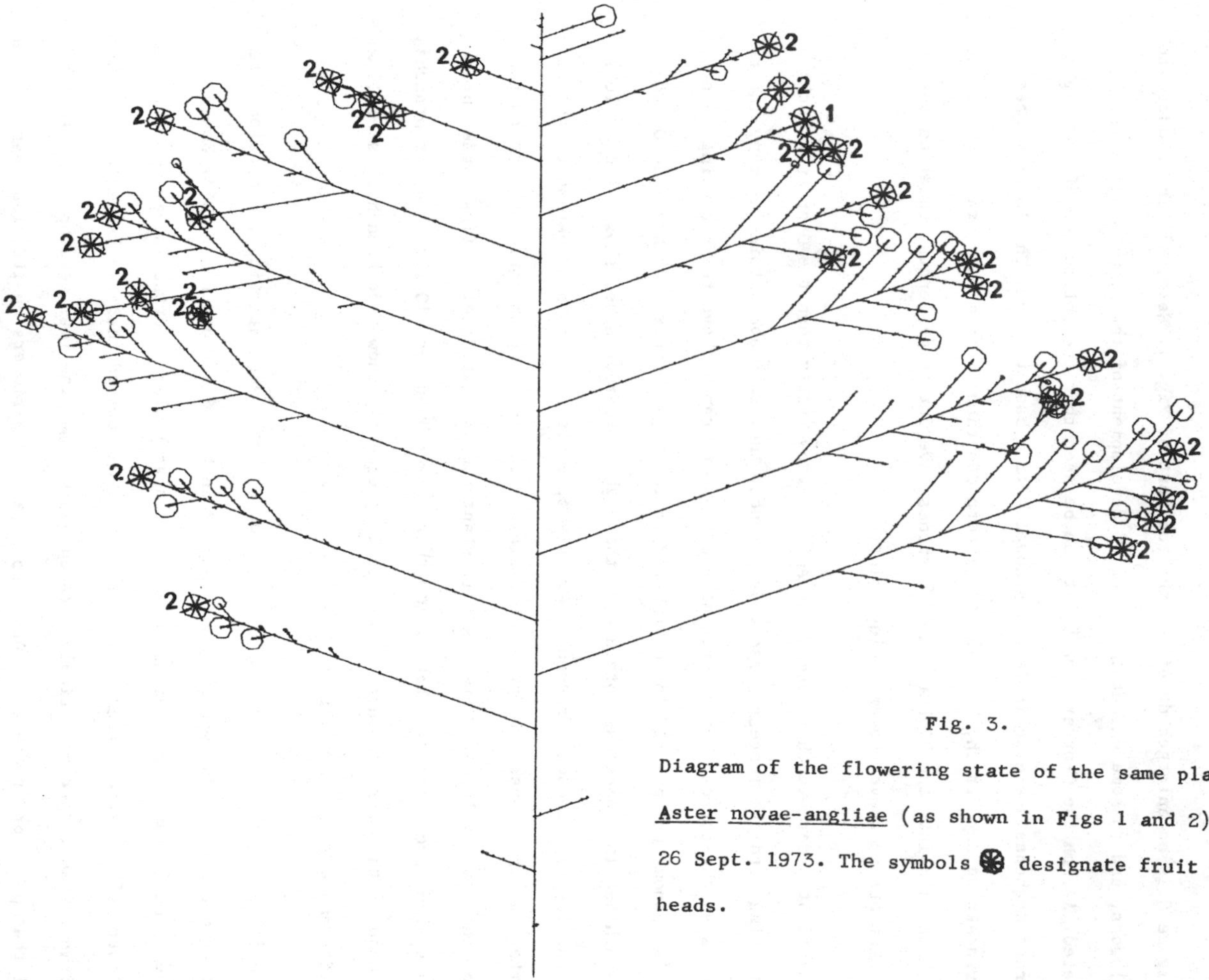

Fig. 3.

Diagram of the flowering state of the same plant of <u>Aster</u> <u>novae-angliae</u> (as shown in Figs 1 and 2), on 26 Sept. 1973. The symbols ⊛ designate fruit bearing heads.

took new measurements of some branches and noticed that several branches had continued to grow, while others had not. It appeared that the branches nearest to the top of their mother branch had grown more than the branches nearest to the base. This phenomenon was strongest near the top of the plant. The flower development had also most strongly proceeded at the top of the plant and on the branches positioned nearest to the top of their mother branches. The data we had gathered about the lengths of the internodes were not complete enough to elaborate them in a new figure. We had gathered, however, all the necessary data of the flowers of the plant. Figure 3, therefore, which is identical to Fig. 2 except for the flower development, shows all floral buds and flowers of the plant at the later stage. A number of flowers had already formed plumed fruits (●) and it was difficult to assign flowering stages to them. One flower, however, had lost its fruits and therefore could definitely be classified as being the most developed flower. All the other plumed fruits were classified equally as second in the flowering order.

<u>The computer model</u>

As mentioned before, Baker and Herman (18, 19, 20) and Liu (21) designed a computer program, called CELIA, to process strings in the way L-systems do. The first version of CELIA was followed by a second, more extensive, version (22), which we used in our model. CELIA consists of a main program which can be instructed by a total number of 16 fixed control and data cards and by several user-written subroutines. We wrote the developmental rules for the model in the (user-written) DELTA subroutine. We found inspiration for the formulation of the rules for our model in the work of Cohen (23). As "cells" or "units" in the sense of L-systems we took already mentioned segments of the plant: internodes, apices, lateral buds, and first internodes on a branch. We instructed CELIA by the control card MODEL to process out organism as a branching $< 1,0 >$ L-system. This latter system is a branching system in which the information for a cell only comes from its own state and that of its first neighbour on the left. The first internode of a branch receives its left neighbour information from the internode on the mother branch which bears the branch in question. The strings were written out in the conventional way, that is, the shoot apex at the right and the base at the left. We introduced four attributes per unit. For the sake of convenience, a unit with its attributes was placed between sharp brackets. The four attributes were, in order of appearance: TYPE, FORS, LONG, and BULK (the whole unit abbreviated as $< T, F, L, B >$).

The variable TYPE can have only three values: 1, standing for an apex or flower; 3, standing for an internode; and 6, standing for a lateral bud or for a first internode on a branch.

FORS is a variable applicable to apices or internodes (it can have values greater than or equal to -2). The FORS value of an apex is simply equal to the number of internodes which were produced by that apex (from the stage of a lateral bud on). The FORS value of an internode is equal to twice the number of internodes produced above it on that branch. The fact that an internode keeps account of the number of internodes produced above it does not necessarily mean that we have here to do with long range communication between parts of a branch. An internode can simply measure the time since its production and the degree of inhibition applicable to that branch and compute from that at any time the number of internodes which have arisen above it. Using twice the number of internodes in FORS is due to our wish to let the growth function of internodes look more realistic, as we shall show later. The negative values for the number of plastochrones were introduced for practical programming reasons, they had no further significance.

The variable LONG can only have values greater than or equal to zero. It stands for the initially determined length of the mother branch of the particular bud or internode. Its value has to do with the degree of inhibition.

We let our plant grow (expand) until a certain stage, at which stage we switch the set of rules. This switch, called "table-switch", is meant to represent the change from vegetative to flowering conditions in the whole plant.

Outside the scope of the table $< 1,0 >$ L-system we make information available concerning the length and inhibition of the branch and of its mother branch. We will argue that this extra information can be deduced to one-step-at-a-time left-sided information transmission, so that it could be fitted into a table < 1,0 > L-system, if we so desired. We will explain later why we thought it was not convenient to do that.

The core of the model: production rules

The most important differences in the rules for the units are based on their first attribute, their TYPE. Therefore we classify the rules according to their TYPE.

A unit (internode or apex) is represented by a quadruple of attributes, < T, F, L, B >. L(L1) designates the value of the attribute LONG of the left neighbour of a unit. The rules which specify how certain quadruples change to other quadruples are shown below. For certain combinations of attributes the same rule is used under both vegetative and floral environmental conditions. For other combinations, the rule which is applicable depends on the environment (vegetative or floral condition). The term "int (F)" indicates the integer portion of the value of the variable F (the lower entire of F).

Rules which apply under both vegetative and floral conditions.

TYPE 3

1. If F is greater than or equal to 6 then

< 3, F, L, B > → < 3, F, L, B >.

This rule states that an internode unit is fully grown when the value of its variable FORS (the number of plastochrones) is greater than or equal to 6.

2. If F is smaller than 6 and int (F) is equal to int (F + 2K) then

< 3, F, L, B > → < 3, F + 2K, L, B >.

This states that an internode unit does not grow (does not increase the value of its variable LONG), but just increases the value of its plastochrone number (the value of the variable FORS) with twice the value of the variable K (the degree of inhibition - the behaviour of which will be explained later -), whenever the value of its variable FORS is smaller than 6 and the value of the lower entire of its variable

F is equal to the value of F + 2K.

3. If F is smaller than 6 and int (F) is smaller than int (F + 2K) then

< 3, F, L, B > → < 3, int(F) + 1, L + L× (int(F) + 1 - 0.15(int(F) + 1)^2), B >.

This states that an internode unit grows and at the same time increases its plastochrone number whenever the value of its variable FORS is smaller than 6 and the value of the lower entire of its variable FORS is smaller than the value of FORS + 2K. The new length of the internode becomes LONG + LONG x (int(FORS) + 1 - - 0.15 (int(FORS) + 1)^2), which can also be written as $x_t = x_{t-1} + x_{t-1}(t - 0.15t^2)$, where x_t is the length of the internode at time t and t is the plastochrone number ($0 \leq t \leq 6$). This formula provides an S-shaped growth curve for the internodes, the derivation of which shall be given later. The new plastochrone number of the internode unit becomes int(FORS) + 1 and not (FORS + 2K) as in the preceding rule. This is in order to make it impossible to let the increase of the plastochrone number amount to more than one integer unit, for this would mean that the growth formula for an internode possibly would not be applied at every integer unit, leading to false results.

<u>TYPE 6</u>

4. If F is greater than or equal to 6 then

< 6, F, L, B > → < 6, F, L, B >.

Similar to Rule 1.

5. If F is smaller than 6 and int(F) is equal to int(F + 2K) then

< 6, F, L, B > → < 6, F + 2K, L, B >.

Similar to Rule 2.

6. If F is smaller than 6 and int(F) is smaller than int(F + 2K) then

< 6, F, L, B > → <6, int(F) + 1, L + L× (int(F) + 1 - 0.15 (int(F) + 1)^2), B >.

Similar to Rule 3.

Rules, which apply only under vegetative conditions

TYPE 1

7. If int(F) is equal to int(F + K) then

$< 1, F, L, B > \rightarrow < 1, F + K, L, B >$.

This rule states that an apical unit does not give rise to new organs, but just increases the value of its plastochrone variable by the value of K (the degree of inhibition), whenever the value of the lower entire of its variable FORS is equal to the value of the lower entire of FORS plus K.

8. If int(F) is smaller than int(F + K) then

$< 1, F, L, B > \rightarrow < 3, -1, L(L1) \times 0.9, B > (: < 6, -2, L(L1), A > :) < 1, F + K, L, B >$.

We state here that an apical unit gives rise to a lateral bud and to an internode, whenever the value of the lower entire of its variable F is smaller than the value of the lower enire of F + K. The unit standing for the lateral bud is placed between parentheses and colons as follows: $(: < 6, F, L, B > :)$. The apex increases the value of its plastochrone number (FORS) by K (the degree of inhibition), as in Rule 7. The newly formed lateral bud gets a FORS value of -2. The value for the length (LONG) of the newly formed lateral bud is equal to the length of the first internode on the left. The lateral bud, therefore, will have the length of the internode, which is going to bear the new branch (Rule 9). The value for the variable BULK of the newly formed lateral bud is equal to the value of A, which is the length of the mother branch of the lateral bud. The behaviour of the variables BULK and A will be explained later. The newly formed internode gets a FORS value of -1. This negative value for the plastochrone number ensures that it will take at least two iterations before the newly formed internode will grow (see the formula given in Rule 3). In the meantime it is very easy to determine the initial length of the next internode which will be formed on the same branch, because the initial length of the previously formed internode on the branch is still available. The LONG value of the newly formed internode is equal to the length of the first internode on the left, multiplied by 0.9. This ensures that the length of the newly formed internode will be somewhat smaller than the length of the previously formed internode on that branch.

TYPE 6

9. If F is equal to -2 then

$$< 6, F, L, B > \rightarrow < 6, -1, \frac{L \times B}{A}, B > < 1, 0, 0, B >.$$

This rule states that a lateral bud unit (with FORS equal to -2) develops into a first internode on a branch and into an apex. The FORS value of the newly formed first internode on this branch is equal to -1 (see Rule 8). The value for the length (LONG) of the newly formed first internode is equal to LONG x BULK, divided by A (the length of the mother branch from base to branching point). Since the variable BULK is equal to the length of the mother branch of the time when the lateral bud is formed (see Rule 8), BULK divided by A implies that the initial length for the newly formed internode depends on the increase in the degree of inhibition (an explanation of this will be given later) which has taken place since the formation of the lateral bud. The FORS and LONG values of the newly formed apex are set equal to zero.

Rules, which apply only under flowering conditions

TYPE 1

10. If $L + \frac{F \times K}{10}$ is greater than or equal to 4, then

$$< 1, F, L, B > \rightarrow < 1, F, L + \frac{F \times K}{10}, B >.$$

An apical unit is considered to be a flower whenever its LONG value is greater than or equal to 4. The value for the plastochrone number of a flower does not increase anymore. The LONG value of this unit now indicates its flowering state. According to the rule, LONG increases by FORS x K divided by 10. The derivation of this formula shall be given later. Under floral induction, the apices also loose gradually their ability to give rise to internodes and to lateral buds, as a consequence of this rule.

11. If $L + \frac{F \times K}{10}$ is smaller than 4 and int(F) is equal to int(F + K) then

$$< 1, F, L, B > \rightarrow < 1, F + K, L + \frac{F \times K}{10}, B >.$$

As Rule 7, this rule also states that an apical unit does not give rise to new organs whenever the value of F ✱ K divided by 10 is smaller than 4 and the value of the lower entire of the variable F is equal to the value of the lower entire of F + K. The FORS value of the apex is increased by K (see Rule 7).

12. If $L + \frac{F \times K}{10}$ is smaller than 4 and int(F) is smaller than int(F + K) then

$$< 1, F, L, B > \rightarrow < \$,-1, L(L1) \times 0.9, B > (: < 6,-2, L(L1), A > :) < 1, F+K, L+\frac{F \times K}{10}, B >.$$

Here we state that an apical unit gives rise to a lateral bud and to a new internode (see Rule 8), whenever the condition of the rule holds. The value for all variables of the apex, the newly formed lateral bud and the internode are equal to the values given for these variables in Rules 8 and 11.

<u>TYPE 6</u>

13. If F is equal to -2 then

$$< 6, F, L, B > \rightarrow < 6, F, L, B >.$$

This states that a lateral bud unit does not develop any further if the plant is under flowering condition. This rule prevents the formation of new branches (Rule 9) when the plant has come under flowering conditions. This restriction is not necessary for the construction of the model. It ensures that the model plant does not become too extensive, which is convenient from the viewpoint of computer processing.

Extra information

Variable A is the sum of the lengths of the internodes of a certain branch and variable K is the degree of inhibition of that branch. We have built a common block of information into the CELIA main program and into the DELTA subroutine. This common block makes it possible to assign to each unit $< T, F, L, B >$ a value for A and a value for K. The computation of A and K at every computing step proceeds from left to right along the filament.

14. If a unit is encountered which is of TYPE 6 and its F value is equal to -2, then the variables A and K assigned to it have the same value which they have in the pre-

vious unit lying on the mother branch. In other words, the values for A and K are not affected by the encounter of a lateral bud as the computation proceeds along the filament.

15. If a unit is encountered with TYPE 6 and an F value which is not equal to -2, then an A value is assigned to this unit equal to the length (LONG) of the first internode on this branch. Further, we assign a value for K equal to the K value of the mother branch times twice the value of BULK, divided by the length of the mother branch from its base to the branching point. (The values for K are always greater than or equal to zero. A value for K of zero stands for complete inhibition, values for K greater than 1 stand for negative inhibition. The main axis always has a K value of 1). In other words, A takes as its value the value of the length of the first internode of that branch, and K determines the degree of inhibition for the branch according to the given formula. The derivation of this formula shall be given later.

16. If a unit is encountered of TYPE 3 or of TYPE 1, then the value of the variable K stays the same as in the previous unit, and the value for the variable A is increased by the length of this unit. In other words, the degree of inhibition (K) for the branch is not affected while the sum of the lengths of the internodes of the branch (A) is increased by the value of the length of the internode we are looking at. When the end of a branch is reached (when a unit of TYPE 1 has been processed), the degree of inhibition (K) and the length of the branch (A) are not carried on any further.

The drawing program

A computer program was also written in order to draw diagrams based on the CELIA output. We used this program to make diagrams of the actual plant as well, where we indicated the lengths of all internodes and the floral states of the apices. The computer program drew the first side branch of a certain branch always at the left hand side and all following side branches alternately to the right and to the left. We had an option in the program for the angles of the branches. In the pictures we allowed the first order branches to make angles of 70 degrees with the main axis, the second order branches to make angles of 30 degrees with the first order branches, and the third and higher order branches to make angles of 20 degrees with their mother branches. The value of the variable LONG of the apices in the model determined the size of the flower (✿). If the value of the variable LONG was greater than 10, we considered the flower to have formed fruits (●). The numbers next to the flowers were handdrawn and give the time order of development of the flowers (according to the value of the variable LONG).

The computations and drawings were carried out by a CDC 6400 (CYBER 73) computer at the University of Utrecht.

<u>Results</u>

Starting with an initial filament of two units $\langle 6, -1, 0.9, 0.5 \rangle$ $\langle 1, 1.0, 0, 0 \rangle$ we expanded the filament for 45 iterations. We let the table-switch from vegetative to floral condition occur at iteration 35. The computer drawing program supplied us with the drawings of the filaments at iterations 5, 15, 25, 35, 40 and 45. The drawings are collected in Figs. 4, 5, 6, and 7. The drawings of the filament at iteration 40 and 45 (Figs. 6 and 7) may be compared with the drawings of the actual plant (Figs. 1, 2 and 3). Comparison with Fig. 1 shows that the computer output does not have the same general appearance as the actual plant. This was mainly due to the absence in the computer model of the long stretch of branchless internodes at the base of the main axis. As we pointed out before, the main axis of the real plant has at its base a part which is quite different in appearance from any higher order branch. When we were building our model we discovered that we could only include this characteristics of the main axis if we adopted a special set of rules for the first part of the development of the plant. This seemed to us unnecessary for our model, so we confined ourselves to building a model of the actual plant without the basal part of the main axis. Our output, therefore, can only be compared with Figs. 2 and 3. Figure 6 is a drawing of the model plant at about the same stage of development as the actual plant in Fig. 2. The two figures can be matched to a

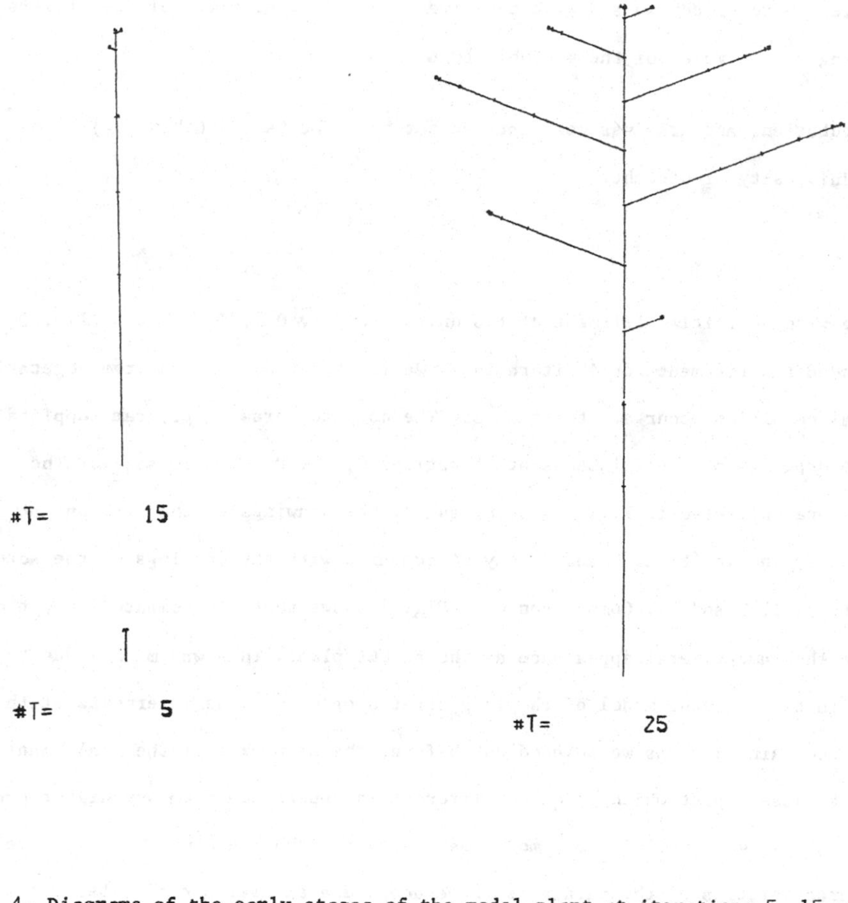

Fig. 4. Diagrams of the early stages of the model plant at iterations 5, 15 and 25.

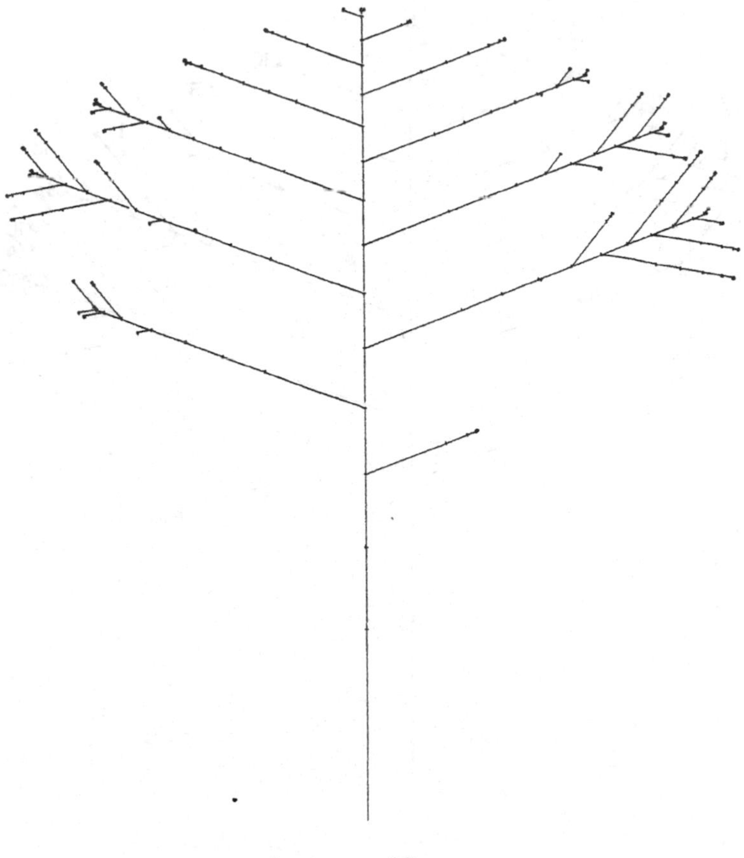

Fig. 5. Diagram of the model plant at the moment of the table-switch from vegetative to flowering condition at iteration 35.

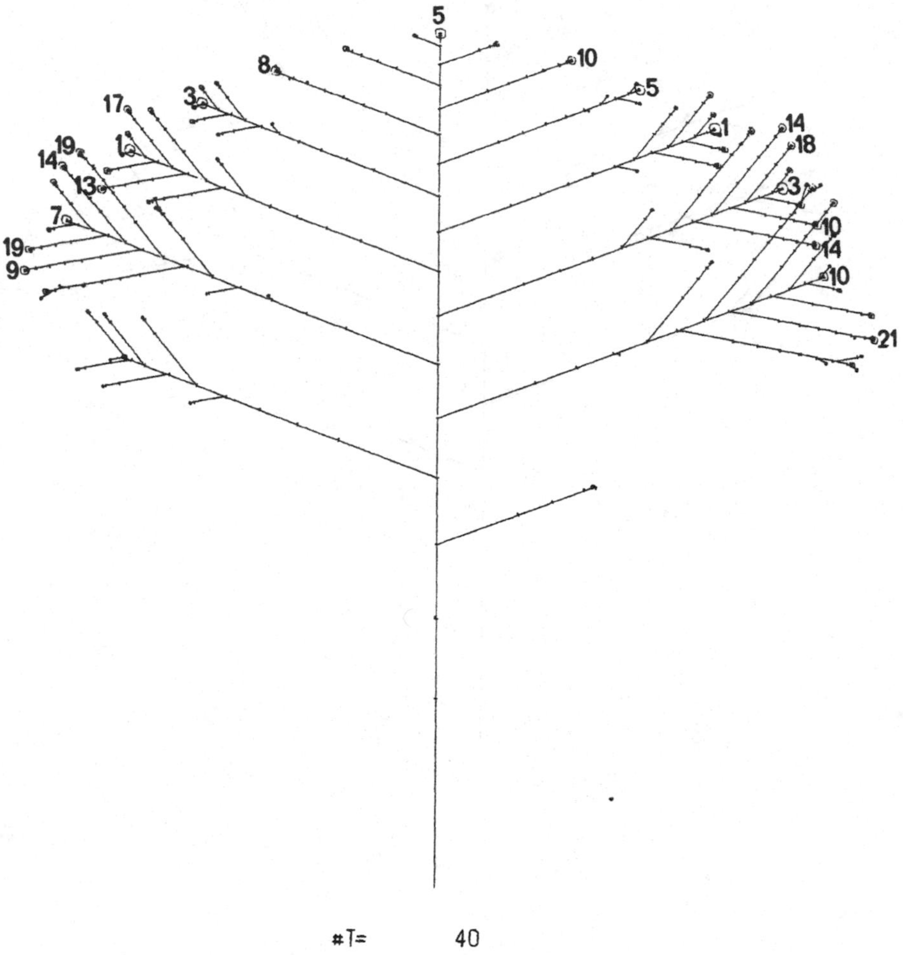

Fig. 6. Diagram of the model plant at iteration 40. (This Figure may be compared with Fig. 2)

considerable extent.The model plant is somewhat smaller than the real plant, but keeping it smaller was more practical for the computer simulation. If we had postponed the table-switch by another 10 iterations, the model plant would have been just as extensive as the actual plant (as we have tested it in some additional simulations). The strictly regular appearance of our model plant is not entirely realistic, namely with respect to the lengths of the internodes, where the higher positioned internodes were always smaller than their preceding ones, and with respect to the lengths of the branches which increased after a certain point to a maximum and decreased very regularly afterwards. These aspects of the model plant are the results of exclusively deterministic values för the constants in the rules; with stochastic values we could introduce more variation into the model. Figs. 4 and 5 could not be compared with the figures of the actual plant, because we did not observe its comparative stages. The figures show how the computer model developed from the initial filament to the stage where it can be compared. Fig. 7 on the other hand, was produced in order to show the progress in the development of the model plant and should be compared with Fig. 3 (except that Fig. 3 is only accurate for floral stages and not for internode lengths at that date of observation).

Discussion: The computer model vs. the actual plant

The rules and notions in our model had to satisfy the following demands: they had to be able to produce the desired pattern, they had to be physiologically reasonable they had to produce stable, but adaptable patterns, which were flexible enough to account for variations in the plants of *Aster novae-angliae* (and even in related species).

The first attribute in our model, TYPE, is assumed to represent the more or less permanently differentiated character of the units which constitute the plant. Clearly, meristematic apices, internodes and flowers (or inflorescences) are both morphologically and developmentally distinct plant organs. We have distinguished between the apices which are born at the tips of branches, and those which are in a lateral position. This distinction was necessary in order to be able to control the further

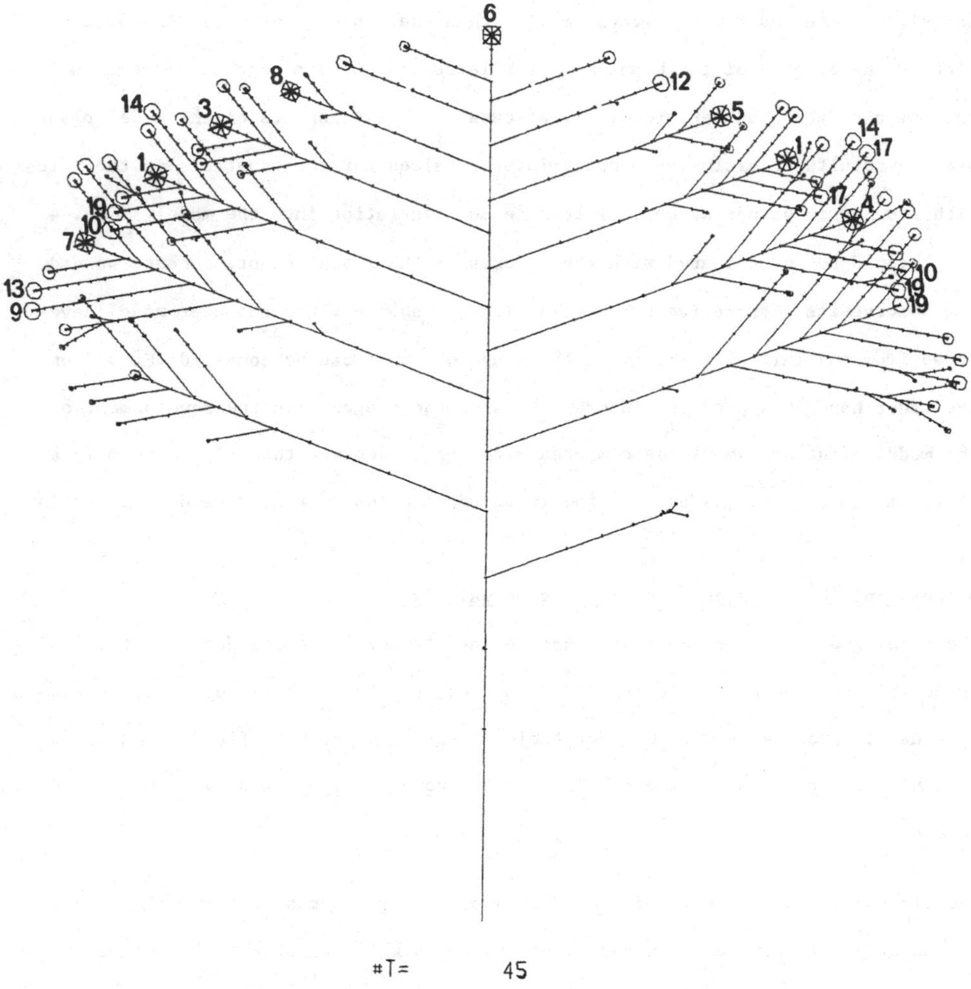

Fig. 7. Diagram of the model plant at iteration 45. (This Figure may be compared with Fig. 3).

growth of the branch which originates from a lateral bud, by assigning it a certain BULK value. We also distinguished between first internodes of branches and later internodes, for the reason that the degree of inhibition for a branch (K) can be determined for the whole branch by using a special formula for the first internode of the branch. This procedure was adopted here for our convenience, another model could easily be constructed without distinction between first and lateral internodes.

Formally, we used only three symbols for designating the TYPE of a unit, namely 1, 3, and 6. The symbol 1 was used to designate apices in terminal positions as well as flowers (no confusion arises from having the same symbols used in these two sense). The symbol 3 was used for internodes, other than first internodes of a branch. The symbol 6 was used to designate lateral buds or first internodes of branches.

The following state transition diagram shows the possible transitions among the differentiated states of organs.

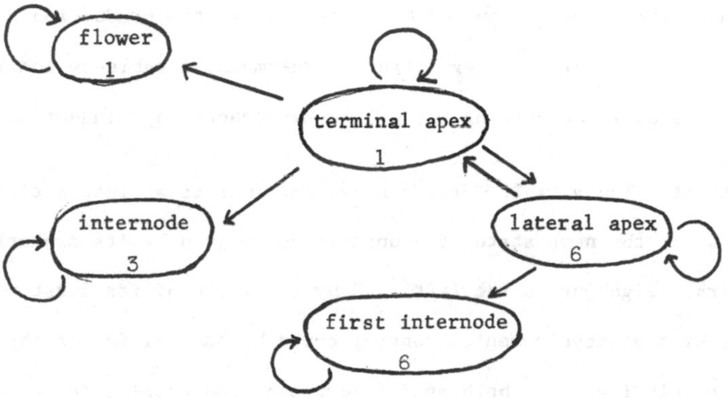

Often other differentiated units may also be recognized. Nozeran, Bancilhon and Neville (5) for example show that at the beginning of the development of the main axis of Phyllanthus amarus another kind of differentiation may take place. The organs formed during this differentiation, when isolated, kept different potentialities. We remarked already, that the basal part of Aster novae-angliae behaved differently from the rest of the plant. This could in our model only be reflected if we would have applied a separate set of rules for the formation of this part of the plant. Apart from the basal part, the main axis was in one more aspect different from the rest of the plant (which is often observed in higher plants) : Its apex sometimes did not form a flower (Figs. 2 and 3). According to our set of rules it would always form a flower, although not necessarily the most vigorous one (Figs. 5 and 6).

The question arises whether this plant could be simulated by a developmental system in which no interactions take place among the constituent parts (as in a $< 0,0 >$ L-system). But then for every lateral bud and its resulting branch there would have to be a different sequence of states, because for every branch the slowing down of its growth seemed to be different and dependent on its position in the plant. Therefore, only interacting systems seemed to be suitable for the simulation of <u>Aster</u>. In addition, we decided to use a table-switch, because we have seen plants of many different sizes in flowering condition which indicates that the production of the flowering stimulus is not internally regulated. Furthermore, a table-switch is physiologically well defendable because of the well-known "short-day" induction mechanism.

We first thought of using a table $< 1,1 >$ L-system. This is an interacting system with tables in which the next state of a unit is determined by its own state, by the state of its first neighbour on the left, and by the state of its first neighbour on the right. This kind of developmental control could be natural from a physiological point of view, namely involving both apical dominance and basal information about the extent of growth. But we decided to try first the simpler system with basal information only. It proved possible to build a model exclusively using basal information, represented by our table $< 1,0 >$ L-system. Further work might prove interesting on the construction of a model with both basal and apical information.

Development with interaction can be modelled not only by $< 1,1 >$ L-systems but also by $< k,\ell >$ L-sysjems, where each cell is influenced by $\underline{k}$ left and $\underline{\ell}$ right neighbours. Since $< k,\ell >$ L-systems can be programmed in CELIA (22), they could provide an opportunity to speed up the flow of information through a filament. The advantages, however, are limited. The rules become much more complicated. We found it easier to introduce common blocks of information in the CELIA program and in the DELTA subroutine rather than to make use of information arriving faster from more distant neighbours.

The slowing down of growth (or inhibition) of branches as function of their position, had to be provided by interaction rules. It was not easy to formulate these rules. We cannot claim that the rules we adopted are the rules which the plant uses. The interaction rules must be of the following kind: First, inhibition must become stronger the further the branching points are left behind the apical meristem which split them off; this relationship is, however, not linear with distance, but is dependent on the size of the whole branch. Secondly, the existing inhibition in a certain branch has to govern the inhibition of its side branches. And thirdly, the side branches near the top of a long branch have to be negatively inhibited, in other words, they had to grow faster than their mother branch, with a factor up to twice.

The first property could only be built into our rules by a rather complicated process. This process involves in the first internode an imprinting (Rules 8 and 12) of the length of its mother branch at the time that the lateral bud is formed (this is stored in the value of the variable BULK). In addition, the rules specify (Rule 15) that the first internode of a branch must keep a measure at all times of the length of its mother branch (from its base to the branching point). And finally, the rules state (Rule 15) that the first internode of a branch must compute the degree of its inhibition from the two previous pieces of information, by dividing the imprinted original length by the new length of the mother branch. This process may be hard to envisage, but it produces the required property and all other methods that we could think of involve far more complicated rules. We got the idea of having an imprinted original length of the mother branch from Sell (15, 16). He demonstrated that buds after isolation showed a different rate of development, depending on their previous position on their mother branch. This implied the imprint of some kind of message.

The second property, that the inhibition of a side branch is controlled by the inhibition of the mother branch, could very easily be built into our rules. This was done by multiplying the inhibition of a particular branch by the inhibition of its mother branch (Rule 15).

The third property, of negative inhibition, could also be easily built into the rules, namely by multiplying the inhibition of any side branch by the factor of two (Rule 15).

Because the growth of the internodes exert an effect on the inhibition of their branches it appears to be important to have a realistic time course for internode growth. From data in the literature (16) we found that full growth of internodes in Coleus takes about 5-7 plastochrone units. Aster novae-angliae may not be much different. More exact data on internode growth, however, were unobtainable. Therefore we compared the 5-7 plastochrone time-units of Coleus with the data of root growth of Zea mays (24). This comparison gives us an indication of the order of length increase which takes place in internodes per time-unit. We obtained a formula which in the case of Zea mays root would push a newly formed internode in 6 plastochrone time-units out of the growth zone : $x_t = x_{t-1} + x_{t-1}\ (t - 0.15\ t^2)$, where x_t the length of the internode at time t and t is expressed in plastochrone time-units ($0 \leq t \leq 6$). We are fully aware that this formula is rather arbitrary for the internode growth of shoots of Aster, but it proved to be adequate (Rules 3 and 6).

Apart from considering the growth rates of internodes we must also deal with different final sizes of internodes throughout the plant. It appeared that the rules must satisfy the following requirements:

First, a certain apex, which gives rise to internodes, must gradually give rise to smaller internodes. Secondly, internodes on a strongly inhibited branch must be smaller than the internodes on the mother branch above the branching point, while not heavily inhibited branches must have internodes of the same size as the mother branch.

The first requirement could be satisfied by letting a newly formed internode be 0.9 times the length of the preceding internode on that branch (Rule 8). The second requirement is satisfied by letting the size of the first internode and consequently all following internodes on a new branch depend upon the inhibition exerted at the time of formation (Rule 9). These rules were simple enough and possibly physiologically defendable.

The last phenomenon, which has to be regulated by the rules, is the process of flowering. The rules for this process must satisfy the following requirements: First, the apices must develop in a particular time sequence dependent on their position in the plant. Secondly, after some time the process has to proceed faster in the higher positioned apices than in the lower positioned ones. Thirdly, the plant must continue to grow after floral induction.

It proved to be possible to satisfy all three requirements based on a principle we call "vigour" (Rules 10, 11, 12). We define "vigour" of a certain apex as the number of plastochrone-units that apex has gone through, multiplied by its inhibition. In the real plant there is an observable connection between branch growth and flower development. Therefore, the parameter "vigour" connects these two in the model. Thanks to repeated observations of a plant of <u>Aster novae-angliae</u> (Figs. 2 and 3, and explanatory text) it was possible to estimate the developmental speed of the flowers against the continuing vegetative growth of the plant. This resulted in the formula for the attribute LONG (as in Rule 10).

As growth continues, "vigour" changes, and it changes in such a way that higher positioned apices in the plant benefit more from it than lower positioned ones. The principle of "vigour", therefore, works so well in our model, that it would not be surprising if the real plants control the development of their flowers in this way. Side branches near to the top of a large branch often bear more developed flowers than the mother branch. This is possible in our model, because the increase in "vigour" is related to the rate of growth of the branch, and branches near to the apex of a large branch can be negatively inhibited up to a factor of two. This means that the "vigour" of those branches can become larger than the "vigour" of their mother branch and consequently that the developmental rate of their flowers is higher than the developmental rate of the flower of the mother branch.

Finally we should require that the model be stable and flexible. In the course of our computer work we tried a variety of values for the constants in the formulas. These provided us with some insight in the stability of the model. Future work with stochastic variables might yield more stable models. The flexibility of the model could bæ tested by investigating the rules for their creative power, i.e., their power to simulate patterns of growth and flowering in related species.

References

1 Lindenmayer, A., 1968, Mathematical models for cellular interactions in development, Part I, Filaments with one-sided inputs, J. Theor. Biol., 18: 280-299.

2 Lindenmayer, A., 1968, Mathematical models for cellular interactions in development, Part II, Simple and branching filaments with two-sided inputs. J. Theor. Biol., 18: 300-315.

3 Lindenmayer, A., 1971, Developmental systems without cellular interactions, their language and grammars, J. Theor. Biol., 30: 455-484.

4 Champagnat, P., 1973, Introduction a l'étude des correlations complexes, manuscript.

5 Nozeran, R., Bancilhon, L.; Neville, P., 1971, Intervention of internal correlations in the morphogenesis of higher plants, Advances in Morphogenesis, 9: 1-66.

6 Troll, W., 1964/1969, Die Infloreszenzen. Typologie und Stellung im Aufbau des Vegetationskörpers. Bd I (1964). Bd II (1969), Gustav Fischer Verlag, Jena.

7 Weberling, F., 1965, Typology of inflorescences, J. Linn. Soc. (Bot.), 59: 215-221.

8 Maresquelle, H.J., 1961, Sur la filiation des inflorescences. Bull. Soc. Bot. Fr., 108: 117-119.

9 Maresquelle, H.J., 1965, Sur la filiation des inflorescences, 2e apport, Ann. Sc. Nat. Bot., 437-446.

10 Maresquelle, H.J., 1964, Sur la filiation des inflorescences, 3e apport, Fleurs de renfort et inflorescences de renfort, Mem. Soc. Bot. Fr., 1964, 96-100.

11 Maresquelle, H.J., 1964, Sur la filiation des inflorescences, 4e apport, La notion de racémisation en morphologie végétale, Mem. Soc. Bot. Fr., 1964, 96-100.

12 Stauffer, H.U., 1963, Gestaltwandel bei Blütenständen von Dicotycedonen, Bot. Jahrbücher, 82: 216-251.

13 Sell, Y., 1969, Les complexes inflorescentiels de quelques Acanthacées. Etude particulière des phénomènes de condensation, de racémisation, d'homogénéisation et de troncature, Ann. Sci. Nat. Bot., 10: 225-300.

14 Maresquelle, H.J., Sell, Y., 1965, Les problèmes physiologiques de la floraison descendante, Bull. Soc. Fr. Physiol. Végét., 11: 94-98.

15 Sell, Y., 1970, Etude préliminaire des rapports entre la floraison descendante et le dévelopement végétatif, Bull. Soc. Bot. Fr., 117: 25-36.

16 Sell, Y., 1970, Rapports entre morphogénèse végétative et morphogénèse florale chez Ruellia lorentziana Griseb. et Justicia simplex D. Don (Acanthacées), Bull. Soc. Bot. Fr., 117: 270-284.

17 Jauffret, F., 1970, Etude de corrélations en régime de floraison descendante, Bull. Soc. Bot. Fr., 117: 21-24.

18 Baker, R., Herman, G.I., 1970, CELIA - a cellular linear iterative array simulator, Proceedings of the Fourth Conference on Applications of Simulations, pp. 64-73.

19 Baker, R., Herman, G.T., 1972, Simulation of organisms using a developmental model, Part I. Basic description, Internat. J. Bio-Med. Computing, 3: 201-215.

20 Baker, R., Herman, G.T., 1972, Simulation of organisms using a developmental model, Part II. The heterocyst formation problem in blue-green algae, Internat. J. Bio-Med. Computing, 3: 251-267.

21 Liu, W.H., 1972, CELIA user's manual, Department of Computer Science, State University of New York at Buffalo.

22 Herman, G.T., Liu, W.H., 1973, The daughter of CELIA, the French flag and the firing squad, Simulation, 21: 33-41.

23 Cohen, D., 1967, Computer simulation of biological pattern generation processes, Nature, 216: 246-248.

24 Erickson, R.O., Sax, K.B., 1956, Elemental growth rate of the primary root of Zea mays, Proc. Amer. Philos. Soc., 100: 487-498.

ADDING CONTINUOUS COMPONENTS TO L-SYSTEMS

A. LINDENMAYER

Theoretical Biology Group, University of Utrecht

Heidelberglaan 2, Utrecht, Netherlands

Summary

Constructions are shown for cellular developmental models with continuous parameters, such as concentration of nutrients or inhibitors, size and age of cells or compartments. It is proposed that we can make use of some of the L-system results for these continuous component models.

Introduction

Developmental descriptions with the help of L-systems are based on discrete symbols which stand for discrete states of cells. In accordance with our present-day understanding of cellular processes, the "state of a cell" at any time is assumed to consist of the "state of the genome" and of the "state of the cytoplasm" at that time. By the "state of the genome" we mean the configuration of active and inactive genes at that time. The genes being discrete entities which are either repressed or not at any one time, the combination of active genes forms a naturally discrete "genomic state". Nevertheless, if the number of genes $\underline{n}$ involved in developmental regulation were large, then the number of possible combinations of active ones, 2^n, could be unmanageable. This, however, does not seem to be the case in the developmental processes investigated so far, not more than a handful of genes being at most implicated in each case.

But the "cytoplasmic states" are an entirely different matter. The cytoplasm consists of thousands of different proteins, nucleic acids, metabolites, and other compounds, each at continuously varying concentrations. Most of these materials are necessary for the normal functioning of the cell and are not involved in developmental regulations. Again, the number of those compounds which are developmentally impor-

tant, such as growth hormones, inducers, cell division regulators and the like, is probably small. Nevertheless, their diffusion and reaction rates must be taken into account, as well as their concentrations, in order to compute their effect on various cells. Ever since the constructions of A.M. Turing's diffusion-reaction model for morphogenesis[1], a considerable number of developmental models have been published with computer instructions and partly based on the production, diffusion, and decomposition of morphogenetically active compounds (morphogens)[*]. Among these we may mention the models of D. Cohen[2] for branching structures, of D.A. Ede and J.T. Law[3] for the early development of chick limbs, of C.P. Raven and J.J. Bezem[4] for the development of snail embryos, of A.H. Veen and A. Lindenmayer[5] for leaf position determination on shoot apices, and of Baker and Herman[6] for heterocyst initiation in blue-green algae. Only the last of these models has to do with simple (unbranched) filaments of cells, so we chose it as the first example to introduce our ideas.
What we propose to show is how developmental models with both discrete genomic and continuous cytoplasmic states can be expressed as counterparts of L-systems, and that in fact these new systems represent a useful extension of the original concepts, with the hope that the results and insights gained on L-systems will carry over to them.
The correspondence between "dynamic" systems (described by differential equations) and discrete algorithmic systems, with reference to diffusion-reaction mechanisms, has recently been commented upon by H.M. Martinez and R.M. Baer[7]: "discreteness can

---

[*] Since the references are mostly to biological papers, we deviate from the format of this volume and list the references at the end of the article.

also be dynamic. It can correspond to the steady states of a physical system maintained far from thermodynamic equilibrium (a dissipative structure). One is accordingly tempted to view this dynamic discreteness as the essential ingredient of any biological process at the cellular level having a programmed nature".
For a more detailed biological justification of L-systems see my review[8], and my chapter in the book of Herman and Rozenberg[9]. For formal definitions and results see Salomaa's chapter on Lindenmayer-systems[10], and the rest of the above m entioned book.

Heterocyst initiation in growing algal filaments of Anabaena

In order to account for the differentiation of heterocysts at more or less regular intervals (every 10 cells or so) in growing filaments of the blue-green alga *Anabaena*, Baker and Herman[6] made the following assumptions (which are widely accepted by biologists).
The heterocysts produce an inhibitor which diffuses along the filament, and into the surrounding medium as well. A cell in which the inhibitor concentration falls below a certain threshold value turns into a heterocyst, and starts producing the inhibitor. Cells which are inhibited from turning into a heterocyst (vegetative cells) can divide upon reaching a certain age.
Diffusion of the inhibitor is governed by the equation

$$\frac{\Delta c}{\Delta t} = k\,(\ell - c) + k\,(r - c) + k\,(e - c)$$

where c is the concentration of inhibitor in the cell under consideration, ℓ, r and e are concentrations of inhibitor in the left and right neighbour cells, and in the environment. From this equation we get

$$\Delta c = k.\Delta t.(\ell + r + e - 3c).$$

Assuming for the present that e = o, and choosing (footnote 1) $\frac{1}{4}$ as the value of $k.\Delta t$, we have then the formula

$$\Delta c = \frac{1}{4}(\ell + r - 3c)$$

which was used in the simulation of Baker and Herman[6]. The fact that e = o means that each cell of the filament continually looses inhibitor to the environment. This is why the inhibitor concentration does not keep increasing in the filament as would be expected since the heterocysts keep producing the inhibitor.

The simulation was carried out by the program CELIA which Baker and Herman[11] and Herman and Liu[12] constructed for generating cellular one-dimensional growing arrays[5]. In the program the state of each cell consists of a certain number of attributes. The next state of the cell, or - if it divides - of its daughter cells, is determined by its present state, and possibly also by the states of its left and right neighbour cells. This means that each attribute has to be computed at each time step for each cell. The instructions used by Baker and Herman[6] in their first simulation in the paper can be given as follows (in a somewhat modified form):

Let $w = (\langle -, x, - \rangle, \langle a, y, u \rangle, \langle -, z, - \rangle)$ be a cell-triple. Then

(1) if $y > t$ and $u > 0$ then $w \rightarrow \langle a, f(x, y, z), (u - 1) \rangle$,

(2) if $y \leq t$ and $u \geq 0$ then $w \rightarrow \langle b, h, 0 \rangle$,

(3) if $y > t$ and $u = 0$ then $w \rightarrow \langle a, f(x, y, z), S^{10\%}_{6000} \rangle \langle a, f(x, y, z), S^{10\%}_{6000} \rangle$.

Finally, let

(4) $\langle b, h, 0 \rangle \rightarrow \langle b, h, 0 \rangle$.

The attributes of each cell are shown between sharp brackets. The first attribute

---

Footnote 1. The diffusion rate constant k is taken here to be the same between cells along the filament, and between cells and the environment. This obviously is a gross simplification. The choice of the value $\frac{1}{4}$ for $k.\Delta t$ has the consequence that if the length of the time step Δt can be estimated from other data then k can also be estimated. Baker and Herman considered $\Delta t \cong 10$ sec. a valid estimate from life cycle data, which gives then $k = 0.025 \text{ sec}^{-1}$ as the estimate for the diffusion rate constant, a rather high rate.

of a cell has only two values, a or b, standing for vegetative cells and heterocysts, respectively. The second attribute is the concentration of the inhibitor, and the third attribute is the age of the cell. The first instruction states that the center cell in state $< a, y, u >$, with its left neighbour having an inhibitor concentration x, its right neighbour an inhibitor concentration z, if y is greater than threshold t and $u > 0$, must go into a cell in state $< a, f (x, y, x), (u - 1) >$. The function f in this case comes from diffusion considerations and is assumed to be

$$f (x, y, z) = y + \frac{1}{4} (x + z - 3y)$$

by using the formula derived previously. The age of the cell is computed by subtracting 1 from u at each step. Thus, as long as the inhibitor concentration remains in a cell above the threshold concentration t (chosen as $t = 3$ in this simulation), the cell remains in the vegetative state a, its inhibitor concentration changes according to the diffusion law, and its (reverse) age decreases by one.

The second instruction specifies that if $y \leq t$ and $u \geq 0$ then the center cell turns into a heterocyst (b), its inhibitor concentration goes to a constant value of h, and its age to 0. According to the fourth instruction, cells of this type remain from then on in the same state.

The third instruction specifies a division of the cell $< a, y, u >$ into two new cells each in the state $<a, f (x, y, z), S^{10\%}_{6000} >$. The term $S^{10\%}_{6000}$ stands for a stochastically chosen value of age from an integer set with average 6000 and standard deviation of 10%. This transformation takes place if $y > t$ and $u = 0$, in other words, when an inhibited vegetative cell reaches age 0.

The genomic states in this developmental system are clearly the states of the first attribute of each cell, a and b, standing for its vegetative and heterocyst condition. The switch from one genomic state to another ($a \rightarrow b$), and the decision for a cell to divide ($a \rightarrow aa$) or not to divide ($a \rightarrow a$), are controlled by the two cytoplasmic attributes (inhibitor concentration and age) with respect to the two threshold values (3 and 0). Once a cell is in state b, it remains so ($b \rightarrow b$).

The simulation of Baker and Herman was successful in generating acceptable heterocyst distributions along growing filaments. For practical reasons they allowed the inhibitor concentration in any cell to assume integer values only, those between 0 and 999 (in the heterocysts the concentration was at the constant value h = 999). The use of integer values did present some difficulties when the inhibitor concentration in the environment had to be varied (e > 0). As we have seen, the instructions of this developmental system were, however, formulated with the help of the continuous function f (x, y, z) and its computations could be carried out to any desired degree of accuracy.

The point we wish to make concerning this developmental system is that it could demonstrably be formulated in a manner analogous to an L-system with twosided inputs (called a "2L-system" or "< 1,1 >L-system") in spite of having continuous and stochastic functions as components. Furthermore, the analogy of this model with L-systems goes much deeper than just a common form of expression. For all practical purposes the computation of the function f (x, y, z) would be carried out only to some finite accuracy, which would mean that the concentration parameter would in fact be discretized (just as Baker and Herman have done it). Any discretized parameter within finite bounds could be regarded as a finite set of states. Thus, although we define the developmental system by a continuous function, we would in reality be working with a discrete state system, in other words, an L-system. The stochastic aspect of the above instructions could also, for most purposes, be replaced by non-deterministic ones.

Once we recognize that certain developmental systems with continuous and / or stochastic components are fundamentally related to certain types of L-systems, the results available for the latter become directly or at least by analogy applicable to the former.

Unfortunately the theory of L-systems with interactions is not sufficiently strong yet to provide many useable results concerning the behaviour or equivalence properties of such systems. The only theorems we might mention are those of Rozenberg[13] concerning the normal forms of L-systems with <u>k</u> left and <u>ℓ</u> right neighbours with inputs. He showed that for any <u>k</u> and <u>ℓ</u>, the class of < k,ℓ > L-languages is identical with the class of < k+ℓ-1,1 > L-languages, or with the class of < 1,k+ℓ-1 > L-languages. Furthermore he proved the existence of a hierarchy of < k,ℓ > L-systems, in the sense that for every $\underline{k}$ and $\underline{\ell}$ one can find a language which cannot be generated by a $< k,\ell >$L-system, but can be generated by a $< k+1,\ell >$L-system. In a simulation, the sizes of $\underline{k}$ and $\underline{\ell}$ correspond to the rates at which active substances can travel along a filament in one or another direction. Thus these results may have a bearing on the simulation parameters chosen in a particular biological model.

The results on growth functions of L systems with interactions[14, 15], may also be eventually useful in answering questions concerning growth rates of filaments when growth is regulated by a process involving interactions among the cells, such as (possibly oriented) diffusion of hormones.

As more properties of L systems with interactions become known, more insights will hopefully be gained of development governed by diffusion-reaction mechanisms, such as the one concerning heterocyst differentiation discussed here.

Branching growth of barley roots

The situation concerning useable L-system results is quite different when we consider developmental processes in which no interaction takes place among the units, as illustrated in the following.

We take as basis of this example the mathematical description by C. Hackett and D. A. Rose[16] of the development of the seminal root of barley. The essential features of their description are: each root member grows at its apex by a constant rate, and produces subapically branches at constant distances from each other. According to their observations: "The development of the root system of barley . . . proceeds in such a manner that relations between the total number, length, surface area and volume of root members remain approximately constant during the vegetative stage of growth. The existence of this property of root development implies that the plasticity of root form so evident to the eye is achieved within a framework of some remarkably constant principles."

In a simplified form, the description of Hackett and Rose consists of giving apical growth rates $v_0, v_1, v_2, \dots$ and branching densities $q_0, q_1, q_2, \dots$ for zero, first, second, etc., order branches. Growth rates v_i are given in terms of mm per day, and branching densities q_i are in terms of branches per mm. They derive approximations of the total numbers and total lengths of first, second and third order branches as functions of time, and attempt to show how these formulas can be fitted to observations by suitable choice of parameters (the v_i and q_i values).

Our purpose is to show that this developmental model can be expressed in a formalism analogous to OL-systems, and that, in spite of the continuous parameters employed, recurrence formulas can be found for the developmental sequence it generates (cf. 17).

Let us assume the following interactionless production rules for all $i \geq 0$:

(1) if $x < \frac{1}{q_i}$ then $< a_i, x > \longrightarrow < a_i, x + v_i >$,

(2) if $x \geq \frac{1}{q_i}$ then $< a_i, x > \longrightarrow < b, \frac{1}{q_i} > \left[< a_{i+1}, 0 > \right] < a_i, x + v_i - \frac{1}{q_i} >$,

(3) $< b, x > \longrightarrow < b, x >$ for all $x \geq 0$.

Each cell in this case represents a root segment, either an apical segment (above the highest branch), or an internodial segment (between two branches), or a basal segment (below the lowest branch and the branching point). The square brackets indicate branches, as in previous articles. The state of each segment consists of two attributes. The first attribute has the value $\underline{a}_i$ and $\underline{b}$, standing for apical segments and for internodial or basal segments, respectively. The second attribute indicates the length of the segment.

The first instruction determines that as long as the length of an apical segment on an $\underline{i}$th order branch is below the required distance between branches $\frac{1}{q_i}$, the segment should grow by an amount v_i.

The second instruction states that once an apical segment on an $\underline{i}$th branch exceeds the required distance $\frac{1}{q_i}$ it should produce a new branch of order $(i + 1)$ with zero length at a point $\frac{1}{q_i}$ distance above the last branch. An internodial segment is cut off this way in state $< b, \frac{1}{q_i} >$, and a new apical segment is formed which receives the left over length of the original segment (which has been extended by v_i).

The third instruction shows that internodial segments do not grow or branch any further.

For the sake of this simple example let us assume that for all $i \geq 0$, $v_i = v$ and $q_i = q$. Consequently we also have $a_i = a$. Let us designate $\frac{1}{q}$ as $\underline{r}$. The constants $\underline{v}$ and $\underline{r}$ may take any positive real value. The term $\lfloor x \rfloor$ designates the lower integer bound of x. The series of integers $k_1, k_2, k_3, \ldots, k_i, \ldots$ are defined as $\lfloor \frac{r}{v} \rfloor$, $\lfloor \frac{2r}{v} \rfloor$, $\lfloor \frac{3r}{v} \rfloor$, $\ldots$, $\lfloor \frac{ir}{v} \rfloor$, $\ldots$.

The following developmental sequence can then be obtained from the axiom $< a, 0>$.

$$S_0 = < a,0 >$$

$$S_1 = < a,v >$$

$$S_2 = < a,2v >$$

$$\vdots$$

$$S_{k_1} = < a,k_1 v >$$

$$S_{k_1+1} = < b,r > [< a,0 >] < a, (k_1+ 1) v - r >$$

$$S_{k_1+2} = < b,r > [S_{k_1-k_1+1}] < a, (k_1 + 2) v - r >$$

$$\vdots$$

$$S_{k_2} = < b,r > [S_{k_2-k_1-1}] <a, k_2 v-r >$$

$$S_{k_2+1} = < b,r > [S_{k_2-k_1}] < b, r> [< a,0 >] < a, (k_2+ 1) v - 2r >$$

$$S_{k_2+2} = < b,r > [S_{k_2-k_1+1}] < b,r > [S_{k_2-k_2+1}] < a, (k_2+ 2) v - 2r >$$

$$\vdots$$

$$S_{k_3} = < b,r > [S_{k_3-k_1-1}] < b,r > [S_{k_3-k_2-1}] < a, k_3 v - 2r >$$

$$S_{k_3+1} = < b,r > [S_{k_3-k_1}] < b,r > [S_{k_3-k_2}] < b,r > [< a,0 >] <a, (k_3 + 1) v - 3r>$$

$$S_{k_3+2} = < b,r > [S_{k_3-k_1+1}] < b,r > [S_{k_3-k_2+1}] < b,r > [S_{k_3-k_3+1}] <a,(k_3+ 2)v - 3r>$$

$$\vdots$$

It is not difficult to see that the following formulas can be obtained, for all integers $\underline{i}$ and $\underline{m}$ such that $i \geq 1$ and $0 < m < (k_{i+1} - k_i)$.

$$S_{k_i} = \mathop{\ast}_{j=1}^{i-1} (< b,r > [S_{k_i-k_{j-1}}]) < a, k_i v - (i - 1) r>$$

$$S_{k_i+m} = \mathop{\ast}_{j=1}^{i} (< b,r > [S_{k_i-k_{j-1}+m}]) < a, (k_i+ m)v - ir >$$

The $\ast$ operator in these formulas indicates concatenation of strings.

The length x of the apical segment (the right-most segment in each string) is always such that $0 \leq x < r$. This we can prove by recognizing that

$$\left\lfloor \frac{ir}{v} \right\rfloor v < ir$$

for any r and v. Thus we also have

$$k_i v - (i - 1) r < r$$

$$\text{and} \quad (k_i + m) v - ir < r$$

The above general formulas apply to strings produced at every step n such that $n > \left\lfloor \frac{r}{v} \right\rfloor$, but they are actually not recurrence formulas, because the difference-terms $(k_{i+1} - k_i)$ and the length-terms of the apical segments may keep changing in an irregular fashion as i increases without bound. However, since in all practical examples $\frac{r}{v}$ is a finite fraction, both the difference-terms and the apical length-terms must follow a cyclically repeating sequence. Thus, if for some r and v values the cycles of terms are determined, we can also obtain true recurrence formulas for these systems.

The availability of recurrence formulas for such continuous component systems is clearly of great advantage. Among others, formulas for total numbers and lengths of different orders of branches are then obtainable.

It is of some interest to ask in general what requirements must a developmental system with continuous components fulfill in order to yield recurrence formulas. One requirement is obviously that no interactions should take place among the units. Another one seems to be that the numerical values which appear in the formulas should remain between certain bounds.

Inflorescence development in Aster

Our third example of a developmental system with continuous components is that constructed by D. Frijters and A. Lindenmayer (in these Proceedings) for the growth and flowering of Aster novae-angliae. This developmental process combines certain aspects of both of our previous examples: branching filamentous growth (as in the root) as well as differentiating structures (like the heterocysts) are involved in it. A new aspect of this process is that an environmentally triggered major change occurs in the course of development: a change from vegetative to flowering condition takes place when the lengths of days under which the plants are growing get shorter than a certain critical value. Asters are namely "short-day" plants, they are induced to flower only when day-length falls below about 10 hours, in late August at our latitude. This major change in developmental program is presented in the form of two tables of instructions, one for vegetative and one for floral development.

Four attributes are used for each segment of the plant. The first attribute (again the controlling genomic attribute) has three values in this case: _1_ for apical segment or flowers, _3_ for internodial segments, and _6_ for lateral buds or for basal segments). The second attribute is a biological age parameter (called here "number of plastochrones", related to the plastochrone index of R.O. Erickson and F.J. Michelini [15]). The third attribute is segment length, just as in the case of root segments. The fourth attribute is "bulk", interpreted as "assimilate intake-capacity", and having a role similar to the inhibitor concentration in the blue-green algal model.

In addition to these four "local" or "cellular" attributes, two other attributes, _A_ and _K_, are also computed for each segment. _A_ is computed as the sum of the lengths of the segments from the nearest branching point to the internodial segment under consideration. _K_ is a variable standing for an inhibition value controlled by the "bulk" value of the first internode on a branch. The value of _K_ thus represents an inhibitory effect imposed on a whole branch depending on the position of the branch.

Sets of instructions are given for both vegetative and floral conditions. Some of the instructions take into account not only the attributes of the segment itself which is being computed, but also those of its nearest left neighbour segment. These two properties of the model, having two "tables" of instructions, and taking the left neighbours into account, would make it a T 1L-system with continuous components, were it not for the fact that the variables A and K are not locally computed . This feature of the model is, however, not essential, A and K values could be carried along as two additional attributes for each segment. This would make the computation less efficient, however.

Assuming that we are dealing here with a continuous counterpart of a T 1L-system, we can make use of the recent results concerning those systems (cf. Lee and Rozenberg[19]).

L-systems with continuous components

We have discussed three examples of developmental descriptions with continuous parameters, the first one a counterpart of a non-deterministic 2L-system, the second one of a deterministic OL-system, and the third one of a deterministic T1L-system (all of them were propagating systems, i.e., without cell death). We might ask what properties, in general, would be required, from a biological point of view, of L-systems with continuous components.

First, let us consider interactionless L-systems (OL- and TOL-systems) with continuous components. We could formulate deterministic production rules in the following completely general form:

$$\langle a_1, a_2, \ldots, a_n \rangle \rightarrow \langle f_1(a_1, \ldots, a_n), f_2(a_1, \ldots, a_n), \ldots, f_n(a_1, \ldots, a_n) \rangle,$$

if no division takes place, or

$$\left.\begin{aligned} \langle a_1, a_2, \ldots, a_n \rangle \rightarrow & \langle d_1(f_1(a_1, \ldots, a_n)), \ldots, d_n(f_n(a_1, \ldots, a_n)) \rangle \\ & \langle d_1(f_1(a_1, \ldots, a_n)), \ldots, d_n(f_n(a_1, \ldots, a_n)) \rangle \ldots \\ \ldots & \langle d_1(f_1(a_1, \ldots, a_n)), \ldots, d_n(f_n(a_1, \ldots, a_n)) \rangle, \end{aligned}\right\} m\text{-times}$$

if division takes place. We let here each cell have n attributes; we allow each attribute to influence the values of all the attributes at each computation step by specifying the functions $f_1, f_2, \ldots, f_n$,; and, finally, when a cell divides into m new cells, we introduce distribution functions $d_1, d_2, \ldots, d_n$ to distribute the new values of the attributes over the newly produced cells.

We are thus proposing here a next-state function $F = (f_1, f_2, \ldots, f_n)$ and a distribution function $D = (d_1, d_2, \ldots, d_n)$ such that for each i, $1 \leq i \leq n$, f_i is a mapping from A^n into A, and d_i is a mapping from A into A^m , where A is the set of values over which the functions range. We have thus

$$F : A^n \times A^n \longrightarrow A^n$$

$$D : A^n \longrightarrow A^m \times A^n$$

The functions $f_1, \ldots, f_n$ may be of very simple form. For genomic attributes they usually consist of simple step-functions, such as represented in the root example by the first-attribute rules for all $i \geq 0$ that : if $x < \frac{1}{q_i}$ then $a_i \rightarrow a_i$,

if $x \geq \frac{1}{q_i}$ then $a_i \rightarrow b\ [a_{i+1}]a_i$.

Similar step-functions with externally determined (constant) thresholds are built into the other two examples discussed. One should in fact, require on biological grounds that in each L-system with continuous components there must be one genomic attribute, and the next-state function for this attribute must be a step-function with one or at most two previously specified thresholds (the thresholds may not be computed). The reason for this requirement is the well-known Jacob-Monod model for gene activation and repression. For the same reason, the genomic attribute should always be a discrete one.

The next-state functions for the other attributes may be freely chosen as long as their values remain non-negative and between finite bounds. In no biological situation would one expect to find a parameter which increases without bound or which becomes negative.

The distribution functions $d_1, \ldots, d_n$ are in most realistic systems rather simple. In our first example the distribution function is the identity function for both new cells as far as the second attribute is concerned (both new cells receive the same inhibitor concentration $f(x, y, z)$). In our second example the distribution function for the second attribute is such that the new length x + v of an apical segment (where x + v exceeds the threshold value) is divided into three portions of lengths r, 0, and x + v - r, respectively, which together add up to x + v, Distribution functions are mostly of one of the above two types, most biological parameters being such that either they appear at the same value in both daughter cells (concentration, temperature, etc.) or they are subdivided among the daughter cells (length, mass, etc.). Occasionally there is also need for an unequal and non-additive distribution function, such as the age assignment (the third attribute) in Baker and Herman's model.

The construction of non-deterministic L-systems with continuous components presents no particular problems. One simply has to specify the set of new cells or strings of cells from which one can choose the next-state of a cell. Similarly, continuous component table L-systems can be easily constructed, as shown by Frijters and Lindenmayer (in these Proceedings).

An additional remark: in a sense the principal effects exerted by next-state functions in interactionless L-systems are timing effects. Certain parameters increase or decrease to a point where they exceed a threshold value, when a new genomic state comes into operation, but no spatial effects can be exerted by them. The fact that OL-systems are composed of timing sequences and cycles was recognized and further elaborated by D. Wood [20].

In systems with interactions we have, in addition to timing sequences, the possibility of sending and extinguishing signals, and setting up oscillations (standing or propagating waves). In continuous component L-systems with interactions the next value of each attribute may, in general, be a function of not only all the attributes of the same cell but also of all the attributes of the neighbouring cells. As shown by the models of Baker and Herman and of Frijters and Lindenmayer, the next-state function of one attribute may depend only on the same attribute in neighbouring cells, or on several attributes. The genomic attribute is usually involved in the functions of all other attributes.

References

1 Turing, A.M., 1952, The chemical basis of morphogenesis. Philos. Transact. Royal Soc. London, Ser. B, 237: 37-72.

2 Cohen, D., 1967. Computer simulation of biological pattern generation processes. Nature, 216: 246-248.

3 Ede, D.A., Law, J.T., 1969. Computer simulation of vertebrate limb morphogenesis. Nature, 221: 244-248.

4 Raven, C.P., Bezem, J.J., 1971/73. Computer simulation of embryonic development, Parts I-VI. Proceedings Kon. Ned. Akad. Wet., Ser. C, 74: 209-233; 75: 20-33; 76: 23-35, 319-340.

5 Veen, A.H., Lindenmayer, A., 1973. Manuscript, part of M.S. thesis of A.H. Veen, A computer model for phyllotaxis: A network of Automata. Univ. of Pennsylvania, Philadelphia.

6 Baker, R., Herman, G.T., 1972. Simulation of organisms using a developmental model. Parts I and II. Internat. J. Bio-Med. Computing, 3: 201-215, 251-267.

7 Martinez, H.M., Baer, R.M., 1973. The algorithmic nature of a reaction-diffusion development process. Bull. Math. Biol. 35: 87-94.

8 Lindenmayer, A., 1974. L-systems in their biological context. Proceedings of conference on "Biologically motivated automata theory", McLean, Virginia.

9 Herman, G.T., Rozenberg, G., with a contribution by Lindenmayer, A., "Developmental Systems and Languages" to be published by North-Holland, Amsterdam.

10 Salomaa, A., 1973. "Formal Languages", Academic Press, New York.

11 Baker, R., Herman, G.T., 1970. CELIA - a cellular linear iterative array simulator. Proceedings Fourth Conference on Applications of Simulation, pp. 64-73.

12 Herman, G.T., Liu, W.H., 1973. The daughter of CELIA, the French flag and the firing squad. Simulation 21: 33-41.

13 Rozenberg, G., 1974. L-system with interactions. J. Computer and System Sciences (in press)

14 Salomaa, A., 1973. On some recent problems concerning developmental languages. Lecture Notes in Computer Science, vol. 2, pp. 23-34, Springer Verlag, Berlin.

15 Vitanyi, P.M.B., 1974. Growth functions of context-dependent Lindenmayer systems, manuscript.

16 Hackett, C., Rose, D.A., 1972. A model of the extension and branching of a seminal root of barley, and its use in studying relations between root dimensions. Part I and II. Austral. J. Biol. Sci., 25: 669-690.

17 Herman, G.T., Lindenmayer, A., Rozenberg, G., 1974. Description of developmental languages using recurrence systems. Math. Systems Theory (in press).

18 Erickson, R.O., Michelini, F.J., 1957. The plastochron index. Amer. J. Bot., 44: 297-305.

19 Lee, K.P., Rozenberg, G., 1974. Table L systems with interactions. Manuscript.

20 Wood, D., 1974. Time-delayed OL languages and sequences. Computer Science Techn. Report 74/3, Dept. of Applied Math., McMaster University, Hamilton.

FORMAL LANGUAGE THEORETICAL APPROACH TO INTRACELLULAR BEHAVIOR

VAHE BEDIAN and GABOR T. HERMAN
Departments of Biophysics and Computer Science
The State University of New York at Buffalo

The fact that a gene in the DNA is a string over the alphabet of 64 codons, which describes a string over the alphabet of 20 amino acids is a great scientific discovery with an obvious relationship to formal language theory. We have begun the process of translating into formal language theoretical terminology the concepts associated with the fact that an organism carries a description of its developmental rules in the DNA of every cell. It is our hope that we shall thus be able to formulate precisely (and possibly answer) some problems related to the origin of life: i.e., how the unique, arbitrary genetic code utilized in organisms today could have first arisen.

For example, one may start with the following definitions.

A molecular soup is a 4-tuple $M = \langle A, C, E, G\rangle$, where
A is a finite nonempty set of constructor units (amino acids),
C is a finite nonempty set of descriptor units (codons),
$E \subset A^+$ is the set of constructors (enzymes),
$G \subset C^+$ is the set of descriptors (genes),
such that $\#A \leq \#C \leq \#E \leq \#G$.

A *production scheme* is a 7-tuple $S = \langle A, C, E, G, F, f_1, f_2 \rangle$, where

$\langle A, C, E, G \rangle$ is a molecular soup, the *soup* of S,

$F \subset E$, $\#F = \#C$,

f_1: $F \to C$,

f_2: $C \to A$.

f_2 can be extended to an f_3 so that f_3: $G \to A^+$, in the usual way.

A *production scheme* $S = \langle A, C, E, G, F, f_1, f_2 \rangle$ is said to be *self-coding* if and only if

(i) f_1 is one-to-one onto,

(ii) f_2 is onto A,

(iii) f_3 is onto F.

Example. Consider the following molecular soup. $M = \langle A, C, E, G \rangle$, where $A = \{a, b\}$, $C = \{0, 1, 2\}$, $E = \{ab, bab, aa, b\}$, $G = \{02, 212, 10, 0, 11\}$. Let F, f_1, f_2, $\bar{F}$, $\bar{f}_1$ and $\bar{f}_2$ be defined as follows.

$F = \{ab, bab, b\}$,

$f_1(ab) = 0$, $f_1(bab) = 1$, $f_1(b) = 2$,

$f_2(0) = b$, $f_2(1) = a$, $f_2(2) = b$,

$\bar{F} = \{ab, bab, aa\}$,

$\bar{f}_1(ab) = 0$, $\bar{f}_1(bab) = 1$, $\bar{f}_1(aa) = 2$,

$\bar{f}_2(0) = a$, $\bar{f}_2(1) = a$, $\bar{f}_2(2) = b$.

It is easy to show that both $\langle A, C, E, G, F, f_1, f_2\rangle$ and $\langle A, C, E, G, \bar{F}, \bar{f}_1, \bar{f}_2\rangle$ are self-coding production schemes whose soup is M.

Using such definitions we can now state precisely problems like the following: "Characterize those molecular soups for which there is one and only one self-coding production scheme of which it is the soup." (This question is related to the uniqueness of the genetic code in living organisms. However, this might not be the only possible way in which a unique code may arise. A more general question is: "How do the formal, time-independent relationships proposed in our definition constrain the real-time, dynamical behavior of a molecular soup, to result in a unique code?")

Because of the finiteness of the domain and range of f_1 and f_2, it is of course decidable for any molecular soup whether or not it is the soup of a unique self coding production scheme.

The systems we have considered so far are quite simple, but they indicate the type of approach we have in mind. We plan to continue to work to improve these definitions so that one can ask really meaningful questions about the origin of the genetic code.

Acknowledgements. The research for this paper has been supported by NSF grant GJ 998. The authors are grateful to Professor Howard Pattee and Silvano Colombano for illuminating discussions.

TOWARDS CHARACTERIZATION RESULTS

THREE USEFUL RESULTS CONCERNING L LANGUAGES WITHOUT INTERACTIONS.

A. EHRENFEUCHT
Department of Computer Science,
University of Colorado at Boulder,
Boulder, Colorado, U.S.A.
and
G. ROZENBERG
Institute of Mathematics,
Utrecht University,
Utrecht, Holland.
Department of Mathematics,
Antwerp University, U.I.A.,
Wilrijk, Belgium.

1. INTRODUCTION.

The theory of L systems and languages (see, e.g., [45], [66], [75] and their references) is one of the fast growing areas of formal language theory. Still it is a rather young field (it originated in 1968 from the work of Lindenmayer, (see [59])) and a number of basic problems remain to be solved. One of the open areas within the theory are characterization results for various subclasses of the class of L languages. The kind of results the absence of which feels rather badly in the theory are the characterization results which would allow one to prove that particular languages do not belong to particular subclasses of the class of L languages. So far, almost exclusively, most of such proofs involved combinatorial arguments directed very much at specific properties of the specific language in question (see, e.g., [81] and [91] for proofs of such a kind). This led to the situation that each time it appeared necessary to prove that a given language is not of a particular kind, a whole new proof, mostly ad hoc, must be produced. (The drastic example of this kind is the proof from [35] of the fact that the language $\{x \in \{a,b\}^*$: the number of occurences of the letter a in x is a power of 2$\}$ is not an E0L language. This proof requires from the reader quite an investment of time to follow involved combinatorial arguments, and yet to prove that a slight variation of the above language is not an E0L language could pose a serious problem to the reader).

In this paper we want to present three results, which, although far from resolving the difficulties discussed above, should significantly contribute to this open area. The first of these results provides a partial characterization for a subclass of ETOL languages (see [89]), the second one provides a partial characterization for a subclass of deterministic ETOL languages (see [89]) and the last one provides a partial characterization for a subclass of EOL languages (see, e.g., [35]). The consequences of these results for comparison of various classes of L languages are also discussed.

In this paper we use standard formal language terminology and notation. In particular Λ denotes the empty word, $|x|$ denotes the length of x and $\#A$ denotes the cardinality of A. Also if x is a word over an alphabet Σ and a is in Σ, then $\#_a(x)$ denotes the number of occurrences of a in x; furthermore if $B \subseteq \Sigma$ then $\#_B(x) = \sum_{a \in B} \#_a(x)$. Finally abs(n) denotes the absolute value of n.

2. ETOL SYSTEMS AND LANGUAGES.

The class of ETOL systems and languages was introduced in [89] and is one of the actively investigated topics in the theory of L systems (see, for example, [6], [16], [27], [71] and [72]).

Definition 1. An ETOL system is a construct $G = \langle V, \Sigma, \mathcal{P}, \omega \rangle$, where
1) V is a finite set (called the alphabet of G).
2) $\mathcal{P}$ is a finite set (called the set of tables of G), $\mathcal{P} = \{P_1, \ldots, P_f\}$ for some $f \geqslant 1$, each element of which is a finite subset of $V \times V^*$. $\mathcal{P}$ satisfies the following (completeness) condition:

$$(\forall P)_{\mathcal{P}} (\forall a)_V (\exists \alpha)_{V^*} (\langle a, \alpha \rangle \in P).$$

3) $\omega \in V^+$ (called the axiom of G).
4) $\Sigma \subseteq V$ (called the target alphabet of G).
(We assume that V, Σ and each P in $\mathcal{P}$ are nonempty sets.)

Definition 2. An ETOL system $G = \langle V, \Sigma, \mathcal{P}, \omega \rangle$ is called:
1) Deterministic if for each P in $\mathcal{P}$ and each a in V there exists exactly one α in V^* such that $\langle a, \alpha \rangle \in P$.
2) An EOL system if $\#\mathcal{P} = 1$.
3) An OL system if $\#\mathcal{P} = 1$ and $(V - \Sigma) = \phi$.

Definition 3. Let $G = \langle V, \Sigma, \mathcal{P}, \omega \rangle$ be an ETOL system. Let $x \in V^+$,

$x = a_1 \dots a_k$, where each a_j, $1 \leq j \leq k$, is an element of V, and let $y \in V^*$. We say that x directly derives y in G (denoted as $x \underset{G}{\Rightarrow} y$) if, and only if, there exist P in $\mathcal{P}$ and $p_1, \dots, p_k$ in P such that $p_1 = \langle a_1, \alpha_1 \rangle$, $p_2 = \langle a_2, \alpha_2 \rangle, \dots, p_k = \langle a_k, \alpha_k \rangle$ and $y = \alpha_1 \dots \alpha_k$. Furthermore $\overset{*}{\underset{G}{\Rightarrow}}$ denotes the reflexive and transitive closure of the relation $\underset{G}{\Rightarrow}$.

Definition 4. Let $G = \langle V, \Sigma, \mathcal{P}, \omega \rangle$ be an ETOL system. The language of G, denoted as L(G), is defined as $L(G) = \{x \in \Sigma^* : \omega \overset{*}{\underset{G}{\Rightarrow}} x\}$.

Definition 5. Let L be a language. L is called an ETOL (deterministic ETOL, EOL or OL) language if, and only if, there exists an ETOL (deterministic ETOL, EOL or OL) system G such that L(G) = L.

Example 1. $G_1 = \langle \{a,b,C,D\}, \{a,b\}, \{P_1,P_2,P_3\}, CD \rangle$, where $P_1 = \{a \to a, b \to b, C \to aCb, D \to Da\}$, $P_2 = \{a \to a, b \to b, C \to Cb, D \to D\}$ and $P_3 = \{a \to a, b \to b, C \to \Lambda, D \to \Lambda\}$, is a deterministic ETOL system such that $L(G) = \{a^n b^m a^n : n \geq 0,\ m \geq n\}$. (Following usual notation we write $x \to \alpha$ for an element $\langle x, \alpha \rangle$ of a table.)

Example 2. $G_2 = \langle \{A_1,B_1,C_1,a_1,b_1,c_1,F,a,b,c\}, \{a,b,c\}, \{P\}, A_1B_1C_1 \rangle$, where $P = \{A_1 \to A_1a_1, B_1 \to B_1b_1, C_1 \to C_1c_1, A_1 \to a, B_1 \to b, C_1 \to c, a_1 \to a, b_1 \to b, c_1 \to c, a \to F, b \to F, c \to F, F \to F\}$ is an EOL system such that $L(G_2) = \{a^n b^n c^n : n \geq 1\}$.

Example 3. $G_3 = \langle \{a\}, \{a\}, p, a \rangle$, where $P = \{a \to a^2\}$ is a OL system such that $L(G_3) = \{a^{2^n} : n \geq 0\}$.

3. ETOL LANGUAGES OVER RARE SUBALPHABETS.

In this section we provide a partial characterization result for a subclass of ETOL languages.

Definition 6. If L is a language over an alphabet Σ and B is a nonempty subset of Σ, then

(1) B is called nonfrequent in L if there exists a constant $C_{B,L}$ such that for every x in L, $\#_B(x) < C_{B,L}$; otherwise B is called frequent in L.

(2) B is called rare in L if for every positive integer k there exists a n_k in N^+ such that for every n larger than n_k, if a word x in L contains n occurrences of letters from B then each two such occurrences are of distance not smaller than k.

Example 4. Let $L = \{(ab^k)^k : k \geqslant 1\}$ and $B = \{a\}$. Then B is frequent in L and also B is rare in L.

Theorem 1. If L is an ET0L language over an alphabet Σ and B is a nonempty subset of Σ which is rare in L, then B is nonfrequent in L.

Here are three examples of applications of Theorem 1.

Corollary 1. Let ψ be a function from positive integers into positive integers such that, for every positive integer n, $\psi(n) \geqslant n$. Then the language $\{(ab^{\psi(n)})^n : n \geqslant 1\}$ is not an ET0L language. Proof: Directly from Theorem 1 and Definition 6.

It is known (see [89], Theorem 19) that the class of ET0L languages is properly included in the class of Λ-free context-free programmed languages (introduced in Rosenkrantz, Programmed grammars and classes of formal languages, Journal of the A.C.M., 16, 107-131). Using Corollary 1 we can provide numerous constructions of Λ-free context-free programmed languages which are not ET0L languages. Thus for instance we have:

Corollary 2. The language $\{(ab^k)^k : k \geqslant 1\}$ is a Λ-free context-free programmed language, but it is not an ET0L language.

Proof. It is not difficult to construct a Λ-free context-free programmed grammar generating $L = \{(ab^k)^k : k \geqslant 1\}$. But $B = \{a\}$ is obviously rare in L whereas it is also frequent in L. Thus by Theorem 1, L is not an ET0L language.

4. DETERMINISTIC ET0L LANGUAGES.

In this section we provide a partial characterization for a subclass of deterministic ET0L languages. First we need a definition.

Definition 7.

(1) Let Σ be an alphabet and $x \in \Sigma^+$. We define $\mu(x)$ as the minimal positive integer n such that any two non-overlapping subwords of x are different.

(2) Let L be a language. L is called exponential if there exists a positive integer C_L larger than 1 such that for every x_1, x_2 in L, if $|x_1| > |x_2|$ then $|x_1| \geqslant C_L|x_2|$.

Example 5. If $\Sigma = \{a,b,c\}$ and $x = abcaba$ then $\mu(x) = 3$. The language $\{x \in \{a,b,c\}^* : |x| = 2^n \text{ for some } n \geq 0\}$ is an exponential language.

Theorem 2. If L is an exponential deterministic ET0L language then there exists a positive integer constant F_L such that, for every x in $L-\{\Lambda\}$, we have $\frac{|x|}{\mu(x)} < F_L$.

As an application of this theorem we can prove now that there exists ET0L languages which are not deterministic ET0L languages. (This was posed as an open problem in [89]). In fact we have even stronger result.

Corollary 4. There exists a 0L language which cannot be generated by an EDT0L system.

Proof. Let $L = \{x \in \{a,b\}^* : |x| = 2^n \text{ for some } n \geq 0\} - \{b\}$. The reader can easily check that L is generated by the 0L system $\langle\{a,b\},\{a,b\},P,a\rangle$ where $P = \{a \to aa, a \to ab, a \to ba, a \to bb, b \to aa, b \to ab, b \to ba, b \to bb\}$ and so L is a 0L language. On the other hand L is exponential, but it does not satisfy the statement of Theorem 2, and so it is not a deterministic ET0L language.

5. E0L LANGUAGES OVER NUMERICALLY DISPERSED SUBALPHABETS.

In this section we provide a partial characterization for a subclass of E0L languages. We start with a definition.

Definition 8. Let L be a language over an alphabet Σ and let B be a nonempty subset of Σ. Let $I_{L,B} = \{n \in N : \text{there exists a word } \omega \text{ in } L \text{ such that } \#_B(\omega) = n\}$.

(1) B is numerically dispersed in L if, and only if, $I_{L,B}$ is infinite and for every positive integer k there exists a positive integer n_k such that, for every u_1, u_2 in $I_{L,B}$, if $u_1 \neq u_2$, $u_1 > n_k$ and $u_2 > n_k$ then $abs(u_1-u_2) > k$.

(2) B is clustered in L if, and only if, $I_{L,B}$ is infinite and there exist positive integers k_1, k_2 both larger than 1 such that, for every word ω in L, if $\#_B(\omega) \geq k_1$, then ω contains at least two occurrences of symbols from B which are of distance smaller than k_2.

Example 6. Let $L = \{x \in \{a,b\}^* : \#_{\{a\}}(x) = 2^n \text{ for some } n \geqslant 0\}$ and let $B = \{a\}$. Obviously B is numerically dispersed in L, but B is not clustered in L. However, the language $\{aba\} \cdot L$ is such that B is clustered in L.

Theorem 3. Let L be an E0L language over an alphabet Σ and let B be a nonempty subset of Σ. If B is numerically dispersed in L, then B is clustered in L.

As an example of the application of Theorem 3 we have the following result. (A language L is called a deterministic T0L language if there exists a deterministic ETOL system $G = \langle V,\Sigma, \ ,\omega\}$ such that $L(G) = L$ and $V = \Sigma$.)

Corollary 5. There exist deterministic T0L languages which are not E0L languages.

Proof. Let $L = \{(ab^m)^{2^n} : m,n \geqslant 0\} \cup \{c^{2^n} : n \geqslant 0\}$. L is a deterministic T0L language, because it is the language of the system $\langle\{a,b\},\{a,b\},\{P_1,P_2,P_3\},c\rangle$ where $P_1 = \{a \to a, b \to b, c \to c^2\}$, $P_2 = \{a \to a, b \to b, c \to a\}$ and $P_3 = \{a \to ab, b \to b, c \to c\}$. On the other hand $\{a\}$ is numerically dispersed in L but it is not clustered in L. Consequently, by Theorem 3, L is not an E0L language.

ON THE SIZE OF DOL LANGUAGES *)

PAUL M.B. VITÁNYI

Mathematisch Centrum, Amsterdam, The Netherlands

ABSTRACT

Languages generated by monogenic (i.e. deterministic) context independent Lindenmayer systems (DOL systems) are investigated. Necessary and sufficient conditions are established under which the language generated by a DOL system is finite. Thus, sharp bounds on the cardinality of such a language are obtained. A feasible solution for the membership problem is given. The problems are solved of what is the minimum sized alphabet over which there is a DOL language of cardinality n and, conversely, what is the maximum sized finite DOL language over an alphabet of m letters. This in turn provides us with some number theoretic functions, interesting in their own right, of which several properties, interrelations and asymptotic approximations are derived.

1. INTRODUCTION

Lindenmayer systems are a class of parallel rewriting systems introduced by Lindenmayer [59,60] as a model for the developmental growth of filamentous organisms. A Lindenmayer system consists of an initial filament, symbolized by a string of letters, and the subsequent stages of development are obtained by rewriting all letters in a string simultaneously at each time step. It is called deterministic if the system is essentially monogenic, i.e. each string has a unique successor. It is called context independent if the rewriting of a letter does not depend on its neighbors.

The study of Lindenmayer systems and the languages they generate has gone a long way since its original biological motivation. It has found its own place within the

---

*) This paper is registered at the Mathematical Center as IW 18/74.

body of formal language theory by the growing interest in parallel processes and the different notions, problems and techniques particular to this field, see e.g. Herman and Rozenberg [45]. For instance, the notion of generating languages by monogenic rewriting systems is altogether foreign to the usual generating grammar approach since there such a language would either be empty of contain one element. It is in this direction that our present investigations take place. We shall be concerned with deterministic context independent Lindenmayer systems and the languages they generate. This family of languages has been studied in detail, e.g. with respect to its place in the Chomsky hierarchy [91,117], (anti)closure properties [91,102], and the growth of word length [111,15,75,98,116]. The membership problem for DOL languages has been solved affirmatively in [14] where a gigantic upper bound on the size of such a language is given in case it is finite.

The present paper consists of two parts. In the first part we establish, by a simple combinatorial argument, necessary and sufficient conditions (with respect to the production rules) under which the language generated by a deterministic context independent Lindenmayer system is finite. These conditions yield sharp bounds on the size of such a language depending on the size of the alphabet and the production rules. Furthermore, a feasible decision procedure for the membership problem is provided and we solve the problems of what is the minimum sized alphabet over which there is a deterministic context independent Lindenmayer language of size n and, conversely, what is the maximum sized finite deterministic context independent Lindenmayer language over an alphabet of m letters. The solutions to these last two problems provide us with some number theoretic functions, interesting in their own right, which form the object of study in the second part of our paper. We derive several properties, interrelations and asymptotic approximations to these functions.

2. FINITE DETERMINISTIC CONTEXT INDEPENDENT LINDENMAYER LANGUAGES

We assume that the standard terminology of formal language theory is familiar. We customarily use, with or without indices, i,j,k,n,m,p,q to range over the set of natural numbers $\mathbb{N} = \{0,1,2,\ldots\}$; a,b,c,d to range over an alphabet W; v,w to range over W^*, i.e. the set of all words over W including the *empty word* λ. A *deterministic context independent Lindenmayer system (DOL system)* is a triple $G = \langle W,\delta,w\rangle$ where W is a finite non-empty *alphabet*, δ is a total mapping from W into W^* called the *set of production rules*, and $w \in WW^*$ is the *axiom*. We extend δ to W^* by defining $\delta(\lambda) = \lambda$ and $\delta(a_1a_2\ldots a_n) = \delta(a_1)\delta(a_2)\ldots\delta(a_n)$. (I.e. δ is a homomorphism on W^*.) δ^i is the composition of i copies of δ and is inductively defined by $\delta^0(v) = v$ and $\delta^i(v) = \delta(\delta^{i-1}(v))$ for $i > 0$. The *DOL language* generated by G is $L(G) = \{\delta^i(w) \mid i \geq 0\}$. A *letter* $a \in W$ is *mortal* ($a \in M$) iff $\delta^i(a) = \lambda$ for some i; *vital* ($a \in V$) iff $a \notin M$; *recursive* ($a \in R$) iff $\delta^i(a) \in W^*\{a\}W^*$ for some $i > 0$; *monorecursive* ($a \in MR$) iff $\delta^i(a) \in$

$\in M^*\{a\}M^*$ for some $i > 0$. Clearly, if $a \in M,R,MR$ then there is an i as above such that $i \leq \#M,\#R,\#MR$, respectively, where $\#Z$ denotes the cardinality of a set Z.

Lemma 1. Let $G = \langle W,\delta,w\rangle$ be a DOL system. If there is an i and a $b \in R-MR$ such that b is a subword of $\delta^i(w)$ then $L(G)$ is infinite.

Proof. If $b \in R-MR$ then there is a $j \leq \#R$ and a $c \in V$ such that $\delta^j(b) = v_1bv_2cv_3$ or $\delta^j(b) = v_1cv_2bv_3$. Hence, if $lg_V(v)$ denotes the number of occurrences of vital letters in a word v, we have

(1) $$lg_V(\delta^{i+nj}(w)) \geq lg_V(\delta^{nj}(b)) > n,$$

and $L(G)$ is infinite. □

Lemma 2. Let $G = \langle W,\delta,w\rangle$ be a DOL system. If there is an $i \geq \#(V-R)$ and a $b \in V-R$ such that b is a subword of $\delta^i(a)$ for some $a \in W$ then there is a $j < i$ and a $c \in R-MR$ such that c is a subword of $\delta^j(a)$.

Proof. There is a sequence of letters $a_0,a_1,\ldots,a_i$ such that $a_0 = a$, $a_i = b$ and a_{j+1} is a subword of $\delta(a_j)$ for $0 \leq j < i$. If $b \in V-R$ then $a_j \in V$ for $0 \leq j \leq i$. Since there are at least $\#(V-R)+1$ a_j's there is one which is recursive and therefore there is a $j_1 < i$ such that $a_{j_1} \in R$. It is easy to see that for a recursive letter d always holds that $\delta^t(d)$ contains a recursive letter as a subword for each t. Therefore, $\delta^{i-j_1}(a_{j_1}) = v_1dv_2bv_3$ or $\delta^{i-j_1}(a_{j_1}) = v_1bv_2dv_3$ where $d \in R$ and $b \in V-R$. Hence $a_{j_1} \in$ $\in R-MR$. By taking c equal to a_{j_1} the lemma is proved. □

Lemma 3. Let $G = \langle W,\delta,w\rangle$ be a DOL system. If $\delta^t(w) \in (M\cup MR)^*$ for $t = \#(V-R)$ then $L(G)$ is finite.

Proof. Suppose

(2) $$\delta^{\#(V-R)}(w) = v_1a_1v_2a_2\ldots v_na_nv_{n+1},$$

where $a_1,a_2,\ldots,a_n \in MR$ and $v_1,v_2,\ldots,v_{n+1} \in M^*$. Now it is easy to see that for each $a_i \in MR$ there is a k_i ($1 \leq k_i \leq \#MR$) and a sequence $a_{i0},a_{i1},\ldots,a_{ik_i}$ such that $a_{i0} =$ $= a_{ik_i} = a_i$, $a_{ij_1} \neq a_{ij_2}$ for $0 \leq j_1 < j_2 < k_i$, and $a_{i\,j+1} \in MR$ is the only vital letter in $\delta(a_{ij})$, $0 \leq j < k_i$. Also,

(3) $$\delta^{\#M}(b) = \lambda \qquad \text{for all } b \in M.$$

Hence, for all $a_i \in MR$ and all $t,t' \geq \#M$ holds

(4a) $$\delta^t(a_i) = \delta^{t'}(a_i) \qquad \text{for } t \equiv t' \bmod k_i,$$

(4b) $\delta^t(a_i) \neq v_1\delta^{t'}(a_i)v_2$ for $t \not\equiv t' \bmod k_i$, for all $v_1,v_2 \in W^*$.

By (2), (3) and (4) we have that for all $t \geq \#(W-R)$ holds:

(5) $\delta^t(w) = \alpha_{1j_1}\alpha_{2j_2}\ldots\alpha_{nj_n}$,

where $\alpha_{ij_i} = \delta^{j_i}(a_i)$, $j_i \equiv t \bmod k_i$ and $\#M \leq j_i < \#M+k_i$, $1 \leq i \leq n$. By (2), (4) and (5):

(6a) $\delta^t(w) \neq \delta^{t'}(w)$ for all t,t' such that $\#(W-R) \leq t < t' < \#(W-R) + \text{l.c.m.}\ (k_1,k_2,\ldots,k_n)$;

(6b) $\delta^t(w) = \delta^{t'}(w)$ for all t,t' such that $t,t' \geq \#(W-R)$ and $t \equiv t' \bmod (\text{l.c.m.}\ (k_1,k_2,\ldots,k_n))$.

Therefore

(7) $\text{l.c.m.}\ (k_1,k_2,\ldots,k_n) \leq \#L(G) \leq \text{l.c.m.}\ (k_1,k_2,\ldots,k_n) + \#(W-R)$. □

We are now ready to state the main theorem of this section.

Theorem 1. Let $G = \langle W,\delta,w\rangle$ be a DOL system. L(G) is finite iff $\delta^t(w) \in (M\cup MR)^*$ for $t = \#(V-R)$.

Proof. "If". By lemma 3.
"Only if".
Case 1. $\delta^t(w) \in W^*(R-MR)W^*$. By lemma 1 L(G) is infinite.
Case 2. $\delta^t(w) \in W^*(V-R)W^*$ for $t = \#(V-R)$. By lemma 2 there is a $t' < t$ such that $\delta^{t'}(w) \in W^*(R-MR)W^*$, and therefore case 1 holds and L(G) is infinite.

Hence, if $\delta^t(w) \in W^*(V-MR)W^*$ for $t = \#(V-R)$ then L(G) is infinite, i.e. if L(G) is finite then $\delta^t(w) \in (M\cup MR)^*$ for $t = \#(V-R)$. □

From the previous lemmas and the theorem we can derive some interesting corollaries.

Corollary 1. L(G) is finite iff $\delta^t(w) \in (M\cup MR)^*$ for all $t \geq \#(V-R)$.

Corollary 2. A DOL language is finite iff all recursive letters which are accessible from the axiom (i.e. which occur in words in the language) are monorecursive.

Since all letters which can be derived from a certain letter (or word) are derived within #W steps, it is easy to determine whether a letter is mortal, vital, recursive, monorecursive. The quickest way is to determine subsequently M, V, R and MR.

Corollary 3. There is an algorithm to determine whether the language generated by a DOL system is finite or not. (Hint: determine M,V,R and MR and apply theorem 1 or corollary 2.)

Next we consider the *membership problem*: given a DOL system $G = \langle W,\delta,w\rangle$ and a word $v \in W^*$, decide whether or not v is in L(G). (Equivalently, is there an i such that $\delta^i(w) = v$). Now assume that L(G) is finite and

$$\delta^{\#(V-R)}(w) = v_1a_1v_2a_2\ldots v_na_nv_{n+1},$$

where $a_1,a_2,\ldots,a_n \in MR$ and $v_1,v_2,\ldots,v_{n+1} \in M^*$. Assume further that $v = \alpha_{1j_1}\alpha_{2j_2}\ldots$ $\ldots\alpha_{nj_n}$ where $\alpha_{ij_i} = \delta^{j_i}(a_i)$ for some j_i such that $\#M \le j_i < \#M+k_i$, $1 \le i \le n$. By (4b) $\delta^{j_i}(a_i) \ne v_1\delta^{j_i'}(a_i)v_2$ for all j_i,j_i' such that $\#M \le j_i < j_i' < \#M+k_i$ and all $v_1,v_2 \in W^*$, $1 \le i \le n$. Therefore, the parse of v (if it exists) is unique and can be executed easily from left to right given $\delta^t(a_i)$ for all t and i, $\#M \le t < \#M+k_i$, $1 \le i \le n$. Since by (4a) $\delta^t(a_i) = \delta^{t'}(a_i)$ for all $t,t' \ge \#M$ such that $t \equiv t' \bmod k_i$ the problem can now be restated as follows: is there a positive integer u such that $u \equiv (j_i-\#M) \bmod k_i$, $1 \le i \le n$. The solution is well known.

Lemma 4. (Chinese remainder theorem [1]). Let $k_1,k_2,\ldots,k_n$ be positive integers and let $t_1,t_2,\ldots,t_n$ be any integers. There is exactly one integer u which satisfies the conditions

$$0 \le u < \text{l.c.m.}\ (k_1,k_2,\ldots,k_n),$$
$$u \equiv t_i \bmod k_i \quad (1\le i\le n)$$
$$\text{iff}\quad t_i \equiv t_j \bmod (\text{g.c.d.}\ (k_i,k_j)) \qquad (1\le i<j\le n).$$

There is no integer $u \equiv t_i \bmod k_i$, $(1\le i\le n)$, if not $t_i \equiv t_j \bmod (\text{g.c.d.}\ (k_i,k_j))$, $(1\le i<j\le n)$.

Therefore, if u exists then $v = \delta^{\#(W-R)+u}(w)$ and $v \ne \delta^t(w)$ for all $t \ge \#(W-R)$ otherwise. If a parse of v as mentioned is not possible then by (5) $v \ne \delta^t(w)$ for all $t \ge \#(W-R)$. Hence we have

Theorem 2. There is an algorithm which solves the membership problem for DOL languages.

Proof. The proof consists in giving an outline of the algorithm.

(i) Determine whether L(G) is finite or not (corollary 3). If L(G) is infinite then generate successively $w,\delta(w),\delta^2(w),\ldots$ and compare each $\delta^i(w)$ with v. Is

[1] See e.g. Knuth,D. *Seminumerical algorithms*. Addison-Wesley, Reading (Mass.)(1969), 256.

$\delta^i(w) \neq v$ for all $i < t_0$ and $\delta^{t_0}(w)$ contains more occurrences of vital letters than does v then $v \notin L(G)$. By (1) $t_0 \leq \#V(lg_V(v) - lg_V(w) + 1)$.

(ii) L(G) is finite. Generate successively $w, \delta(w), \ldots, \delta^{\#(W-R)}(w)$ and compare each $\delta^i(w)$ with v. Is $\delta^i(w) \neq v$ for all i such that $0 \leq i \leq \#(W-R)$ then try to parse v as discussed above. Is the parse successful then apply the Chinese remainder theorem. Depending on whether or not an integer u, as stated in the theorem, exists v does or does not belong to L(G). If the parse is not successful then $v \notin L(G)$. □

The decision procedure for the membership problem for DOL languages we gave above is unusual under mathematical decision procedures in that it is *feasible*, i.e. gives answers to reasonable questions within a reasonable time[2], as testified by an ALGOL 60 implementation, Vitányi [114]. Of course, if L(G) is finite we can test for membership by generating the whole of L(G). But as will appear from the next corollary and the asymptotic approximations in section 4, even for a modest alphabet of, say, a hundred letters, this may turn out not to be feasible.

By the inequality (7) we can easily determine the cardinality of a finite DOL language.

Example. Let $G = \langle\{a,a_1,a_2,a_3,b_1,b_2,c_1,c_2,c_3\}, \{\delta(a) = c_1a_1b_1c_3, \delta(a_1) = c_1a_2, \delta(a_2) = c_2a_3, \delta(a_3) = c_3c_3a_1, \delta(b_1) = c_1b_2c_1, \delta(b_2) = c_2b_1c_1, \delta(c_1) = c_2c_3, \delta(c_2) = c_3, \delta(c_3) = \lambda\}, c_1ac_3a_1b_2c_2\rangle$.

Then:

$$M = \{c_1,c_2,c_3\},$$
$$V = \{a,a_1,a_2,a_3,b_1,b_2\},$$
$$R = MR = \{a_1,a_2,a_3,b_1,b_2\}.$$

Since a does not occur in a value of δ, $\delta^{\#(V-R)}(c_1ac_3a_1b_2c_2) \in (M \cup MR)^*$: L(G) is finite. The different *periods* k_1,k_2 are 2 and 3. Therefore, by (7)

$$\text{l.c.m.}\ (2,3) \leq \#L(G) \leq \text{l.c.m.}\ (2,3) + 9-5,$$

or,

$$6 \leq \#L(G) \leq 10.$$

By writing out L(G) we see that $\#L(G) = 10$.

From the inequality (7) we obtain the following corollary (see also [114]) which forms the basis of the sequel.

---

[2] See e.g. Parikh, R. *Existence and feasibility in arithmetic*, J.Symb.Logic. 34 (1971), 494 - 508.

<u>Corollary 4</u>. (i) Let $P: \mathbb{N} \to \mathbb{N}$ be defined as follows. $P(m)$ is the largest natural number n which is the least common multiple of $k_1, k_2, \ldots, k_q$, for all possible partitions of m into $q = 1,2,\ldots,m$ positive integral summands, plus the number of summands equal to 1. By (7) $P(m)$ is the maximum cardinality of a finite DOL language over an alphabet of m letters.
(ii) Let $S: \mathbb{N} \to \mathbb{N}$ be defined as follows. $S(n)$ is the smallest natural number m such that there exists a partition of m into positive integral summands $k_1, k_2, \ldots, k_q$, $q \leq m$, and l.c.m. $(k_1, k_2, \ldots, k_q) + \#\{i \mid k_i = 1\} = n$. By (7) $S(n)$ is the minimum cardinality of an alphabet over which there is a DOL language of cardinality n.

The remainder of the paper will be concerned with the investigation of the number theoretic functions S, P and some variants. Thus we derive lower bounds on the size of the alphabet as a function S of the size of a finite DOL language over such an alphabet, and upper bounds on the size of a finite DOL language as a function P of the size of the alphabet.

3. FUNCTIONS WHICH RELATE SIZE OF LANGUAGE WITH SIZE OF ALPHABET

The number theoretic functions S and P of corollary 4 have a much broader setting than just their connection with DOL systems. Imagine a process which starts by counting until some number d and then initializes some number q of periodic counters. Then $S(n)$ and $P(m)$ have a natural interpretation as the smallest number of states needed to generate a prescribed number n of distinguishable configurations and the largest number of distinguishable configurations which can be generated by using a prescribed number m different states, respectively. If we have the additional restriction $d = 0$ then, in the latter case, we ask in effect for the maximum order of a permutation of the m-th degree. (The order of a permutation of the m-th degree is the exponent of the smallest power of a permutation on m elements which is equal to the identity permutation.) Already Landau[3] investigated the maximum order $f(m)$ of a permutation of a given degree m. I.e. $f: \mathbb{N} \to \mathbb{N}$ where $f(m)$ is defined as the maximum of the least common multiple of $k_1, k_2, \ldots, k_q$ for all possible partitions of m into $q = 1,2,\ldots,m$ positive integral summands. We shall return to this connection with Landau's work in section 4.

According to corollary 4,

$$(8) \qquad S(n) = \min\{ \sum_{i=1}^{q} k_i + d \mid \text{l.c.m. } (k_1, k_2, \ldots, k_q) + d = n\},$$

---

[3] Landau, E. *Über die Maximalordnung der Permutationen gegebenen Grades*, Archiv der Math. und Phys., Dritte Reihe, <u>5</u> (1903), 92 - 103.

(9) $$P(n) = \max\{\text{l.c.m.}\ (k_1,k_2,\ldots,k_q) + d \mid \sum_{i=1}^{q} k_i + d = n\}.$$

For the smallest values of n we find:

n	1	2	3	4	5	6	7	8	9	10	11	12	13	14
S(n)	1	2	3	4	5	5	6	7	8	7	8	7	8	9
P(n)	1	2	3	4	6	7	12	15	20	30	31	60	61	84

For instance,

$$S(14) = 2+7 = 4+3+2 = 9 \qquad \text{since } 14 = 2*7 = 4*3 + 2.$$

$$P(14) = 2*2*3*7 = 4*3*7 = 84 \qquad \text{since } 14 = 2+2+3+7 = 4+3+7.$$

Hence, the corresponding representations of S(n) and P(n) in $k_1,k_2,\ldots,k_q,d$ are not unique. Clearly, in (8) and (9) the $\bar{k}_1,\bar{k}_2,\ldots,\bar{k}_{\bar{q}}$ for which the extrema are reached for a given n will be relatively prime. Suppose we can factorize a $\bar{k}_i$, $1 \le i \le \bar{q}$, into two relatively prime factors $\bar{k}_{i1}$ and $\bar{k}_{i2}$:

$$\bar{k}_i = \bar{k}_{i1}*\bar{k}_{i2}, \qquad \bar{k}_{i1} > 1, \qquad \bar{k}_{i2} > 1.$$

Then

$$\bar{k}_i - (\bar{k}_{i1}+\bar{k}_{i2}) = \bar{k}_{i1}*\bar{k}_{i2} - (\bar{k}_{i1}+\bar{k}_{i2}) = (\bar{k}_{i1}-1)(\bar{k}_{i2}-1) - 1 \ge 0.$$

Therefore, it suffices to look for $\bar{k}_1,\bar{k}_2,\ldots,\bar{k}_{\bar{q}}$ which are powers of distinct primes.

Hence we replace (8) and (9) by

(10) $$S(n) = \min\{\Sigma p^{\alpha} + d \mid \Pi p^{\alpha} + d = n\},$$

(11) $$P(n) = \max\{\Pi p^{\alpha} + d \mid \Sigma p^{\alpha} + d = n\},$$

where p denotes some prime. To obtain a canonical representation for S(n) and P(n) we take the representation with the smallest d for which the extrema are reached. By the unique factorization property of the natural numbers this representation will be unique. Additionally we define

(12) $$S'(n) = \min\{\Sigma p^{\alpha} + d \mid \Pi p^{\alpha} + d \ge n\},$$

(13) $$P'(n) = \max\{\Pi p^{\alpha} + d \mid \Sigma p^{\alpha} + d \le n\}.$$

(Then S'(n) is the number of letters in the smallest alphabet over which there is a finite DOL language of at least cardinality n and P'(n) is the cardinality of the largest finite DOL language over an alphabet of at most n letters.) It is convenient to introduce also

(14) $$s(n,d) = \Sigma p^{\alpha} + d \quad \text{such that } \Pi p^{\alpha} = n-d,$$

since by the unique factorization property s(n,d) is found immediately; and we see that

(15) $$S(n) = \min\{s(n,d) \mid 0 \le d \le n\}.$$

The first 2000 values of S(n) were determined by computer and showed a quite erratic behavior. E.g. S(1971) = 61, S(1972) = 50, S(1973) = 51 and S(2000) = 39. (Østerby[4] contains a detailed computer analysis of S(n) for $1 \le n \le 5 \cdot 10^{11}$. Furthermore, S'(n) and P(n) are computed for a large number of values. He considers e.g. the question in how many different ways S(n) can be obtained from n.)

Now let us take a closer look at the general behavior and interrelations of our functions. It is at once apparent that, since $P(n+1) \ge P(n)+1$ for all n, P is strictly increasing and therefore P' = P. $S(n+1) \le S(n)+1$ and S(8) = S(10) = 7 while S(9) = = 8. Therefore, S is not monotonic. By its definition S' is monotonic increasing and $S'(n) \le S(n)$ for all n. A crude approximation gives us (for n > 1):

(16a) $$P(n) < n^n;$$

(16b) $$S(n)^{S(n)} > n;$$

(16c) $$S'(n)^{S'(n)} > n.$$

From (16b) and (16c) it follows that $S(n) \to \infty$ and $S'(n) \to \infty$ for $n \to \infty$. In section 4 we shall derive asymptotic approximations for P, S' and inf S; it will appear that these functions are intimately related to the distribution of the prime numbers. We use the notation $f(x) \sim g(x)$ for f(x) is *asymptotic* to g(x), i.e. $\lim_{x\to\infty} f(x)/g(x) = 1$. It is well known[5] that the number of primes $\pi(x)$ not exceeding x is asymptotic to x/log x: $\pi(x) \sim x/\log x$. Furthermore, the i-th prime p_i is asymptotic to i log i: $p_i \sim i \log i$. It then follows from (16a) that $e^{\log P(n)} \le e^{n \log n}$ and therefore $\log P(n) \le n \log n \sim p_n$. Since $S'(n)^{S'(n)} \ge n$, similarly $\log n \le S'(n) \log S'(n)$.

---

[4] Østerby, O. *Prime decompositions with minimum sums*. Univ. of Aarhus, Comp. Sci. Dept. Tech. Rept. DAIMI-PB 19 (1973).

[5] Hardy, G.H. & Wright, E.M. *An introduction to the theory of numbers*, Oxford University Press (1945), 9 - 10.

By noting[6] that x/log x is asymptotic to the function inverse of x log x we have that $S'(n) \geq g(n)$ for some function $g(n) \sim \frac{\log n}{\log\log n} \sim \pi(\log n)$. Therefore, $S(n) \geq g(n)$ also.

Since P is strictly increasing and $P(6) = 7$, $P(7) = 12$: $P\colon \mathbb{N} \to \mathbb{N}$ is an injection but no surjection; since $S(n+1) \leq S(n)+1$ and $S'(n+1) \leq S'(n)+1$ for all n, $S(n) \to \infty$ and $S'(n) \to \infty$ for $n \to \infty$, $S(5) = S'(5) = S(6) = S'(6) = 5$: $S,S'\colon \mathbb{N} \to \mathbb{N}$ are surjections but no injections. From the definitions we would expect S and S' to be some kind of an inverse of P. Since P is the maximum size language over an alphabet of n letters, and since P is strictly increasing, an alphabet of size n is the minimum size alphabet over which there is a language of (at least) size P(n). Therefore, if we denote the set of values of P by $A = \{P(i) \mid i \geq 0\}$ we obtain $S(P(n)) = S'(P(n)) = n$ for all $n \in \mathbb{N}$. Hence the restrictions of S and S' to A are the inverse of P:

$$(17) \qquad S_{/A} = S'_{/A} = P^{-1}.$$

From the definitions we also see that between two consecutive values of P, S' is constant (S' is monotonic, $S'(P(n)) = n$ for all n, $S'(P(n)+1) = n+1$ for all n) and therefore:

$$(18) \qquad S'(m) = P^{-1}(n) \quad \text{for all } m, \quad P(P^{-1}(n)-1) < m \leq n,$$

where $n \in A$. Since $S'(n) \leq S(n)$ for all n we have therefore by (17)

$$(19) \qquad S(n) = S'(n) = P^{-1}(n) \quad \text{and} \quad S(m) \geq P^{-1}(n),$$

for all $n \in A$ and all $m > P(P^{-1}(n)-1)$.

Therefore, S' is a stepfunction where every step of 1 takes place at a value of P. Furthermore, S' is the greatest monotonic increasing function which is a lower bound on S.

In looking at the function S and trying to distinguish its features we readily notice that if n is a prime or the power of a prime then $S(n) = S(n-1)+1$. The way S is defined, however, does not give us a general method, to find the value of S for a certain argument, better than by trial and error. The following theorem is one of the main results of this section and provides an inductive definition of S.

<u>Theorem 3</u>.

$$S(n) = \begin{cases} n & \text{for } n = 0,1,2,3,4,5. \\ \min\{S(n-1)+1,\ s(n,0)\} & \text{for } n > 5. \end{cases}$$

---

[6] Hardy & Wright. Op. cit. 9–10.

Proof. By induction on n. The theorem holds for n = 0,1,2,3,4,5. Suppose the theorem is true for all $n \le m$. Since

$$S(m+1) = \min\{s(m+1,d) \mid 0 \le d \le m+1\},$$

and

$$s(m'+1,d') = s(m',d'-1)+1 ,$$

for all m' and all d' such that $0 < d' \le m'+1$, we have

$$S(m+1) = \min\{S(m)+1,\ s(m+1,0)\}. \ \square$$

The following corollary of theorem 3 is also stated by Østerby[7] and gives a recursive definition of S(n). By theorem 3 we have for all n:

$$S(n) = \min\{s(n,0),\ s(n-1,0)+1,\ldots,s(1,0)+n-1,\ n\}.$$

Since for all k such that $n \ge k > S(n)$ holds $S(n) < s(n-k,0)+k$, we have:

Corollary 5. $S(n) = \min\{s(n,0),\ s(n-1,0)+1,\ldots,s(n-S(n),0)+S(n)\}$.

Hence we only have to compute s(n,d), i.e. the sum of the highest powers of primes in the factorization of n-d, for $d = 0,1,\ldots,k_0$ where k_0 is the minimum of the previously computed values of s(n,d)+d.

The analogue of theorem 3 for P is

$$P(n) = \begin{cases} n & \text{for } n = 0,1,2,3,4 \\ \max\{P(n-1)+1,\ \max\{m \mid s(m,0) = n\}\} & \text{for } n > 4. \end{cases}$$

This does not help us very much, essentially because although the factorization of a natural number is unique, a partition is not. If we assume that the following conjecture by Landau[8] is true, viz. $P(\Sigma_{i=1}^{k} p_i) = \Pi_{i=1}^{k} p_i$ for all k, then since P is strictly increasing we can slightly limit the number of m's which have to be investigated:

$$P(n) = \begin{cases} n & \text{for } n = 0,1,2,3,4 \\ \max\{P(n-1)+1,\ \max\{m \mid s(m,0) = n \text{ and } \prod_{i=1}^{k} p_i < m \le \prod_{i=1}^{k+1} p_i\}\} & \text{for } \sum_{i=1}^{k} p_i < n \le \sum_{i=1}^{k+1} p_i, \end{cases}$$

7 Østerby, Op. cit.

8 Landau, Op. cit.

where we denote by p_i the i-th prime and $p_1 = 2$.

4. ASYMPTOTIC APPROXIMATIONS

In this section we investigate the asymptotic behavior of our functions. Landau[9] proves that for $f(n) = \max\{\Pi p^\alpha \mid \Sigma p^\alpha \le n\}$:

$$(20) \qquad \log f(n) \sim \sqrt{n \log n}\ .$$

<u>Theorem 4</u>. $\log P(n) \sim \sqrt{n \log n}$.

<u>Proof</u>. By (20) $\log f(n) \sim \sqrt{n \log n}$, i.e.

$$\lim_{n\to\infty} \frac{\log f(n)}{\sqrt{n \log n}} = 1\ .$$

Also,

$$\lim_{n\to\infty} \frac{\log (f(n)+n)}{\sqrt{n \log n}} = 1 + \lim_{n\to\infty} \frac{\log (1+n/f(n))}{\sqrt{n \log n}} = 1.$$

Since by (11) and the definition of f(n) we have:

$$f(n) \le P(n) < f(n)+n, \text{ i.e., } \log f(n) \le \log P(n) < \log (f(n)+n),$$

and we proved above that

$$\log f(n) \sim \log (f(n)+n) \sim \sqrt{n \log n}\ ,$$

we have

$$\log P(n) \sim \sqrt{n \log n}\ . \quad \square$$

<u>Corollary 6</u>. $\log P(n) \sim \sqrt{p_n}$, where p_n is the n-th prime.

<u>Theorem 5</u>. $S'(n) \sim \dfrac{\log^2 n}{\log \log^2 n}$.

<u>Proof</u>. If $\log y = \sqrt{x \log x}$, then $\log^2 y = x \log x$ and

$$\log \log^2 y = \log x + \log \log x \sim \log x.$$

---

[9] Landau, Op. cit.

Since

$$x = \frac{\log^2 y}{\log x} \quad \text{we have } x \sim \frac{\log^2 y}{\log \log^2 y} .$$

By this argument and since $\log P(m) \sim \sqrt{m \log m}$ it follows:

$$m \sim \frac{\log^2 P(m)}{\log \log^2 P(m)}$$

or

$$P^{-1}(n) \sim \frac{\log^2 n}{\log \log^2 n} \quad \text{for } n \in \{P(i) \mid i \geq 0\}.$$

Denote $\log^2 n/\log \log^2 n$ by $h(n)$. By (18) $S'(n) \sim h(n)$ for n in the range of P. This cannot tell us anything about the sup $S'(n)$ since the restriction to special values of n can only yield a lower bound but not an upper bound. According to (18), however, we have for all pairs of consecutive values of P, say n_1, n_2:

$$S'(n_1) \leq S'(m) \leq S'(n_2) = S'(n_1)+1, \quad n_1 \leq m \leq n_2.$$

Since h is strictly increasing,

$$\begin{aligned}
\lim_{m\to\infty} S'(m)/h(m) &\geq \lim_{m\to\infty} S'(m)/h(n_2) \\
&\geq \lim_{m\to\infty} (S'(n_2)-1)/h(n_2) \\
&= \lim_{n_2\to\infty} (S'(n_2)/h(n_2) - 1/h(n_2)) \\
&= 1 - \lim_{n_2\to\infty} 1/h(n_2) = 1.
\end{aligned}$$

Analogous we prove that $\lim_{m\to\infty} S'(m)/h(m) \leq 1$, and therefore $S'(m) \sim h(m)$ for all $m \in \mathbb{N}$. □

<u>Corollary 7</u>. $S'(n) \sim \pi(\log^2 n)$.

The greatest monotonic increasing function which is a lower bound on S is $S'(n) \sim h(n)$. Therefore:

<u>Corollary 8</u>. $\inf S(n) \sim \dfrac{\log^2 n}{\log \log^2 n}$.

Because of theorem 3 $\inf S(n) \sim \inf s(n,0)$ and we have:

Corollary 9. The greatest monotonic increasing function which is a lower bound on the sum of the greatest powers of primes in the factorization of n, i.e. s(n,0), is asymptotic to h(n). Hence:

$$\inf s(n,0) \sim \frac{\log^2 n}{\log \log^2 n}\,.$$

As is to be expected, this lower bound is reached for the special sequence of values $n = \prod_{i=1}^{k} p_i$, $k \in \mathbb{N}$.

Lemma 5. $\sum_{i=1}^{k} p_i \sim \frac{\log^2 n}{\log \log^2 n}$, where $n = \prod_{i=1}^{k} p_i$ and $k \in \mathbb{N}$.

Proof. The number of factors in a factorization of a natural number n is denoted by $\omega(n)$. According to Hardy & Wright[10]

$$\omega(n) \sim \frac{\log n}{\log \log n}\,.$$

Therefore, $\Sigma_{i=1}^{k} p_i \sim \Sigma_{i=1}^{\omega(n)} i \log i$. Bounding this discrete summation on both sides by an integral we obtain:

$$\int_1^{\omega(n)} i \log i \, di \le \sum_{i=1}^{\omega(n)} i \log i \le \int_2^{\omega(n)+1} i \log i \, di,$$

$$\frac{1}{2}\Big[i^2 \log i - i^2/2\Big]_1^{\omega(n)} \le \sum_{i=1}^{\omega(n)} i \log i \le \frac{1}{2}\Big[i^2 \log i - i^2/2\Big]_2^{\omega(n)+1},$$

$$\frac{1}{2}(\omega(n)^2(\log \omega(n) - \tfrac{1}{2}) + \tfrac{1}{2}) \le \sum_{i=1}^{\omega(n)} i \log i \le \frac{1}{2}((\omega(n)+1)^2(\log(\omega(n)+1) - \tfrac{1}{2}) - 4 \log 2 + 2).$$

Hence if $n \to \infty$ through this particular series of values we have

$$\begin{aligned}\sum_{i=1}^{k} p_i &\sim \frac{1}{2}(\omega(n)^2 \log \omega(n) - \omega(n)^2/2)\\ &\sim \frac{1}{2}\omega(n)^2 \log \omega(n)\\ &\sim \frac{\log^2(n)\,(\log \log n - \log \log \log n)}{2\,(\log \log n)^2}\\ &\sim \frac{\log^2 n}{2 \log \log n} = \frac{\log^2 n}{\log \log^2 n}\,. \quad \Box\end{aligned}$$

---

[10] Hardy & Wright, Op. cit., 355.

A numerical verification shows:

$$(2+3+5)/(\log^2 (2*3*5)/\log\log^2 (2*3*5)) \approx 0.47$$

$$(2+3+\ldots+17)/(\log^2 (2*3*\ldots*17)/\log\log^2 (2*3*\ldots*17)) \approx 0.58$$

$$(2+3+\ldots+97)/(\log^2 (2*3*\ldots*97)/\log\log^2 (2*3*\ldots*97)) \approx 0.75$$

$$(2+3+\ldots+173)/(\log^2 (2*3*\ldots*173)/\log\log^2 (2*3*\ldots*173)) \approx 0.79.$$

Resuming the results of this section we have:

$$\log P(n) \sim \sqrt{n \log n} \sim \sqrt{p_n} ;$$

$$S'(n) \sim \inf S(n) \sim \inf s(n,0) \sim \frac{\log^2 n}{\log\log^2 n} \sim \pi(\log^2 n);$$

and, furthermore,

$$s(n,0) \sim \frac{\log^2 n}{\log\log^2 n} ,$$

for $n \to \infty$ through the particular series of values $n = \Pi_{i=1}^{k} p_i$.

Acknowledgement. I thank O. Østerby and D. Wood for critical comments.

GENERATIVELY DETERMINISTIC L LANGUAGES. SUBWORD POINT OF VIEW

A. EHRENFEUCHT
Department of Computer Science, University of Colorado, at Boulder,
K.P. LEE [1)]
Department of Computer Science, S.U.N.Y. at Buffalo,
and
G. ROZENBERG
Institute of Mathematics, Utrecht University, and
Department of Mathematics, Antwerp University, UIA

INTRODUCTION

The notion of a "deterministic machine" or a "deterministic language" (as opposed to their nondeterministic counterparts) is one of the oldest and most investigated in the theory of computation and in formal language theory. One can however observe that whereas the notion of a deterministic machine is usually the natural one (in every situation there is at most one possible "move" the machine can make), the notion of a deterministic language is often not natural at all. In fact a deterministic language is almost always defined as a language which can be recognized by a deterministic machine, although in many cases the languages themselves are being defined by grammars rather than by machines. The typical situation is of the following kind: first a class of languages $\mathcal{L}$ is defined by a class of grammars $\mathcal{G}$, then one finds an "equivalent" class of machines $\mathcal{M}$, and then by considering the deterministic subclass $\mathcal{M}_D$ of the class $\mathcal{M}$ one obtains the deterministic subclass $\mathcal{L}_D$ of the class $\mathcal{L}$. What subclass of $\mathcal{G}$ generates $\mathcal{L}_D$ is mostly not understood at all, or, in the best case, it is the "translation" of $\mathcal{M}_D$ into the subclass of $\mathcal{G}$, which could neither be called natural nor give any insight into the nature of the deterministic restriction. The basic difficulty lies in the fact that the notion of a deterministic language is defined via recognizers whereas the languages themselves are often defined in terms of generative devices.

In this paper we want to point out several classes of languages for which the notion of "generative determinism" (deterministic restriction defined in terms of grammars rather than recognizers) is not only a very natural one but it also lends itself to mathamatical treatment.

The theory of L systems and languages originated with the work of

---

1) This paper is based on part of this author's Ph.D. thesis.

Lindenmayer [59], [60]. Its purpose was to model the growth of filamentous organisms. From the formal language theory point of view, L systems are string rewriting systems. They have provided us with an alternative to the now standard Chomsky framework for defining languages. Basically L systems differ from Chomsky grammars in the lack of nondeterminals and in the totally parallel manner of rewriting (meaning that in a single derivation step one must rewrite all occurrences of all the symbols in the string being rewritten). For more detailed discussion see, for example, [45] or [66]. In the theory of L systems the deterministic restriction arose for a number of natural and "practical" reasons. Its investigation has led to novel fields like growth functions (see [75] and its references) and to new research on rather established topics like the deterministic simulation of one kind of system by another (see, for example, [12]). This paper continues the study of the role determinism plays in various classes of L systems.

A possible division line in the theory of L systems is the distinction between systems without interactions and systems with interactions. Accordingly the present paper is divided into two parts. In the first part we treat systems without interactions, while the second part is concerned with systems with interactions.

PART I
L systems without interactions

In an L system without interactions, the rewriting of a letter in a string does not depend on the context in which the letter occurs (in other words, each occurrence of the same letter may be rewritten in the same way).

I.1 TOL systems and languages.

TOL systems and languages were divised to model special cases of development in which no cell interaction takes place but there is a finite number of possible environments. In different environments, the behaviour of the same cell may be different. TOL systems were introduced in [81]. Their formal definitions and basic properties can be found there. (TOL systems, or languages, abbreviates "table L systems, or languages, without interactions".)

A T0L system has the following components[2]:

(i) A finite set of symbols Σ, the <u>alphabet</u>.

(ii) A finite set $\mathcal{P}$ of <u>tables</u> of productions. Each production in a table is usually written in the form $a \to \alpha$, where $a \in \Sigma$ and $\alpha \in \Sigma^*$. The meaning of $a \to \alpha$ is that an occurrence of the letter a in a string may be replaced by α (where each replacement is "context-free"). In general, a table may contain several productions for each symbol. In every step of a derivation, all symbols in a string must be simultaneously replaced according to the production rules of one arbitrarily chosen table.

(iii) A starting string, σ, the <u>axiom</u>.

Thus a T0L system G is usually specified as $G = \langle \Sigma, \mathcal{P}, \sigma \rangle$. The <u>language generated by G</u>, denoted as L(G), consists of σ and all strings which can be derived from σ in a finite number of steps. A language L is called a <u>T0L language</u> if there exists a T0L system G such that L = L(G).

<u>Example 1</u>. Let $G = \langle \{a,b\}, \{\{a \to a^2, b \to b^2\}, \{a \to a^3, b \to b^3\}\}, ab \rangle$. Then

$L(G) = \{a^{2^n 3^m} b^{2^n 3^m} \mid n,m \geq 0\}$.

I.2. Deterministic T0L languages. A limit theorem.

If we view T0L systems as models of development, then each table of the system represents a particular environment. A T0L system is called deterministic if in each environment there is only one choice for the next developmental step. This means that each next string in a derivation starting from the axiom is uniquely determined by the previous one and the table applied.

Formally the deterministic restriction is defined as follows.

<u>Definition 1</u>. A T0L system $G = \langle \Sigma, \mathcal{P}, \sigma \rangle$ is called <u>deterministic</u> if, for each P in $\mathcal{P}$ and each a in Σ, there exists exactly one α in Σ^* such that $a \to \alpha$ is in P. A language L is called a <u>deterministic T0L language</u> if there exists a deterministic T0L system G such that L = L(G).

It is not difficult to construct examples of languages which can

---

2) Throughout this paper we shall use standard formal language notation, as for example in (Hopcroft & Ullman, <u>Formal Languages and their Relation to Automata</u>, Addison-Wesley, 1969). We use $|x|$ for the length of a string x and #A for the cardinality of a set A. The empty string is denoted by the symbol Λ. If we write that L is a language over an alphabet Σ, or just $L \subseteq \Sigma^*$, then we also mean that each letter of Σ occurs in a word of L.

be generated by a nondeterministic TOL system but cannot be generated by deterministic TOL systems. One would like however to find a non-trivial (and hopefully interesting) property which would be inherent to the class of deterministic TOL languages.

Investigating the set of words generated by a particular grammar is one of the most basic activities in formal language theory. It is however often interesting and well motivated physically to investigate the set of all subwords (subpatterns) generated by a particular grammar. Quite often one is interested in just the number of different subwords of a particular length encountered in a given language.

It turns out that the ability to generate an arbitrary number of subwords of an arbitrary length is a property of a TOL system which disappears when the deterministic restriction is introduced. More precisely, if L is a deterministic TOL language over an alphabet containing at least two letters, then the ratio of the number of different subwords of a given length k occurring in the words of L to the number of all possible words of length k tends to zero as k increases. Formally this is stated as follows.

Theorem 1. Let Σ be a finite alphabet such that $\#\Sigma = n \geq 2$. If L is a deterministic TOL language, $L \subseteq \Sigma^*$, then

$$\lim_{k\to\infty} \frac{\pi_k(L)}{n^k} = 0,$$

where $\pi_k(L)$ denotes the number of all subwords of length k occurring in the words of L.

The proof of Theorem 1 appears in [17] .
All other results presented in this paper have not yet been published before.

Note that this result is not true if $\#\Sigma = 1$ (the language $\{a^{2^n} \mid n \geq 1\}$ is a deterministic TOL language). Neither is it true for nondeterministic TOL languages (Σ^* is a TOL language for every alphabet Σ).

We believe that the above results is a fundamental one for characterizing deterministic TOL languages. It can be used, for example, in both intuitive and formal proofs that some languages are not deterministic TOL languages (an example of such an application is a proof that if $\Sigma = \{a,b\}$ and F is a finite language over Σ, then Σ^*-F is not in the class of deterministic TOL languages).

One has however to be careful in understanding this result. Note for example that if $\Sigma = \{a_1, \ldots, a_n\}$ for some $n \geq 2$, then the deterministic TOL system $G = \langle \Sigma, \{P_1, \ldots, P_{n-1}\}, a_n \rangle$, where

$P_i = \{a_n \to a_n a_i\} \cup \{a_j \to a_j | 1 \leq j \leq n-1\}$ for $1 \leq i \leq n-1$ is such that, for each $k \geq 1$, $\pi_k(L(G)) \geq (n-1)^k$. The ramifications of Theorem 1 will be discussed in more detail below.

I.3. Some subclasses of the class of TOL languages.

We will explore now further the subword point of view of the deterministic restriction in TOL systems. In particular we will see that this way of viewing deterministic TOL systems and languages possesses one very pleasant and desirable feature. It is "very sensitive" to various structural changes imposed on the class of TOL systems. In fact we will be able to classify a number of subclasses of the class of TOL systems according to their subword generating efficiency.

First we need some definitions.

Definition 2. A TOL system $G = < \Sigma, \mathcal{P}, \sigma >$ is called:

1) a OL system if $\# \mathcal{P} = 1$,

2) propagating, if for every P in $\mathcal{P}$, $P \subset \Sigma \times \Sigma^+$,

3) everywhere growing, if for every P in $\mathcal{P}$ and every α in Σ^*, whenever $a \to \alpha$ is in P (for arbitrary a in Σ), then $|\alpha| > 1$,

4) uniform, if there exists an integer $t > 1$ such that, for every P in $\mathcal{P}$ and every α in Σ^*, if $a \to \alpha$ is in P (for arbitrary a in Σ), then $|\alpha| = t$.

Definition 3. A TOL language L is called propagating, everywhere growing, uniform or a OL language if $L = L(G)$ for a propagating TOL system, everywhere growing TOL system, uniform TOL system or a OL system, respectively.

We will use the letters P, G and U to denote the propagating, everywhere growing, and uniform restrictions respectively. Thus, for example, a UTOL system means a uniform TOL system and a deterministic GOL system means a deterministic everywhere growing OL system. It should be obvious to the reader that a GTOL system (language) is also a PTOL system (language) and that each UTOL system (language) is also a GTOL system (language).

Example 2.

1) $G = < \{a\}, \{\{a \to a, a \to aa\}\}, a >$ is a POL system. It is not deterministic. Thus $\{a\}^+$ is a POL language.

2) The TOL system from Example 1 is a deterministic GTOL system. Thus $\{a^{2^n 3^m} b^{2^n 3^m} | n,m \geq 0\}$ is a deterministic GTOL language.

We would like to point out that the restrictions which have been defined in this section (propagating, 0L, etc.) were not introduced for the purpose of this paper; they have already been studied earlier in the theory of L systems.

I.4. Everywhere growing deterministic T0L languages.

As has been indicated at the end of section I.1, even deterministic PT0L systems can generate "a lot" of subwords (say, for each $k \geq 0$, at least $(n-1)^k$ out of the total number n^k of possible subwords of length k in an alphabet of size $n \geq 2$). The situation is however quite different for deterministic GT0L languages.

Theorem 2.

1) If L is a deterministic GT0L language, then there exist positive constants α and β, such that, for every $k > 0$, $\pi_k(L) \leq \alpha k^\beta$.

2) For every positive number ℓ, there exists a deterministic UT0L language L such that if α, β are positive constants such that, for every $k > 0$, $\pi_k(L) \leq \alpha k^\beta$, then $\beta > \ell$.

I.5. Deterministic 0L languages.

The class of deterministic 0L systems is one of the most important and most intensively studied classes of L systems (see, e.g., [45], [75], [82] and [95]). In this section we shall investigate the "subword complexity" of deterministic 0L languages as well as how various structural restrictions on the class of deterministic 0L systems influence the subword complexity of the corresponding classes of languages.

As to the whole class of deterministic 0L languages we have the following result.

Theorem 3.

1) For every deterministic 0L language L there exists a constant α_L such that, for every $k > 0$, $\pi_k(L) \leq \alpha_L k^2$.

2) For every positive number ℓ there exists a deterministic P0L language L such that $\pi_k(L) \geq \ell . k^2$ for infinitely many positive integers k.

If we restrict ourselves to languages generated by deterministic 0L systems in which each letter is rewritten as a word of length at least 2, then we get the following subword complexity class.

Theorem 4.

1) For every deterministic G0L language L there exists a positive constant α_L such that, for every $k > 0$, $\pi_k(L) \leq \alpha_L.k.\log k$.

2) For every positive number ℓ there exists a deterministic G0L language L such that $\pi_k(L) \geq \ell.k.\log k$ for infinitely many positive integers k.

Further restriction to deterministic uniform 0L systems yields us a class of generative devices with very limited ability of subword generation.

Theorem 5.

1) For every deterministic U0L language L there exists a positive constant α_L such that, for every $k > 0$, $\pi_k(L) \leq \alpha_L.k$.

2) For every positive number ℓ, there exists a deterministic U0L language L such that $\pi_k(L) \geq \ell.k$ for infinitely many positive integers k.

PART II
L systems with interactions

In an L system with interaction, the rewriting of a letter in a string depends on the context in which the letter occurs (in other words, two occurrences of the same letter may have to be rewritten in different ways if they are in different contexts).

This part of the paper will be organized in more or less the same way as Part I so that the reader can more easily compare and contrast the results for L systems without interactions and those for L systems with interactions.

II.1. TIL systems and languages.

Whereas T0L systems attempt to model growth in different environments but with no cell interactions, TIL systems also allow interaction among cells to take place in addition to environmental changes. They were introduced in (Lee & Rozenberg)[3], where the relevant formal definitions and basic properties can be found. (TIL systems, or languages, abbreviates "table L systems, or languages, with interactions".)

A TIL system G has four components, $G = \langle \Sigma, \mathcal{P}, \sigma, g \rangle$, where

(i) Σ is the alphabet,

3) Lee & Rozenberg: TIL systems and languages, submitted for publication.

(ii) σ is the axiom, as in the TOL case.
(iii) The symbol g is a new symbol, called the environment symbol. It represents the environment and its usage will be clear from the following description of productions in G.
(iv) $\mathcal{P}$ is a finite set of tables of productions. Each production is of the form $< \alpha,a,\beta > \to \gamma$, where $a \in \Sigma, \alpha \in g^*\Sigma^*, \beta \in \Sigma^*g^*, \gamma \in \Sigma^*$. For each particular system G, there are numbers $k,\ell \geq 0$ such that $|\alpha| = k$ and $|\beta| = \ell$ for all productions in G. The meaning of $< \alpha,a,\beta > \to \gamma$ is that an occurrence of the letter a in a word, with the string of letters α immediately to its left and the string of letters β immediately to its right, may be replaced by the string γ . α and β are thus the left and right contexts for a, respectively. Productions for letters at the edges of a string will have an appropriate number of environment symbols g in the context. A string x is said to derive a string y if the letters of x in $g^k x g^\ell$ can be rewritten in the above way to produce the string y, where all productions are from an arbitrarily chosen table.

The language generated by a TIL system G, denoted as L(G), consists of σ and all strings which can be derived from σ in a finite number of steps. A Language L is called a TIL language if there exists a TIL system G such that L = L(G).

Example 3. Let $G = < \{a\},\{\{ < g,a,\Lambda > \to a^3, < a,a,\Lambda > \to a^2\}, \{ < g,a,\Lambda > \to a^5, < a,a,\Lambda > \to a^3\}\},a^5,g >$. Then $L(G) = \{a^{2^n 3^{m-1}} | n,m \geq 1\}$. Here the amount of left context is k = 1 and the amount of right context is $\ell = 0$.

It should be noted that TOL systems can be identified with those TIL systems whose productions are of the form $< \Lambda,a,\Lambda > \to \alpha$.

II.2. Deterministic TIL systems.

A TIL system is called deterministic if for each particular environment, a letter in a given context can be replaced by only one string. Formally, the deterministic restriction is defined for TIL systems as follows.

Definition 4. A TIL system $G = < \Sigma,\mathcal{P},\sigma,g >$ is called deterministic if the following condition holds: For each $P \in \mathcal{P}$, each $a \in \Sigma$, if $< \alpha,a,\beta > \to \gamma_1$ and $< \alpha,a,\beta > \to \gamma_2$ are productions for a in P in the context of α and β, then $\gamma_1 = \gamma_2$. A language L is called a deterministic TIL language if there exists a deterministic TIL system G such that L = L(G).

In the rest of Part II we shall look at the role determinism plays in TIL systems from the subword point of view.

First we may remark that the analogue of Theorem 1 for deterministic TIL languages does not hold. It is an easy exercise to construct, for any alphabet Σ (with $\#\Sigma = n$), a deterministic TIL language L such that $\pi_k(L) = n^k$ for every $k \geqslant 0$; hence for this L,

$$\lim_{k\to\infty} \frac{\pi_k(L)}{n^k} = 1.$$

II.3. Some subclasses of the class of TIL languages.

Analogous to the TOL case, we have the following definition.

Definition 5. A TIL system $G = \langle \Sigma, \mathcal{P}, \sigma, g \rangle$ is called

1) an IL system if $\#\mathcal{P} = 1$.

2) propagating if for every $P \in \mathcal{P}$, $P \subset g^*\Sigma^* \times \Sigma \times \Sigma^* g^* \times \Sigma^+$.

3) everywhere growing if for every $P \in \mathcal{P}$ and every $\gamma \in \Sigma$, whenever $\langle \alpha, a, \beta \rangle \to \gamma$ is in P (for some $a \in \Sigma$, $\alpha \in g^*\Sigma^*$, $\beta \in \Sigma^*\beta^*$), then $|\gamma| > 1$.

4) uniform if there exists an integer $t > 1$ such that for every $P \in \mathcal{P}$ and $\gamma \in \Sigma^*$, if $\langle \alpha, a, \beta \rangle \to \gamma$ is in P (for some $a \in \Sigma$, $\alpha \in g^*\Sigma^*$, $\beta \in \Sigma^*\beta^*$) then $|\gamma| = t$.

Definition 6. A TIL language L is called propagating, everywhere growing, uniform or an IL language if L = L(G) for a propagating TIL system, everywhere growing TIL system, uniform TIL system or an IL system G, respectively.

We shall also use the letters P, G, and U to denote the propagating, everywhere growing and uniform restrictions respectively, as explained for the TOL case.

Example 4.

1) The TIL system G from Example 3 is a deterministic GTIL system. Thus the language $\{a^{2^n 3^m - 1} \mid n,m \geqslant 1\}$ is a deterministic GTIL language.

2) Let $G = \langle \{a\}, \{\{ \langle \Lambda, a, g \rangle \to a^2, \langle \Lambda, a, a \rangle \to a\}\}, a, g \rangle$. Then G is a deterministic PIL system and so $\{a\}^+$ is a deterministic PIL language.

II.4. Everywhere growing deterministic TIL languages.

At the end of section II.2, we have remarked that given any alphabet Σ a deterministic TIL system can be found generating all possible subwords over Σ. The addition of the everywhere growing restriction reduces this subword generating ability as in the case of L systems without interactions. In fact the analogue of Theorem 2 (concerning deterministic GT0L languages) for deterministic GTIL languages holds.

Theorem 6.

1) If L is a deterministic GTIL language, then there exist positive constants α and β, such that, for every $k > 0$, $\pi_k(L) \leq \alpha k^\beta$.

2) For every positive number ℓ, there exists a deterministic UTIL language L such that if α, β and positive constants such that, for every $k > 0$, $\pi_k(L) \leq \alpha k^\beta$, then $\beta > \ell$.

II.5. Deterministic IL languages.

Theorem 3 states that for a deterministic 0L language L, the number of subwords of length k is proportional to k^2. Thus the subword generating ability of a 0L system is reduced from n^k (where n is the cardinality of the alphabet) to k^2 by the addition of the deterministic restriction. The situation is different concerning IL languages. Vitanyi (personal communication) has a construction which, for any alphabet Σ, produces a DIL system G with alphabet $\Sigma \cup \{a,b\}$ (where a,b are new symbols) which generates all possible subwords over Σ. Thus the following theorem is true.

Theorem 7. Given any integer $n > 2$, there exists a DIL language L such that, for any $k \geq 0$, $\pi_k(L) \geq (n-2)^k$.

The above theorem says that the addition of determinism to IL systems (in general) reduces only slightly their subword generating ability. Despite this, we find that deterministic GIL and deterministic G0L systems, as well as deterministic UIL and deterministic U0L systems, have the same subword generating power. This can be seen from the following two theorems and Theorems 4 and 5.

Theorem 8.

1) For every deterministic GIL language L there exists a positive constant α_L such that, for every $k > 0$, $\pi_k(L) \leq \alpha_L . k . \log k$.

2) For every positive number ℓ there exists a deterministic GIL language such that $\pi_k(L) \geq \ell . k . \log k$ for infinitely many positive integers k.

Theorem 9.

1) For every deterministic UIL language L there exists a positive constant α_L such that, for every $k > 0$, $\pi_k(L) \leqslant \alpha_L . k$.

2) For every positive number ℓ, there exists a deterministic UIL language L such that $\pi_k(L) \geqslant \ell . k$ for infinitely many positive integers k.

GROWTH OF STRINGS IN CONTEXT DEPENDENT LINDENMAYER SYSTEMS *)

PAUL M.B. VITÁNYI

Mathematisch Centrum, Amsterdam, The Netherlands

ABSTRACT

Growth functions of context dependent Lindenmayer systems are investigated. Bounds on the fastest and slowest growth in such systems are derived, and a method to obtain (P)D1L growth functions from (P)D2L growth functions is given. Closure of context dependent growth functions under several operations is studied with special emphasis on an application of the firing squad synchronization problem. It is shown that, although all growth functions of DILs using a one letter alphabet are DOL growth functions, there are growth functions of PDILs using a two letter alphabet which are not. Several open problems concerning the decidability of growth equivalence, growth type classification etc. of context dependent growth are shown to be undecidable. As a byproduct we obtain that the language equivalence of PDILs is undecidable and that a problem proposed by Varshavsky has a negative solution.

1. INTRODUCTION

Lindenmayer systems, L systems for short, are a class of parallel rewriting systems. They were introduced by Lindenmayer [59,60] as a model for the developmental growth in filamentous organisms. These systems have been extensively studied, see e.g. Herman & Rozenberg [45], and, from the formal language point of view, form an alternative to the usual generative grammar approach. A particularly interesting topic in this field, both from the viewpoint of the biological origins and in its own right, is the study of the growth of the length of a filament as a function of time. An L system consists of an initial string of letters, symbolizing an initial one di-

*) This paper is registered at the Mathematical Center as IW 19/74.

mensional array of cells (a filament), and the subsequent strings (stages of development) are obtained by rewriting all letters of a string simultaneously at each time step. When the rewriting of a letter may depend on the m letters to its left and the n letters to its right we talk about an *(m,n)L system.* When each letter can be rewritten in exactly one way in each context of m letters to its left and n letters to its right we talk about a *deterministic (m,n)L system.* All L systems considered in this paper are deterministic (i.e. essentially monogenic rewriting systems) since this allows a cleaner theory of growth to be developed. However, most of the results concerning growth types and decidability we shall derive hold under appropriate interpretation also for nondeterministic L systems.

The general family of deterministic L systems is called the *family of deterministic context dependent L systems* or *DIL systems.* The best investigated subfamily is that of the D(0,0)L (i.e. DOL) or deterministic context independent L systems. Growth of the length of strings in this latter class has been extensively studied, cf. section 2, and almost all questions posed have been proved to be decidable by algebraic means [111,75,98] and some by combinatorial arguments [116]. The study of the growth of length of strings in the general case of context dependent L systems has been more or less restricted to the observation that the corresponding problems here are still open, cf. [45, chapter 15], [75] and [102]. We shall investigate the growth of length of strings in context dependent L systems and we shall solve some of the open problems by quite elementary means. By a reduction to the printing problem for Turing machines we are able to show that e.g. the growth type of a context dependent L system is undecidable, even if no production is allowed to derive the empty word; that the growth equivalence problem for these systems is unsolvable; and that the corresponding questions for the growth ranges have similar answers. (As a byproduct we obtain the results that the language equivalence for PD1Ls is undecidable and that a problem proposed by Varshavsky has a negative solution.)

Furthermore, we derive bounds on the fastest and slowest growth in such systems; we give a method for obtaining growth functions of systems with a smaller context from systems with a larger context; it is shown that all bounded growth functions of context dependent L systems are within the realm of the context independent growth functions whereas for each type of unbounded context dependent growth functions there are growth functions which are not; similarly, all growth functions of context dependent L systems using a one letter alphabet are growth functions of context independent L systems whereas this is not the case for growth functions of the simplest context dependent L systems using a two letter alphabet; we give an application of the firing squad synchronization problem, etc.

The paper is divided in three parts. In section 2 we prepare the ground by giving a cursory review of some results on growth functions of context independent L systems. In sections 3.1-3.3 we develop outlines for a theory of context dependent growth functions and give some theorems and illuminating examples. In section 3.4

we prove the undecidability of several open problems in this area.

2. GROWTH FUNCTIONS OF CONTEXT INDEPENDENT L SYSTEMS

We assume that the usual terminology of formal language theory is familiar. Except where defined otherwise we shall customarily use, with or without indices, i,j, k,m,n,p,r,t to range over the set of natural numbers $\mathbb{N} = \{0,1,2,\ldots\}$; a,b,c,d,e to range over an alphabet W; v,w,z to range over W^* i.e. the set of all words over W including the *empty word* λ. #Z denotes the *cardinality* of a set Z; lg(z) the *length* of a word z and $lg(\lambda) = 0$.

An L system is called deterministic context independent (DOL system) if the rewriting rules are deterministic and the rewriting of a letter is independent of the context in which it occurs. With each DOL system G we can associate a growth function f_G where $f_G(t)$ is the length of the generated string at time t. Growth functions of DOL systems were studied first by Szilard [111], later by Doucet [15], Paz & Salomaa [75], Salomaa [98] and Vitányi [116,115].

A *semi DOL system (semi DOL)* is an ordered pair $S = \langle W,\delta \rangle$ where W is a finite nonempty *alphabet* and δ is a total mapping from W into W^* called the *set of production rules*. A pair $(a,\delta(a))$ is also written as $a \to \delta(a)$. We extend δ to a homomorphism on W^* by defining $\delta(\lambda) = \lambda$ and $\delta(a_1a_2\ldots a_n) = \delta(a_1)\delta(a_2)\ldots\delta(a_n)$, $n > 0$. δ^i is the composition of i copies of δ and is inductively defined by $\delta^0(v) = v$ and $\delta^i(v) = \delta(\delta^{i-1}(v))$ for $i > 0$. A *DOL system (DOL)* is a triple $G = \langle W,\delta,w \rangle$ where W and δ are as above and $w \in WW^*$ is the *axiom*. The *DOL language* generated by G is $L(G) = \{\delta^i(w) \mid i \geq 0\}$. The *growth function* of G is defined by $f_G(t) = lg(\delta^t(w))$. Clearly, for each DOL $G = \langle W,\delta,w \rangle$, if $m = \max\{lg(\delta(a)) \mid a \in W\}$ then $f_G(t) \leq lg(w)\, m^t$. Hence the fastest growth possible is exponentially bounded. We classify the growth of DOLs as follows [116]:
A growth function f_G is *exponential (type 3)* if $\lim_{t\to\infty} f_G(t)/x^t \geq 1$ for some $x > 1$; f_G is *polynomial (type 2)* if $\lim_{t\to\infty} f_G(t)/p(t) \geq 1$ and $\lim_{t\to\infty} f_G(t)/q(t) \leq 1$ for some unbounded polynomials[1] p and q; f_G is *limited (type 1)* if $0 < f_G(t) \leq m$ for some constant m and all t; f_G is *terminating (type 0)* if $f_G(t) = 0$ but for a finite number of initial arguments.

By an application of the theory of homogeneous linear difference equations with constant coefficients, Salomaa [98] gave an algorithm to derive an explicit formula of the following form for the growth function of an arbitrary DOL G:

$$(1) \qquad f_G(t) = \sum_{i=1}^{n} p_i(t)\, c_i^t,$$

---

[1] A function f(t) is said to be *unbounded* if for each n_0 there is a t_0 such that $f(t) > n_0$ for all $t > t_0$.

where p_i is an r_i-th degree polynomial with complex algebraic coefficients and c_i a complex algebraic constant, $1 \le i \le n$, $\Sigma_{i=1}^{n}(r_i+1) = \#W$. From this it follows that the above classification is exhaustive in the DOL case; that the growth type of a DOL can be determined and that the growth equivalence for two DOLs is decidable (two DOLs G, G' are said to be growth equivalent iff $f_G(t) = f_{G'}(t)$ for all t).

The approach of [98] becomes too complicated for large alphabets and does not tell us anything about the *structure* of growth, viz. the local properties of production rules which are responsible for types of growth [116]. By considering DOLs with one letter axioms we can talk about growth types of letters, and clearly the growth type of a DOL is the highest numbered growth type of the letters in its axiom. Given a semi DOL, different types of growth may result from different choices of the axioms; therefore the growth type of a semi DOL is a combination of the growth types possible for different choices of the axiom. (Written from left to right according to decreasing digits, e.g. 3210, 321, 21.)

Example 1.

$G = \langle\{a\},\{a \to a^2\},a\rangle$: growth type 3.

$G = \langle\{a,b\},\{a \to b, b \to ab\},a\rangle \quad f_G(t) = \frac{\sqrt{5}+1}{2\sqrt{5}}\left(\frac{1+\sqrt{5}}{2}\right)^t + \frac{\sqrt{5}-1}{2\sqrt{5}}\left(\frac{1-\sqrt{5}}{2}\right)^t$: growth type 3.

($f_G(t)$ is the t-th term of the Fibonacci sequence)

$G = \langle\{a,b\},\{a \to ab, b \to b\},a\rangle \quad f_G(t) = t+1$: growth type 2.

$S = \langle\{a,b,c,d\},\{a \to a^2b, b \to bc, c \to cd, d \to \lambda\}\rangle$: growth type 3210.

The following theorem, [116], tells us which combinations may occur in the DOL case.

Theorem 1. Type 2 never occurs without type 1. All other combinations are possible. (I.e. there are no semi DOLs of growth type 320, 32, 20 or 2).

It is, however, easy to show that growth type 2 may occur without growth type 1 for the simplest context dependent L systems, i.e. the one letter alphabet PD1Ls. (cf. example 2, section 3).

Furthermore, in the DOL case, necessary and sufficient conditions for the growth type of a letter $a \in W$ under a set of production rules are obtained from the emptyness of the intersection of the set of letters, derivable from a, with three disjoint classes of recursive letters, where a letter $b \in W$ is *recursive* if $\delta^i(b) = v_1bv_2$ for some $i > 0$ and some $v_1,v_2 \in W^*$, [116].

3. GROWTH FUNCTIONS OF CONTEXT DEPENDENT L SYSTEMS

The general form of a context dependent L system was introduced by Rozenberg [86]. We define a *deterministic (m,n)L system (D(m,n)L)* as a triple $G = \langle W,\delta,w\rangle$, where W is a finite nonempty *alphabet*, the *set of production rules* δ is a total mapping from $\bigcup_{i=0}^{m} W^i \times W \times \bigcup_{j=0}^{n} W^j$ into W^* and $w \in WW^*$ is the *axiom*. δ induces a total mapping $\bar{\delta}$ from W^* into W^* as follows: $\bar{\delta}(\lambda) = \lambda$ and $\bar{\delta}(a_1a_2\ldots a_k) = \alpha_1\alpha_2\ldots\alpha_k$ if for each i such that $1 \leq i \leq k$ we have

$$\delta(a_{i-m}a_{i-m+1}\ldots a_{i-1},a_i,a_{i+1}a_{i+2}\ldots a_{i+n}) = \alpha_i,$$

where we take $a_j = \lambda$ for $j < 1$ and $j > k$. The composition of i copies of $\bar{\delta}$ is inductively defined by $\bar{\delta}^0(v) = v$ and $\bar{\delta}^i(v) = \bar{\delta}(\bar{\delta}^{i-1}(v))$, $i > 0$. When no confusion can result we shall write δ for $\bar{\delta}$. The *D(m,n)L language* generated by G is $L(G) = \{\delta^i(w) \mid i \geq 0\}$, and the *growth function* of G is $f_G(t) = lg(\delta^t(w))$.

A *semi D(m,n)L* is a D(m,n)L without the axiom. A *propagating D(m,n)L (PD(m,n)L)* is a D(m,n)L $G = \langle W,\delta,w\rangle$ such that $\delta(v) \neq \lambda$ for all $v \in WW^*$. In the literature a D(0,0)L is usually called a DOL, a D(1,0)L or D(0,1)L is usually called a D1L, a D(1,1)L is usually called a D2L and a D(m,n)L (m,n≥0) a DIL. The corresponding semi L systems are named accordingly.

Example 2. $S = \langle W,\delta\rangle$ is a semi PD(0,1)L where $W = \{a\}$ and $\delta(\lambda,a,\lambda) = a^2$, $\delta(\lambda,a,a) = a$. It is easily verified that for every axiom a^k, $k > 0$, S yields the growth function $f(t) = k+t$. (At each time step the letter on the right end of the string generates aa while the remaining letters generate a.) Therefore, even for PD1Ls using a one letter alphabet growth type 2 can occur without growth type 1 and all combinations of growth types 0,1,2,3 are possible. (Contrast this with the situation for DOLs in theorem 1.)

In section 2 we defined growth types 3,2,1,0 which were exhaustive for the DOL case. However, as will appear in the sequel, this is not so for DILs. Therefore we define two additional growth types to fill the gaps between types 1 and 2, and types 2 and 3. We call the growth in a DIL G *subexponential (type 2½)* iff the growth is not exponential and there is no unbounded polynomial p such that $f_G(t) \leq p(t)$ for all t; *subpolynomial (type 1½)* iff f_G is unbounded and for each unbounded polynomial p holds that $\lim_{t\to\infty} f_G(t)/p(t) = 0$.

For DOLs the following types of problems have been considered and solved effectively (cf. section 2 and the references contained therein).

(i) Analysis problem. Given a DIL, describe its growth function in some fixed predetermined formalism.

(ii) Synthesis problem. Given a function f in some fixed predetermined formalism and some restriction x on the family of DILs. Find a DIL which satisfies x and whose growth function is f. Related to this is the problem of which growth functions can be growth functions of DILs satisfying restriction x.

(iii) Growth equivalence problem. Given two DILs, decide whether or not they have the same growth function.

(iv) Classification problems. Given a DIL or a semi DIL, decide what is its growth type.

(v) Structural problems. What properties of production rules induce what types of growth?

Furthermore we have the hierarchy problem. Is the set of DOL growth functions a proper subset of the D1L growth functions and similar problems?

In section 3.4 we shall show that even for PD1Ls the problems (i)-(v) are recursively unsolvable.

3.1. Bounds on unbounded growth

Since it is difficult to derive explicit formulas for growth functions of the more involved examples of DILs, and according to section 3.4 impossible in general, we avail ourselves of the following notational devices.

$\lfloor f(t) \rfloor$ is the *lower entier* of f(t), i.e. for each t, $\lfloor f(t) \rfloor$ is the largest integer not greater than f(t).

$f(t) \sim g(t)$: f(t) is *asymptotic* to g(t), i.e. $\lim_{t\to\infty} f(t)/g(t) = 1$.

$f(t) \approx\!> g(t)$: f(t) *slides onto* g(t) (terminology provided by G. Rozenberg) iff for each maximum argument interval [t',t"] on which g(t) has a constant value holds that f(t) = g(t) for all t and some t"' such that $t' \le t''' \le t \le t''$.

As in the DOL case, for each DIL G = <W,δ,w> holds that $f_G(t) \le lg(w)\, m^t$ where $m = \max\{lg(\delta(v_1,a,v_2)) \mid v_1,v_2 \in W^* \text{ and } a \in W\}$. Hence the fastest growth is exponential, and for each DIL there is a DOL which grows faster. We shall now investigate what is the slowest unbounded growth which can occur. Remember that a function f is unbounded if for each n_0 there is a t_0 such that $f(t) > n_0$ for $t > t_0$.

Theorem 2.

(i) For any PDIL G = <W,δ,w> such that f_G is unbounded holds:

$$\lim_{t\to\infty} f_G(t)/\log_r t \ge 1 \qquad \text{where } r = \#W > 1.$$

(ii) For any DIL G = <W,δ,w> such that f_G is unbounded holds:

$$\lim_{t\to\infty} \sum_{i=0}^{t} f(t) / \sum_{i=0}^{t} \lfloor \log_r((r-1)i+r) \rfloor \ge 1 \qquad \text{where } r = \#W > 1.$$

Proof.

(i) Order all strings in WW^* according to increasing length. The number of strings of length less than k is given by $t = \Sigma_{i=1}^{k-1} r^i$, $i = \#W$. Hence $t = \frac{r^k - r}{r-1}$ and therefore $k = \log_r((r-1)t+r)$. If we define $f(t)$ as the length of the t-th string in WW^* then, clearly, $f(t) = \lfloor \log_r((r-1)t+r) \rfloor$ and $\lim_{t\to\infty} f(t)/\log_r t = 1$. The most any PDIL system with an unbounded growth function can do is to generate all strings of WW^* in order of increasing length and without repetitions. Therefore $\lim_{t\to\infty} f_G(t)/\log_r t \geq 1$.

(ii) The most any DIL with an unbounded growth function can do is to generate all strings of WW^* in some order and without repetitions. Therefore, $\lim_{t\to\infty} \Sigma_{i=0}^{t} f_G(t)/\Sigma_{i=0}^{t} f(i) \geq 1$. □

In the sequel of this section we shall show that theorem 2 is optimal.

Example 3. Let $G_1 = \langle W,\delta,w \rangle$ be a PD(0,1)L such that $W = \{0,1,2,\ldots,r-1,¢,s\}$ $(r>1)$; $\delta(\lambda,¢,i) = ¢$ for $0 \leq i \leq r-1$, $\delta(\lambda,¢,s) = ¢0$, $\delta(\lambda,i,\lambda) = \delta(\lambda,i,s) = i+1$ for $0 \leq i < r-1$, $\delta(\lambda,s,\lambda) = 1$, $\delta(\lambda,s,0) = \delta(\lambda,s,1) = 0$, $\delta(\lambda,r-1,\lambda) = \delta(\lambda,r-1,s) = s$, $\delta(\lambda,i,j) = i$ for $0 \leq i,j \leq r-1$; $w = ¢0$.

The starting sequence is: $¢0$, $¢1$, ..., $¢\,r-1$, $¢s$, $¢01$, ..., $¢0\,r-1$, $¢0s$, $¢11$, ..., $¢\underbrace{r-1\ldots r-1}_{k\ \times}$, $¢\underbrace{r-1\ldots r-1}_{k-1\ \times}s$, $¢\underbrace{r-1\ldots r-1}_{k-2\ \times}s1$, ..., $¢s00\ldots$, $¢0000\ldots$, ...

Observe that G counts all strings over an alphabet of r letters. When an increment of the length k is due on the left side it needs k extra steps. Furthermore, there is an additional letter ¢ on the left. Therefore,

$$f_{G_1}(t) = \lfloor \log_r((r-1)t+r - \lfloor \log_r((r-1)t/r+1) \rfloor) \rfloor + 1$$

$$\approx \lfloor \log_r((r-1)t+r) \rfloor + 1.$$

Hence $f_{G_1}(t) \sim \log_r t$. Hence, with a PD1l using r+2 letters we can reach the slowest unbounded growth of a PDIL using r letters.

Some variations of Example 3 are the following:

Example 4. Let G_2 be a PD(0,1)L defined as G_1 but with $\delta(\lambda,¢,s) = ¢1$. Then, essentially, G_2 counts on a number base r and

$$f_{G_2}(t) = 2, \qquad 0 \leq t < r$$

$$f_{G_2}(t) = \lfloor \log_r(t - \lfloor \log_r t/r \rfloor) \rfloor + 2$$

$$\approx \lfloor \log_r t \rfloor + 2, \qquad t \geq r.$$

Example 5. Let $G_3 = \langle\{0,1,2,\ldots,r-1\} \times \{0,¢,s\}, \delta_3, (0,¢)\rangle$ be such that the action is as in G_1 but with ¢ and s coded in the appropriate letters. Then,

$$f_{G_3}(t) = \lfloor \log_r((r-1)t+r - \lfloor \log_r((r-1)t/r+1)\rfloor)\rfloor$$

$$\approx \lfloor \log_r((r-1)t+r)\rfloor$$

Example 6. Let G_4 be as G_2 with the modifications of G_3. Then

$$f_{G_4}(t) = 1, \qquad 0 \le t < r$$

$$f_{G_4}(t) = \lfloor \log_r(t-\lfloor \log_r t/r\rfloor)\rfloor + 1$$

$$\approx \lfloor \log_r t\rfloor + 1, \qquad t \ge r.$$

Examples 3-6 all corroborate the fact that for any PDIL with an unbounded growth function there is a PD1L with an unbounded growth function which grows slower, although not slower than logarithmic. That theorem 2 (ii) cannot be improved upon follows from the following lemma, implicit in van Dalen [12] and Herman [33].

Lemma 1. For a suitable standard formulation of Turing machines [2], e.g. the quintuple version, holds that for any deterministic Turing machine T with symbol set S and state set Q we can effectively construct a D2L $G_5 = \langle W_5, \delta_5, w_5\rangle$ which simulates it in real time. I.e. the t-th instantaneous description of T is equal to $\delta_5^t(w_5)$. There is a required G_5 with $W_5 = S \cup Q$ and a required propagating G_5 with $W_5 = Q \cup (S \times Q)$.

Since T can expand its tape with at most one tape square per move we see that $f_{G_5}(t+1) \le f_{G_5}(t)+1$.

It is well known that a Turing machine can compute every recursively enumerable set $A = \{1^{f(t)} \mid f(t)$ is a 1:1 total recursive function$\}$. We can do this in such a way that for each t when f(t) has been computed the Turing machine erases everything else on its tape. Subsequently, it recovers t from f(t) by f^{-1}, adds 1 and computes f(t+1). In particular, the simulating D2L G_5 can, instead of replacing all symbols except the representation of f(t) by blank symbols, replace all the superfluous blank letters by the empty word λ. Suppose that A is nonrecursive. Then, clearly, it is not the case that for each n_0 we can find a t_0 such that $f_{G_5}(t) > n_0$ for $t > t_0$, although such a t_0 exists for each n_0. Hence theorem 2 (ii) is optimal for D2Ls, and as will appear from the next lemma also for D1Ls.

[2] For results and terminology concerning these devices see e.g. M. Minsky, *Computation: finite and infinite machines*. Prentice-Hall, London (1967).

Lemma 2.

(i) Let $G = \langle W,\delta,w\rangle$ be any D2L. We can effectively find a D1L $G' = \langle W',\delta',w'\rangle$ such that for all t holds: $\delta'^{2t}(w') = ¢\delta^t(w)$ for some $¢ \notin W$.

(ii) Let $G = \langle W,\delta,w\rangle$ be any PD2L. We can effectively find a PD1L $G'' = \langle W'',\delta'',w''\rangle$ such that for all t holds: $\delta''^{2t}(w'') = ¢\delta^t(w)\$^t$ for some $¢,\$ \notin W$.

Proof.

(i) Let $G = \langle W,\delta,w\rangle$ be any D2L. Define a D(0,1)L $G' = \langle W',\delta',w'\rangle$ as follows:

$$W' = W \cup (W \times (W\cup\{\lambda\})) \cup \{¢\}, \quad ¢ \notin W; \quad w' = ¢w;$$
$$\delta'(\lambda,a,c) = (a,c), \qquad \delta'(\lambda,¢,(a,c)) = ¢\delta(\lambda,a,c),$$
$$\delta'(\lambda,¢,c) = ¢, \qquad \delta'(\lambda,(a,\lambda),\lambda) = \lambda,$$
$$\delta'(\lambda,(a,b),(b,c)) = \delta(a,b,c),$$

for all $a,b \in W$ and all $c \in W\cup\{\lambda\}$. (The arguments for which δ' is not defined, shall not occur in our operation of G'.)

For all words $v \in WW^*$, $v = a_1a_2\ldots a_k$, holds:

$$\delta'^2(¢a_1a_2\ldots a_k) = \delta'(¢(a_1,a_2)(a_2,a_3)\ldots(a_k,\lambda)) =$$
$$= ¢\delta(\lambda,a_1,a_2)\delta(a_1,a_2,a_3)\ldots\delta(a_{k-1},a_k,\lambda) =$$
$$= ¢\delta(a_1a_2\ldots a_k).$$

Since, furthermore, $\delta'^2(¢) = ¢$ we have therefore $\delta'^{2t}(w') = ¢\delta^t(w)$ for all t.

(ii) Let $G = \langle W,\delta,w\rangle$ be any PD2L. Define a PD1L $G'' = \langle W'',\delta'',w''\rangle$ as follows:

$$W'' = W \cup (W \times (W\cup\{\lambda\})) \cup \{¢,\$\}, \quad ¢,\$ \notin W; \quad w'' = ¢w;$$
$$\delta''(\lambda,a,c) = (a,c), \qquad \delta''(\lambda,(a,b),(b,c)) = \delta(a,b,c),$$
$$\delta''(\lambda,a,\$) = (a,\lambda), \qquad \delta''(\lambda,¢,(a,c)) = ¢\delta(\lambda,a,c),$$
$$\delta''(\lambda,\$,\$) = \$, \qquad \delta''(\lambda,(a,\lambda),\lambda) = \delta''(\lambda,(a,\lambda),\$) = \$,$$
$$\delta''(\lambda,¢,d) = ¢, \qquad \delta''(\lambda,\$,\lambda) = \$,$$

for all $a,b, \in W$, all $c \in W\cup\{\lambda\}$ and all $d \in W\cup\{\lambda,\$\}$. Analogous with the above we prove that if $\delta^t(w) \neq \lambda$ for all t then $\delta''^{2t}(w'') = ¢\delta^t(w)\$^t$. □

Theorem 3.

(i) If $f(t)$ is a D2L growth function then $g(t) = f(\lfloor t/2\rfloor)+1$ is a D1L growth function.

(ii) If $f(t)$ is a PD2L growth function then $g(t) = f(\lfloor t/2\rfloor)+\lfloor t/2\rfloor+1$ is a PD1L growth function.

(iii) If $f(t)$ is a PD2L growth function then $g(t) = f(\lfloor t/2\rfloor)$ is a D1L growth function.

(iv) If $f(t)$ is a PD2L growth function then $g(t) = f(\lfloor t/2\rfloor)+\lfloor t/2\rfloor$ is a PD1L growth function.

Proof. (i) and (ii) follow from lemma 2 and its proof. (iii) and (iv) follow from lemma 2 and its proof by the observation that we can encode the left end marker ¢ in the leftmost letter of a string and keep it there in the propagating case. □

Note that by lemma 2 the transition in theorem 3 is effective, i.e. given a D2L G, of which f is the growth function, we can construct a required D1L G' such that $f_{G'} = g$.

3.2. Synthesis of growth functions

In the last section we saw that if f(t) is the growth function of a D2L G then $g(t) = f(\lfloor t/2 \rfloor)+1$ is the growth function of a D1L G' and there is a uniform method to construct G' given G. In this sense we shall treat some methods for obtaining growth functions. We consider operations under which families of growth functions are closed. An important tool here is an application of the *Firing Squad Synchronization Problem*[3]. Stated in the terminology of L systems it is the following. Let $S = \langle W_S, \delta_S \rangle$ be a semi PD2L such that $\lg(\delta_S(a,b,c)) = 1$ for all $b \in W_S$ and all $a,c \in W_S \cup \{\lambda\}$, and there is a letter m in W_S such that $\delta_S(m,m,\lambda) = \delta_S(m,m,m) = m$. The problem is to design an S satisfying the restrictions above such that $\delta^{k(n)}(m^n) = f^n$, $f \in W_S$, for all natural numbers n and a minimal function k of n, while $\delta^t(m^n) \in (W_S - \{f\})^n$ for all t, $0 \le t < k(n)$. Balzer[4] proved that there is a minimal time solution $k(n) = 2n-2$. In the PD2L case we can achieve a solution in e.g. $k(n) = n-1$ by dropping the restriction $\delta_S(m,m,\lambda) = m$ and having both letters m on the ends of an initial string act like "soldiers receiving the firing command from a general" in the firing squad terminology. Assume that $S = \langle W_S, \delta_S \rangle$ is such a semi PD2L simulating a firing squad with $k(n) = n-1$. Let $G = \langle W, \delta, w \rangle$ be any (P)D2L. We define the (P)D2L $G' = \langle W', \delta', w' \rangle$ as follows:

$$W' = W \times W_S;$$

$$w' = (a_1,m)(a_2,m)\dots(a_k,m) \qquad \text{for } w = a_1a_2\dots a_k,$$

$$\delta'((a,a'),(b,b'),(c,c')) = (b,b'') \qquad \text{for } \delta_S(a',b',c') = b'' \text{ and } a'b'c' \neq fff,$$

$$\delta'((a,f),(b,f),(c,f)) = \begin{cases} (b_1,m)(b_2,m)\dots(b_h,m) & \text{for } \delta(a,b,c) = b_1b_2\dots b_h, \\ \lambda & \text{for } \delta(a,b,c) = \lambda. \end{cases}$$

We easily see that if $\delta(v) = v'$ for $v,v' \in W^*$ then

---

[3] See e.g. Minsky, Op. cit., 28-29.

[4] Balzer, R., *An 8 state minimal solution to the firing squad synchronization problem*, Inf. Contr. 10 (1967), 22-42.

$$\delta'^{\lg(v)}((a_1,m)(a_2,m)\dots(a_k,m)) = (b_1,m)(b_2,m)\dots(b_h,m)$$

where $v = a_1a_2\dots a_k$ and $v' = b_1b_2\dots b_h$; and $\delta'^{\lg(v)}((a_1,m)(a_2,m)\dots(a_k,m)) = \lambda$ for $v' = \lambda$. Therefore we have:

Lemma 3. Let G be any (P)D2L. We can effectively find a (P)D2L G' such that

$$(2)\qquad f_{G'}(t) = \begin{cases} f_G(0) & \text{for all } t \text{ such that } 0 \le t < f_G(0), \\ f_G(\tau+1) & \text{for all } t \text{ such that } \sum_{i=0}^{\tau} f_G(i) \le t < \sum_{i=0}^{\tau+1} f_G(i). \end{cases}$$

Since we can simulate an arbitrary (but fixed) number of r firing squads in sequence plus a number j of production steps of G' for each production step of G, we can effectively find a (P)D2L G' for each (P)D2L G such that:

$$f_{G'}(t) = \begin{cases} f_G(0) & \text{for all } t \text{ such that } 0 \le t < r\, f_G(0) + j \\ f_G(\tau+1) & \text{for all } t \text{ such that } r\sum_{i=0}^{\tau} f_G(i)+(\tau+1)j \le t < \\ & \qquad r\sum_{i=0}^{\tau+1} f_G(i)+(\tau+2)j. \end{cases}$$

Let us call the operation to obtain a growth function $f_{G'}$ from f_G as defined in (2) *FSS*. Then $f_{G'} = \mathrm{FSS}(f_G)$.

A cascade of r firing squads working inside each other, such that one production step of a (P)D2L G is simulated if the outermost squad fires, gives us a (P)D2L G' such that $f_{G'} = \mathrm{FSS}^r(f_G)$, i.e.

$$(3)\qquad f_{G'}(t) = \begin{cases} f_G(0) & \text{for all } t \text{ such that } 0 \le t < f_G(0)^r \\ f_G(\tau+1) & \text{for all } t \text{ such that } \sum_{i=0}^{\tau} f_G(i)^r \le t < \sum_{i=0}^{\tau+1} f_G(i)^r. \end{cases}$$

Example 7. Suppose that f_G is exponential, say $f_G(t) = 2^t$. Then $\mathrm{FSS}(f_G) = f$ where $f(t) = 2^{\tau+1}$ for $\Sigma_{i=0}^{\tau} 2^i \le t < \Sigma_{i=0}^{\tau+1} 2^i$. Hence $f(2^{\tau+1}-1) = 2^{\tau+1}$ and $f(t) = 2^{\lfloor \log_2 t \rfloor}$, i.e. $f(t) \asymp t$.[5] We can obtain analogous results for arbitrary exponential functions.

[5] $f \asymp g$ asserts that f is of the same *order of magnitude* as g, i.e. $c_1 g(t) < f(t) < c_2 g(t)$ for all t and some constants c_1, c_2.

Example 8. Suppose that f_G is polynomial, e.g. $f_G(t) = p(t)$ where $p(t)$ is a polynomial of degree r. Then $FSS(f_G) = f$ where $f(\Sigma_{i=0}^{t} p(i)) = p(t+1)$. Since $\Sigma_{i=0}^{t} p(i) = q(t)$ where $q(t)$ is a polynomial of degree r+1 we have $f(t) \asymp t^{r/r+1}$. By (3) we see that $FSS^j(f_G) = f$ where $f(t) \asymp t^{r/(r+j)}$.

Hence we have:

Theorem 4. For each rational number r, $0 < r \leq 1$, we can effectively find a PD2L G such that $f_G(t) \asymp t^r$.

Proof. Since $r = r'/r''$ such that r'', r' are natural numbers and $r'' \geq r'$, and according to Szilard [111] we can, for every monotonic ultimately polynomial function g, find a PDOL G' such that $f_{G'} = g$, by example 8 we can find a PD2L G such that $f_G(t) \asymp t^{r'/r''}$.
□

Example 9. Let $f_G(t) = \lfloor \log_2 t \rfloor$. Then $FSS(f_G) = f$, where $f((t-1)2^{t+1}+4) = t+1$, i.e. $f(t) \asymp \log t$.

Hence we see that the relative slowing down gets less when the growth function is slower.

By theorem 3 everything we have obtained for D2Ls holds for D1Ls if we substitute $\lfloor t/2 \rfloor$ for t in the expression for the growth function and add 1. However, even for D1Ls we can achieve a greater slowing down. Let G be some D2L. We can construct a D1L G' which simulates G such that for each production step of G, G' does the following.

(a) G' counts all strings of length $f_G(t)$ over an r letter alphabet by the method of example 3. When an increase of length is due on e.g. the left side,
(b) G' initializes a firing squad, making use of the simulation technique of lemma 2. When the firing squad fires, G' simulates one production step of G and subsequently starts again at (a).

Hence, if $h(t) \leq f_G(t) \leq g(t)$ for a D2L G and monotonic increasing functions h and g then we can effectively find a D1L G' such that $f_{G'}(\Sigma_{i=0}^{t} r^{h(i)}) < g(t+1)$. For instance, if $f_G(t) = t$ then $f_{G'}(t) < \log_r t$, $t > 1$.

We can combine processes like the above to obtain stranger and stranger, slower and slower growth functions. Similar to the above application of the Firing Squad Synchronization Problem we could apply the *French Flag Problem* (see e.g. [37]).

The next theorem tells us under what operations the family of growth functions is closed. In particular, the subfamilies of (P)D2L, (P)D1L and (P)DOL growth functions are closed under (i)-(iii).

Theorem 5. Growth functions are closed under (i) addition, (ii) multiplication with a natural number $r > 0$, (iii) entier division of the argument by a natural number $r > 0$, (iv) FSS. Growth functions are not closed under (v) subtraction, (vi) division, (vii) composition.

Proof.

(i) Let $G_1 = \langle W_1, \delta_1, w_1 \rangle$ and $G_2 = \langle W_2, \delta_2, w_2 \rangle$ be two DILs with disjoint alphabets. Define $G_3 = \langle W_1 \cup W_2, \delta_3, w_1 w_2 \rangle$. Then it is easy to construct δ_3, given δ_1 and δ_2, such that $f_{G_3} = f_{G_1} + f_{G_2}$.

(ii) Follows from (i).

(iii) Let $G_1 = \langle W_1, \delta_1, w_1 \rangle$ be a DIL. Define $G_2 = \langle W_2, \delta_2, w_2 \rangle$ such that $f_{G_2}(t) = f_{G_1}(\lfloor t/r \rfloor)$. This is easily achieved by introducing a cycle of length r for each direct production of G_1.

(iv) By lemma 3.

(v)-(vi) Trivial.

(vii) 2^t is a growth function while $2^{(2^t)}$ is not. □

We conclude this section with some conjectures. The evidence in favor of in particular conjecture 1 is overwhelming, but we have not been able to derive a formal proof.

Conjecture 1. Growth functions are not closed under multiplication. (E.g. $2^{t+\lfloor \log_2 t \rfloor}$ can hardly be a growth function.)

Conjecture 2. Unbounded growth functions are closed under function inverse. (E.g. $f(t) = r^t$ is a growth function for r is a constant. $g(t) \sim f^{-1}(t) = \log_r t$ is a growth function too.)

Conjecture 3. There are no PD1L growth functions $f(t) \asymp t^r$ where r is not a natural number. (It is hard to see how a string can determine its length in the PD1L case.)

3.3. Hierarchy

The first PD1L growth function of growth type $1\frac{1}{2}$ was "Gabor's sloth" in [75, p.338]. Examples 3-6 and section 3.2. provide us with an ample supply of this growth type. A more difficult problem is to construct a DIL of growth type $2\frac{1}{2}$. The first (and until now only) DIL of growth type $2\frac{1}{2}$ is the PD2L of Karhumäki [50] with growth function f where $2^{\sqrt{t}} \le f(t) \le (2^{\sqrt{3}})^{\sqrt{t}}$. By lemma 2 we can construct a PD1L G such that $2^{\sqrt{\lfloor t/2 \rfloor}} + \lfloor t/2 \rfloor \le f_G(t) \le (2^{\sqrt{3}})^{\sqrt{\lfloor t/2 \rfloor}} + \lfloor t/2 \rfloor$. From these results and theorem 5 (i) follows:

Theorem 6. There are PD1L growth functions of growth types $1\frac{1}{2}, 2, 2\frac{1}{2}, 3$ which are not DOL growth functions.

Hence the family of (P)DOL growth functions is properly contained in the family of (P)D1L growth functions. However, if we restrict ourselves to the bounded growth functions the situation is different.

Theorem 7. Let G be any DIL such that f_G is of (i) growth type 0, or, (ii) growth type 1. Then we can construct a DOL G' such that $f_{G'} = f_G$.

Proof.

(i) Let $f_G(t) > 0$ for all $t \le t_0$ for some t_0 and $f_G(t) = 0$ otherwise. Then $f_{G'} = f_G$ where $G' = \langle W', \delta', w' \rangle$ is a DOL constructed as follows:

$$W' = \{a_0, a_1, \ldots, a_{t_0}, b\};\ w' = a_0 b^{f_G(0)-1};$$

$$\delta'(a_i) = a_{i+1} b^{f_G(i+1)-1} \qquad \text{for all } i,\ 0 \le i < t_0,$$

$$\delta'(b) = \delta'(a_{t_0}) = \lambda.$$ [6]

(ii) If f_G is of growth type 1 for some DIL G then f_G is ultimately periodic, i.e. $f_G(t) = f_G(t-u)$ for all $t > t_0+u$ for some t_0 and u. The construction of the appropriate DOL G' is similar to the construction in (i). □

Corollary 1. The family of bounded (P)DIL growth functions coincides with the family of bounded (P)DOL growth functions.

Theorem 8. Let $G = \langle W, \delta, w \rangle$ be a *unary* (i.e. #W = 1) DIL. Then there is a DOL G' such that $f_{G'} = f_G$.

Proof. Suppose f_G is bounded. By theorem 7 the theorem holds. Suppose f_G is unbounded, and let G be a D(m,n)L. Furthermore, let $p = \lg(\delta(a^m, a, a^n))$, $x = \Sigma_{i=0}^{m-1} \lg(\delta(a^i, a, a^n)) + \Sigma_{j=0}^{n-1} \lg(\delta(a^m, a, a^j))$. Since f_G is unbounded there is a t_0 such that $f_G(t_0) \ge 2(m+n)+x+1$. For all $t \ge t_0$ the following equation holds:

$$(4) \qquad f_G(t+1) = p(f_G(t)-m-n) + x.$$

Case 1. $p = 0$. Then $f_G(t) \le (m+n)y$ where $y = \max\{\lg(\delta(v_1, a, v_2)) \mid v_1, v_2 \in W^*\}$. Therefore f_G is bounded: contradiction.

Case 2. $p = 1$. Then $x-m-n > 0$ since f_G is bounded otherwise. It is easy to construct a DOL G' such that $f_{G'} = f_G$ in this case.

Case 3. $p > 1$. Construct a DOL $G'' = \langle W'', \delta'', w'' \rangle$ as follows:

$$W'' = \{a_0, a_1, a_2, a_3\};\ \delta''(a_0) = \lambda,\ \delta''(a_1) = a_0 a_1 a_3^{p-2},\ \delta''(a_2) = a_2 a_3^{x+p-1},$$

$$\delta''(a_3) = a_3^p;\ w'' = (a_0 a_1)^{m+n} a_2 a_3^{f_G(t_0)-2(m+n)-1}$$ [6]

It is easy to prove by induction on t that $f_{G''}(t) = f_G(t+t_0)$ for all t. By using

[6] We define δ for DOLs as in section 2.

theorem 7 we construct a DOL $G' = <W',\delta',w'>$ such that $W'' \subseteq W'$, $\delta'' \subseteq \delta'$, $\delta'^{t_0}(w') = w''$ and $f_{G'}(t) = f_G(t)$ for $0 \leq t < t_0$. Then $f_{G'} = f_G$. □

It may be worthwhile to note that the solution to the difference equation (4) is given by:

$$f_G(t) = \begin{cases} f_G(t_0) + (x-m-n)(t-t_0) & \text{for } p = 1, \\ p^{t-t_0} f_G(t_0) + (x-p(m+n)) \dfrac{1-p^{t-t_0}}{1-p} & \text{for } p > 1, \end{cases}$$

for all $t > t_0$.

Therefore, the growth function of a unary DIL is either linear or purely exponential, which by equation (1) gives us

Corollary 2. The family of growth functions of unary DILs is properly contained in the family of growth functions of DOLs.

Theorem 9. There is a *binary* PD1L $G = <W,\delta,w>$, (i.e. $\#W = 2$), with a one letter axiom such that there is no DOL G' such that $f_{G'} = f_G$.

Proof. Let $G = <W,\delta,w>$ be a PD(1,0)L where

$$W = \{a,b\};\ w = a;\ \delta(\lambda,a,\lambda) = b,\ \delta(\lambda,b,\lambda) = aa,\ \delta(a,a,\lambda) = a,$$
$$\delta(b,a,\lambda) = b,\ \delta(b,b,\lambda) = b,\ \delta(a,b,\lambda) = aa.$$

The initial sequence of produced strings is:

$a, b, aa, ba, aab, baaa, aabaa, ba^3ba, a^2ba^4b, ba^3ba^5, a^2ba^4ba^4, ba^3ba^5ba^3, a^2ba^4ba^6ba^2, ba^3ba^5ba^7ba, a^2ba^4ba^6ba^8b, ba^3ba^5ba^7ba^9, \ldots\ldots$

Every second time step one b is introduced on the left and starts moving along the string to the right. Every time step b moves one place to the right and leaves a string a^2 on the place it formerly occupied. When a letter b reaches the right end of the string it disappears in the next step leaving aa. Therefore, on the one hand, every second production step there enters a length increasing element in the string; on the other hand, with exponentially increasing time intervals one of these elements disappears. The strings where a b has just disappeared in the above sequence are:

$$\delta^5(a) = baaa,\ \delta^9(a) = ba^3ba^5,\ \delta^{15}(a) = ba^3ba^5ba^7ba^9.$$

Now introduce the notational convenience $\Pi_{i=1}^{x}\ v(i)$ where $v(i)$ is a function from $\mathbb{N}$ into W^*. E.g. if $v(i) = a^ib^{2i}$ then $\Pi_{i=1}^{3}\ v(i) = ab^2a^2b^4a^3b^6$.

<u>Claim</u>. $\delta^{t(x)}(a) = \prod_{i=1}^{2^x} ba^{2i+1}$ where $t(x) = 2^{x+1} + 2x + 3$.

<u>Proof of claim</u>. By induction on x.

$x = 0$. $\delta^5(a) = ba^3$.

$x > 0$. Suppose the claim is true for all $x \leq n$. Then

$$\delta^{t(n)}(a) = \prod_{i=1}^{2^n} ba^{2i+1} = \ldots ba^{2.2^n+1}.$$

This last occurence of b will just have disappeared at time $t' = t(n) + 2.2^n + 2 = t(n+1)$. The distance with the preceding occurence of b was 2.2^n-1 and therefore

$$(5) \qquad \delta^{t(n+1)}(a) = \ldots ba^{2.2^n-1 + 2(2.2^n+2) - 2(2^n+1)} = \ldots ba^{2.2^{n+1}+1}.$$

At time t(n) the total number of occurences of b in the string was 2^n; at time t(n+1) this is $2^n+2^n+1-1 = 2^{n+1}$ and

$$(6) \qquad \delta^{t(n+1)}(a) = ba^3b\ldots .$$

Since it is easy to see that for all $t \geq 0$ holds if $\delta^t(a) = v_1ba^{i_1}ba^{i_2}bv_2$ for some v_1,v_2 then $i_2 = i_1+2$, it follows from (5) and (6) that $\delta^{t(n+1)}(a) = \prod_{i=1}^{2^{n+1}} ba^{2i+1}$, which proves the claim.

Hence,

$$f_G(t(x)) = \sum_{i=1}^{2^x} 2(i+1) = 2^x(2^x+3) = 1/4(t(x)-2x-3)(t(x)-2x+3)$$

$$= 1/4\ t(x)^2-x\ t(x)+x^2 - 9/4.$$

Since $t(x) = 2^{x+1}+2x+3$ we have $x \approx \lfloor \log_2 t(x)/2 \rfloor$ and therefore:

$$(7) \qquad f_G(t(x)) \approx 1/4\ t(x)^2 - \lfloor \log_2 t(x)/2 \rfloor t(x) + \lfloor \log_2 t(x)/2 \rfloor^2 - 9/4.$$

From (7) and the general formula for a DOL growth function (1) it follows that f_G cannot be a DOL growth function since

$$f_G(t) - 1/4\ t^2 \sim t \log t. \quad \square$$

That context dependent L systems using a two letter alphabet cannot yield all DOL growth functions is ascertained by the counterexample $f(0) = f(1) = f(2) = 1$ and

$f(t) = t$ for $t > 2$, which is surely a (P)D0L growth function.

Corollary 3. The family of binary (P)D1L growth functions has nonempty intersections with the family of (P)D0L growth functions and neither contains the other.

An open problem in this area is: does the family of (P)D1L growth functions coincide with the family of (P)D2L growth functions. A proof of conjecture 3 would show that the family of PD1L growth functions is properly contained in the family of PD2L growth functions.

Using a similar technique as in lemma 2 we can, however, say the following.

Theorem 10.

(i) If $f(t)$ is a PD2L growth function then $f(t)$ is a D(2,0)L growth function.

(ii) If $f(t)$ is a D2L growth function then $f(t)+1$ is a D(2,0)L growth function.

Proof.

(i) Let $G = \langle W,\delta,w\rangle$ be a PD2L. Define a D(2,0)L $G' = \langle W',\delta',w'\rangle$ as follows.

$$W' = W \cup W \times \{\text{¢}\} \text{ where } \text{¢} \notin W;\ w' = a_1a_2\ldots a_{n-1}(a_n,\text{¢}) \text{ for } w = a_1a_2\ldots a_n;$$

$$\delta'(ab,c,\lambda) = \delta(a,b,c), \qquad \delta'(\lambda,c,\lambda) = \lambda,$$

$$\delta'(ab,(c,\text{¢}),\lambda) = \delta(a,b,c)a_1a_2\ldots a_{m-1}(a_m,\text{¢}) \quad \text{if } \delta(b,c,\lambda) = a_1a_2\ldots a_m,$$

$$\delta'(\lambda,(c,\text{¢}),\lambda) = a_1a_2\ldots a_{m-1}(a_m,\text{¢}) \quad \text{if } \delta(\lambda,c,\lambda) = a_1a_2\ldots a_m,$$

for all $b,c \in W$ and all $a \in W\cup\{\lambda\}$.

Then $\delta'^t(w') = b_1b_2\ldots b_{m-1}(b_m,\text{¢})$ if $\delta^t(w) = b_1b_2\ldots b_m$, and therefore $f_{G'} = f_G$.

(ii) Let $G = \langle W,\delta,w\rangle$ be a D2L. Define a D(2,0)L $G' = \langle W',\delta',w'\rangle$ as follows.

$$W' = W\cup\{\text{¢}\} \text{ where } \text{¢} \notin W;\ w' = w\text{¢};$$

$$\delta'(ab,c,\lambda) = \delta(a,b,c),\ \delta'(\lambda,c,\lambda) = \lambda,$$

$$\delta'(ab,\text{¢},\lambda) = \delta(a,b,\lambda)\text{¢},\ \delta'(\lambda,\text{¢},\lambda) = \text{¢},$$

for all $b,c \in W$ and all $a \in W\cup\{\lambda\}$.

Then $\delta'^t(w') = \delta^t(w)\text{¢}$ and therefore $f_{G'}(t) = f_G(t)+1$. □

Rozenberg [86] proved that a D(m,n)L can be simulated in real time by a D(k,ℓ) if $k+\ell = m+n$ and $k,\ell,m,n > 0$. Therefore, by using the same trick as above we have the following:

Corollary 4.

(i) If $f(t)$ is a PD(m,n)L growth function then $f(t)$ is a D(k,ℓ) growth function where $k+\ell = m+n$.

(ii) If f is a D(m,n)L growth function then f(t)+1 is a D(k,ℓ) growth function where $k+\ell = m+n$.

In particular, (i) and (ii) hold for $k = m+n$ and $\ell = 0$ and vice versa.

3.4. Decision problems

According to section 2 and the beginning of section 3 (and the references contained therein) the analysis, synthesis, growth equivalence, classification and structural problems all have a positive solution for context independent growth, i.e. there is an algorithm which gives the required answer or decides the issue. (This is not completely true for the synthesis problem, see theorem 33 in Paz & Salomaa [75].) The corresponding problems for the general case of DIL systems have been open. It will be shown here that for DILs these problems all have a negative solution essentially because already PD1Ls can simulate any effective process. (Note that by theorems 8 and 9 the above problems have a positive solution if we restrict ourselves to unary DILs or to DILs with a bounded growth function.) Furthermore, we shall show that similar questions concerning growth ranges of DILs have similar answers. First we need the notion of a *Tag system*[7]. A Tag system is a 4 tuple $T = \langle W,\delta,w,\beta\rangle$ where W is a finite nonempty *alphabet*, δ is a total mapping from W into W^*, $w \in WW^*$ is the *initial string*, and β is a positive integer called the *deletion number*. The operation of a Tag system is inductively defined as follows: the initial string w is generated by T in 0 steps. If $w_t = a_1a_2\ldots a_n$ is the t-th string generated by T then $w_{t+1} = a_{\beta+1}a_{\beta+2}\ldots a_n\delta(a_1)$ is the (t+1)-th string generated by T.

<u>Lemma 4 (Minsky)</u>. It is undecidable for an arbitrary Tag system T with $\beta = 2$ and a given positive integer k whether T derives a string of length less than or equal to k. In particular it is undecidable whether T derives the empty word.

We shall now show that if it is decidable whether or not an arbitrary PD1L has a growth function of growth type 1 then it is decidable whether or not an arbitrary Tag system with deletion number 2 derives the empty word λ. Therefore, by lemma 4 it is undecidable whether a PD1L has a growth function of type 1.

Let $T = \langle W_T,\delta_T,w_T,2\rangle$ be any Tag system with deletion number 2. Define a PD(1,0)L $G = \langle W,\delta,w\rangle$ as follows:[8]

$$W = W_T \cup W_T' \cup W_T \times W_T \cup \{¢,\$\},$$

where $W_T' = \{\underset{\sim}{a} \mid a \in W_T\}$, $W_T' \cap W_T = \phi$ and $¢,\$ \notin W_T \cup W_T'$;

---

[7] Minsky, Op. cit.

[8] The idea of simulating Tag systems with 1Ls occurs already in the first papers on L systems i.e. [33] and [12].

$w = w_T ¢;$

$\delta(\lambda,a,\lambda) = \delta(\$,a,\lambda) = \delta(\$,(a,b),\lambda) = \underset{\sim}{a},$

$\delta(\lambda,\underset{\sim}{a},\lambda) = \delta(\$,\underset{\sim}{a},\lambda) = \delta(\lambda,\$,\lambda) = \delta(\$,\$,\lambda) = \delta(\$,¢,\lambda) = \delta(\lambda,¢,\lambda) = \$,$

$\delta(a,b,\lambda) = \delta(\underset{\sim}{a},(b,c),\lambda) = \delta(a,(b,c),\lambda) = b,$

$\delta(a,¢,\lambda) = ¢,$

$\delta(\underset{\sim}{b},c,\lambda) = \delta((a,b),c,\lambda) = (c,b),$

$\delta(\underset{\sim}{b},¢,\lambda) = \delta((a,b),¢,\lambda) = \delta_T(b)¢,$

for all $a,b,c \in W_T$ and all $\underset{\sim}{a},\underset{\sim}{b}, \in W_T'$.

A sample derivation is:

T	G
$a_1a_2a_3a_4a_5$	$a_1a_2a_3a_4a_5¢$
$a_3a_4a_5\delta_T(a_1)$	$\underset{\sim}{a}_1a_2a_3a_4a_5¢$
$a_5\delta_T(a_1)\delta_T(a_3)$, etc.	$\$(a_2,a_1)a_3a_4a_5¢$
	$\$\underset{\sim}{a}_2(a_3,a_1)a_4a_5¢$
	$\$\$a_3(a_4,a_1)a_5¢$
	$\$\$\underset{\sim}{a}_3a_4(a_5,a_1)¢$
	$\$\$\$(a_4,a_3)a_5\delta_T(a_1)¢$
	$\$\$\$\underset{\sim}{a}_4(a_5,a_3)\delta_T(a_1)¢$, etc.

In the simulating PD1L G signals depart from the left, with distances of one letter in between, and travel to the right at an equal speed of one letter per time step. Therefore, the signals cannot clutter up. It is clear that if the Tag system T derives the empty word, then there is a time t_0 such that $\delta^{t_0}(w) = \$^k¢$ and $\delta^t(w) = \$^{k+1}$ for some k and for all $t > t_0$. Conversely, the only way for G to be of growth type 1 is to generate a string of the form $\$^k¢$. (If the string always contains letters other than \$ and ¢ then at each second production step there appears a new occurrence of \$ and the string grows indefinitely long.) Therefore, T derives the empty word iff G is of growth type 1. Since it is undecidable whether or not an arbitrary Tag system with deletion number 2 derives the empty word it is undecidable whether or not a PD1L is of growth type 1.

Theorem 11.

(i) It is undecidable whether or not an arbitrary PD1L is of growth type i, $i \in \{1,1\frac{1}{2},2,2\frac{1}{2},3\}$.

(ii) It is undecidable whether or not an arbitrary D1L is of growth type i, $i \in \{0,1,1\frac{1}{2},2,2\frac{1}{2},3\}$.

(iii) It is undecidable whether an arbitrary PD1L has an unbounded growth function.

Proof.

(i) Let $G_1 = \langle W_1, \delta_1, w_1\rangle$ be a PD(1,0)L simulating a Tag system T as discussed above. Let $G_2 = \langle W_2, \delta_2, w_2\rangle$ be a PD(1,0)L of growth type i, $i \in \{1, 1\frac{1}{2}, 2, 2\frac{1}{2}, 3\}$ such that $W_2 \cap W_1 = \phi$. Define $G_3 = \langle W_3, \delta_3, w_3\rangle$ as follows:

$$W_3 = W_2 \cup \{\$\};\ w_3 = w_2;$$
$$\delta_3 = \delta_2 \cup \{\delta_3(\$,\$,\lambda)=\delta_3(\lambda,\$,\lambda)=\$\} \cup \{\delta_3(\$,a,\lambda)=\delta_2(\lambda,a,\lambda) \mid a \in W_2\}.$$

Clearly, $f_{G_3} = f_{G_2}$. Now construct a PD(1,0)L $G_4 = \langle W_4, \delta_4, w_4\rangle$ as follows:

$$W_4 = W_3 \cup W_1;\ w_4 = w_1;$$
$$\delta_4 = \delta_3 \cup (\delta_1 - \{\delta_1(\$,¢,\lambda)=\$\}) \cup \{\delta_4(\$,¢,\lambda) = w_3\}.$$

If there is a time t_0 such that $\delta_1^{t_0}(w_1) = \$^k¢$ for some k then $\delta_4^{t_0}(w_4) = \$^k¢$ and $\delta_4^{t+t_0+1}(w_4) = \$^k\delta_3^t(w_3)$ for all t, i.e. $f_{G_4}(t+t_0+1) = f_{G_2}(t)+k$. If there is no such time t_0 then $f_{G_4}(t) = f_{G_1}(t)$ for all t. In this latter case it is easy to see that $f_{G_1}(t) \asymp t$, i.e. G_4 is of growth type 2. By the previous discussion it is undecidable whether such a time t_0 exists and therefore whether f_{G_4} is of growth type i or 2.

(ii) Follows by a similar argument if we talk about D(1,0)Ls instead of PD(1,0)Ls, change everywhere $\delta_.(\lambda,\$,\lambda) = \$$ into $\delta_.(\lambda,\$,\lambda) = \lambda$, and let i range over $\{0, 1, 1\frac{1}{2}, 2, 2\frac{1}{2}, 3\}$.

(iii) Follows from (i). □

Corollary 5. There is no algorithm which, for an arbitrary PD1L G, gives an explicit expression for f_G in a formalism we can use.

The undecidability of whether a (P)D1L is of a certain growth type holds (because of the proof method) also for future refinements of the classification. We could have proved theorem 11 by simulating Turing machines with PD1Ls (cf. lemmas 1 and 2) and reducing everything to the printing problem for Turing machines. This, however, would have caused some difficulties with the slow growth types.

Theorem 11 has some interesting corollaries. Two DIL systems G_1, G_2 are said to be *language equivalent* if $L(G_1) = L(G_2)$. Now it is known that the language equivalence for e.g. OL languages is undecidable. The status of the language equivalence problem for DOL languages is unknown as yet. (Cf. [5,99,84].) By the special tractable nature of PD1L systems it might well be that the language equivalence problem is decidable in this case. However, in the proof of theorem 11 (i) it is clearly undecidable whether $L(G_4) = L(G_1)$. Therefore we have:

Corollary 6. The language equivalence of PD1L languages is undecidable. (According to theorem 12 this is even the case if we are informed in advance that both PD1Ls concerned are of the same growth type i, $i \in \{2, 2\frac{1}{2}, 3\}$.)

V.I. Varshavsky proposed the following problem: "Consider the class of D2L grammars producing strings which stabilize at a certain length. Make some reasonable assumptions about the maximal production length (e.g. 2) and axiom length (e.g. 1) and find the maximal stable string length as a function of the number of letters in the alphabet."[9] The restrictions as stated in the above problem are no restrictions on the generating power of any usual subfamily of DILs since it is clear that by enlarging the alphabet we can simulate any DIL G_1 by a DIL G_2 where G_2 takes k_1 production steps to generate the axiom of G_1 and takes a constant number k_2 of productions steps of G_2 to simulate one production step of G_1, i.e. $\delta_2^{k_1+k_2 t}(w_2) = \delta_1^t(w_1)$ for all t. (This is similar to deriving e.g. the Chomsky Normal Form for context free grammars.) Suppose we restrict ourselves to the family of PD1Ls and there is a function as proposed by Varshavsky where, moreover, this function is computable. Then it would also be decidable whether or not a PD1L G simulating a Tag system T ever generates a string of the form $\$^k¢$ for some k: contradicting lemma 4. Therefore, we have

Corollary 7. Let V_i be the family of PD1Ls $G = \langle W, \delta, w \rangle$ such that $\#W = i$, $w \in W$, $lg(\delta(a,b,\lambda)) \leq 2$ for all $b \in W$ and $a \in W \cup \{\lambda\}$, and $lg(\delta^{t_0+t}(w)) = lg(\delta^{t_0}(w))$ for some t_0 and all t. Let $v(i) = \max\{lg(v) \mid v \in L(G) \text{ and } G \in V_i\}$. There is no computable function f such that $v(i) \leq f(i)$ for all i, i.e. v increases faster than any computable function and hence Varshavsky's problem has a negative solution.

Theorem 12.

(i) It is undecidable whether or not two PD1Ls are growth equivalent even if we have the advance information that they are of the same growth type i, $i \in \{2, 2\frac{1}{2}, 3\}$.

(ii) It is undecidable whether or not two D1Ls are growth equivalent even if we have the advance information that they are of the same growth type i, $i \in \{1\frac{1}{2}, 2, 2\frac{1}{2}, 3\}$.

(iii) The growth equivalence of two DILs is decidable if we have the advance information that they both have bounded growth functions.

Proof. Take an arbitrary Tag system T and simulate it with a PD1L G_1 as in the proof of theorem 11.

(i) Now construct two variants of G_1, called G_2 and G_3, which act like G_1 until $\$¢$ occurs in a string. Then G_2 and G_3 start different growths albeit of the same

[9] In: *Unusual automata theory*. Univ. of Aarhus, Comp. Sci. Dept. Tech. Rept. DAIMI PB-15 (1973), 20.

growth type i, $i \in \{2, 2\frac{1}{2}, 3\}$. Now let f be another growth function of type i. Since PD1L growth functions are closed under addition (theorem 5) both $g = f_{G_2} + f$ and $h = f_{G_3} + f$ are PD1L growth functions of type i, say of G_4 and G_5. If $\$¢ never occurs in a string then $f_{G_4} = f_{G_5} = f_{G_1} + f$ and $f_{G_1}(t) \asymp t$. If \$¢ occurs in a string then $f_{G_4} \neq f_{G_5}$. Since it is undecidable whether \$¢ occurs in a string it is undecidable whether or not $f_{G_4} = f_{G_5}$, where it is known that both f_{G_4} and f_{G_5} are of growth type i, $i \in \{2, 2\frac{1}{2}, 3\}$.

(ii) Similar to (i). Since we talk here about D1Ls we can slow the growth function f_{G_1} down to $f_{G'_1}$ where $f_{G'_1} < \log_r t$, $r > 1$, (cf. discussion after example 9).

(iii) Trivial. □

Note that the theorem above leaves open the decidability of the question of two PD1Ls being growth equivalent if we are informed in advance that they are both of growth type $1\frac{1}{2}$. This is because in our simulation method of Tag systems all simulating PD1Ls are either of growth type 1 or growth type 2.

<u>Theorem 13</u>. It is undecidable whether two PD2Ls are growth equivalent even if we are informed in advance that they are both of growth type $1\frac{1}{2}$.

<u>Proof</u>. Take a PD2L G_1 simulating a Tag system T. Construct a PD2L G_2 which simulates G_1 such that $f_{G_2}(t) < \log_r f_{G_1}(t)$ (cf. discussion after example 9). Since $f_{G_1}(t) \asymp t$ or $f_{G_1}(t) \leq m$ for some constant m, f_{G_2} is of growth type $1\frac{1}{2}$ or 1. Then use the method of proof of theorem 12 (i). □

Theorems 11-13 have analogues for the growth ranges of DIL systems. The *growth range* of a DIL G is defined by $R(G) = \{lg(v) \mid v \in L(G)\}$. Although the results on growth ranges are not corollaries of theorems 11-13 they follow by the same proof method. Two DILs G_1 and G_2 are said to be *growth range equivalent* iff $R(G_1) = R(G_2)$.

<u>Theorem 14</u>. The growth range equivalence is undecidable for two PD1Ls G_1 and G_2 even if we have advance information that they both are of growth type i, $i \in \{2, 2\frac{1}{2}, 3\}$.

<u>Proof</u>. The proof of theorem 12 (i) will do since we can choose f_{G_1} and f_{G_2} such that they are strictly increasing at different rates iff a substring \$¢ occurs. □

Under appropriate interpretation we can prove the undecidability of growth range type classification etc. analogous to theorem 11-13. Note, however, that the growth range type can be different from the growth function type of a DIL. E.g. $f_G(t) = 2^{\lfloor \log_2 t \rfloor}$ is of growth type 1 whereas $R(G) = \{2^i \mid i \geq 0\}$ and therefore is exponential.

A fortiori all undecidability results above hold under appropriate interpretation also for nondeterministic context dependent L systems.

SOME GROWTH FUNCTIONS OF CONTEXT-DEPENDENT L-SYSTEMS

J. KARHUMÄKI

Department of Mathematics, University of Turku, Finland

1. Introduction

Lindenmayer systems or shortly L-systems were introduced by Lindenmayer, [59] and [60], for describing the development of filamentous organisms. Because of this biological origin one interesting aspect in the study of deterministic L-systems is the theory of growth functions. It is known, [75] and [104], that if a DOL-system grows faster than any polynomial it grows exponentially. In [50] there is an example which shows that the same does not hold for D2L-systems. Here we deal with this example shortly.

Functions $f(n)=k^n$ and $g(n)=n^k$, where k is a natural number, are DOL growth functions. The inverse functions of these, i.e., logarithm functions and fractional powers, are D2L growth functions, cf. [104], but they are not DOL growth functions. So after we have established the existence of a D2L-system with the growth type $2\frac{1}{2}$, a natural question arises: is there any context-dependent DL-system such that its growth function lies between logarithm functions and fractional powers? In Section 4 of this paper we shall give a positive answer to this question.

For more backround material concerning growth functions the reader is referred to [75], [104] and [116].

2. Preliminaries

We use standard formal language notations, cf. [102]. Here we define only growth types of deterministic L-systems. We say that the growth in a DL-system with the growth function f(n) is exponential or type 3 iff there exist n_o and a constant $t > 1$ such that

$$f(n) \geq t^n \qquad \text{for } n \geq n_o .$$

Iff there are polynomials $p_1(n)$ and $p_2(n)$ (with positive rational coefficients) such that f(n) satisfies the condition

$$p_1(n) \leq f(n) \leq p_2(n)$$

we say that the growth is polynomial or type 2. In the case, where the empty word does not belong to the sequence and the growth function is bounded by a constant, we say that the growth is of type 1. Iff the growth function becomes ultimately 0 we say that the growth is of type 0.

This classification is exhaustive for DOL-systems, cf. [104]. The same does not hold for context-dependent DL-systems. As we mentioned, logarithm functions and fractional powers, which lie between growth types 1 and 2, are D2L growth functions. We say that this kind of growth is of type $1\frac{1}{2}$. Furthermore we say that the growth is of type $2\frac{1}{2}$ iff the growth function is neither bounded by a polynomial nor of type 3.

3. Growth type $2\frac{1}{2}$

In this section we give an example of a PD2L-system with the growth type $2\frac{1}{2}$. First we informally describe the development of our organism.

At certain intervals our organism is of the form $(ga^k)^m g$. Thus, consider the word $ga^k g$. The letter g is called a node. These nodes always send messengers b and $\bar{b}$ to the right and to the left, respectively.

At the same time g changes to an inactive form $\bar{g}$ (which does not send any messengers). While moving on, messengers b and $\bar{b}$ duplicate every letter. When b and $\bar{b}$ meet, they create a new node which is in the inactive form. Furthermore, b and $\bar{b}$ disappear and new messengers f and $\bar{f}$ are born. They travel to the right and to the left, respectively.

At the beginning, g sends to the right also another messenger (letters c and d). This messenger travels at the rate which is only half of the rates of the other messengers. When this messenger and $\bar{f}$ meet, this slow messenger changes to the messenger f. Now we have three messengers travelling on. Moreover, these are synchronized in the sense that they reach each an inactive node simultaneously. When this happens, they disappear and transform the nodes to the active form g.

During this process, we increase the number of a's between letters g by one. So the word ga^kg has changed to the form $ga^{k+1}ga^{k+1}g$, i.e., it has essentially duplicated. Note that the time in which the organism duplicates its length increases linearly.

The development, described above, can be obtained as follows. Consider a PD2L-system with the following productions:

$$a_a{}^{g} \to \bar{b}a \ ,$$
$$g_a{}^{a} \to ab \ ,$$
$$b_a{}^{a} \to ab \ ,$$
$$a_a{}^{\bar{b}} \to \bar{b}a \ ,$$
$$b_a{}^{\bar{b}} \to \bar{f}\bar{h}f \ ,$$
$$d_a{}^{x} \to c \qquad \text{if } x{=}a \text{ or } x{=}b,$$
$$f_a{}^{x} \to f \qquad \text{for all } x,$$
$$x_a{}^{\bar{f}} \to \bar{f} \qquad \text{for all } x,$$
$$a_a{}^{e} \to \bar{f} \ ,$$
$$e_a{}^{a} \to f \ ,$$
$$\bar{h}_b{}^{a} \to d \ ,$$
$$a_b{}^{a} \to a \ ,$$
$$a_b{}^{\bar{b}} \to \bar{f}\bar{g} \ ,$$

$a_{\bar{b}}\bar{h} \to a\,,$

$a_{\bar{b}}a \to a\,,$

$b_{\bar{b}}a \to f\,,$

$a_{c}\bar{\bar{f}} \to e\,,$

$x_{c}y \to d \qquad \text{if } x \neq a \text{ or } y \neq \bar{\bar{f}},$

$a_{d}\bar{\bar{f}} \to \bar{\bar{f}}\,,$

$x_{d}y \to a \qquad \text{if } x \neq a \text{ or } y \neq \bar{\bar{f}},$

$x_{e}y \to a \qquad \text{for all } x \text{ and } y,$

$x_{f}y \to a \qquad \text{for all } x \text{ and } y,$

$d_{\bar{\bar{f}}}a \to f\,,$

$x_{\bar{\bar{f}}}y \to a \qquad \text{if } x \neq d \text{ or } y \neq a,$

$\alpha_{g}a \to \bar{g}d\,,$

$a_{g}\alpha \to a\bar{g}\,,$

$a_{g}a \to a\bar{g}d\,,$

$x_{\bar{g}}\bar{\bar{f}} \to h \qquad \text{for all } x,$

$f_{\bar{g}}x \to h \qquad \text{for all } x,$

$\alpha_{h}a \to \bar{h}b\,,$

$a_{h}\alpha \to \bar{b}\bar{h}\,,$

$a_{h}a \to \bar{b}\bar{h}b\,,$

$x_{\bar{h}}\bar{\bar{f}} \to g \qquad \text{for all } x,$

$f_{\bar{h}}x \to g \qquad \text{for all } x,$

$y_{x}z \to x \qquad \text{otherwise.}$

Above α is the input from the environment. To simplify the growth function we use two kinds of nodes, g and h. The details of the following are in [50]. If we take ga^4g to the 19th word of our system, then after $3n^2$ steps, where $n \geq 3$, the organism is of the form

$$(ha^{2n-1})^{2\,4^{n-3}}h \quad .$$

So the growth function f(n) satisfies the condition

$$f(3n^2) = 2n\,2^{2n-5} + 1 \quad , n \geq 3 \, .$$

From this we obtain easily, because our system is λ-free, the result that there exists n_o such that

$$2^{\sqrt{n}} \leq f(n) \leq (2^{\sqrt{3}})^{\sqrt{n}} \quad , n \geq n_o .$$

So our system is indeed of the growth type $2\frac{1}{2}$.

4. Growth between logarithm functions and fractional powers

In this section we show, how we can obtain PD1L growth functions which lie between logarithm functions and fractional powers. Particularly, we show that there is a PD1L-system such that its growth function is asymptotically equal to the function $({}^2\log n)^2$. The development of our organism can be described as follows.

The organism consists of two parts. The left one is called the growing part and the right one is called the control part. The growing part is a DL-system, and it determines essentially the length of the organism. The purpose of the control part is to tell to the growing part when it has to take one step. This can be accomplished by means of a messenger which is sent at certain intervals by the control part and which travels through the growing part.

In the next example the control part will be a PD1L-system with the growth function asymptotically equal to the function ${}^2\log n$. Furthermore, the growing part will be a PDOL-system which grows asymptotically like the function n^2. So it is needed 2^n steps to change the length of the organism from n^2 to $(n+1)^2$.

Now we go to the formal example. Let H be the following PDOL-system

$$H = (\{a,b,c\},\ v_1 = cc,\ \{a \to a,\ b \to ba,\ c \to cba\}).$$

(Note that we have not specified the axiom v_o). Using the methods of [98], one can easily see that the growth function g(n) of this system satisfies the equation

$$g(n) = (n+1)^2 - (n+1) \quad , n \geq 1 .$$

This will be the growing part of our system.

Now we define the whole system G. The alphabet V is

$$V = \{e,0,1,S\} \cup V_1 \cup \bar{V}_1 ,$$

where $V_1 = \{a,b,c\}$ and $\bar{V}_1 = \{\bar{a},\bar{b},\bar{c},\bar{e}\}$. The input from the environment is g. The axiom is not specified, but w_3 is the word cce0. The productions are as follows:

$$
\begin{array}{lll}
\bar{a}^x \to a & \text{for all } x \in V, \\
\bar{b}^x \to ba & \text{for all } x \in V, \\
\bar{c}^x \to cba & \text{for all } x \in V, \\
\bar{e}^x \to e & \text{for all } x \in V, \\
e^S \to \bar{e}0 , & \\
x^{\bar{y}} \to \bar{x} & \text{for all } x \in V_1 \text{ and } \bar{y} \in \bar{V}_1, \\
0^g \to 1 , & \\
0^S \to 1 , & \\
1^g \to S , & \\
1^S \to S , & \\
S^g \to 1 , & \\
S^0 \to 0 , & \\
S^1 \to 0 , & \\
x^y \to x & \text{otherwise.}
\end{array}
$$

<u>Assertion 1</u>. Let P be an arbitrary word over V. Then for all $i \geq 1$, the following two conditions hold

(i) $P01^i \Rightarrow^{2^i} P'1^{i+1}$ and

(ii) if $P01^i \Rightarrow^k P'XQ$, where $k < 2^i$, $X \in V$ and $lg(Q) = i$, then X differs from the letter S.

<u>Proof</u>. Because the productions for the letters S, 0 and 1 are length preserving, the word P above derives exactly the word P′ in both cases. Moreover, the rewriting of our system depends only on the right neighbour of a letter. Thus, we may assume that P and P′ are empty words.

Consider the derivations

$01 \Rightarrow 0S \Rightarrow 11$,

$011 \Rightarrow 01S \Rightarrow 0S1 \Rightarrow 10S \Rightarrow 111$ and

$0111 \Rightarrow 011S \Rightarrow 01S1 \Rightarrow 0S0S \Rightarrow 1011 \Rightarrow 101S \Rightarrow 10S1 \Rightarrow 110S \Rightarrow 1111$.

So the Assertion is true if $i \leq 3$.

Assume now that the Assertion is true for every $k \leq i-1$, where $i > 3$. Consider now the derivation starting from the word 01^i. Let j be the least natural number such that $i+1 \leq 2^j$. Then clearly $3 \leq j \leq i-1$. After i+1 steps the word 01^i has changed to the form 10R. So by the induction hypothesis, the considered derivation begins as follows:

$$
\begin{array}{ll}
01^{i-4}1111 & \\
01^{i-4}111S & \\
01^{i-4}11S1 & \\
01^{i-4}1S0S & \\
01^{i-4}S011 & \\
\text{---------} & 2^2 + \ldots + 2^{j-1} \quad \text{steps} \\
10^{i-j}1^j & \\
\text{-------} & 2^j + \ldots + 2^{i-2} \quad \text{steps} \\
101^{i-1} &
\end{array}
$$

Note that during this part of the derivation the leftmost symbol differs from S. During the next 2^{i-1} steps the second letter from the left differs from S by induction hypothesis. So the leftmost symbol differs from 1. Furthermore, the word 01^{i-1} changes to the word 1^i.

Thus, the word 01^i has changed in

$$1 + 1 + 2 + \ldots + 2^{i-1} = 2^i$$

steps to the word 1^{i+1}, and in every stage the leftmost symbol differs from S. So we have proved Assertion 1.

Assertion 2. For all $i \geq 1$, the following is true

(i) $e1^i \Rightarrow^{2^{i+1}} e1^{i+1}$ and

(ii) if $e1^i \Rightarrow^k EQ$, where $k < 2^{i+1}$ and $E \in \{e, \bar{e}\}$, then $E = \bar{e}$

if and only if $k = i + 1$.

Proof. One can easily see that the Assertion is true if $i \leq 3$. If $i > 3$, the derivation starting from the word $e1^i$ begins as follows.

$$e1^{i-4}1111 \Rightarrow e1^{i-4}111S \Rightarrow e1^{i-4}11S1 \Rightarrow e1^{i-4}1S0S \Rightarrow e1^{i-4}S011 .$$

Now S is travelling on to the left. At each step it changes to 0 and the next 1 changes to S. When S meets e, it disappears and e changes to the word $\bar{e}0$. At the next step this bar disappears.

By Assertion 1, the (i+1)st letter from the right differs from S during the first

$$1 + 1 + 2 + \dots + 2^i = 2^{i+1}$$

steps. Thus, by Assertion 1, the word $e1^i$ changes in 2^{i+1} steps to the word $e1^{i+1}$. Clearly, the claim (ii) is also true.

Let E(H) and E(G) be the sequences generated by H and G, respectively. Denote

$$E(H) = v_o, v_1 = cc, v_2, \dots$$
$$E(G) = w_o, w_1, w_2, w_3 = cce0, w_4, \dots \quad .$$

The whole derivation according to G is as follows:

$$
\begin{aligned}
w_3 &= cce0 \\
w_4 &= cce1 \\
& cceS \\
& cc\bar{e}01 \\
& c\bar{c}e0S \\
w_8 &= \bar{c}cbae11 \\
& cbacbae1S \\
& cbacbaeS1 \\
& cbacba\bar{e}00S \\
& cbacb\bar{a}e011 \\
& cbac\bar{b}ae01S \\
& cba\bar{c}baae0S1
\end{aligned}
$$

$$
\begin{array}{ll}
 & cb\bar{a}cbabaae10S \\
w_{16} = & c\bar{b}acbabaae111 \\
 & \bar{c}baacbabaae11S \\
 & v_3e1S1 \\
 & ------ \\
w_{32} = & \ldots e1111 \\
 & v_4e111S \\
 & -------- \\
w_{64} = & v_5e11111 \\
 & -------- \\
w_{2^{i+1}} = & v_ie1^i \\
 & -----
\end{array}
$$

The word $v_{i-1}e1^{i-1}$ changes in $(i+1) + lg(v_{i-1})$ steps to the word v_iEP, where $E\in\{e,\bar{e}\}$. Thus, it follows from the fact

$$2^i \geq (i+1) + (i^2-i) \quad , i \geq 5$$

that the general formula for $w_{2^{i+1}}$ is indeed as above.

If f(n) is the growth function of our system, then

$$f(2^{i+1}) = (i+1)^2 \quad , i \geq 5 .$$

Assume $n\in[2^{i+1},2^{i+2}]$. Then, because our system is λ-free, the following approximations are true for $n \geq 32$

$$f(n) \leq f(2^{i+2}) = (i+2)^2 \leq ({}^2\log(n) + 1)^2 \text{ and}$$

$$f(n) \geq f(2^{i+1}) = (i+1)^2 \geq ({}^2\log(n) - 1)^2 .$$

Thus, the function f(n) is asymptotically equal to the function $({}^2\log n)^2$.

We can generalize the above example as follows. Let p and r be natural numbers. The function $(n+1)^r-(n+1)$ is a PD0L growth function, cf. [111]. Moreover, there exists a PD1L-system with the growth function asymptotically equal to the function ${}^p\log n$ (P. Vitányi, personal communication). So the above construction gives us a PD1L-system with the growth function asymptotically equal to the function $({}^p\log n)^r$.

DOL SYSTEMS WITH RANK

A. EHRENFEUCHT
Department of Computer Science
University of Colorado at Boulder, Boulder,
Colorado, U.S.A.

G. ROZENBERG
Department of Mathematics, Utrecht University,
Utrecht, Holland
and
Department of Mathematics, Antwerp University,
UIA, Wilrijk, Belgium.

INTRODUCTION

L systems (also called Lindenmayer systems or developmental systems) have recently gained considerable attention in both formal language theory and theoretical biology (see, e.g., [45], [60], [66] and their references). Among the developmental systems which are under active investigation now are the so called DOL systems (see, e.g., [14], [45], [75], [82], [83] and [95]). One of the most interesting and physically best motivated topics in the theory of L systems is that of "local versus global properties". It is concerned with explaining on the local level (sets of productions) global properties (i.e., those properties of the language or of the sequence generated by an L system whose formulation is independent on the L system itself). Examples of papers in this direction are [95] and [116].

This paper is concerned with the topic of "local versus global properties" in the case of DOL systems. It provides structural characterization of those DOL systems whose growth functions (see, e.g., [98] and [111]) are polynomially bounded.

We use standard formal-language theoretical terminology and notation. (Perhaps the only unusual notation is " $\#_a(x)$" meaning "the number of occurrences of the letter a in the word x".)

1. DOL SYSTEMS, SEQUENCES AND LANGUAGES

In this section we introduce basic definitions and terminology concerning DOL systems.

Definition 1. A deterministic L system without interactions, abbreviated DOL system, is a triple $G = \langle \Sigma, \delta, \omega \rangle$ where Σ is a finite nonempty set (the alphabet of G), ω is a nonempty word over Σ (the axiom of G) and δ (the transition function of G) is a homomorphism from Σ into Σ^*. G is called a propagating DOL system, abbreviated PDOL system, if δ is a homomorphism from Σ into Σ^+.

Definition 2. Let $G = \langle \Sigma, \delta, \omega \rangle$ be a DOL system and let, for $i \geqslant 0$, δ^i denote the i-folded composition of δ (with δ^0 being the identity function on Σ^*). The sequence of G, denoted $\mathcal{E}(G)$, is the sequence $\omega_0, \omega_1, \ldots$ of words over Σ^* such that $\omega_0 = \omega$ and $\omega_i = \delta^i(\omega)$ for every $i \geqslant 0$. The language of G, denoted $\mathcal{L}(G)$, is defined by $\mathcal{L}(G) = \{x \in \Sigma^* : \delta^i(\omega) = x \text{ for some } i \geqslant 0\}$. A letter a from Σ is called useful (in G) if a occurs in $\delta^i(\omega)$ for some $i \geqslant 0$.

Definition 3. Let K be a language (a sequence of words). K is called a DOL or a PDOL language (sequence) if for some DOL system G or for some PDOL system G respectively $\mathcal{L}(G) = K$ ($\mathcal{E}(G) = K$).

Definition 4. Let $G = \langle \Sigma, \delta, \omega \rangle$ be a DOL system and a be in Σ. We say that a is limited (in G) if there exists a constant C such that, for every $i \geqslant 0$, $|\delta^i(a)| < C$.

Definition 5. Let $G = \langle \Sigma, \delta, \omega \rangle$ be a DOL system. We say that G is polynomially bounded if there exists a polynomial p such that, for all $i \geq 0$, $|\delta^i(\omega)| \leq p(i)$.

Example 1. Let $G = \langle \Sigma, \delta, \omega \rangle$ where $\Sigma = \{a\}$, $\omega = a$ and δ is such that $\delta(a) = a^2$. Then G is a PDOL system, $\mathcal{E}(G) = a, a^2, a^4, \ldots$, $\mathcal{L}(G) = \{a^{2^i} : i \geq 0\}$ and G is not a polynomially bounded system.

Example 2. Let $G = \langle \Sigma, \delta, \omega \rangle$ where $\Sigma = \{a,b,c,d\}$, $\omega = cab$ and δ is such that $\delta(a) = cab$, $\delta(b) = b$, $\delta(c) = \Lambda$ and $\delta(d) = d$. Then G is a DOL system (but it is not a PDOL system), $\mathcal{E}(G) = cab, cab^2, cab^3, \ldots$, $\mathcal{L}(G) = \{cab^n : n \geq 1\}$ and G is polynomially bounded. The letters b and c are limited but the letter a is not limited. The letter d is not useful.

2. DOL SYSTEMS WITH RANK

In this section basic notions concerning DOL systems with rank (the subject of investigation of this paper) are introduced.

Definition 6. Let $G = \langle \Sigma, \delta, \omega \rangle$ be a DOL system. The rank of a letter a in G, denoted $\rho_G(a)$, is defined inductively as follows:

(i) If a is limited in G, then $\rho_G(a) = 1$.

(ii) Let $\Sigma_0 = \Sigma$ and $\delta_0 = \delta$. Let, for $j \geq 1$, δ_j denote the restriction of δ to $\Sigma_j = \Sigma - \{a : \rho_G(a) \leq j\}$. For $j \geq 1$, if a is limited in $\langle \Sigma, \delta_j, a \rangle$ then $\rho_G(a) = j+1$.

Definition 7. Let G be a DOL system. We say that G is a DOL system with rank if every letter which is useful in G has a rank. If G is a DOL system with rank then the rank of G is defined as the largest of the ranks of letters useful in G.

Example 3. Let G be the DOL system from Example 1. Then the letter a has no rank and consequently G is not a DOL system with rank.

Example 4. Let G be the DOL system from Example 2. Then $\rho_G(b) = \rho_G(c) = \rho_G(d) = 1$ and $\rho_G(a) = 2$. Consequently G is a DOL system with rank and the rank of G equals 2.

3. RESULTS

In this section main results concerning DOL systems with rank are stated.

First of all it turns out that the notion of a DOL system with rank is an effective one in the following sense.

Theorem 1. It is decidable whether an arbitrary DOL system is a DOL system with rank.

The language (or sequence) equivalence problem for DOL systems (i.e., whether two arbitrary DOL systems produce the same language or sequence) is one of the most intriguing and the longest open problems in the theory of L systems. At the time of writing of this paper we were not able to settle this question for arbitrary DOL systems with rank. However for propagating DOL systems with rank we have the following result.

Theorem 2. There exists an algorithm which given two arbitrary PDOL systems with rank G_1 and G_2 will decide whether or not $\mathcal{L}(G_1) = \mathcal{L}(G_2)$ $(\mathcal{E}(G_1) = \mathcal{E}(G_2))$.

Thus PDOL systems with rank constitute at the present time the largest nontrivial subclass of the class of DOL systems for which the language (and sequence) equivalence problem is decidable.

One of the interesting features of DOL systems with rank is that the sequence of Parikh vectors corresponding to a DOL system with rank always has an ultimately periodic polynomial description in the following sense.

Theorem 3. Let $G = \langle \Sigma, \delta, \omega \rangle$ be a DOL system with rank. For every letter a which is useful in G there exist integers s, r and a sequence $p_0, p_1, \ldots, p_{r-1}$ of polynomials (with rational coefficients and with positive leading coefficients) such that, for every $j > s$, $\#_a(\delta^{(ir+t)}(\omega)) = p_t(i)$, where $j = ir+t$ and $0 \leq t < r$.

The notion of a DOL system with rank is an important one as it provides the structural characterization of polynomially bounded DOL systems.

Theorem 4. A DOL system is polynomially bounded if and only if it is a DOL system with rank.

In fact the rank of a DOL system characterizes quite precisely the growth of a polynomially bounded DOL system, as is shown by the following result.

Theorem 5. If $G = \langle \Sigma, \delta, \omega \rangle$ is a DOL system, a is in Σ and n is a nonnegative integer, then $\rho_G(a) = n+1$ if and only if there exist polynomials $p_a(i)$, $q_a(i)$ of degree n, such that, for all $i \geq 0$, $p_a(i) \leq |\delta^i(a)| \leq q_a(i)$. Moreover one can, by exploiting the structural properties of G, effectively construct polynomials $p_a(i)$ and $q_a(i)$ with this property.

As corollaries of Theorem 4 we get a number of results concerning polynomially bounded DOL systems. For example, we have the following.

Corollary 1. There exists an algorithm which given two arbitrary polynomially bounded PDOL systems G_1 and G_2 will decide whether or not $\mathcal{L}(G_1) = \mathcal{L}(G_2)$ $(\mathcal{E}(G_1) = \mathcal{E}(G_2))$.

<u>Corollary 2</u>. If $G = \langle \Sigma, \delta, \omega \rangle$ is a polynomially bounded DOL system, then there exist integers s,r and a sequence $p_0, p_1, \ldots, p_{r-1}$ of polynomials (with rational coefficients and with positive leading coefficient) such that, for every $j > s$, $|\delta^{(ir+t)}(\omega)| = p_t(i)$, where $j = ir+t$ and $0 \leqslant t < r$.

NEW ATTACKS ON DOL EQUIVALENCE PROBLEM

EQUIVALENCE OF L-SYSTEMS

Mogens Nielsen
Department of Computer Science
University of Aarhus
Aarhus, Denmark

This paper summarizes some results concerning decidability of various kinds of equivalence problems for classes of L-systems - primarily DOL-systems. The reader is assumed to be familiar with some standard definitions and notations from the theory of L-systems.

For any finite alphabet, $\Sigma = \{\sigma_1, \sigma_2, \ldots, \sigma_n\}$, let π_Σ denote the mapping that associates with each word from Σ^* its corresponding Parikh-vector, i.e., for every word $x \in \Sigma^*$, $\pi_\Sigma(x)$ is the vector, in which the i'th component is the number of occurrences of σ_i in x.

For any class of deterministic L-systems, you may consider equivalence with respect to

WL(WS) : the set (sequence) of words generated

PL (PS) : the set (sequence) of Parikh-vectors associated with the words generated

NL (NS) : the set (sequence) of lengths of the words generated

Note that WL-, PL-, and NL-equivalence are also well-defined for nondeterministic L-systems.

The decidability of the corresponding six equivalence problems for DOL-systems is considered in [70]. The following result is proved ($|\Sigma|$ denotes the cardinality of Σ):

Theorem 1

For any two DOL-systems over some alphabet Σ, generating sequences of words $\{w_i\}$ and $\{v_i\}$ respectively:

1) $\forall$ i, $0 \le i$: $\pi_\Sigma(w_i) = \pi_\Sigma(v_i)$

iff

2) $\forall$ i, $0 \le i \le |\Sigma|$: $\pi_\Sigma(w_i) = \pi_\Sigma(v_i)$

A direct consequence of Theorem 1 is

Theorem 2

PS-equivalence is decidable for DOL-systems.

Furthermore, the following two theorems are proved in [70]:

Theorem 3

PL-equivalence is decidable for DOL-systems.

Theorem 4

WL-equivalence is decidable for DOL-systems iff WS-equivalence is decidable for DOL-systems.

These theorems leave open one of the main open questions in the theory of L-systems, namely the decidability of WL- and WS-equivalence for DOL-systems. It is known that these equivalence problems are decidable for some subclasses of DOL, e.g., ([41]):

Theorem 5

WL-equivalence is decidable for any class of unary L-systems (systems over a one-letter alphabet).

The following result is fairly easy to prove (a stronger version of the theorem has been proved by P. Johansen):

Theorem 6

WS-equivalence is decidable for locally catenative ([95]) DOL-systems.

Furthermore, G. Rozenberg has proved:

Theorem 7

WS-equivalence is decidable for DOL-systems with polynomial growth ([75]).

On the other hand, WL- and WS-equivalence are also known to be undecidable for some classes of systems, that include DOL. The following two theorems are proved in [80], [84], and [99]:

Theorem 8

WL-equivalence is undecidable for POL-systems.

Theorem 9

WL-equivalence is undecidable for PDTOL-systems.

Furthermore, using an idea suggested by P. Vitanyi (originally to prove undecidability of NS-equivalence) you can prove:

Theorem 10

All six equivalence problems considered in this paper are undecidable for D1L-systems.

It seems likely, however, that WS- and thereby WL-equivalence is decidable for DOL-systems. The following two results which are somewhat related to the problems are proved in [70]:

Theorem 11

There exists an algorithm that will produce for any reduced ([70]) DOL-system over an alphabet Σ, all (finitely many) systems over Σ, which are PL-(PS-) equivalent to the given system.

Theorem 12

Let S_1 and S_2 be two WS-equivalent DOL-systems over an alphabet Σ, for which the first $|\Sigma|$ generated Parikh-vectors are linearly independent, then $S_1 = S_2$.

(Note that the property "reduced" is decidable for OL-systems, but not for 1L-systems ([33])).

The following conjecture is suggested:

Conjecture

There exists a computable function f, mapping integers to integers, such that for any two DOL-systems over some alphabet Σ, generating sequences of words $\{w_i\}$ and $\{v_i\}$:

1) $\forall$ i, $0 \le i$: $\quad w_i = v_i$

iff

2) $\forall$ i, $0 \le i \le f(|\Sigma|)$: $\quad w_i = v_i$

This conjecture implies, of course, the decidability of WS-equivalence for DOL-systems. Note the similarity between the conjecture and Theorem 1, which states that for sequences of Parikh-vectors generated, the conjecture is true with f as the identity-function. That this is not the case for sequences of words generated, is seen from the following example.

Example

Consider the two DOL-systems, S_1 and S_2, over the alphabet $\Sigma \doteq \{a_i, b_i \mid 1 \le i \le n\}$.

	S_1	S_2
axiom	$a_1\ b_1$	$a_1\ b_1$
productions	$a_1 \rightarrow a_2$	$a_1 \rightarrow a_2$
	$b_1 \rightarrow b_2$	$b_1 \rightarrow b_2$
	$\vdots$	$\vdots$
	$a_{n-1} \rightarrow a_n$	$a_{n-1} \rightarrow a_n$
	$b_{n-1} \rightarrow b_n$	$b_{n-1} \rightarrow b_n$
	$a_n \rightarrow a_1\ b_1\ b_1$	$a_n \rightarrow a_1\ b_1\ b_1\ a_1\ a_1\ b_1\ b_1$
	$b_n \rightarrow a_1\ a_1\ b_1\ b_1\ a_1$	$b_n \rightarrow a_1$

It is easy to verify that the sequences of words generated by these two systems coincide until the 3n'th generated word and no longer. This implies that if the above conjecture is true, then $f(i) > 1\frac{1}{2} \cdot i$ for every integer i.

Finally, concerning length-equivalence of DOL-systems [75]:

<u>Theorem 13</u>

NS-equivalence is decidable for DOL-systems.

Decidability of NL-equivalence is still an open question for DOL-systems. In [70] the following theorem was proved.

<u>Theorem 14</u>

NL-equivalence is decidable for PDOL-systems.

But the proof of Theorem 14 builds essentially on the propagating property of the systems, and furthermore, J. Karhumaki has shown that there exists a DOL-system for which the range of its growth-function is not the range of the growth-function of any PDOL-system.

THE SYNTACTIC INFERENCE PROBLEM FOR D0L-SEQUENCES

P.G. DOUCET

Afdeling Theoretische Biologie, Rijksuniversiteit Utrecht.

SUMMARY

The syntactic inference problem consists of deciding, for a given set of words, whether there exists a grammar such that its language includes these given words; and also of actually finding any such grammars. In this paper, the problem is considered for D0L-systems. The stress is on the second, constructive, part of the problem.
The initial information may have various forms. Most of the results deal with cases in which

- the words are given as a sequence (i.e., with their rank order numbers), which may be either consecutive or scattered.
- the size of the alphabet is given.

From the decidability point of view most of the results are not new. The proposed decision method, however, represents a considerable speed-up by passing the initial data through a number of algebraic "sieves" which turn out to be quite dense.
The method depends on there being enough information to establish a linear dependence relation between the Parikh-vectors of the given words.
Several variants of the problem are discussed. One subcase of a hitherto open problem is solved; other problems remain open.

0. INTRODUCTION

Suppose a not-too-large set of words, say, $S = \{ab, aabc, a^6bbc\}$ is given. One can ask whether there exists a D0L-system G such that $S \subseteq L(G)$. This is perhaps the simplest form of the syntactic in-

ference problem. It is one of the 36 such problems for L-systems posed by Feliciangeli and Herman [28] , and one of the 6 which are still open. There may, however, be some additional information. The alphabet may be given, and there may be some information on the order of appearance of the words; either general (only the order) or specific (the precise rank order numbers). Feliciangeli and Herman make a different distinction. They only consider ordered, but not precisely numbered, sets; within this domain they distinguish sets of consecutive words, sets of scattered, but equally spaced, words and unspecified ordered sets of words.
I shall mainly discuss those cases where the aphabet is given as well as the rank order numbers. Actually, the inference problem is known to be decidable as soon as the alphabet is given: it is not difficult to see that in that case the number of (reduced) DOL-systems is finite, and one can simply try them all out. I intend to present an algorithm which is able to discard the vast majority of combinations at an early stage. It can be roughly described by the following sequence of steps:

1. take the Parikh-images of the given words
2. find a linear dependence relation and its associated polynomial $\psi(x)$
3. find a divisor of $\psi(x)$
4. find a growth matrix
5. find a set of production rules.

Essentially, the method makes use of the number of letters present in each given word (as opposed to their order) for as long as possible. This allows one to apply algebraic methods to the resulting vectors, these being generally more powerful than the combinatorial approach. The method works only if sufficient words are given to establish a linear dependence relation between their Parikh-vectors. Even then, a certain amount of trial-and-error work is necessary.

1. PRELIMINARIES

I shall assume the reader to be acquainted with the notion of a DOL-system such as outlined by Rozenberg and Doucet [91] or Salomaa [102]. I shall denote a DOL-system G by the triple $< \Sigma, P, w_0 >$, where Σ is

the alphabet, P the set of production rules, and w_0 the axiom. $\mathcal{E}(G)$ denotes the infinite sequence of words generated by G, in order of appearance. If a sequence of words is equal to $\mathcal{E}(G)$ for some DOL-system G, it is called a DOL-sequence. Any subsequence of a DOL-sequence is called a DOL-subsequence. Most DOL-subsequences occurring in the sequel will be finite. They may either be consecutive (such as w_4, w_5, w_6, w_7) or scattered (such as w_0, w_3, w_4, w_{20}).
Unless specified otherwise, any sequence will be a sequence of numbered words, i.e. a subset of $\mathbb{N} \times \Sigma^*$; it may be finite or infinite. Sequences will be denoted by script letters.
$\#S$ denotes the number of elements of a set S.
$|w|$ denotes the length (= number of letters) of a word w.
If $\Sigma = \{\sigma_1,\ldots,\sigma_k\}$, then the Parikh-vector $\bar{w}$ assigned to a word w is defined as a vector in $\mathbb{N}^k$ with its ith coordinate equal to the number of occurrences of σ_i in w. Example: if $\Sigma = \{a,b,c\}$ and w = cacaa, then $\bar{w} = (3,0,2)^T$. The superscript denotes the transposition operator, since vectors will be written as column vectors. All vectors will be distinguishable by a bar.
The length of a vector $\bar{a} = (\alpha_1,\ldots,\alpha_k)^T$ is defined as $|\bar{a}| = \Sigma\alpha_i$. This definition is compatible with the earlier definition of word length: $|w| = |\bar{w}|$.
Without the details of a formal definition it will be clear that in a similar way the set P of production rules can be mapped into a k×k matrix $A_P = ((c_{ij}))$, where c_{ij} gives the number of occurrences of σ_i in $P(\sigma_{ij})$; in other words, the j-th column of A_P equals the Parikh-vector of $P(\sigma_j)$. A_P is called the growth matrix of P or G; it is also called the production matrix. If no confusion is likely, A_P is also written A.
If $\mathcal{S}$ is any sequence of words $w_{i_1}, w_{i_2},\ldots$, then its Parikh-image $\bar{\mathcal{S}}$ denotes the sequence of vectors $\bar{w}_{i_1}, \bar{w}_{i_2},\ldots$. Similarly, $\bar{\mathcal{E}}(G)$, the Parikh-sequence of G, is defined as $\bar{w}_0, \bar{w}_1, \bar{w}_2,\ldots$. $\mathbb{N}$, $\mathbb{Z}$, $\mathbb{Q}$, $\mathbb{R}$, and $\mathbb{C}$ denote the sets of natural, integer, rational, real and complex numbers, respectively. R[x] denotes the set of all polynomials in x with coefficients in the set R.

2. RECURRENCE RELATIONS SATISFIED BY PARIKH-SEQUENCES.

Let $G = \langle \Sigma, P, w_0 \rangle$ be a DOL-system with $\#\Sigma = k$, and let A be G's growth matrix. The Parikh-mapping $\sigma_1 \mapsto (1,0,\ldots,0)^T,\ldots,\sigma_k \mapsto (0,\ldots,0,1)^T$ maps words over the alphabet Σ into the k-dimensional vector space R over the field $\mathbb{Q}$*). The growth matrix A is a linear mapping

of R into itself.
In G's Parikh-sequence $\bar{\mathcal{E}} = \bar{w}_0, \bar{w}_1, \bar{w}_2, \ldots$ some vectors are linearly dependent. Let such a dependence be given by a <u>recurrence relation</u> like

$$\bar{w}_8 + \bar{w}_6 - 3\bar{w}_5 + 4\bar{w}_0 = \bar{0}. \qquad (1)$$

This can also be written as

$$(A^8+A^6-3A^5+4I)\bar{w}_0 = \bar{0}$$

(I is the k×k identity matrix), or

$$\psi(A)\bar{w}_0 = \bar{0},$$

where $\psi(x) = x^8 + x^6 - 3x^5 + 4$.
I shall call $\psi(x)$ the <u>associated polynomial</u> of the recurrence relation (1), and vice versa. (The customary term "characteristic polynomial" may lead to confusion).
This section deals with the question: what recurrence relations obtain in $\bar{\mathcal{E}}(G)$? Most of the answers come by way of their associated polynomials.
Three polynomials connected with A or G are of special importance.
First, the <u>characteristic polynomial of A</u>, $\phi_A(x)$, defined by $\phi_A(x) = \det(xI-A)$.
Second, the <u>minimal polynomial of A</u>, $m_A(x)$, defined as the lowest-degree monic**) polynomial in $\mathbb{Q}[x]$ for which $m_A(A) = O$ (the null matrix).
Third, the <u>minimal polynomial of G</u>, $\mu_G(x)$, defined as the lowest-degree monic polynomial in $\mathbb{Q}[x]$ for which $\mu_G(A)\bar{w}_0 = \bar{0}$.
Observe that $\phi_A(x)$ and $m_A(x)$ depend on A only; $\mu_G(x)$ depends on both A and $\bar{w}_0$.
The following lemmas summarize a few standard facts from matrix theory.
<u>Lemma 2.1</u> $\phi_A(x)$, $m_A(x)$ and $\mu_G(x)$ are unique.
<u>Lemma 2.2</u> $m_A(x)$ contains the same linear factors $x-\lambda_i$ ($\lambda_i \in \mathbb{C}$) as $\phi_A(x)$; their multiplicaties may, however, be lower. If $\phi_A(x) = 0$ has no multiple roots in $\mathbb{C}$, then $m_A(x) = \phi_A(x)$.

---

*) It might be more elegant to construct the more restricted module R over the ring $\mathbb{Z}$, but the present approach will do.

**) i.e., with leading coefficient 1.

<u>Lemma 2.3</u> $m_A(x)$ divides every polynomial $\psi(x)$ for which $\psi(A) = O$.
<u>Lemma 2.4</u> $\mu_G(x)$ divides every polynomial $\psi(x)$ for which $\psi(A)\bar{w}_0 = \bar{0}$.
<u>Lemma 2.5</u> There exist algorithms for finding $m_A(x)$ and $\mu_G(x)$.
For further information, I refer the reader to standard texts like Gantmacher, Chs. IV and VII*). Furthermore, I will need two theorems from algebra:

<u>Lemma 2.6</u> If factorization in an integral domain R is unique, so is factorization in R[x].

<u>Lemma 2.7</u> A polynomial in $\mathbb{Z}[x]$ which can be factored in polynomials in $\mathbb{Q}[x]$ can already be factored in polynomials in $\mathbb{Z}[x]$.

Both lemmas can, e.g., be found in Birkhoff and Maclane, Ch. III**). Since $\phi_A(x) \in \mathbb{Z}[x]$, $\mu_G(x) \in \mathbb{Q}[x]$, $m_A(x) \in \mathbb{Q}[x]$, and $\mathbb{Z}$ has unique factorization, lemmas 2.6 and 2.7 can be applied, giving

<u>Lemma 2.8</u> $m_A(x)$ and $\mu_G(x)$ have integer coefficients.

<u>Theorem 2.9</u> If in a DOL-sequence $\mathcal{E}(G)$ some vectors from $\bar{\mathcal{E}}(G)$ satisfy a recurrence relation, then they also satisfy a monic recurrence relation with integer coeeficients.

<u>Proof</u> Suppose the recurrence relation $w_r + \alpha_{r-1}\bar{w}_{r-1}+....+\alpha_0\bar{w}_0 = \bar{0}$ is given, with all $\alpha_i \in \mathbb{Q}$.
If m is the degree of G's minimal polynomial $\mu_G(x)$, then $r < m$ is impossible; for r = m the theorem is trivially true (by lemma 2.1), so $r > m$ remains to be examined.
All α_i are rational, so one can find a number M such that

$$M\bar{w}_r + M\alpha_{r-1}\bar{w}_{r-1}+...+M\alpha_0\bar{w}_0 = \bar{0} \qquad (2)$$

has only integer coefficients. $\bar{w}_r$ can be expressed in $\bar{w}_{r-1},...,\bar{w}_{r-m}$ by means of the recurrence relation associated with $\mu_G(x)$, which has integer coefficients. By subtracting this relation M-1 times from (2), one obtains a relation of the required form. ⊠

The subspace of $\mathbb{Q}^k$ spanned by the vectors $\bar{w}_0,\bar{w}_1,\bar{w}_2,...$ is of dimension m, since, from rank order number m on, each vector linearly depends on the previous vectors. Hence

<u>Theorem 2.10</u> If $\mu_G(x)$ has degree m, then any set of m vectors from $\bar{\mathcal{E}}(G)$ is linearly dependent.

---

*) F.R. Gantmacher, The theory of matrices. New York: Chelsea, 1959 (Translated from the Russian).

**) G. Birkhoff and S. Maclane. A survey of modern algebra. New York: Mac Millan, 1953.

Let G be a DOL-system with minimal polynomial $\mu_G(x)$, of degree m. Then $\mathcal{E}(G) = w_0, w_1, w_2, \ldots$. All Parikh-vectors $\bar{w}_r$ from $\bar{\mathcal{E}}(G)$ can be expressed in terms of the first m Parikh-vectors $\bar{w}_0, \ldots, \bar{w}_{m-1}$. In the sequel, this initial subsequence will be denoted by $\bar{\mathcal{E}}_0$. These m vectors can also be collected in the matrix E_0, with k rows and m columns. Thus each vector $\bar{w}_r \in \bar{\mathcal{E}}(G)$ can be written as

$$\bar{w}_r = E_0 \bar{c}_r,$$

where $\bar{c}_r$, the <u>coefficient vector</u> of the word w_r (or the vector $\bar{w}_r$) is an m-vector. So $\bar{c}_r$ is just another way of representing the recurrence relation by which $\bar{w}_r$ can be expressed in the first m Parikh-vectors. Observe that

(i) For each r, $\bar{c}_r$ is unique and has integer coefficients.

(ii) The associated polynomial of $\bar{c}_r$ (with obvious definition) is equal to $x^r (\mathrm{mod}\ \mu_G(x))$.

(iii) If some set of Parikh-vectors satisfies a recurrence relation

$$\bar{w}_r + \alpha_{r-1}\bar{w}_{r-1} + \ldots + \alpha_0 \bar{w}_0 = \bar{0},$$

then, since E_0 is non-singular, their coefficient vectors satisfy the same relation:

$$\bar{c}_r + \alpha_{r-1}\bar{c}_{r-1} + \ldots + \alpha_0 \bar{c}_0 = \bar{0}.$$

3. THE BASIC INFERENCE PROBLEM

The simplest problem is the following.
Given an alphabet of size k and a sequence $\mathcal{S} = w_0, \ldots, w_k$, find all DOL-systems G for which $\mathcal{S}$ is the initial subsequence of $\mathcal{E}(G)$.
To solve the problem, first form the Parikh-images of the words: $\bar{\mathcal{S}} = \bar{w}_0, \ldots, \bar{w}_k$. If $\mathcal{S}$ is to be the initial subsequence of some $\mathcal{E}(G)$, then the following relation must hold:

$$A \begin{pmatrix} \bar{w}_0 & \cdots & \bar{w}_{k-1} \\ | & & | \\ | & & | \end{pmatrix} = \begin{pmatrix} \bar{w}_0 & \cdots & \bar{w}_k \\ | & & | \\ | & & | \end{pmatrix} \qquad (3)$$

or $$AS = T \qquad (4)$$

(A is the growth matrix of G).
One may now distinguish two cases, depending on S.

First, if S is non-singular (which, incidentally, means that $\phi_A(x) = m_A(x) = \mu_G(x)$), then A is uniquely determined by

$$A = TS^{-1}$$

Second, if rank (S) = k-r with r > 0, then A can be written

$$A = A_0 + \lambda_1 A_1 + \ldots + \lambda_q A_q,$$

where - A_0 is some solution of AS = T

- $A_1, \ldots, A_q$ are mutually independent solutions of AS = O; $q \leq k.r.$
- $\lambda_1, \ldots, \lambda_q$ are otherwise arbitrary numbers such that A has only positive elements.

The last condition leads to q linear unequalities in $\lambda_1, \ldots, \lambda_q$, with finitely many solutions (perhaps none). Properly speaking, the number of solutions can indeed be infinite, but only if (and as far as) letters not occurring in $\mathcal{S}$ are concerned. The complication is completely formal, since such a letter will never appear at all if it did not appear in $\mathcal{S}$; it may, if desired, be formally eliminated by only admitting reduced G's.

Once an admissible growth matrix A is found, one returns from Parikh-vectors to words.

Lemma 3.1 The growth matrix and the first $\# \Sigma+1$ words of a DOL-sequence uniquely determine the useful production rules.

Proof The restriction to useful production rules (i.e. rules which are at all applied in $\mathcal{E}$) should be obvious.

Let $w_0 = \sigma_{01} \ldots \sigma_{0p}$.

One can then parse w_1 in p subwords, starting from the left-hand side:

$$w_1 = P(\sigma_{01}) * \ldots * P(\sigma_{0p}),$$

where the subword lengths $|P(\sigma_{0i})|$ can be looked up in A, being equal to the lengths of the column vectors $\overline{P(\sigma_{0i})}$ of A.

By this procedure, $P(\sigma_{0i})$ is found for all letters in w_0. The procedure is then continued for the one-step derivations $w_1 \Rightarrow w_2, \ldots, w_{k-1} \Rightarrow w_k$. Any letter which has not appeared by then will not appear at all. ⊠

Theorem 3.2 For a given k×k matrix A and a word sequence $\mathcal{S} = w_0, \ldots, w_k$ over a k-letter alphabet there is at most one reduced DOL-system G with the properties

(i) A is the growth matrix of G.

(ii) $\mathcal{S}$ is the initial subsequence of $\mathcal{E}(G)$.

G can be effectively constructed.

Proof The theorem follows from lemma 3.1 by observing that the construction of the set of production rules P from A and $\mathcal{S}$ does not depend on the fact that A is a growth matrix or $\mathcal{S}$ is a D0L-subsequence. ⊠

During the construction of P several things may happen, in this order:

1 The total length of $P(w_i)$ as found from A is not equal to the length of the given word w_{i+1}.

2 After parsing w_{i+1} in $|w_i|$ subwords the Parikh-vectors of the individual subwords are not equal to the appropriate columns of A, even though the lengths may match.

3 For some letter σ, $P(\sigma)$ as found from one instance of σ somewhere in the derivation may differ from $P(\sigma)$ as found from some other instance of σ, even though both Parikh-vectors are equal (and consistent with A).

In each case, A is rejected as a growth matrix for $w_0,\ldots,w_k$. Whether in case 3 $w_0,\ldots,w_k$ must also be rejected as a D0L-subsequence is not yet quite clear to me.

If the matrix A happens to be non-singular (which is the rule rather than the exception), theorem 3.2 has interesting consequences, which can be formulated in various ways. Let the order of a recurrence relation $\psi(A)\bar{w}_0 = \bar{0}$ be defined as the degree of the polynomial $\psi(x)$.

Corollary 3.3 If a D0L-subsequence $\mathcal{S}$ does not satisfy any recurrence relation of order lower than $\#\Sigma$, then there is only one G with $\mathcal{S} = \mathcal{E}(G)$.

Corollary 3.4 If a sequence $\mathcal{S}$ of k+1 words over a k-letter alphabet does not satisfy any recurrence relation of order lower than k, then there exists at most one D0L-system G such that $\mathcal{S}$ is the initial subsequence of $\mathcal{E}(G)$.

Corollary 3.5 Two different (and reduced) D0L-systems G and H can only produce the same sequence if

$$\mu_G(x) = \mu_H(x) \neq \phi_G(x) = \phi_H(x).$$

4. Inference from a scattered sequence.

Like in the previous section, the alphabet Σ is regarded as given; $\# \Sigma = k$. The given sequence of words, however, has the form $\mathcal{S} = w_{i_1}, w_{i_2}, \ldots, w_{i_p}$, with $i_0 < i_1 < \ldots < i_p$ and p arbitrary, instead of $\mathcal{S} = w_0, w_1, \ldots, w_k$. After a few remarks on notation I shall first describe the algorithm which produces all possible G's from $\mathcal{S}$, then go into its justification, and next give two examples. The section is concluded by a flow diagram indicating the acceptance/rejection structure of the algorithm.

Three different sequences will appear in the sequel:

- the given sequence $\mathcal{S} = w_{i_1}, w_{i_2}, \ldots, w_{i_p}$.
- the initial DOL-subsequence $\mathcal{E}_0 = w_0, w_1, \ldots, w_{m-1}$, where m is the degree of G's minimal polynomial.
- the next-to-initial DOL-subsequence $\mathcal{E}_1 = w_1, w_2, \ldots, w_m$.

Each of these sequences can be collected in a matrix. They will be denoted by S, E_0 and E_1, respectively; they are elements of $\mathbb{N}^{k \times p}$ and $\mathbb{N}^{k \times m}$ (twice).

As described at the end of section 2, the elements of $\bar{\mathcal{S}}$ can all be expressed in the elements of $\bar{\mathcal{E}}_0$, each $\bar{w}_j$ by means of its coefficient vector $\bar{c}_j$. The coefficient vectors of $\mathcal{S}$ can again be collected in a matrix, C, which is an element of $\mathbb{Z}^{m \times p}$.

The construction procedure now runs as follows:

1. Find some recurrence relations within $\bar{\mathcal{S}}$. Determine the greatest common divisor of their associated polynomials, say, $\psi(x)$.
2. Find a monic divisor of $\psi(x)$, with integer coefficients and degree $\leq k$. Let $\chi(x)$, with degree m, be such a divisor. The next steps will investigate whether $\chi(x) = \mu_G(x)$ for some G such that $\mathcal{S} \subseteq \mathcal{E}(G)$.
3. Compute the coefficient matrix C from $\chi(x)$ and the index set of $\mathcal{S}$.
4. Find $E_0 \in \mathbb{N}^{k \times m}$ satisfying the matrix equation $S = E_0 C$.
5. Determine $\bar{w}_m$ from $\bar{w}_0, \ldots, \bar{w}_{m-1}$ as found in E_0 and from $\chi(x)$'s associated recurrence relation. Now one can compose E_1 from E_0 and $\bar{w}_m$. Next find $A \in \mathbb{N}^{k \times k}$ satisfying the matrix equation $E_1 = A\, E_0$.
6. Determine all powers of the production rules P needed to produce the words of $\mathcal{S}$ from one another by first computing the appropriate powers of A and then using these to parse the words of $\mathcal{S}$ (as in the basic inference problem from section 3).
7. By combinatorial means, find the set of production rules P from the growth matrix and the various powers of P found in step 6.

Ad 1. $\bar{\mathcal{S}}$ may or may not satisfy a recurrence relation. Of course it always does if $\mathcal{S}$ contains k+1 or more words, but this is not a necessary condition. If $\overline{\mathcal{S}}$ does not satisfy a recurrence relation, the whole procedure simply doesn't work. If it does, there may be several, and it is helpful (though not necessary) to find them all. If $\mathcal{S}$ is part of a DOL-sequence &(G), then the associated polynomials of these recurrence relations are all multiples of $\mu_G(x)$; so is their greatest common divisor, $\psi(x)$. If the associated polynomial of any of the discovered recurrence relations does not (in its monic form) have integer coefficients, then $\mathcal{S}$ is no DOL-subsequence (by theorem 2.9).

Example: If $\mathcal{S}$ consists of w_2 = acd, w_3 = abba and w_5 = acbbdaa, then $2\overline{w}_2 + \overline{w}_3 - 2\overline{w}_5 = \overline{o}$; the associated polynomial (in monic form) is $x^5 - \frac{1}{2}x^3 - x^2$, which does not satisfy theorem 2.9. Hence $\mathcal{S}$ is not a DOL-subsequence.

<u>Ad 2</u>. $\mu_G(x)$ must have the following properties:

(i) it divides $\psi(x)$

(ii) it is monic and has integer coefficients (by lemma 1.8).

(iii) it has degree k or less.

Step 2 consists of finding all polynomials $\chi(x)$ with these properties, by trial and error. That this is a finite enterprise is ensured by

<u>Lemma 4.1</u>. For a given polynomial $\psi(x) \in \mathbb{Z}[x]$ bounds can be found for the coefficients of all $\psi(x)$'s divisors of given degree m.

<u>Proof</u>. By a well-known theorem from algebra, all complex roots y_j of a polynomial

$$\psi(x) = x^n + \alpha_{n-1}x^{n-1} + \dots \alpha_1 x + \alpha_0$$

are either smaller than 1 or are bounded by

$$|y_j| \leq M = n \cdot \max_i \{\alpha_i\}.$$

Since in our case $|\alpha_i| \geq 1$ for all i, $|y_j| \leq M$ holds in all cases. Any divisor $\chi(x)$ of $\psi(x)$ of degree m can be written as

$$\chi(x) = (x-y_1)\dots(x-y_m) = x^m + \beta_{m-1}x^{m-1} + \dots + \beta_0,$$

where

$$|\beta_{m-1}| = |y_1+\dots+y_m| \leq mM$$

$$|\beta_{m-2}| = |\sum_{i\neq j} y_i y_j| \leq m(m-1)M$$

etc.

Thus each β_i of $\chi(x)$ can be bounded in terms of m and M. (To be sure, the bounds so obtained are often not very practical, and may be considerably improved by using the fact that $\beta_i \in \mathbb{Z}$; for example, β_0 must, by lemma 2.7, be a factor of α_0). ⊠

Ad 3. The construction of the various $\overline{c}_i$ was described at the end of section 2.

Ad 4. The matrix C may be singular, so there may be several (though only finitely many) E_0 satisfying the equation $S = E_0C$.

Ad 5. Like in the basic inference problem of section 3, several (though only finitely many) growth matrices A may be found.

Ad 6. Knowing A, one can now parse w_{i_1} into $|w_{i_0}|$ subwords, each of length found from the appropriate column vector length of $A^{i_1-i_0}$, and thus infer some rules from $P^{i_1-i_0}$. In contrast with the basic problem, the absence of a letter in $\mathcal{S}$ does not mean that it is never used at all. It may have been used in the words in between the given words, and it may be indispensable.

Ad 7. The information obtained from step 6 does not always uniquely determine P.

As an example, consider the following problem:

Find all DOL-systems over the alphabet {a,b,c,d} such that $\mathcal{E}(G)$ includes w_1 = d, w_3 = dac, w_5 = accbd, w_9 = cbddacdacaccbd. To solve the problem, follow the steps of the procedure:

1. The sequence $\mathfrak{Z}$ consists of $\overline{w}_1 = (0,0,0,1)^T$, $\overline{w}_3 = (0,1,1,1)^T$, $\overline{w}_5 = (1,1,2,1)^T$, $\overline{w}_9 = (3,2,5,4)^T$.

The only recurrence relation obtaining in $\mathfrak{Z}$ is $\overline{w}_9-3\overline{w}_5+\overline{w}_3-2\overline{w}_1 = \overline{o}$. Its associated polynomial is $\psi(x) = x^9-3x^5+x^3-2x$.

2. $\psi(x) = x(x^2+2)(x^3-x-1)^2$. Its set of divisors of degree $\leqslant 4$ (= Σ) exhausts the possibilities for G's minimal polynomial; it consists of x, x^2+2, $x(x^2+2)$, x^3-x-1 and $x(x^3-x-1)$.

Of these x can be immediately discarded. So can x^2+2 (which is associated with the impossible recurrence relation $\overline{w}_2 = -2\overline{w}_0$) and $x(x^2+2)$. Two polynomials remain, x^3-x-1 and x^4-x^2-x.

3. First try $\chi(x) = x^3-x-1$. $\chi(x)$ is associated with $\overline{w}_3 = \overline{w}_1 + \overline{w}_0$, and iteration produces

$$\overline{w}_4 = \overline{w}_2 + \overline{w}_1$$

$$\overline{w}_5 = \overline{w}_3 + \overline{w}_2 = \overline{w}_2 + \overline{w}_1 + \overline{w}_0$$

$$\vdots$$

$$\overline{w}_9 = 3\overline{w}_2 + 4\overline{w}_1 + 2\overline{w}_0$$

So $\overline{c}_1 = (0,1,0)^T$, $\overline{c}_3 = (1,1,0)^T$, $\overline{c}_5 = (1,1,1)^T$ and $c_9 = (2,4,3)^T$;

$$C = \begin{pmatrix} 0 & 1 & 1 & 2 \\ 1 & 1 & 1 & 4 \\ 0 & 0 & 1 & 3 \end{pmatrix}$$

4. E_0 must now be solved from $S = E_0C$, or $\begin{pmatrix} 0 & 0 & 1 & 3 \\ 0 & 1 & 1 & 2 \\ 0 & 1 & 2 & 5 \\ 1 & 1 & 1 & 4 \end{pmatrix} = E_0 \begin{pmatrix} 0 & 1 & 1 & 2 \\ 1 & 1 & 1 & 4 \\ 0 & 0 & 1 & 3 \end{pmatrix}$.

E_0 must also be in $\mathbb{N}^{4\times 3}$.

There happens to be precisely one solution : $E_0 = \begin{pmatrix} 0 & 0 & 1 \\ 1 & 0 & 0 \\ 1 & 0 & 1 \\ 0 & 1 & 0 \end{pmatrix}$.

This supplies the three initial vectors of $\overline{\mathcal{E}}(G)$.

5. The fourth vector of $\overline{\mathcal{E}}(G)$ is found from the first three and from G's minimal recurrence relation : $\overline{w}_3 = \overline{w}_1 + \overline{w}_0 = (0,1,1,1)^T$. Now E_1 is also known, and the growth matrix $A (\in \mathbb{N}^{4\times 4})$ can be solved from

$$AE_0 = A_1, \text{ or } A \begin{pmatrix} 0 & 0 & 1 \\ 1 & 0 & 0 \\ 1 & 0 & 1 \\ 0 & 1 & 0 \end{pmatrix} = \begin{pmatrix} 0 & 1 & 0 \\ 0 & 0 & 1 \\ 0 & 1 & 1 \\ 1 & 0 & 1 \end{pmatrix}$$

There are solutions, $A = \begin{pmatrix} 0 & 0 & 0 & 1 \\ 1 & 0 & 0 & 0 \\ 1 & 0 & 0 & 1 \\ 0 & 0 & 1 & 0 \end{pmatrix}$ and $A = \begin{pmatrix} 0 & 0 & 0 & 1 \\ 1 & 0 & 0 & 0 \\ 1 & 0 & 0 & 1 \\ 1 & 1 & 0 & 0 \end{pmatrix}$

6. First try the first A. The powers of A relevant for are A^2(for $\overline{w}_1 \overset{2}{\Rightarrow} \overline{w}_3$ and $\overline{w}_3 \overset{2}{\Rightarrow} \overline{w}_5$) and A^4(for $\overline{w}_5 \overset{4}{\Rightarrow} \overline{w}_9$).

$$A^2 = \begin{pmatrix} 0 & 0 & 1 & 0 \\ 0 & 0 & 0 & 1 \\ 0 & 0 & 1 & 1 \\ 1 & 0 & 0 & 1 \end{pmatrix} \text{ and } A^4 = \begin{pmatrix} 0 & 0 & 1 & 1 \\ 1 & 0 & 0 & 1 \\ 1 & 0 & 1 & 2 \\ 1 & 0 & 1 & 1 \end{pmatrix} .$$

These induce the following parsing in $\mathcal{S}$:

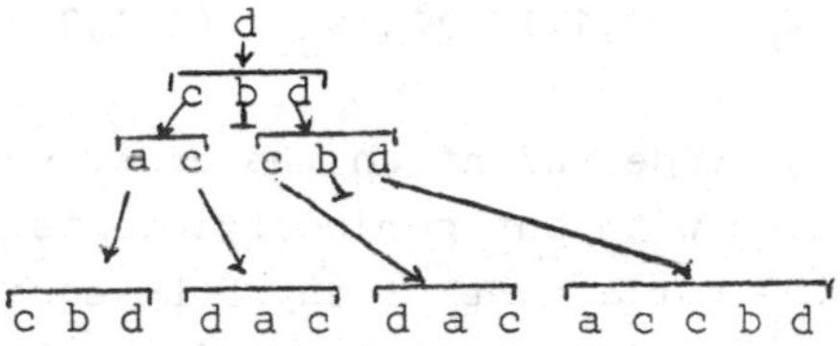

The parsing is consistent, both internally and with A, and produces the following information :

$$P^2(d) = cbd \; ; \; P^4(a) = cbd, \; P^4(c) = dac, \; P^4(d) = accbd.$$

7. Combining the data from step 6 with the growth matrix A, one obtains one set of production rules :

$\{a \to cb, \; b \to \lambda, \; c \to d, \; d \to ac\}$ and two possible axioms: $w_0 = b_c$ or $w_0 = cb$.

6,7 Now try the other A left over from step 5. In the same fashion, one set of production rules is produced, again with two possible axioms :

$P = \{a \to cbd, \; b \to d, \; c \to \lambda, \; d \to ac\}$; $w_0 = bc$ or $w_0 = cb$.

3,4,5,6,7 One more $\chi(x)$ was left over from step 3 : $\chi(x) = x^4 - x^2 - x$.

It first produces $C = \begin{pmatrix} 0 & 0 & 0 & 0 \\ 1 & 0 & 1 & 2 \\ 0 & 0 & 1 & 3 \\ 0 & 1 & 0 & 2 \end{pmatrix}$, then $E_0 \begin{pmatrix} \alpha_0 & 0 & 1 & 0 \\ \alpha_1 & 0 & 0 & 1 \\ \alpha_2 & 0 & 1 & 1 \\ \alpha_3 & 1 & 0 & 1 \end{pmatrix}$ with

the α_i (the axiom's coordinates) arbitrary.
In step 5, two solutions for A appear, together with further restrictions on the axiom :

$$A = \begin{pmatrix} 0 & 0 & 0 & 1 \\ 1 & 0 & 0 & 0 \\ 1 & 0 & 0 & 1 \\ 0 & 0 & 1 & 0 \end{pmatrix} \quad \text{with } \overline{w}_0 = (1,\lambda,0,0)^T \ (\lambda \text{ arbitrary})$$

or

$$A = \begin{pmatrix} 0 & 0 & 0 & 1 \\ 1 & 0 & 0 & 0 \\ 1 & 0 & 0 & 1 \\ 1 & 1 & 0 & 0 \end{pmatrix} \quad \text{with } \overline{w}_0 = (1,0,\lambda,0)^T \ (\lambda \text{ arbitrary}).$$

In steps 6 and 7 the same two P's as before are produced ; the axioms are, however, sligthly different :
$P = \{a \to cb,\ b \to \lambda,\ c \to d,\ d \to ac\}$ with $w_0 = b^m cb^n$ (m,n arbitrary),
$P = \{a \to cbd,\ b \to d,\ c \to \lambda,\ d \to ac\}$ with $w_0 = c^m bc^n$.
This concludes the example.
Another example may show the procedure's speed to advantage.
Let $\mathcal{S}$ be given, consisting of w_1 = b, w_4 = acb, w_6 = ddab, w_9 = abcaddab, and w_{11} = aabbccddabcd. $\Sigma = \{a,b,c,d\}$. Is $\mathcal{S}$ part of a DOL-sequence ?
Step 1 : $w_1 = (0,1,0,0)^T$, $w_4 = (1,1,1,0)^T$, $w_6 = (1,1,0,2)^T$, $w_9 = (3,2,1,2)^T$, $w_{11} = (3,3,3,3)^T$.

Now $\overline{w}_{11}$ is of course dependent on the other vectors, but not by a monic relation with integer coefficients.

Hence $\mathcal{S}$ is (by theorem 2.9) not a part of any DOL-sequence.
Observe that this remains true if the alphabet is not given.

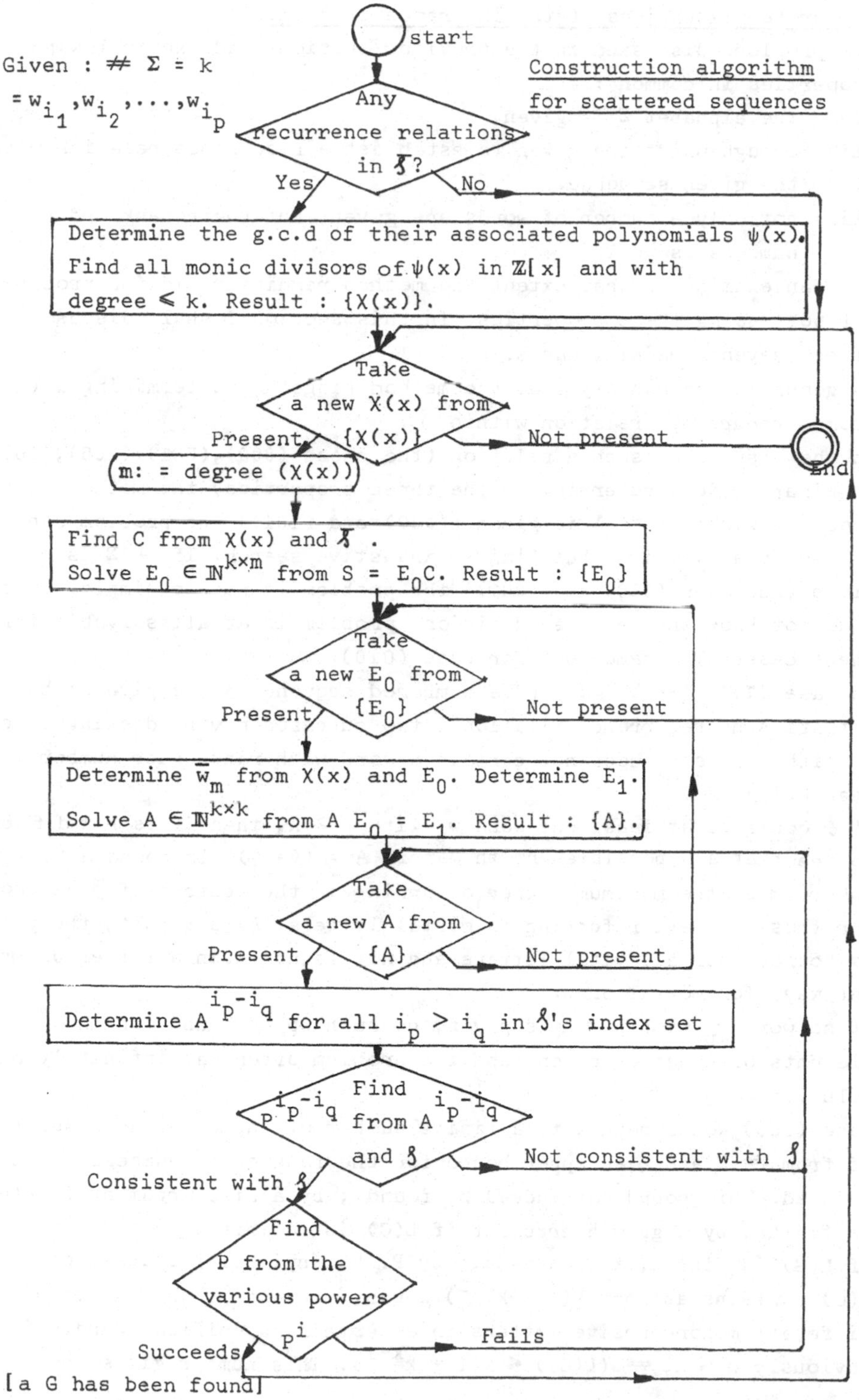
start
Given : # Σ = k
= w_{i_1}, w_{i_2}, ..., w_{i_p}
Construction algorithm for scattered sequences
Any recurrence relations in 𝔖?
Yes
No
Determine the g.c.d of their associated polynomials ψ(x). Find all monic divisors of ψ(x) in ℤ[x] and with degree ≤ k. Result : {χ(x)}.
Take a new χ(x) from {χ(x)}
Present
Not present
End
m: = degree (χ(x))
Find C from χ(x) and 𝔖. Solve E_0 ∈ ℕ^{k×m} from S = E_0 C. Result : {E_0}
Take a new E_0 from {E_0}
Present
Not present
Determine w̄_m from χ(x) and E_0. Determine E_1. Solve A ∈ ℕ^{k×k} from A E_0 = E_1. Result : {A}.
Take a new A from {A}
Present
Not present
Determine A^{i_p - i_q} for all i_p > i_q in 𝔖's index set
Find P^{i_p - i_q} from A^{i_p - i_q} and 𝔖
Not consistent with 𝔖
Consistent with 𝔖
Find P from the various powers P^i
Fails
Succeeds
[a G has been found]

5. Further extensions of the inference problem.

The problems discussed in the previous sections had the following properties in common :

(i) the alphabet Σ is given.

(ii) enough words are given to establish a recurrence relation within the given sequence.

(iii) not only a number of words are given, but their rank order numbers as well.

One can examine to what extent the method remains valid for problems not possessing these properties. In this section I shall discuss some of the seven remaining cases.

In general, one can say that the method hinges on determining $\mu_G(x)$ from a recurrence relation within $\mathcal{S}$.

In the absence of such a relation (the cases (000),(001),(100),(101); in binary code , referring to the three properties) the method simply does not work; If $\# \Sigma$ is given ((100) and (101)) the problem can be solved by a laborious but finite exhaustive search. If $\# \Sigma$ is not given (subcases (000) and (001)) the problem is not so simple. In fact, I do not know whether the decision problem is at all solvable for these cases. The same goes for case (010).

In case (101) ($\# \Sigma = k$ and a numbered sequence $\mathcal{S}$ are given ; but $\overline{\mathcal{S}}$ satisfies no recurrence relation), two subcases may be distinguished: $\mathcal{S}$ either does or does not certain a word with rank order number larger than k.

If $\mathcal{S}$ contains at least one word w_p with $p \geq k$, then it is not difficult to see that any possible growth matrix $A = ((a_{ij}))$ is bounded by $a_{ij} \leq M$ (where M is the maximum number occurring in the vectors of $\overline{\mathcal{S}}$), except for those numbers referring to mortal letters. As a result, the problem is bounded for all vital letters and not bounded (in a rather unimportant way) for mortal ones.

If no word w_p with $p \geq k$ is given, no such upper bound for the elements of A can be given, and the problem often has infinitely many solutions.

Case (100) would reduce to a finite number of the previous cases (101) if from $\# \Sigma$ and $\mathcal{S}$ an upper bound for the rank order numbers could be deduced. This bound can indeed be found ; by a size argument if L(G) is finite, by a growth argument if L(G) is infinite.

If L(G) is finite, then a result by P. Vitányi [114] states that L(G) contains at most $k(1 + k^{n-1})$ words, where n is the number of different monorecursive letters in a certain, specified, word. Since obviously $n \leq k$, $\# (L(G)) \leq k(1 + k^{k-1})$. This number gives the

required upper bound, since any higher rank order number refers to a duplicate of an earlier word.
If, on the other hand, L(G) is infinite, then $|w_{n+k}| \geq |w_n| + 1$ for every n. Consequently, an upper bound for the rank order numbers {i} in the given set of words S is given by

$$i \leq k \cdot \max \{|w| : w \in S\}$$

So case (100) can be reduced to case (101) ; hence the case is solvable. The indicated procedure is of course not nearly a practical method.
In case (011) a recurrence relation can be found in $\overline{\mathcal{S}}$, but Σ may be larger than the "observed" Σ_{obs}.
The inference algorithm of section 4 applies during the first steps, where no knowledge of Σ is necessary.
In step 4 problems may arise. First, the degree of $\mu_G(x)$ can never be larger then $\# \Sigma$. So, if it turns out that $\deg(\mu_G(x)) = m > \# \Sigma_{obs}$, Σ must be larger than Σ_{obs}. Now simply extend Σ_{obs} to Σ in the minimal way : namely, such that

$$\# \Sigma = k = \max(\# \Sigma_{obs}, m),$$ and then apply

step 4 : find a matrix $E_0 \in \mathbb{N}^{k \times m}$ satisfying $S = E_0 C$.
From the pictorial representation

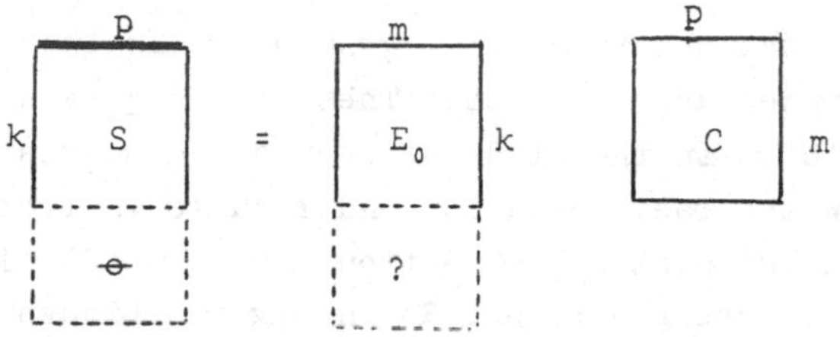

it is not difficult to see that increasing $\# \Sigma$ beyond k cannot have any other effect than adding mortal letters to solutions already obtained with Σ. In other words : if there are no solutions for E_0 with this minimal Σ, then there are none.
That Σ can indeed be larger than Σ_{obs} can be seen from this very simple example : Find a DOL-system such that $w_0 = a$, $w_4 = aaa$.
$\psi(x) = x^4 - 3$, with no other divisors. If $\psi(x)$ is to be G's minimal polynomial, then $\# \Sigma \geq 4$. In fact, $p = \{a \to b, b \to c, c \to d, d \to aaa\}$ provides a solution.
Case (110) can be regarded as a more favorable subcase of (100), involving considerably less guesswork.
Of the variants discussed, (011) may be the most interesting one, since it solves a subcase of the hitherto open problem (Feliciangeli and Herman [28]) of finding G from $\mathcal{S}$ if Σ is not given.

FREE GROUPS IN LINDENMAYER SYSTEMS

PETER JOHANSEN AND ERIK MEILING

Datalogisk institut, Københavns Universitet

Abstract. Locally catenative equations are defined in the free group. It is shown that if the free group generated by a DOL sequence is finitely generated then there exists a locally catenative equation in the free group which defines the DOL sequence. An algorithm is given which finds the generators of the free group if it is finitely generated.

A conjecture is stated in terms of the existence of a certain group. The conjecture implies the solvability of the DOL equivalence problem.

1. Introduction.

Techniques from the theory of free groups are in this paper applied to the study of Lindenmayer systems. These techniques have previously been used by the authors in the study of regular languages [1,2]. In the preliminaries follow the basic notation and results in free groups. No previous knowledge is assumed. In section 3 we consider locally catenative equations in the free group. See Rozenberg and Lindenmayer [95]. We define an equivalence group of two DOL systems and show that if there exists a finitely generated equivalence group then we can decide if the two systems are equivalent. Here we consider the sequence equivalence problem. See Mogens Nielsen [70] for a proof that this problem is equivalent to the language equivalence problem.

---

1. Peter Johansen, An Algebraic Normal Form for Regular Events, Polyteknisk Forlag, Lyngby 1972.
2. J.Clausen, J.Hammerum, E.Meiling, T.Skovgaard, Automata Theory in Free Groups, manuscript to be submitted to Acta Informatica.

We are not able to prove that a finitely generated equivalence group exists in the general case, nor that it can be effectively constructed. In special cases, however, it can be found. It is conjectured that it can be found in the general case. Section 4 presents an algorithm which finds the generators of the group closure of a DOL sequence if it is finitely generated.

We have, unfortunately, at present no way of deciding when this occurs. The algorithm is being implemented in LISP 1.5 on IBM/360.

2. Preliminaries.

For definitions and basic results in Lindenmayer systems and free groups the reader is referred to Herman and Rozenberg [45] and Hall (1952)[3].

In the following $H = \langle \Sigma, h, w_o \rangle$ and $G = \langle \Sigma, g, w_o \rangle$ will denote DOL systems. $h^i(w_o)$ will be denoted w_i when reference to H is implicit. The language generated by H is denoted $L(H) = \{w_o, w_1, \ldots, w_n, \ldots\}$ The sequence generated by H is denoted $E(H) = w_o, w_1, \ldots, w_n, \ldots$

The free group $F(\Sigma)$ is defined as follows: Let $\Sigma = \{a, b, \ldots, z\}$. Define a shadow alphabet $\bar{\Sigma} = \{\bar{a}, \bar{b}, \ldots, \bar{z}\}$. Define an equivalence relation D on the free semigroup $(\Sigma \cup \bar{\Sigma})^*$ as the transitive, symmetric, and reflexive closure of the adjacency relation A:

$$xAy \Leftrightarrow \exists u, v \in (\Sigma \cup \bar{\Sigma})^*, \exists c \in \Sigma \text{ such that}$$

$$x = uv \text{ and } (y = uc\bar{c}v \text{ or } y = u\bar{c}cv)$$

$F(\Sigma)$ is the set of equivalence classes of D. Group composition is $D(x)\cdot D(y) = D(xy)$. The 1-element is the class $D(\lambda)$. The inverse of the class $D(a_1, a_2 \ldots a_n)$ where $a_i \in (\Sigma \cup \bar{\Sigma})$ is the class $D(\bar{a}_n \ldots \bar{a}_2\, \bar{a}_1)$. Here $\bar{\bar{a}}_i$ denotes a_i.

---

3. M.Hall. <u>The Theory of Groups,</u> The Macmillan Company, New York, 1959.

It can be shown that each equivalence class contains precisely one word which does not contain any adjacent occurrences of a letter and its inverse. This word is called a reduced word. An equivalence class is often denoted by its reduced representative.

Let $S \subset F(\Sigma)$. $[S]$ denotes the smallest subgroup of $F(\Sigma)$ which contains S. S is called a generator set of $[S]$. $[S]$ is called the group closure of S. Let $T \subset F(\Sigma)$ be a subgroup. If there exists a finite set S such that $[S] = T$ then T is finitely generated. $y(s_1, s_2, \ldots, s_n)$ means an element of $[s_1, s_2, \ldots, s_n]$.

The main result on free groups is the following:

Let $A \subset F(\Sigma)$ be a group. There exists a set of generators $a_1, a_2, \ldots$, called free generators, such that $[a_1, a_2, \ldots] = A$ and such that any element from A can be written as a unique product of generators and their inverses. Any set with this property has the same cardinality, called the rank of A. The cardinality of any set of generators is at least the rank of A. $\{a_i\}$ can furthermore be chosen such that $a_i = u_i s_i \bar{v}_i$, $i = 1,2\ldots$ where no letters from s_i or s_j are cancelled in any products $a_i^{\pm 1} a_j^{\pm 1}$. s_i is called the significant factors of a_i.

Example 1:

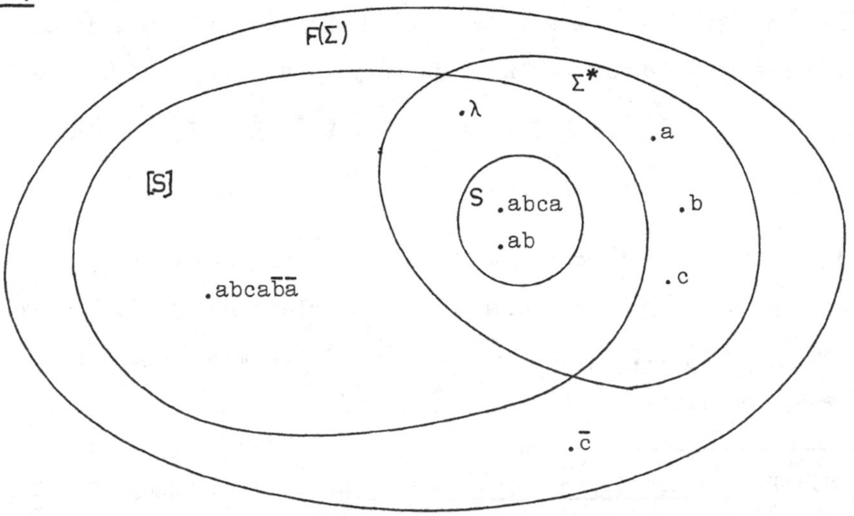

Example 2:

$$A = [a\underset{\wedge}{b}\bar{a},\ a\underset{\wedge}{c}] = [a\underset{\wedge}{b}c,\ ac] = [a\underset{\wedge}{b}\underset{\wedge}{c}ac,\ ac]$$

Significant factors are marked by $\wedge$.

Example 3:

$$F(\Sigma) = [\underset{\wedge}{a}, \underset{\wedge}{b}] \quad S = [a\underset{\wedge}{a},\ a\underset{\wedge}{b}\bar{a},\ \underset{\wedge}{b}]$$

$$T = [aab,\ aaaabb,\ \ldots\ ,(aa)^{2^n} b^{2^n},\ \ldots\ ]$$

$$T \subset S \subset F(\Sigma).$$

This example shows that the rank of a subgroup may be greater than the rank of the group itself:

rank $(F(\Sigma)) = 2$; rank $(S) = 3$; rank $(T) = \infty$.

That rank $(T) = \infty$ can be seen this way:

Let $s_n = (aa)^{2^n} b^{2^n}$. $T = [s_0, s_1, \ldots]$

Define $t_n = s_n \bar{s}_{n-1}$ for $n = 1, 2, \ldots$ and $t_0 = s_0$.

This gives $t_n = (aa)^{2^n} b^{2^n} \bar{b}^{2^{n-1}} (\bar{a}\bar{a})^{2^{n-1}}$

$$= (aa)^{2^n} b^{2^{n-1}} (\bar{a}\bar{a})^{2^{n-1}}$$

It is seen that $T = [t_0, t_1, \ldots]$ because $s_n = t_n t_{n-1} t_{n-2} \cdots t_0$. Also it is seen that the occurrences of b in t_n constitute significant factors. Hence rank$(T) = \infty$.

3. Locally catenative equations in the Free Group.

First the case is studied where $[L(H)]$ is finitely generated. An equivalence group of two DOL-systems is defined. Theorem 2 shows that if a finitely generated equivalence group can be found for two systems, then the equivalence problem is solved. Then it is conjectured that a finitely generated equivalence group always exists, and can effectively be constructed.

Theorem 1:

$[L(H)]$ is finitely generated

$\Updownarrow$

There exists a locally catenative equation in $F(\Sigma)$:

$$w_n = eq(w_{n-1}, \dots, w_{n-r}) \text{ for } n \geq cut$$

Proof:

$\Downarrow$: Let $[L(H)] = [g_1, \dots, g_n]$. Each g_k, $k=1, \dots, n$, is a product $g_k(w_o, w_1, \dots, w_{q_k-1})$ for some q_k. Let r be the maximum of all q_k. Then $[L(H)] = [w_o, w_1, \dots, w_{r-1}]$. From this it follows that $w_r \in [w_o, w_1, \dots, w_{r-1}]$ and $w_r = eq(w_{r-1}, \dots, w_o)$ Since h is a homomorphism of $F(\Sigma)$ this part follows by induction.

$\Uparrow$: From the recursion equation it follows by induction that $[L(H)]$ is generated by $\{w_o, w_1, \dots, w_{r-1}\}$.

At this point a natural question arises:
If the rank of $[L(H)]$ is r, can we then choose the first r elements from E(H) as generators? We have been unable to prove this, but believe it to be true.

Small conjecture.

$[L(H)]$ is finitely generated of rank r

$\Updownarrow$

$[L(H)]$ is freely generated by $\{w_o, w_1, \dots, w_{r-1}\}$

This conjecture is mentioned again in section 4 in connection with the algorithm to find free generators of L(H). Here we shall point out a consequence of this small conjecture, which follows immediately from the unique factorization in the free group.

Consequence of small conjecture.

[L(H)] is finitely generated of rank r

$\Updownarrow$

There exists a unique locally catenative equation in the free groups of minimal cut with cut = r and depth $\leq$ r.

Example 4:

E(H) = ab, abab, ...

E(H) = [ab] of rank 1

$w_1 = abab = w_o w_o$

recurrence equation

$w_n = w_{n-1} w_{n-1}$

Example 5:

H = < {a,b}, {a→a, b→ab}, b>

E(H) = b, ab, aab, ...

G = <{a, b}, {a→a, b→ba}, b>

E(G) = b, ba, baa, ...

[L(H)] = [L(G)] = [a,b] of rank 2

recurrence equation in common:

$w_n = w_{n-1} \bar{w}_{n-2} w_{n-1}$, cut=2

E(H) defined by $w_o = b$, $w_1 = ab$

E(G) defined by $w_o = b$, $w_1 = ba$.

Example 6:

G = < {a, b, c}, {a→cba, b→a, c→cc}, b>

$w_o = b$

$w_1 = a$

$w_2 = cba$

Since $a = w_1$, $b = w_o$, and $c = w_2 \bar{w}_1 \bar{w}_o$ we know that $[L(H)] \supset F(\Sigma)$ and therefore $[L(H)] = F(\Sigma)$.

$$w_3 = ccacba$$

It then follows that w_3 can be expressed in terms of w_o, w_1, and w_2 by substitution:

$$w_3 = (w_2\bar{w}_1\bar{w}_o)(w_2\bar{w}_1\bar{w}_o)\ w_1(w_2\bar{w}_1\bar{w}_o)\ w_o w_1$$

$$= (w_2\bar{w}_1 w_o)^2\ w_1 w_2$$

The recurrence equation becomes

$$w_n = (w_{n-1}\bar{w}_{n-2}\bar{w}_{n-3})^2\ w_{n-2}w_{n-1}$$

Example 7:

$H = \langle \{a,b\}, \{a \to aa,\ b \to bb\}, aab \rangle$

$[L(H)]$ is of infinite rank as shown in example 3. By theorem 1 it follows that there does not exist a locally catenative recurrence equation defining $E(H)$. Example finished.

We shall in what follows attempt to formulate a generalization of theorem 1. We have to present it as a conjecture since we are unable to prove it.

Definition: An equivalence group for the two DOL systems H and G is a group Q with the properties

(i) $w_o \in Q$

(ii) $h(Q) \subset Q$ and $g(Q) \subset Q$

(iii) $(\forall q \in Q)[(\forall i)\ h^i(w_o) = g^i(w_o)] \Rightarrow [(\forall i)\ h^i(q) = g^i(q)]$

Lemma 1:

For any DOL systems such that $[L(H)] = [L(G)]$, $[L(H)]$ is an equivalence group.

Proof:

(i) and (ii) are trivially fulfilled. To verify (iii), assume that H and G are equivalent.

Let $q \in [L(H)]$. $h^i(q) = h^i(q(w_o, h(w_o), \dots, h^j(w_o), \dots))$

$= q(h^i(w_o), h^{i+1}(w_o), \dots)$

Since $h^j(w_o) = g^j(w_o)$ for all j, we get

$= q(g^i(w_o), g^{i+1}(w_o), \dots)$

$= g^i(q(w_o, g(w_o), \dots))$

$= g^i(q(w_o, h(w_o), \dots)) = g^i(q)$

Lemma 2:

There exists only one DOL-system H which generates E(H).

$\Updownarrow$

$F(\Sigma)$ is an equivalence group for all DOL systems G.

Proof:

$\Downarrow$: Obvious because (iii) is vacuously fulfilled.

$\Uparrow$: Obvious because (iii) implies that g and h are identical on the generators of $F(\Sigma)$.

Example 8:

The DOL-system from example 7 is uniquely determined by E(H). Hence [a,b] is an equivalence group for all DOL-systems G.

The significance of equivalence groups is due to the next theorem.

Theorem 2:

If there exists a finitely generated equivalence group $Q = [q_1, \dots, q_n]$ for two DOL-systems G and H then G and H are equivalent if and only if

(*) $h(q_i) = g(q_i)$ for $i = 1, 2, \dots, n$

Proof:

Assume G and H equivalent; then (iii) implies the theorem.

Assume (*). We are going to prove $\forall i \geq o\ [h^i(w_o) = g^i(w_o)]$. (*) implies, that $\forall q \in Q\ [h(q) = g(q)]$

Since Q is closed under the homomorphisms G and H we conclude that

$\forall_{i \geq o} \forall q \in Q \; [h^i(q) = g^i(q)]$

The result follows now from the fact that $w_o \in Q$.

Corollary 1:

If $[L(H)] = [L(G)] = [w_o, h(w_o), \ldots, h^{r-1}(w_o)]$

then G and H are equivalent if and only if

$$h^i(w_o) = g^i(w_o) \quad i = o, 1, \ldots, r$$

Proof:

Follows from lemma 1 and theorem 2.

Example 9:

Using corollary 1 we can, with reference to example 6, deduce that two DOL-sequences which have the common initial terms

$$w_o = b$$
$$w_1 = a$$
$$w_2 = cba$$
$$w_3 = ccacba$$

must be identical.

Example 10:

$H = \langle \{a, b, c, d\}, \{a \to aa, b \to b, c \to c, d \to bd\}, acd \rangle$

$G = \langle \{a, b, c, d\}, \{a \to aa, b \to b, c \to cb, d \to d\}, acd \rangle$

$E(G) = E(H) = acd, aacbd, aaaacbbd, \ldots, (aa)^{2^n} cb^n d, \ldots$

We notice that the occurrences of c constitute significant factors. Hence the rank of $[L(H)]$ is infinite and the equivalence group $[L(H)]$ is infinitely generated. Lemma 2 tells us that $[a, b, c, d]$ is not an equivalence group.

All powers of h and g coincide on a and on b, and

$$h^i(cd) = g^i(cd) = cb^i d \text{ for } i = o, 1, \ldots$$

From this follows that $T = [a, b, cd, cbd, cb^i d, \ldots]$ is an equivalence group. .

$$T = [\hat{a}, \hat{b}, \hat{cd}, \hat{cb\bar{c}}] \text{ since } cb^i d = (cb\bar{c})^i cd$$

We have found a finitely generated equivalence group for G and H even if [L(G)] = [L(H)] is infinitely generated.
We proceed to formulate a conjecture.

Main conjecture:

For any two DOL-systems H and G a finitely generated equivalence group can be effectively constructed.
Because of theorem 2, a proof of this conjecture will solve the equivalence problem for DOL-systems.

A consequence of the conjecture is that for any DOL sequence H the set of all free group elements x, with the property that if G is equivalent with H then $\langle \Sigma, h, x \rangle$ is equivalent with $\langle \Sigma, g, x \rangle$, is a finitely generated group. This follows because the intersection of two finitely generated subgroups of $F(\Sigma)$ is finitely generated, and because there exists only a finite number of DOL systems equivalent to H. (M. Nielsen [70]).

4. An algorithm to find [L(H)].

This section presents an algorithm which finds a set of generators for [L(H)] if this group is finitely generated. If this is not so, the algorithm yields a still larger subset of an infinite set of free generators with significant factors. We have at present no available test to decide between the two possibilities. It is no surprise that this algorithm exists. Nielsen's algorithm is known from free group theory. It finds a set of free generators with significant factors from a finite set of generators.
Let Nielsen (W) be a procedure which has a finite set W as argument and which as result delivers a set of free generators with significant factors of [W].

Our algorithm is then as follows:

```
begin
    Y_o := {w_o} ;
    n  := 1;
    while  w_n ∉ [Y_{n-1}] do
    begin Y_n := Nielsen (Y_{n-1} ∪ {w_n});
          n  := n+1

    end
end
```

At exit from the algorithm, $w_n \in [Y_{n-1}]$. It follows that $[L(H)] = [Y_{n-1}]$. It is believed, and stated as the small conjecture in section 3, that the rank of $[L(H)]$ equals n at exit from the algorithm. The sore point is of course that if $[L(H)]$ has infinite rank then the algorithm never exits. In this case $[L(H)] = \bigcup_{i=o}^{\infty} [Y_i]$. An adaptation of the algorithm, which takes into account that the sequence is generated by a homomorphism is being implemented in LISP 1.5 on IBM/360. In the next examples, Z_n denotes $[Y_n]$.

Example 11:

This example shows the successive values of Z_n for the following DOL-system

$$H = \langle \{a,b,c\},\{a\to ab, b\to ca, c\to ac\}, ac\rangle$$

The first elements of the sequence are

ac
abac
abcaabac
abcaacababcaabac

Z_o = [ac]

Z_1 = [ac,abac] = [ac,ab]

Z_2 = [ac,ab,abcaabac] = [ac,ab,ca]

Z_3 = [ac,ab,ca,abcaacababcaabac] = [ac,ab,ca,λ] = Z_2

Now the chain $Z_o \subset Z_1 \subset Z_2$ ... will stay constant forever and [L(H)] = Z_2. From theorem 1 we know that the sequence is locally catenative. From lemma 1 we know that [L(H)] is an equivalence group for any other DOL-system that generates the same sequence.

From an algorithmic point of view it would be convenient to find generators for Z_n as an extension of the generators found for Z_{n-1}, and this is always possible since Z_n is an extension of Z_{n-1}. In this example it is even possible to obtain significant factors in the extended set of generators. This is not always possible as will be shown in example 12.

We know that the DOL-system H is locally catenative but we have not found a locally catenative formula. Such a formula can be found by keeping track of the relation between the generators of Z_n (in the following denoted w'_o, ... ,w'_{n-1}) and the elements of the sequence (w_o, ... ,w_n, ..). We will also use the fact that

$$Z_n = [w'_o, \ldots ,w'_{n-1}, h(w'_{n-1})]$$

Using this method we get

<u>step 0</u>

w_o = ac $\qquad\qquad$ $w'_o = w_o$

$Z_o = [w'_o]$ = [ac]

<u>step 1</u>

$h(w'_o)$ = abac

$w'_1 = h(w'_o)\overline{w}'_o$ = ab $\qquad\qquad$ $w'_1 = w_1\overline{w}_o$

$Z_1 = [w'_o,w'_1]$ = [ac,ab]

<u>step 2</u>

$h(w_1') = abca$

$w_2' = \bar{w}_1' h(w_1') = ca$ $\qquad\qquad$ $w_2' = w_o\bar{w}_1 \cdot w_2\bar{w}_1$

$Z_2 = [w_o', w_1', w_2'] = [ac, ab, ca]$

<u>step 3</u>

$h(w_2') = acab$

$w_3' = \bar{w}_1'\bar{w}_o' h(w_2') = \lambda$ $\qquad\qquad$ $w_3' = w_o\bar{w}_1 \cdot \bar{w}_o \cdot w_1\bar{w}_2 w_3\bar{w}_2$

$Z_3 = [w_o', w_1', w_2', w_3'] = [ac, ab, ca]$

From the calculations in step 3 we get

$$\lambda = w_o\bar{w}_1\bar{w}_o w_1\bar{w}_2 w_3\bar{w}_2 \quad \Leftrightarrow$$

$$w_3 = w_2\bar{w}_1 w_o w_1\bar{w}_o w_2$$

Hence the locally catenative formula

$$w_n = w_{n-1}\bar{w}_{n-2} w_{n-3} w_{n-2}\bar{w}_{n-3} w_{n-1} \qquad , cut=3$$

Notice that the example agrees with the small conjecture.

<u>Example 12:</u>

This example shows the methods used in example 11 on the DOL-system

$$H = \langle\{a,b,c\},\{a\to abc, b\to a, c\to c\}, ab\rangle$$

<u>step 0</u>

$w_o' = ab$ $\qquad\qquad$ $w_o' = w_o$

$Z_o = [ab]$

<u>step 1</u>

$h(w_o') = abca$

$w_1' = ca$ $\qquad\qquad$ $w_1' = \bar{w}_o w_1$

$Z_1 = [ab, ca]$

<u>step 2</u>

$h(w_1') = cabc$

$w_2' = bc$ $\qquad\qquad$ $w_2' = \bar{w}_1 w_o\bar{w}_1 w_2$

$Z_2 = [ab, ca, bc]$

step 3

$h(w'_2) = ac$

$w'_3 = ac$ $\qquad\qquad w'_3=\bar{w}_2 w_1 \bar{w}_2 w_3$

$Z_3 = [ab, ca, bc, ac]$

At this point w'_3 has no significant factors, and we have to change some of the previously found generators to obtain significant factors.

This situation occurs exactly in the case where the new generator is a catenation of an initial subword and a final subword of the generators previously found. We mention, without stating the proof, that [L(H)] in this case is finitely generated. According to the algorithm we now should change the generators to obtain significant factors. But since we know that the group is finitely generated we might as well carry on until we get the locally catenative formula. Notice that although the generators found do not contain significant factors they are still free generators of the group in agreement with the small conjecture.

step 4

$h(w'_3) = abcc$

$w'_4 = cc$ $\qquad\qquad w'_4=\bar{w}_0 \bar{w}_3 w_2 \bar{w}_3 w_4$

$Z_4 = [ab, ca, bc, ac, cc]$

step 5

$h(w'_4) = cc$

$w'_5 = \lambda$ $\qquad\qquad w'_5=\bar{w}_4 w_3 \bar{w}_2 w_3 w_0 \cdot \bar{w}_1 \bar{w}_4 w_3 \bar{w}_4 w_5$

From this we get

$$w_5=w_4 \bar{w}_3 w_4 w_1 \bar{w}_0 \bar{w}_3 w_2 \bar{w}_3 w_4$$

And the locally catenative formula

$$w_n=w_{n-1} \bar{w}_{n-2} w_{n-1} w_{n-4} \bar{w}_{n-5} \bar{w}_{n-2} w_{n-3} \bar{w}_{n-2} w_{n-1}$$

Notice, that although w_4 is of length 24 we only have to operate on a word w'_4 of length 2. One can say that we for each word have extracted the new information, and the methods used in these examples reduce the hard work involved dealing with fast growing systems.

Acknowledgement.

The main part of the work described in this paper was developed during a workshop on Lindenmayer systems in Aarhus. The authors wish to thank the participants for a most stimulating working atmosphere. We are grateful to Bente Rasmussen for typing the final version.

Notes on PRE-SET PUSHDOWN AUTOMATA

Jan van Leeuwen

Department of Computer Science
State University of New York at Buffalo
Amherst, New York 14226

Department of Mathematics
University of Utrecht
Utrecht, The Netherlands

ABSTRACT. Motivated by practical implementation-methods for recursive program-schemata we will define and study presetting techniques for push-down automata. The main results will characterize the languages of preset pda's in terms of types of iterated substitution languages. In particular when conditions of "locally finiteness" and of "finite returning" are imposed we get a feasible machine-model for a class of developmental languages. The accepted family extends to the smallest AFL enclosing it when we drop the condition of locally finiteness. At the same time this family will be the smallest such full AFL. If all conditions are removed, preset pda's exactly represent the family of iterated regular substitution languages, a sub-family of the indexed languages. Deterministic preset pda's are also studied, and the language-family they define is shown to be closed under complementation, generalizing a classical result.

> "Any theory ... formulates an ideal average which abolishes all exceptions at either end of the scale and replaces them by an abstract mean."
>
> in C. G. Jung: The Undiscovered Self.

---

* This work has in part been supported by the Center for Mathematical Methods in the Social, Biological, and Health Sciences (SUNY at Buffalo), by NSF grant GJ 998, and by NATO grant 574.

1. INTRODUCTION

Eventually we like to introduce what might be called: "developmental systems - a programmer's point of view", but we will not immediately emphasize it here. We rather follow the original approach which led to such implications and start with analyzing some automaton-theoretic concepts.

Push-down automata represent the execution-mechanism of parameter-less recursion. They were successfully used in context-free language theory, occasionally in the theory of (monadic) program-schemata, and the deterministic version has been extensively analyzed in parsing.

There has been a twofold motivation for presetting the amount of storage in machine-models with a stack-like external memory. First of all in most implementations there is a definite series of locations allocated as a push-down register, whenever it is required. Secondly familiar types of (single variable) recursion can most efficiently be simulated when the stack is implicitly used as a counter at the same time. In the latter type of application the machine will basicly recognize/execute instruction-sequences which appear on the input-tape, a not very common but certainly useful interpretation of input.

By presetting a push-down automaton we mean that at the very beginning of a computation a certain stack-square is allocated as the maximum location (or "highest" point) to which the stack may grow during that computation.

We wish to remark that if this were all, the accepted languages would still be context-free, but not all computations would terminate because the allocated space might be insufficient. The new feature is to let an overflow-indicator (or "interrupt") actively influence the computation.

Therefore the machine-model will have two transition-functions: δ (to be used whenever the stack is not maximal) and δ_{top} (to be used when the stack reached its preset maximum), both having well-known formats.

There is one more practical concept never mentioned for ordinary pda's but relevant when the stack is going to be used as implicit parameter-value. It is the concept of an "empty" location, but this can only be argumented with more information about how we look at what can occupy locations. In the "squares" on the stack are pieces of program (or rather, pointers to subroutines).

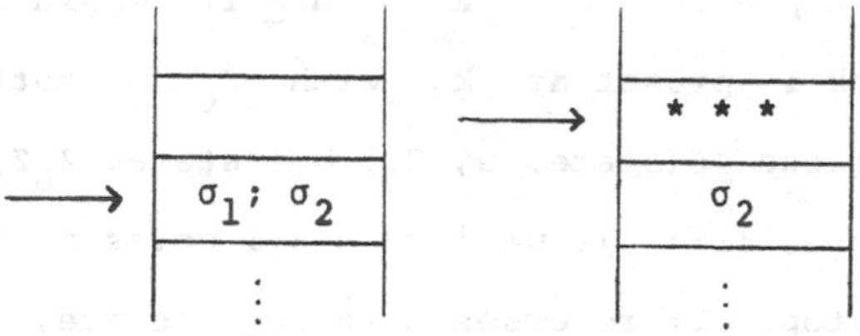

When σ_1 is a recursive call, it will be removed from the current (top-most) location and the procedure-body called for will be pushed in the next one. When we return and find that σ_2 is a recursive call as well, an "empty" location is created and no garbage-collectioning should happen as it would improperly destroy the counting. Empty locations in the body of the stack are filled with ϕ.

2. PRESET PUSHDOWN AUTOMATA

We give a formal description of the general model.

<u>Definition</u>. A preset pda is an 8-tuple $\mathfrak{A} = \langle Q, \Sigma, \Gamma, \delta, \delta_{top}, q_0, Z_0, F \rangle$ with Q (states), Σ (inputs), Γ (stack-symbols), q_0 (initial state), Z_0 (initial stack-contents), F (final states) as usual, and for all $p \in Q$, $a \in \Sigma \cup \{\lambda\}$, $\gamma \in \Gamma$ $\delta(p, a, \gamma)$ a finite set of instructions of the form (q, ϕ), (q, A), $(q, \phi A)$, (q, AB) $(A, B \in \Gamma)$ and, similarly, $\delta_{top}(p, a, \gamma)$ a finite set of instructions of the form (q, ϕ), (q, A).

There can be more general definitions that allow for writing longer words per move, but it can be shown (see [55]) that there is no gain in power. Observe that this version is close to the program-cruncher we motivated it with, and δ_{top} for instance never writes beyond the permissible limit. The given version is a normal form.

Here is an example of a preset-pda, with notions of acceptability defined (as usual) by empty store and final state.

<u>Example</u>. A preset pda for $L = \{a^{n^2} \mid n \geq 1\}$ would operate as follows. Say the stack is preset at k, with Z_0 as bottom-marker. With instructions $\delta(\text{state}, a, Z_0) = \{(\text{state}, Z_0 Z)\}$, $\delta(\text{state}, a, Z) = \{(\text{state}, \phi Z)\}$ it will make k-1 moves on input a and push a Z to the top. It reverses with $\delta_{top}(\text{state}, a, Z) = \{(\text{state}, \phi)\}$ and returns to the (first) Z_0 it finds downwards on λ-input. Then it lifts Z_0 two locations higher (on λ-input) and repeats the same cycle as before over and over again. When, lifting Z_0, it would have passed the preset limit it stops in a non-accepting state, otherwise it goes on until at last Z_0 is lifted into the maximal location and sweeps down on $\delta_{top}(\text{state}, a, Z_0) = \{(\text{final state}, \phi)\}$.

At a successful termination $k + (k - 2) + \ldots + 1 = (\frac{k+1}{2})^2$ (an integer) moves on input a were made, and the machine will accept all and exactly all the squares.

Instantaneous descriptions of a preset pda are of the form (state, remaining input, push-down contents, n), where n is the presetting relevant and constant for the particular computation.

<u>Definition</u>. A language L is called a preset pda-language if and only if a preset pda $\mathfrak{A}$ as above exists such that

$L = \{x \in \Sigma^* \mid \exists_{q \in F}(q_0, x, Z_0, n) \overset{*}{\vdash} (q, \lambda, \phi, n)$ for at least one $n \geq 1\}$.

In the definition it is emphasized that more than one presetting might actually be appropriate for acceptance.

As usual for non-deterministic machines there may be both accepting and rejecting computations for an input-string, but it will still be counted in the language.

3. THE LANGUAGES OF PRESET PDA'S

Here we will develop a generative (as opposed to analytic) description of preset pda's in terms of their languages. The general theory rightaway leads into the algebraic F-iteration grammars developed in [57] and made more explicit in [103]. Most general results proved for various parallel rewriting systems follow from a few theorems in this area ([57]). Here we only give a few of the abstract concepts that were developed and found useful.

A family of languages will be defined as usual, but in addition we always assume closure under isomorphism.

Definition. Let F be a family of languages. The hyper-algebraic extension of F consists of all languages of the form

$\bigcup_{k \geq 0} \tau^k(\$) \cap \Sigma^*$, where τ is an F-substitution and Σ an alphabet.*)

When F is a quasoid (i.e. containing C^* and closed under $\cap R$ and finite substitution), the hyper-algebraic extension becomes an AFL closed under iterated F-substitution. Several algebraic

*) Footnote. In later generalizations hyper-algebraic extensions were defined differently and more widely!

results were obtained.

The characterization theorem we will prove for preset pda languages is an interesting analogue of a classically known theorem for context-free languages (which can be described as the algebraic extension of the family of regular languages*)).

<u>THEOREM</u>. The family of preset pda languages is the hyper-algebraic extension of the regular languages.

<u>Proof</u>.

Let τ be a regular substitution, $\mathcal{A}_a = \langle Q_a, \Sigma, \delta_a, q_a, F_a \rangle$ a finite automaton for $\tau(a)$. $\mathcal{A}_a$ may have λ-transitions, and we will in fact for simplicity assume that always $q_a \notin F_a$. Non-empty stack-locations will have a contents as shown below.

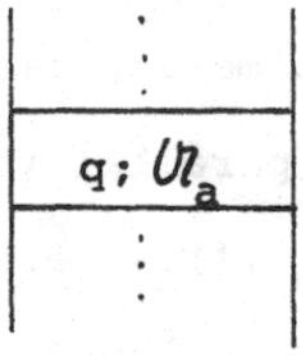

where $q \in Q_a$, representing that in generating a member of $\tau(a)$ we got as far as q in the finite automaton for it.

The idea is not to generate the word from $\tau(a)$ immediately as a whole, but symbol by symbol and each time a next symbol is generated to use it to expand its τ-image to the preset top first before proceeding with the next symbols. Thus we generate $\tau(S)$ in strictly leftmost manner and use the finite automata as a finite code for the (possibly) arbitrarily long strings we can rewrite individual symbols with.

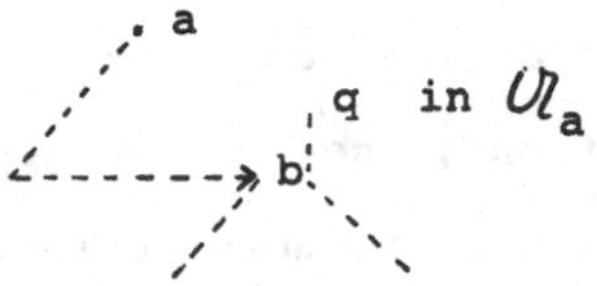

*) Footnote. See van Leeuwen, J., "A generalization of Parikh's theorem in formal language theory", Tech. Rep. 71, Dept. of Comp. Sciences, SUNY, Buffalo, 1974.

Here is how the instructions look like. We only give their basic schemes. First realize that expansion to the present top is entirely on λ-input, only δ_{top} checks input. Therefore

$\delta(\text{state}, \lambda, [q; \mathcal{U}_a]) = \{(\text{state}, [r; \mathcal{U}_a]) \mid r \in \delta_a(q, \lambda)\} \cup$

$\{(\text{state}, \phi) \mid \exists_{r \in F_a}\ r \in \delta_a(q, \lambda)\} \cup$

$\{(\text{state}, [r; \mathcal{U}_a][q_b; \mathcal{U}_b]) \mid b \in \Sigma \text{ and } r \in \delta_a(q, b)\} \cup$

$\{(\text{state}, \phi[q_b; \mathcal{U}_b]) \mid b \in \Sigma \text{ and } \exists_{r \in F_a}\ r \in \delta_a(q,b)\}.$

Note that we may or may not stop in a final state when generating a word of $\tau(a)$. When the preset maximum (which actually stands for how far we iterate) is reached, then $\delta_{top}(\text{state}, b, [q; \mathcal{U}_a]) =$

$\{(\text{state}, [r; \mathcal{U}_a]) \mid r \in \delta_a(q, b)\} \cup$

$\{(\text{state}, \phi) \mid \exists_{r \in F_a}\ r \in \delta_a(q, b)\}$

and the obvious rules on λ-input for traversing possible λ-transitions. Successful termination now is actually on empty store but as standard we may non-deterministically send the machine in a final state at the same time.

The formal proof of the reverse is tedious but follows the same lines as the restricted case worked out in detail in [55]. Here we give the basic type of constructs.

Let $\mathcal{U} = \langle Q, \Sigma, \Gamma, \delta, \delta_{top}, q_0, Z_0, F\rangle$ be a preset pda recognizing L. The iterated (regular) substitution τ for L will have basic symbols of the form

$[p, A, B, q]$ $(p, q \in Q, A \in \Gamma, B \in \Gamma \cup \{\phi\})$

with the following semantics.

$[p, A, B, q]$ $(B \in \Gamma)$: when in state p with A under the pointer, (after a local move) it will write B and move upwards, later returning in state q (which will then continue on the B)

$[p, A, \phi, q]$: similarly, but (after a local move) it will empty the location and move upwards, later sweeping down in state q.

Thus "variables" will represent recursions. The "terminal" symbols will actually be coded as $\bar{a}$, and later finish with the well-known cycle $\bar{a} \to a \to \not{c}$ (where $\not{c} \to \not{c}$ and $\not{c}$ outside the terminal range) to enforce synchronous termination. There is a problem there when subsequent expansions and δ_{top}-instructions are on λ-input, which in the iteration would be an untimely termination of that branch. However, the hyper-algebraic extension of regular languages is closed under arbitrary homomorphisms (from a more general result in [57]), and we may as well let the machine read \$ instead of λ all the time and erase it later from the language.

Replacement rules become

$[p, A, B, q] \to \{\bar{w}_1[p_1, A_1, B_1, q_1]\bar{w}_2 \ldots \bar{w}_k[p_k, A_k, \phi, q]\} \mid$ starting in state p with A on the stack $\mathfrak{A}$ will do a (local) computation on $\bar{w}_1$ input and recur in state p_1 writing BA_1 on the stack, then all possible strings w_i for local computation from q_{i-1} on B_{i-1} leading to p_i with A_i on the stack (note the final return state)$\}$ $\cup$

$\{\bar{w}_1[p_1, A_1, B_1, q_1]\bar{w}_2 \ldots \bar{w}_k[p_k, A_k, B_k, q_k]\bar{w}_{k+1} \mid$ similarly, but now w_{k+1} also inducing a local computation from q_k on B_k emptying the location and returning in state q$\}$ $\cup$

$\{\bar{w}_1[p_1, A_1, q] \mid w_1$ inducing a local computation from p on A eventually leading to state p_1 and stacking $BA_1\}$.

It is straightforward that the (possibly infinite) set of strings by which [p, A, B, q] may be rewritten is a <u>regular</u> language. The construction goes through for $B = \phi$ as well. Note that by previous assumption now all $\bar{w}_i$'s are $\neq \lambda$.

The symbols [p, A, q] represent when δ_{top} has to be used.

The rules are

$[p, A, q] \to \{w \mid$ (unbarred this time) w induces a local computation with δ_{top} from p and A finally emptying the location and returning in state q (w is $\neq \lambda$ by assumption)$\}$

With appropriate start rules (a presetting 1 is to be treated separately, but there is closure under union) the generated iteration-language is exactly L.

It follows that preset pda languages form an AFL (even a full AFL). Later we will see when or when not you get an AFL with the restricted preset pda-models.

COROLLARY. Preset pda languages are indexed, and (hence) strictly included in the context-sensitive languages. (see [56])

4. DETERMINISTIC PRESET PDA'S

As opposed to classical machine-models this time it is not immediately clear when a preset pda should be called deterministic. Obviously δ and δ_{top} have to yield applicable instructions unambiguously and should be chosen as for deterministic pda's, i.e., with regards to the present modifications. But what about presetting? It can be shown that as far as computational power is concerned, the stack in preset pda's need never grow more than linear in the length of input strings and that would reasonably limit choices when we were to preset the stack functionally in the input (in global theory it may be different). We will argue that another form of "determinism" is more useful here, but illustrate it with an example first.

Example. A preset pda for $L = \{ww^R \mid w \in \Sigma^*\}$ would operate as follows. It copies input in the stack until the presetting is reached, then with δ_{top} it changes mode and removes symbols from the stack while checking against input.

It is important to observe that for any word $ww^R \in L$ there can be only one presetting of the given machine which would lead to acceptance. In fact, the machine for $\{a^{n^2} \mid n \geq 1\}$ designed before had the same feature and was structurally strong enough to "enforce" the appropriate presetting of the stack.

<u>Definition</u>. L is called a weakly deterministic preset pda language if there is a preset pda $\mathfrak{A}$ with deterministic δ and δ_{top} accepting L such that $\forall_{w \in L} \exists_{!\, n}\ (q_0, w, Z_0, n) \overset{*}{\vdash} (q, \lambda, \gamma, n)$ for some $q \in F$, with the preset maximum location reached at least once.

All deterministic context-free languages are weakly deterministic preset pda, but we get many more.

The next result is a generalization of a classical theorem on deterministic pda's.

<u>THEOREM</u>. The family of weakly deterministic preset pda languages is closed under complementation.

The main step in the proof is to eliminate non-terminating computations on λ-input at run-time (there can be no pre-calculation as is the classical proof for ordinary deterministic pda's). Tables stored in all locations to record past symbol-state configurations at that location are used to check for periodicities.

5. LOCALLY FINITENESS AND FINITE RETURNING

Returning to the original motivation, preset pda's as formalized so far may not yet be what computer scientists would call "practical". Further restrictions that are necessary were extensively discussed in [55], and basically relate to the original idea that in the stack-locations procedure-bodies would be stored. Implementation leads to bounds on size and, in slightly informal terminology, we would like preset pda's to have the following properties:

<u>locally finiteness</u> - a fixed bound on the length of local computations, i.e., with non-moving pointer.

<u>finite returning</u> - a fixed bound on how many recursions there can be from a base-location.

Here is the relation to developmental systems.

<u>THEOREM</u>. The family of languages defined by locally finite preset pda's which have the finite return property coincides with the family CR0L (or E0L).

The proof is in [55] but follows the same lines as the general result in section 3.

This representation for CR0L-languages is very powerful, and of interest also from a schematologist's point of view.

Finite returning imposed alone would permit machines to do arbitrary long calculations on the same location.

<u>THEOREM</u>. (Representation theorem) L can be accepted with a preset pda that has the finite return property if and only if there is a λ-free regular substitution τ and a language $L' \varepsilon$ CR0L such that $L = \tau(L')$.

The virtue of this theorem, that it directly uses the machine-representation and the previous result, contrasts with more abstract approaches.

In particular, the following results can now be derived very easily. They were independently also given in [7] in an entirely different approach.

THEOREM. The least AFL enclosing CR0L at the same time is the least such full AFL.

THEOREM. (Representation theorem) L belongs to the least full AFL enclosing CR0L if and only if $L = \tau(L')$ for some $L' \in$ CR0L and λ-free regular substitution τ.

The results were found through the machine-approach.

RECURRENCE SYSTEMS

G. T. HERMAN

Department of Computer Science

The State University of New York at Buffalo

The purpose of this paper is to demonstrate that recurrence systems provide a useful approach to the theory of developmental systems and languages. The demonstration is done by providing a simple proof of the important theorem of Ehrenfeucht and Rozenberg on the equivalence of the family of E0L languages with the family of images under coding of 0L languages.

1. Introduction.

Recurrence systems have already been introduced elsewhere [42, alternatively see 45], and we are not going to repeat the detailed biological motivation behind the definition. Our purpose in this paper is to demonstrate the usefulness of recurrence systems as a tool for simplifying the proofs of mathematical theorems concerning developmental languages. By the way of demonstration we shall provide an alternative proof of an important theorem of Ehrenfeucht and Rozenberg [20]. We begin with a discussion of the Ehrenfeucht and Rozenberg theorem and its significance.

E0L languages were introduced in [35], as those languages which are the intersections of 0L languages and Δ^*, for some alphabet Δ. This corresponds to introducing the notion of a "terminal alphabet" into L system theory. E0L languages were found mathematically tractable and interesting and have been discussed in a number of other papers. In particular, it was shown in [39] that E0L languages are a natural extension of ALGOL-like languages.

Although such theorems are interesting from a mathematical point of view, their biological significance is not inherent in their statements, but are a consequence of the Ehrenfeucht and Rozenberg theorem. This is because, even though 0L languages are well motivated from a biological point of view and the creation of a language from another language by intersection with Δ^* is a standard procedure in formal language theory, the intersection of a 0L language with Δ^* does not seem to make any biological sense. After all, why should we exclude certain developmental stages from the language of an organism just because of the appearance of certain cellular states? The answer is provided by the following discussion.

Clearly, the experimental verification of our developmental systems should inlcude, among other features, the identification of the individual cellular states (corresponding to the symbols of the alphabet) which occur in the model. In some cases, no morphological or biochemical distinction can be made among the cells in the course of development, and thus only the temporal and spatial distribution of the cell divisions can be tested against observations. In other cases, there are irreversibly differentiated cells in the organism, and the spatio-temporal occurrences of such cells can be ascertained and compared with those given by the model. It should be the goal of developmental studies that eventually all cellular states, not only the irreversibly differentiated ones, postulated by the models should also be experimentally distinguishable. The goal is however very far from being realized, and in the meantime we must ask the question: what class of developmental systems (class of 0L systems, for instance) will satisfy a certain observed distribution of cell divisions and of differentiated cells? This problem can also be phrased in the following way. Our observations provide us with "images" of the actual developmental sequences. We are trying to find the class of developmental systems which generates a sequence whose "image" is the observed developmental sequence.

For example, in a description of the development of a compound branching pattern in [42] we denoted each cell by c, i.e., we made no distinction between cells in different states. Even though it is quite possible that experimental observations do not provide us a method by which we can distinguish states, it is clearly reasonable to postulate the existence of different states when trying to explain the development. We have therefore proposed a 0L system with ten different possible cell states. This system is sufficient to explain the observed development, inasmuch that if we replace each digit in the sequence generated by the system by c, then we get exactly the observed sequence. We can formalize this as follows.

<u>Definition</u>. A coding of an alphabet Σ into an alphabet Δ is a homomorphism which maps a single letter of Σ into a single letter of Δ.

Our discussion above can now be restated as follows. Due to our lack of ability to distinguish always cells in different states, when presented with a language L describing an organism as observed, we should look not only for systems which generate L, but also for systems which generate a language K such that L is the image of K under a coding. In particular, the family of all languages which are images of 0L languages under coding is in some sense biologically more important than the family of 0L languages.

A major justification for studying E0L languages is provided by the following result of Ehrenfeucht and Rozenberg [20].

<u>Theorem</u>. A language is an E0L language if, and only if, it is the image of a 0L language under some coding.

This is the theorem we are going to prove using recurrence systems.

2. Definition of basic recurrence systems.

For our proof we do not need the full generality of recurrence systems. We therefore define a more restricted concept which we call a basic recurrence system.

Definition. A basic recurrence system (BR system) is a 5-tuple

$$S = \langle \Sigma, \Omega, A, F, \omega \rangle,$$

where

(1) Σ is a finite non-empty set of symbols (the alphabet),

(2) Ω is a finite non-empty set (the index set),

(3) A is a function, associating with each $x \in \Omega$ a finite set $A(x)$ (of axioms) such that $A(x) \subset \Sigma^+$,

(4) F is a function, associating with each $x \in \Omega$ a finite non-empty set $F(x)$ (of recurrence formulas) such that $F(x) \subset \Omega^+$,

(5) $\omega \in \Omega$ (the distinguished index).

For any $x \in \Omega$ and for any positive integer y, we define $L_{x,y}(S)$ as follows.

$$L_{x,1}(S) = A(x).$$

If $y > 1$,

$$L_{x,y}(S) = \bigcup_{k_1 \cdots k_f \in F(x)} L_{k_1,y-1}(S) \cdots L_{k_f,y-1}(S).$$

Then

$$L(S) = \bigcup_{y=1}^{\infty} L_{\omega,y}(S)$$

is said to be the language generated by S. A language which is generated by a BR system, is said to be a BR language.

(In the terminology of [42], a BR system is a Λ-free depth 1 recurrence system in which the recurrence formulas do not contain constants.)

Example. Let $S = \langle\{a, b\}, \{1, 2, 3, 4, 5\}, A, F, 1\rangle$, where

$A(1) = A(2) = A(3) = \emptyset$, $A(4) = \{a\}$, $A(5) = \{b\}$,

$F(1) = \{35, 45\}$,

$F(2) = \{2\}$,

$F(3) = \{22, 33, 44\}$,

$F(4) = \{2\}$,

$F(5) = \{1\}$.

The following are the top four lines of a semi-infinite table which gives the values of $L_{x,y}(S)$.

y \ x	1	2	3	4	5
1	∅	∅	∅	a	b
2	ab	∅	aa	∅	∅
3	∅	∅	aaaa	∅	ab
4	aaaaab	∅	aaaaaaaa	∅	∅

It is easy to prove by induction that $L(S) = \{a^{f(n)}b \mid n \geq 1\}$, where $f(n) = (2^{2n} - 1)/3$.

Definition. A BR system $S = \langle\Sigma, \Omega, A, F, \omega\rangle$ is said to be ϕ-free if and only if, for all $x \in \Omega$, $A(x) \neq \emptyset$. In such a case $L(S)$ is said to be a ϕ-free BR language.

The example given above is not a ϕ-free BR system. However the language can be generated by a ϕ-free BR system as will be shown in the next section. The more complicated BR system S will be used below to demonstrate our results.

3. Some results on basic recurrence systems.

Lemma 1. If F is a finite set of non-empty strings over an alphabet Σ_0, d is a non negative integer, and, for $1 \leq i \leq d$, $S_i = <\Sigma_i, \Omega_i, A_i, F_i, \omega_i>$ is a ϕ-free BR system, such that $L = F \cup \bigcup_{i=1}^{d} L(S_i) \neq \emptyset$, then L is a ϕ-free BR language.

Proof. If L is not empty we can assume without loss of generality that F is not empty. We may also assume that the Ω_i's are pairwise disjoint, for $1 \leq i \leq d$. We are now going to construct a ϕ-free BR system $S = <\Sigma, \Omega, A, F, \omega>$ such that $L = L(S)$.

$$\Sigma = \bigcup_{i=0}^{d} \Sigma_i.$$

$$\Omega = \bigcup_{i=1}^{d} \Omega_i \cup \{\omega\}, \quad \text{where} \quad \omega \notin \bigcup_{i=1}^{d} \Omega_i.$$

$$A(\omega) = F, \quad A(x) = A_i(x) \quad \text{if} \quad x \in \Omega_i.$$

$$F(\omega) = \{\omega, \omega_1, \ldots, \omega_d\}, \quad F(x) = F_i(x) \quad \text{if} \quad x \in \Omega_i.$$

It is easy to see that S is a ϕ-free BR system. It can be shown by induction that

$$L_{\omega,1}(S) = F,$$

and, for all $y > 1$,

$$L_{\omega,y}(S) = F \cup \bigcup_{z=1}^{y-1} \bigcup_{i=1}^{d} L_{\omega_i,z}(S_i).$$

Therefore,

$$L(S) = \bigcup_{y=1}^{\infty} L_{\omega,y}(S) = F \cup \bigcup_{i=1}^{d} L(S_i) = L.$$

Note that the proof of Lemma 1 is constructive.

Lemma 2. Every BR language is a ϕ-free BR language.

Proof. If L is a BR language, then there exists a BR system $S = <\Sigma, \Omega, A, F, \omega>$ such that $L = L(S)$.

For $y \geq 1$, we define

$$E(y) = \{x \mid L_{x,y}(S) = \emptyset\}.$$

It is easy to see from the definition of $L_{x,y}$ that if $E(y_1) = E(y_2)$, then $E(y_1 + 1) = E(y_2 + 1)$. Also, since $E(y) \subset \Omega$, there must be a y_1 and y_2 such that $E(y_1) = E(y_2)$, and $y_1 \neq y_2$.

Let p and q be the smallest positive integers such that $p < q$ and $E(p) = E(q)$. Let $d = q - p$.

$$L(S) = \bigcup_{y=1}^{p-1} L_{\omega,y}(S) \cup \bigcup_{i=0}^{d-1} \left(\bigcup_{z=0}^{\infty} L_{\omega,p+i+zd}(S)\right).$$

In view of Lemma 1, it is sufficient to show that for $0 \leq i \leq d - 1$, $L_i = \bigcup_{z=0}^{\infty} L_{\omega,p+i+zd}(S)$ is either $\emptyset$ or is a ϕ-free BR language. We shall do this by constructing a ϕ-free BR system S_i such that if $L_i \neq \emptyset$, then $L_i = L(S_i)$.

$S_i = \langle \Sigma, \Omega - E(p + i), A_i, F_i, \omega \rangle$, where, for $x \in \Omega - E(p + i)$, $A_i(x) = L_{x,p+i}(S)$, and $F_i(x)$ is defined as follows.

Since F is a finite substitution of elements of Ω by non-empty finite sets of strings over Ω, for any positive integer k, F^k is well defined and is a finite substitution of the same kind. Thus, in particular, $F^d(x) \subset \Omega^+$ for any x in Ω^+. We define, for $0 \leq i \leq d - 1$, $x \in \Omega - E(p + i)$, $F_i(x) = F^d(x) \cap (\Omega - E(p + i))^+$.

In order to show that S_i is a ϕ-free BR system all we need to show is that for all $x \in \Omega - E(p + i)$, $A_i(x)$ is not empty and $F_i(x)$ is not empty. The former is obvious from the definition of $E(p + i)$. To see the latter, all we have to show is that for all $x \in \Omega - E(p + i)$, $F^d(x)$ contains at least one string over $\Omega - E(p + i)$. But if this was not the case we would have

$$L_{x,q+i}(S) = \bigcup_{k_1 \ldots k_f \in F^d(x)} L_{k_1,p+i}(S) \ldots L_{k_f,p+i}(S) = \emptyset,$$ contradicting the fact that $x \notin E(p + i) = E(q + i)$.

Each of the S_i is therefore a ϕ-free BR system. It is now easy to show by induction that for all $z \geq 0$ we have that, for all $x \in \Omega - E(p + i)$,

$$L_{x,p+i+zd}(S) = L_{x,z+1}(S_i).$$

In particular,

$$L_i = \bigcup_{z=0}^{\infty} L_{\omega,p+i+zd}(S) = \bigcup_{z=0}^{\infty} L_{x,z+1}(S_i) = L(S_i).$$

This completes the proof of our lemma. We note that the proof is constructive, given a BR system S, we can effectively produce a finite set F, a positive integer d and ϕ-free BR systems $S_0, \ldots, S_{d-1}$ such that

$$L(S) = F \cup \bigcup_{i=0}^{d-1} L(S_i).$$

From these we can use the construction of Lemma 1 to produce a ϕ-free BR system S' such that $L(S) = L(S')$.

We demonstrate this on the example of the last section. $E(1) = \{1, 2, 3\}$, $E(2) = \{2, 4, 5\}$, $E(3) = \{1, 2, 4\}$, $E(4) = \{2, 4, 5\}$. Thus, $p = 2$, $q = 4$ and $d = 2$. $F = L_{\omega,1}(S) = \emptyset$.

$L_0 = \bigcup_{z=0}^{\infty} L_{\omega,2+zd}(S) = L(S_0)$, where S_0 will be defined below.

$L_1 = \bigcup_{z=0}^{\infty} L_{\omega,3+zd} = \emptyset$. Hence $L(S) = L(S_0)$, where $S_0 = \langle\{a, b\}, \{1, 3\}, A_0, F_0, 1\rangle$, where $A_0(1) = \{ab\}$, $A_0(3) = \{aa\}$, $F_0(1) = \{331\}$ and $F_0(3) = \{3333\}$. The semi-infinite table associated with S_0 begins with

y \ x	1	3
1	ab	aa
2	aaaaab	aaaaaaaa
3	$a^{21}b$	a^{32}
4	$a^{85}b$	a^{128}

In the case of this example we did not have to make use of the construction of Lemma 1.

Those familiar with the definition of recurrence systems [42, or 45], will appreciate the following consequence of Lemma 2.

Corollary. Every recurrence language is a ϕ-free recurrence language.

Lemma 3. Every ϕ-free BR language is the image of a 0L language under some coding.

Proof. If L is a ϕ-free BR language, then there exists a ϕ-free BR system $S = \langle\Sigma, \Omega, A, F, \omega\rangle$ such that $L = L(S)$. We define a 0L system $G = \langle\Delta, P, \sigma\rangle$ as follows.

$\Delta = \Omega \times \Sigma \cup \overline{\Omega \times \Sigma} \cup \{S_1, S_2, \ldots, S_k\}$, where k is a positive integer such that there is a word of L of length k. (By our definition of a ϕ-free BR language, there is at least one such integer.)

$\sigma = S_1 S_2 \ldots S_k$.

P consists of the following productions.

$S_1 \rightarrow \langle\omega, a_1\rangle\langle\omega, a_2\rangle \ldots \langle\omega, a_t\rangle$, for all $a_1, a_2, \ldots, a_t$ in Σ such that $a_1 a_2 \ldots a_t \in A(\omega)$.

$S_i \to \Lambda$, for $2 \leq i \leq k$.

$\overline{\langle x, a\rangle} \to y$, for all $x \in \Omega$, $a \in \Sigma$ and $y \in f(F(x))$,

where f is a finite substitution which associates with every $z \in \Omega$ the set of all strings $\overline{\langle z, a_1\rangle}\langle z, a_2\rangle \ldots \langle z, a_t\rangle$, where $a_1, a_2, \ldots, a_t$ are in Σ and $a_1 a_2 \ldots a_t \in A(z)$.

$\overline{\langle x, a\rangle} \to \Lambda$, for all $x \in \Omega$ and $a \in \Sigma$.

Let $a_1 a_2 \ldots a_k$ be a word of length k in L. Let h be the coding defined by

$h(S_i) = a_i$, for $1 \leq i \leq k$,

$h(\overline{\langle x, a\rangle}) = h(\langle x, a\rangle) = a$, for all $x \in \Omega$ and $a \in \Sigma$.

We claim that $L(S) = h(L(G))$. This claim has a reasonably standard inductive proof and is therefore omitted. (See for example the proofs of Lemmas 2 and 3 in [39].) Instead, we demonstrate our claim on the BR system S_0, which is described following Lemma 2.

In this case $\Delta = \{\langle 1, a\rangle, \langle 3, a\rangle, \langle 1, b\rangle, \langle 3, b\rangle, \overline{\langle 1, a\rangle}, \overline{\langle 3, a\rangle}, \overline{\langle 1, b\rangle}, \overline{\langle 3, b\rangle}, S_1, S_2\}$ and $\sigma = S_1 S_2$. P has the following productions:

$S_1 \to \overline{\langle 1, a\rangle}\langle 1, b\rangle$

$S_2 \to \Lambda$

$\overline{\langle 1, a\rangle} \to \overline{\langle 3, a\rangle}\langle 3, a\rangle\overline{\langle 3, a\rangle}\langle 3, a\rangle\overline{\langle 1, a\rangle}\langle 1, b\rangle$

$\overline{\langle 1, b\rangle} \to \overline{\langle 3, a\rangle}\langle 3, a\rangle\overline{\langle 3, a\rangle}\langle 3, a\rangle\overline{\langle 1, a\rangle}\langle 1, b\rangle$

$\overline{\langle 3, a\rangle} \to \overline{\langle 3, a\rangle}\langle 3, a\rangle\overline{\langle 3, a\rangle}\langle 3, a\rangle\overline{\langle 3, a\rangle}\langle 3, a\rangle\overline{\langle 3, a\rangle}\langle 3, a\rangle$

$\overline{\langle 3, b\rangle} \to \overline{\langle 3, a\rangle}\langle 3, a\rangle\overline{\langle 3, a\rangle}\langle 3, a\rangle\overline{\langle 3, a\rangle}\langle 3, a\rangle\overline{\langle 3, a\rangle}\langle 3, a\rangle$

$\langle x, u\rangle \to \Lambda$ for $x \in \{1, 3\}$ and $u \in \{a, b\}$.

A derivation in $G = \langle \Delta, P, \sigma\rangle$ looks as follows:

$S_1 S_2$

$\overline{\langle 1, a\rangle}\langle 1, b\rangle$

$\overline{\langle 3, a\rangle}\langle 3, a\rangle\overline{\langle 3, a\rangle}\langle 3, a\rangle\overline{\langle 1, a\rangle}\langle 1, b\rangle$

$(\overline{\langle 3, a\rangle}\langle 3, a\rangle)^4(\overline{\langle 3, a\rangle}\langle 3, a\rangle)^4(\overline{\langle 3, a\rangle}\langle 3, a\rangle)^2\ \overline{\langle 1, a\rangle}\langle 1, b\rangle$

If the coding h is now applied to this derivation $(h(S_1) = a, h(S_2) = b)$ we get the following strings

ab

ab

aaaaab

$a^{21}b$

4. Proof of the Ehrenfeucht-Rozenberg Theorem.

It has been proved in [42, Corollary 7], that the image of a 0L language under any homomorphism (and hence under any coding) is an E0L language. We are now going to prove the converse.

Using the results of [42] (especially Theorem 7 and Corollary 3) it is easy to show that for every E0L language L there exists a BR system S, such that $L(S) = L - \{\Lambda\}$. By Lemma 2, $L - \{\Lambda\}$ is a ϕ-free BR language and hence, by Lemma 3, it is the image of a 0L language under some coding. Hence L, which is either $L - \{\Lambda\}$, or $(L - \{\Lambda\}) \cup \{\Lambda\}$ is also the image of a 0L language under some coding.

This completes the proof of the theorem. We note that it can easily be made constructive.

It should also be pointed out that even though we have shown that for every E0L language L there is a 0L system G such that $L = h(L(G))$ for some coding h, the G we have produced during the proof (see proof of Lemma 3) is biologically somewhat undesirable. It has the property that in every step a cell either dies or divides into (usually) many cells, most of which (usually) die in the next step. The same criticism applies to the original Ehrenfeucht and Rozenberg proof of their theorem (see [20]). It would be interesting to see whether or not a similar theorem would still be valid regarding a biologically reasonable restriction of 0L systems.

5. Conclusion.

Recurrence systems provide us with a powerful tool for proving theorems about developmental systems and languages.

Acknowledgement. The research for this paper has been supported by NSF grant GJ 998. The work has been highly influenced by the cooperation of the author with Professors A. Lindenmayer and G. Rozenberg, this cooperation has been supported by NATO grant 574.

ADULT LANGUAGES OF L SYSTEMS AND THE CHOMSKY HIERARCHY

Adrian Walker
Department of Computer Science
State University of New York at Buffalo

Introduction

The concept of an L system was first introduced by Lindenmayer [59, 60] as "a theoretical framework within which intercellular relationships can be discussed, computed, and compared". The concept has proved to be a fruitful one, and has opened up a new area of interdisciplinary research. Much of the work to date on L systems is reported in Herman and Rozenberg [45]. The motivation for the present paper is the thought that, since L systems are proving so useful as a framework for studying biological growth and development, perhaps they can also be used to study the ways in which organisms achieve and maintain relatively stable adult states. Thus while the emphasis in work on L systems to date has been on all the strings derivable from an initial string, we shall focus in this paper on just those strings which renew themselves dynamically once they have been derived.

Notation

We write λ for the empty string, $|\alpha|$ for the length of a string α (e.g. $|\lambda| = 0$), and $\#V$ for the number of elements in a set V. If α is a string we write the set of symbols occurring in α as sym α, e.g. sym abbac = {a, b, c}. If L is a set of strings we write sym L for $\bigcup_{\alpha \in L}$ sym α. We write the number of occurrences of the symbol a in a string α as $\#_a(\alpha)$, e.g. $\#_a(\text{abbac}) = 2$.

We abbreviate context free grammar, context sensitive grammar, linear bounded automaton, and Turing machine as CFG, CSG, LBA and TM respectively. We require that if $\alpha \to \beta$ is a production of a CSG then $|\alpha| \leq |\beta|$. We write the classes of context free, context sensitive languages not containing λ, and recursively enumerable languages as L(CF), L(CS) and L(RE) respectively. Otherwise we use the notation of Hopcroft and Ullman† for phrase structure grammars.

If δ is a mapping from a set of strings into a set of sets of strings, we say that $\delta^0(\alpha) = \{\alpha\}$, and for each $i \geq 0$ $\delta^{i+1}(\alpha) = \delta\delta^i(\alpha)$. We say that $\delta^*(\alpha) = \bigcup_{i=0}^{\infty} \delta^i(\alpha)$.

Definitions

A <u>0L system</u> is a 3-tuple $H = \langle V, \delta, S\rangle$ where V is an alphabet, $S \in V$ and δ is a mapping from V^* into the finite subsets of V^* defined as follows. There is a table Q of productions $Q \subset V \times V^*$ such that for each $b \in V$ there is a $\beta \in V^*$ such that $\langle b, \beta\rangle \in Q$. $\delta(\lambda) = \{\lambda\}$ and for $\alpha = a_1 \ldots a_n$, $\delta(\alpha) = Q(a_1) \ldots Q(a_n)$. If for each production $\langle b, \beta\rangle \in Q$ $\beta \neq \lambda$ we say that H is a propagating 0L system, or <u>P0L system</u> for short.

A <u>2L system</u> is a 4-tuple $H = \langle V, \delta, g, S\rangle$ where V and S are as in a 0L system, g is a symbol not in V, and δ is a mapping from V^* into the finite subsets of V^* defined as follows. There is a table Q of productions $Q \subset V_g V V_g \times V^*$, where $V_g = V \cup \{g\}$ such that for each $abc \in V_g V V_g$ there is a $\beta \in V^*$ such that $\langle abc, \beta\rangle \in Q$. $\delta(\lambda) = \{\lambda\}$, and for $\alpha = a_1 \ldots a_n$, $\delta(\alpha) = Q(a_0 a_1 a_2) \ldots Q(a_{j-1} a_j a_{j+1}) \ldots Q(a_{n-1} a_n a_{n+1})$ where a_0 and a_{n+1} stand for g.

---

† Hopcroft, J. E., J. D. Ullman, <u>Formal Languages and their Relation to Automata</u>, Addison-Wesley, Reading, Mass., 1969. From now on we refer to this book simply as H & U.

If for each production $<abc, \beta> \in Q$ $\beta \neq \lambda$ we say that H is a <u>P2L system</u>.

If H is an L system with mapping δ and initial symbol S, we define the <u>adult language</u> of H as $A(H) = \{\alpha \in \delta^*(S) \mid \delta(\alpha) = \{\alpha\}\}$.

Phrase Structure Grammars

We now summarize some results about phrase structure grammars which we shall need later.

We follow Aho and Ullman† in saying that a CFG $G = <V_N, V_T, P, S>$ is <u>proper</u> if

(i) for each $A \in V_N$ it is not the case that $A \overset{+}{\Rightarrow} A$,

(ii) either P has no productions of the form $A \to \lambda$, or $S \to \lambda$ is the only such production and S never appears on the right of a production, and

(iii) for each $B \in V_N$ there exist $\alpha, \beta, \gamma \in V_T^*$ such that $S \overset{*}{\Rightarrow} \alpha B \gamma \overset{*}{\Rightarrow} \alpha\beta\gamma$.

The following result is obtainable by algorithms 2.8-2.11 of Aho and Ullman†.

<u>Lemma 1</u> There exists an algorithm which takes as input any CFG G and produces as output a proper CFG G' such that $L(G) = L(G')$.

<u>Lemma 2</u> There exists an algorithm which takes as input any grammar G and produces as output a grammar G' such that

(i) if $\alpha' \to \beta'$ is a production of G' then $|\alpha'| \in \{1, 2\}$,

(ii) if $\alpha' \to \lambda$ is a production of G', then $|\alpha'| = 1$,

---

† Aho, A. V., J. D. Ullman, <u>The Theory of Parsing, Translating and Compiling</u>, volume 1, Prentice Hall, Englewood Cliffs, 1972.

(iii) if G is a CSG then so is G', and

(iv) $L(G) = L(G')$.

Proof Let $G = \langle V_N, V_T, P, S\rangle$ be a grammar. It is easy to see that we lose no generality by assuming that if $\alpha \underset{P}{\rightarrow} \lambda$ then $|\alpha| = 1$. Then to construct $G' = \langle V_N', V_T, Q, S\rangle$, place each production in P having a left side of length 1 or 2 directly in Q. For each production $A_1 \ldots A_m \underset{P}{\rightarrow} B_1 \ldots B_n$ where $A_i, B_j \in (V_N \cup V_T)$ and $m \geq 3$, Q contains $A_1A_2 \rightarrow B_1C_2$, $Z \rightarrow \lambda$, and in addition

(i) $C_iA_{i+1} \rightarrow B_iC_{i+1}$ $(2 \leq i \leq m-2)$ and
$C_{m-1}A_m \rightarrow B_{m-1} \ldots B_n$, if $m \leq n$;

(ii) $C_iA_{i+1} \rightarrow B_iC_{i+1}$ $(2 \leq i \leq n-1)$ and
$C_nA_m \rightarrow B_nZ$, if $m = n+1$;

(iii) $C_iA_{i+1} \rightarrow B_iC_{i+1}$ $(2 \leq i \leq n)$,
$C_iA_{i+1} \rightarrow ZC_{i+1}$ $(n < i \leq m-2)$, and
$C_{m-1}A_m \rightarrow Z$, if $m \geq n+2$.

In this construction the C_i's are new symbols, and if productions $p_1, p_2 \in P$ give rise to subsets Q_1, Q_2 of Q, then the C_i's in Q_1 and Q_2 are distinct.

It is straightforward to check that our construction has the required properties.∎

Adult Languages of 0L Systems

In order to characterize the adult languages of 0L systems, we first derive a property of the productions which must hold in order for a string to map only into itself. Note that it is not necessarily the case that $a \rightarrow a$ for each letter in such a string, e.g. if $a \rightarrow ab$, $b \rightarrow c$ and $c \rightarrow \lambda$, then $\delta(abc) = \{abc\}$. (When $\delta(\alpha) = \{\beta\}$ we shall write simply $\delta(\alpha) = \beta$.)

Lemma 3 If $H = \langle V, \delta, S\rangle$ is a 0L system, $\Sigma = \text{sym } A(H)$, and $m = \#\Sigma$, then for each $a \in \Sigma$ there is a unique $\beta \in \Sigma^*$ such that $\delta^*\delta^m(a) = \beta$.

Proof

1. For each $a \in \Sigma$, $\#\delta(a) = 1$ and $\delta(a) \in \Sigma^*$: if $a \in \Sigma$ then there exist $\alpha_1, \alpha_2 \in \Sigma^*$ such that $\delta(\alpha_1 a \alpha_2) = \alpha_1 a \alpha_2 = \delta(\alpha_1)\delta(a)\delta(\alpha_2)$.

2. If $a \in \Sigma$ then $\#_a\delta(a) \in \{0, 1\}$: if $a \in \Sigma$ then there exist $\alpha_1, \alpha_2 \in \Sigma^*$ such that $\delta(\alpha_1 a\alpha_2) = \alpha_1 a\alpha_2 = \delta(\alpha_1)\delta(a)\delta(\alpha_2)$. Hence if $\#_a\delta(a) = k$ then $\#_a\delta^i(\alpha_1 a\alpha_2) \geq k^i$ for each $i \geq 0$. Since $\delta^*(\alpha_1 a\alpha_2) = \alpha_1 a\alpha_2$ and $\#_a(\alpha_1 a\alpha_2) \leq |\alpha_1 a\alpha_2|$ it is obvious that we must have $k \leq 1$.

3. If $a \in \Sigma$ and $\#_a\delta(a) = 0$ then $\delta^m(a) = \lambda$: suppose that for all $i \geq 0$, $\delta^i(a) \neq \lambda$. Since $a \in \Sigma$ we have $a \in \text{sym } \gamma$ for some γ such that $\delta(\gamma) = \gamma$. Since $\#_a\delta(a) = 0$, we can write either (i) $\gamma = u\delta(a)\, v\, a\, w$ for some $u, v, w \in \Sigma^*$, or (ii) $\gamma = uav\delta(a)w$ for some $u, v, w \in \Sigma^*$. Hence, since $\delta(\gamma) = \gamma$ we can show that $|\delta^i(\gamma)| \geq |\delta^0(a)\ldots\delta^i(a)|$ for each $i \geq 0$. But then $|\delta^{|\gamma|}(\gamma)| \geq |\delta^0(a)\ldots\delta^{|\gamma|}(a)| > |\gamma|$, a contradiction since $\delta^{|\gamma|}(\gamma) = \gamma$. So it must be the case that for some $i \geq 0$, $\delta^i(a) = \lambda$. From this it is easy to show by path length arguments that $\delta^m(a) = \lambda$.

4. For each $a \in \Sigma$ such that $\#_a\delta(a) = 1$, there is a unique $\beta \in \Sigma^+$ such that $\delta^*\delta^m(a) = \beta$: since $\#_a\delta(a) = 1$ we can write $\delta(a) = \alpha a\bar{\alpha}$ for some $\alpha, \bar{\alpha} \in (\Sigma - \{a\})^*$. If $\delta^i(\alpha\bar{\alpha}) \neq \lambda$ for all $i \geq 0$ then it is easy to see that for any ℓ there exists a j such that $|\delta^j(a)| > \ell$, which is impossible since a occurs in a string γ such that $\delta(\gamma) = \gamma$. So there is an i such that $\delta^i(\alpha\bar{\alpha}) = \lambda$, and hence by 3. we have that $\delta^m(\alpha\bar{\alpha}) = \lambda$. Let r, s be the greatest integers less than or equal m such that $\delta^r(\alpha) \neq \lambda$, $\delta^{r+1}(\alpha) = \lambda$,

$\delta^s(\bar{\alpha}) \neq \lambda$, and $\delta^{s+1}(\bar{\alpha}) = \lambda$. Then it is easy to see that if we write $\beta = \delta^r(\alpha) \ldots \delta^0(\alpha)a\delta^0(\bar{\alpha}) \ldots \delta^s(\bar{\alpha})$ then $\delta^*\delta^m(a) = \beta$. The lemma now follows from 2, 3, and 4. ■

We shall need to know how to find sym A(H) for any 0L system H.

Lemma 4 There exists an algorithm which takes as input any 0L system H and produces as output the set sym A(H).

Proof Let $H = \langle V, \delta, S \rangle$ be a 0L system, and let $\Sigma = \text{sym } A(H)$, $m = \#\Sigma$, and $n = \#V$. Let $L = \{\alpha \in \delta^i(S) \mid i \leq 2^n + m, \delta(\alpha) = \alpha\}$. We claim that $\Sigma = \text{sym } L$.

Obviously sym $L \subset \Sigma$. Suppose $b \in \Sigma$. Then there is an $\alpha \in A(H)$ such that $b \in \text{sym } \alpha$. So $\alpha \in \delta^*(S) \cap \{u \mid \delta(u) = u\}$. Hence there exists an $i \geq 0$ such that $\alpha \in \delta^i(S)$ and $\alpha \in \delta^{i+m}(S)$. But it is easy to check that if $\alpha \in \delta^i(S)$, there exists an $\bar{\alpha} \in \delta^{2^n}(S)$ such that sym α = sym $\bar{\alpha}$. Hence by Lemma 3 there exists an $\bar{\bar{\alpha}} \in \delta^m(\bar{\alpha})$ such that sym $\bar{\bar{\alpha}}$ = sym α and $\delta(\bar{\bar{\alpha}}) = \bar{\bar{\alpha}}$. So $\bar{\bar{\alpha}} \in L$ and hence $b \in \text{sym } L$. ■

We can use the last two lemmas to put any 0L system in a form in which $\delta(a) = a$ for each letter a which occurs in the adult language.

Lemma 5 There exists an algorithm which takes as input any 0L system G and produces as output a 0L system H such that $A(G) = A(H)$ and for each $a \in \text{sym } A(H)$, $\delta_H(a) = a$.

Proof Let $G = \langle V, \delta_G, S \rangle$ be a 0L system. Let $\Sigma_G = \text{sym } A(G)$, and let $m = \#\Sigma_G$.

If $\Sigma_G = \emptyset$ then we are done, so suppose $\Sigma_G \neq \emptyset$. Let $H = \langle V, \delta_H, S\rangle$ be a 0L system constructed from G as follows. Define a mapping $\theta: V \to V^*$ by

$$\theta(a) = \begin{cases} a, & \text{if } a \in V - \Sigma_G \\ \delta_G^m(a), & \text{if } a \in \Sigma_G, \end{cases}$$

extend θ to domain V^* by $\theta(\lambda) = \lambda$ and $\theta(a\alpha) = \theta(a)\theta(\alpha)$, and further to domain 2^{V^*} in the obvious manner. Then define $\delta_H: V \to 2^{V^*}$ by

$$\delta_H(a) = \begin{cases} \theta\delta_G(a), & \text{if } a \in V - \Sigma_G \\ a, & \text{if } a \in \Sigma_G. \end{cases}$$

By lemmas 3 and 4, H is well-defined. We claim that $A(G) = A(H)$.

1. For every $t \geq 0$ and $\beta \in V^*$, $\beta \in \delta_H^t(S)$ iff there exists an $\alpha \in V^*$ such that $\alpha \in \delta_G^t(S)$ and $\theta(\alpha) = \beta$: this is straightforward to prove by induction on t.

2. $A(G) \subset A(H)$: Let $\alpha = a_1 \dots a_n \in A(G)$. Then $a_j \in \Sigma_G$. Let $\delta_G^m(a_j) = \delta_G^{m+1}(a_j) = \beta_j$. Since $\delta_G^m(\alpha) = \alpha$, we have $\beta_1 \dots \beta_n = \alpha$, and so $\theta(\alpha) = \beta_1 \dots \beta_n = \alpha$. Since $\alpha \in \delta_G^*(S)$ we have from 1. that $\theta(\alpha) \in \delta_H^*(S)$. But $\theta(\alpha) = \alpha$, so $\alpha \in \delta_H^*(S)$. Also, since $\alpha \in \Sigma_G^*$ it follows from the construction of δ_H that $\delta_H(\alpha) = \alpha$. Hence $\alpha \in A(H)$.

3. $A(H) \subset A(G)$: Let $\beta \in A(H)$. Then $\beta \in \delta_H^*(S)$. So it follows from 1. that there exists an α such that $\alpha \in \delta_G^*(S)$ and $\theta(\alpha) = \beta$. Let $\alpha = \alpha_0 A_1 \alpha_1 \dots \alpha_{n-1} A_n \alpha_n$, where $\alpha_j \in \Sigma_G^*$, $A_j \in (V - \Sigma_G)$, and $n \geq 0$. Since $\alpha_j \in \Sigma_G^*$ it follows from Lemma 3 that there is a $\beta_j \in \Sigma_G^*$ such that $\delta_G^m(\alpha_j) = \delta_G^{m+1}(\alpha_j) = \beta_j$. It follows from this and the definition of θ that $\theta(\alpha) = \beta_0 A_1 \beta_1 \dots \beta_{n-1} A_n \beta_n$. Since $\beta_j \in \Sigma_G^*$, we have from the construction of δ_H that $\delta_H(\beta_j) = \beta_j$. Since $\beta \in A(H)$, we have $\delta_H(\beta) = \beta$. Since $\delta_H(\beta) = \beta$ and $\delta_H(\beta_j) = \beta_j$ it is clear that $\delta_H(A_j) = A_j$. Since $A_j \notin \Sigma_G$, if $\gamma_j \in \delta_G(A_j)$

then $\theta(\gamma_j) \in \delta_H(A_j)$, and so $\theta(\gamma_j) = A_j$. But this is only possible if $\gamma_j = A_j$. Hence $\delta_G(A_j) = A_j$. Now since $\delta_G(\beta_j) = \beta_j$ and $\beta = \theta(\alpha) = \beta_o A_1 \beta_1 \ldots \beta_{n-1} A_n \beta_n$, we have $\delta_G(\beta) = \beta$. Moreover, since $\delta_G^m(\alpha_j) = \beta_j$ and $\delta_G^m(A_j) = A_j$, we have $\delta_G^m(\alpha) = \beta$. Hence $\beta = \delta_G(\beta) \in \delta_G^m(\alpha) \in \delta_G^*(S)$, and so $\beta \in A(G)$.

2. and 3. together establish our claim that $A(H) = A(G)$. ■

We shall use Lemmas 4 and 5 to characterize the class $A(0L)$ of adult languages of 0L systems. First we need the following notation. If $G = \langle V_N, V_T, P, S\rangle$ is a CFG with $V_N \cup V_T = V$ we define a mapping $\psi_G: V \to 2^{V^*}$ by

$$\psi_G(a) = \begin{cases} a, & \text{if } a \in V_T \\ \{\beta \mid a \underset{P}{\to} \beta\} & \text{if } a \in V_N, \end{cases}$$

and we extend ψ_G to domain V^* by $\psi_G(\lambda) = \lambda$ and $\psi_G(a\alpha) = \psi_G(a)\psi_G(\alpha)$. It is easy to check that $L(G) = \psi_G^*(S) \cap V_T^*$.

<u>Lemma 6</u> There exists an algorithm which takes as input any 0L system H and produces as output a CFG G such that $A(H) = L(G)$.

<u>Proof</u> Let $H = \langle V, \delta_H, S\rangle$ be a 0L system, let $\Sigma = \text{sym } A(H)$, and assume without loss of generality that $S \in V - \Sigma$. By Lemma 5 we may also assume that for each $a \in \alpha$, $\delta_H(a) = a$. Let $G = \langle V - \Sigma, \Sigma, P, S\rangle$ be a CFG constructed from H, where $P = \{A \to \alpha \mid A \in V - \Sigma$ and $\alpha \in \delta_H(A)\}$. By Lemma 4 we can compute Σ from H, so our construction is effective.

Now it is easy to check from our construction that for each $i \geq 0$, $\delta_H^i(S) = \psi_G^i(S)$. Hence $\delta_H^*(S) = \psi_G^*(S)$. So $\delta_H^*(S) \cap \Sigma^* = \psi_G^*(S) \cap \Sigma^*$. But since $\delta_H(a) = a$ for each $a \in \Sigma$, it is easy to see that $A(H) = \delta_H^*(S) \cap \Sigma^*$, and it is a property of our notation ψ_G that $L(G) = \psi_G^*(S) \cap \Sigma^*$, hence $A(H) = L(G)$. ■

We can prove the converse of Lemma 6.

Lemma 7 There exists an algorithm which takes as input any CFG G and produces as output a 0L system H such that $L(G) = A(H)$.

Proof Let $G = \langle V_N, V_T, P, S\rangle$ be a CFG. By Lemma 1 we may assume that G is proper. Let $H = \langle V, \delta_H, S\rangle$ be constructed from G by $V = V_N \cup V_T$, and

$$\delta_H(a) = \begin{cases} \{\alpha \mid a \underset{P}{\rightarrow} \alpha\}, & \text{if } a \in V_N \\ a, & \text{if } a \in V_T \end{cases}$$

Clearly the construction is effective, and since G is proper $\delta: V \rightarrow 2^{V^*}$ is everywhere defined, so H is a 0L system.

It follows from our construction that for each $i \geq 0$, $\psi_G^i(S) = \delta_H^i(S)$. Hence $\psi_G^*(S) = \delta_H^*(S)$. Now it follows from the fact that G is proper that $\psi_G(\alpha) = \alpha$ iff $\alpha \in V_T^*$. Hence from our construction, $\delta_H(\alpha) = \alpha$ iff $\alpha \in V_T^*$. So $A(H) = \{\alpha \in \delta_H^*(S) \mid \delta_H(\alpha) = \alpha\} = \delta_H^*(S) \cap V_T^*$. Hence from the property $L(G) = \psi_G^*(S) \cap V_T^*$ of our notation ψ_G, we have $A(H) = L(G)$. ∎

We can now characterize the class A(0L) of adult languages of 0L systems in terms of the class L(CF) of context free languages.

Theorem 1 $A(0L) = L(CF)$.

Proof Immediate from Lemmas 6 and 7. ∎

Let us say of two classes $\mathcal{L}_1$ and $\mathcal{L}_2$ of languages that $\mathcal{L}_1 \overline{\overline{\lambda}} \mathcal{L}_2$ if $\{L \cup \{\lambda\} \mid L \in \mathcal{L}_1\} = \{L \cup \{\lambda\} \mid L \in \mathcal{L}_2\}$. Then we have the following result for propagating 0L systems.

<u>Theorem 2</u> $A(P0L) =_{\lambda} L(CF)$.

<u>Proof</u> By Lemma 6, we have $A(P0L) \subset L(CF)$. Suppose $L \in L(CF)$. Then there is a proper CFG such that $L = L(G)$. It follows from Lemma 7 and the construction in its proof that we can construct a P0L system H such that $(L - \{\lambda\}) = A(H)$, i.e. such that $L = L(G) = A(H) \cup \{\lambda\}$. ■

Thus we have effective constructions which take us from any 0L system to a corresponding CFG, and vice versa. We have also shown that the propagating restriction makes little difference for adult languages of 0L systems, i.e. $A(0L) =_{\lambda} A(P0L)$. We shall see however that the propagating restriction is very important in 2L systems.

Adult Languages of 2L Systems

We now look at adult languages of 2L systems with and without the propagating restriction, and their relationship to the phrase structure languages of the Chomsky hierarchy.

<u>Lemma 8</u> There exists an algorithm which takes as input any grammar G and produces as output a 2L system H such that $L(G) = A(H)$. Moreover if G is a CSG, then H is a P2L system.

<u>Proof</u> Let $G = \langle V_N, V_T, P, S\rangle$ be a grammar. By Lemma 2 we may assume without loss of generality that if $\alpha \underset{P}{\to} \beta$ then $|\alpha| \in \{1, 2\}$ and that if $\alpha \underset{P}{\to} \lambda$ then $|\alpha| = 1$. We shall show how to construct from G a 2L system H such that $A(H) = L(G)$. The idea behind the construction is as follows.

Our construction will be such that if $S \overset{*}{\underset{G}{\Rightarrow}} \gamma$, where $\gamma = C_1C_2 \ldots C_n$ and $\gamma \notin L(G)$, then a string $\vec{C}_1C_2 \ldots C_n$ is derivable in H. The $\rightarrow$ will then move to the right along the string, allowing local rewriting according to the productions of P which have a single symbol on the left. When $\rightarrow$ reaches the right end of the string, it changes to $\leftarrow$. The $\leftarrow$ then moves to the left along the string, allowing local rewriting according to the productions of P which have two symbols on the left. When $\leftarrow$ reaches the left end of the string, it changes to $\rightarrow$ or to $\Rightarrow$. If the change is to $\rightarrow$, then the above process is repeated. If the change is to $\Rightarrow$ then two things can happen. If the string is in V_T^+, then $\Rightarrow$ moves all the way to the right and vanishes, yielding a string in A(H). If the string contains a symbol from V_N, then $\Rightarrow$ moves as far as that symbol, then changes to $\leftarrow$, and rewriting continues as above.

Formally, our construction of a 2L system H from the grammar $G = \langle V_N, V_T, P, S\rangle$ is as follows.

A) $V = V_N \cup V_T \cup \{X\}$, where X is a symbol not in $V_N \cup V_T$.

$V_g = V \cup \{g\}$, where g is a symbol not in V.

B) $\vec{V}$, $\overleftarrow{V}$, $\overset{\Rightarrow}{V}$ and $\hat{V}$ are mutually disjoint sets, which are individually disjoint from $V \cup \{g\}$, defined by

$$\vec{V} = \{\vec{A} \mid A \in V\}$$

$$\overleftarrow{V} = \{\overleftarrow{A} \mid A \in V\}$$

$$\overset{\Rightarrow}{V} = \{\overset{\Rightarrow}{A} \mid A \in V\}$$

$$\hat{V} = \{[C\gamma] \mid AB \underset{P}{\rightarrow} C\gamma \text{ where } A, B, C \in V \text{ and } \gamma \in V^*\}$$

C) $W = V \cup \vec{V} \cup \overleftarrow{V} \cup \overset{\Rightarrow}{V} \cup \hat{V}$

$W_g = W \cup \{g\}$.

D) $Q_1 = \{L\vec{A}B \rightarrow \gamma \mid A, B \in V, L \in V_g, \gamma \in V^*, \text{ and } A \underset{P}{\rightarrow} \gamma\}$

$Q_2 = \{L\vec{A}g \rightarrow \overleftarrow{C}\gamma \mid A, B, C \in V, \gamma \in V^*, \text{ and } A \underset{P}{\rightarrow} C\gamma\}$

$Q_3 = \{L\vec{A}g \rightarrow \overleftarrow{X} \mid L \in V_g, A \in V, A \underset{P}{\rightarrow} \lambda\}$

$Q_4 = \{L\overleftarrow{X}R \rightarrow \lambda \mid L, R \in V_g\}$

$Q_5 = \{L A \overleftarrow{B} \to [C\gamma] \mid A, B, C \in V, L \in V_g, \gamma \in V^*$ and
$AB \underset{P}{\to} C\gamma\}$

$Q_6 = \{L[C\gamma]B \to \overleftarrow{C} \mid B, C, \in V, L \in V_g$, and $[C\gamma] \in \hat{V}\}$

$Q_7 = \{[C\gamma]BR \to \gamma \mid B, C \in V, R \in V_g$, and $[C\gamma] \in \hat{V}\}$

$Q_8 = \{\overrightarrow{A}BR \to \overrightarrow{B} \mid A, B \in V$ and $R \in V_g\}$

$Q_9 = \{L\overrightarrow{A}B \to A \mid L \in V_g$ and $A, B \in V\}$

$Q_{10} = \{L\overleftarrow{B}g \to \overleftarrow{B} \mid L \in V_g$ and $B \in V_N\}$

$Q_{11} = \{LA\overleftarrow{B} \to \overleftarrow{A} \mid L \in V_g$ and $A, B \in V\}$

$Q_{12} = \{A\overleftarrow{B}R \to B \mid A, B \in V$ and $R \in V_g\}$

$Q_{13} = \{g\overleftarrow{A}R \to \overset{\Rightarrow}{A} \mid A \in V_T$ and $R \in V_g\}$

$Q_{14} = \{g\overleftarrow{A}R \to \overleftarrow{A} \mid A \in V$ and $R \in V_g\}$

$Q_{15} = \{L\overset{\Rightarrow}{A}R \to A \mid L, R \in V_g$ and $A \in V\}$

$Q_{16} = \{\overset{\Rightarrow}{A}\overleftarrow{B}R \to \overset{\Rightarrow}{B} \mid A, B \in V_T$ and $R \in V_g\}$

$Q_{17} = \{\overset{\Rightarrow}{A}\overleftarrow{B}R \to \overleftarrow{B} \mid A \in V, B \in V_N$ and $R \in V_g\}$

$Q_{18} = \{LAR \to A \mid L, R \in W_g, A \in W,$ and there is no $\gamma \in W^*$ such that $(LAR \to \gamma) \in \bigcup_{k=1}^{17} Q_k\}$

E) $Q = \bigcup_{k=1}^{18} Q_k$

F) $H = \langle W, \delta, g, S\rangle$, where δ is defined by Q.

H is a 2L system, since our construction is such that for each $LAR \in W_gWW_g$ there exists a $\gamma \in W^*$ such that $LAR \underset{Q}{\to} \gamma$.

From the construction it is straightforward to write out a detailed proof that $L(G) = A(H)$. (A full proof is given in Walker†).

It remains to be shown that if G is a CSG then H is propagating. Suppose G is a CSG. If Q contains a production of the form $LAR \to \lambda$, then by inspection this production is in $Q_1 \cup Q_4 \cup Q_7$. But then it follows from the construction that there is a

† Walker, A. D., Formal Grammars and the Stability of Biological Organisms, Ph.D. thesis, Department of Computer Science, State University of New York at Buffalo, 1974.

production $\alpha \underset{P}{\to} \beta$ for which $|\alpha| > |\beta|$, a contradiction. ■

In the next lemmas we shall use the following notation. If M is an LBA we denote the language accepted by M as $L(M)$, and if T is a TM we denote the language accepted by T as $L(T)$.

<u>Lemma 9</u> There exists an algorithm which takes as input any P2L system H and produces as output an LBA M such that $A(H) = L(M)$.

<u>Proof</u> Let $H = \langle V, \delta, g, S\rangle$ be a P2L system. Let M be an LBA constructed from H to operate as follows.

The tape of M has three tracks. If a string α is placed on the top track of the tape, M decides whether or not $\alpha \in L(M)$ in the following way.

(i) M tests whether or not $\delta(\alpha) = \alpha$. If so, M does (ii) below. If not, M rejects α and halts.

(ii) M writes S in the middle track and proceeds, nondeterministically, to see if $\alpha \in \delta^*(S)$, using the lower track as workspace. If M discovers that $\alpha \in \delta^*(S)$, then M accepts α and halts. If, in simulating a derivation $S = \alpha_0, \alpha_1, \ldots, \alpha_k$ where $\alpha_k \in \delta^k(S)$ M finds that $|\alpha_k| > |\alpha|$, M rejects α and halts.

From the above description it is a straightforward task to write down formally an algorithm which constructs M from H, and to show that $L(M) = A(H)$. ■

<u>Lemma 10</u> There exists an algorithm which takes as input any 2L system H and produces as output a Turing machine T such that $A(H) = L(T)$.

Proof is similar to that of Lemma 9, except that in step (ii) there is no limit on the length of an intermediate string α_k. Hence not every computation by T terminates. However, because of the way in which L(T) is defined for a Turing machine T, it is the case that A(H) = L(T). ■

We can now characterize the classes A(P2L) of adult languages of P2L systems and A(2L) of adult languages of 2L systems in terms of the classes L(CS) of context sensitive languages and L(RE) of recursively enumerable languages.

Theorem 3 A(P2L) = L(CS).

Proof That A(P2L) $\subset$ L(CS) follows from Lemma 9 and the fact that for each LBA M there is a CSG G such that L(M) = L(G); see e.g. H & U, Theorem 8.2. It is immediate from Lemma 8 that L(CS) $\subset$ A(P2L). ■

Theorem 4 A(2L) = L(RE).

Proof That A(2L) $\subset$ L(RE) follows from Lemma 10 and the fact that for each TM T there is a grammar G such that L(T) = L(G); see e.g. H & U, Theorem 7.4. It is immediate from Lemma 8 that L(RE) $\subset$ A(2L). ■

This completes our characterization of 2L systems. We note that while the propagating restriction made little difference for 0L systems, in the sense that A(0L) $=_{\lambda}$ A(P0L), it makes a fundamental difference for 2L systems, since A(P2L) $\subsetneq$ A(2L).

Conclusions

Theorems 1 - 4 give us a satisfactory analysis of L systems from the point of view of the adult languages they generate, for they establish direct correspondences with three of the four main classes of languages in the Chomsky hierarchy. The remaining class is that of the regular languages, and it is an easy exercise to restrict the form of the productions of a 0L system to ensure that its adult language is regular. In Walker† it is shown that the result for 2L systems can be extended to $<k, \ell>L$ systems (see Herman and Rozenberg [45] for the definition of such systems) with $k + \ell \geq 1$, and that the result for P2L systems can be extended to $P<k, \ell>L$ systems with $k, \ell \geq 1$.

From the point of view of formal language theory, we have given a new characterization, by totally parallel grammars, of each of the classes of languages in the Chomsky hierarchy. From the point of view of biological model building, we have gained access to many of the established results of formal language theory.

Acknowledgements

The author wishes to thank Professors G. T. Herman, A. Lindenmayer, and G. Rozenberg for their help and encouragement. This work is supported by NSF Grant GJ 998 and NATO Research Grant 574.

---

† Walker, A. D., Formal Grammars and the Stability of Biological Organisms, Ph.D. thesis, Department of Computer Science, State University of New York at Buffalo, 1974.

STRUCTURED OL-SYSTEMS

K. ČULÍK II

Department of Applied Analysis
and Computer Science
University of Waterloo
Waterloo, Ontario, Canada
and
Geselschaft für Mathematik und Datenverarbeitung Bonn

ABSTRACT A new type of Lindenmayer systems, called Structured OL-systems (SOL systems), is studied which gives a formal tool for investigation of structured organisms and structurally dependent developments. It is shown that a restricted version of SOL-systems is equivalent to codings (length-preserving homomorphisms) of OL-Languages. The properties of unrestricted SOL-systems are then studied. It is for example shown that the languages generated by them properly include the languages generated by extended table OL-Systems.

1. Introduction.

Lindenmayer systems have been the object of extensive study during recent years. The systems, also called developmental systems, were introduced in connection with a theory proposed to model the development of filamentous organisms. The stages of development are represented by strings of symbols correspondings to states of individual cells of an organism. The developmental instructions are modelled by grammar-like productions. These productions are applied simultaneously to all symbols to reflect the simultanity of the growth in the organism. This parallelism is the main difference between Lindenmayer systems and ordinary generative grammars. Another difference is that in most of the versions of Lindenmayer systems only one type of symbols (terminals) is considered which means that all the intermediate strings in a derivation are strings in the generated language. The simplest type of Lindenmayer systems are the OL-Systems [61] in which every symbols is rewritten independently of its neighbours.

When we compare OL-systems and the corresponding class of grammars, context-free grammars, we see that OL-systems are missing one important feature of context-free grammars, namely they are not structuring the generated strings. A derivation in a context-free grammar can be represented as a derivation-tree which describes the structure of a string with respect to this derivation. We can consider the analogous derivation tree for a derivation in an OL-system but in this case the branching nodes are labelled by terminal symbols rather than nonterminals (grammatical categories) and the tree does not reflect the possibly interesting structure of an organism.

In this paper we introduce <u>Structured OL systems</u> (SOL-systems) which not only allow to describe the structure of generated strings but also give a formal tool to study the cases when the development is structurally dependent. A simple example is the case when all the stages of a developing organism consist of certain fixed number of partes and there are different development rules for every part of the organism. From a mathematical point of view the SOL-systems give another interesting type of context-sensitivity in parallel rewriting (compare with |CO| †). A structured organism is represented in an SOL-system as a labelled tree. The labels of the leaves of the tree represent the individual cells of an organism, the labels of its branching nodes represent the structural "units" of the organism.

An SOL-system is given by a single starting structure and a finite number of developmental rules. At every stage of the development the rules are applied simultaneously to all cells and structural units (nonterminals) of an organism. According the rules each structural unit can change its state or disappear (but not divide) and every cell can be replaced by a substructure, i.e. it can divide into several parts each of which can be either a single cell or another structured part. At every step a cell can divide only into a limited number of subparts but there is generally no limit on the number of subparts of a structural unit which can be created during the

† |CO| : K. Čulik II and J. Opatrný, Context in parallel rewriting, in this volume.

development, i.e. there is generally no limit on the number of sons of a branching node.

Types of structural units will be represented by labels from an alphabet which corresponds to the nonterminals of a context-free grammar. We will define SOL-systems in such a way that rewriting of a nonterminal may depend on its father but not on its sons in a tree. We consider parallel rewriting; at every step of a derivation all labels in a tree must be simultaneously rewritten. The language generated by an SOL-system is the set of all frontiers of the generated trees.

We will consider a special subfamily of SOL-systems, called simple SOL-systems, in which essentially only labels on leaves (individual cells) are rewritten, i.e. in a simple SOL-system it is possible to create new structural units but once a unit is created it never changes its state. We will show that the languages generated by simple SOL-systems are exactly length preserving homomorphisms (coding) of OL-languages [10,20]. Then we will investigate the properties of the family generated by unrestricted SOL-systems (SOL). We will show that SOL is closed under Kleene operation $(\cup,.,*)$ and under ε-free homomorphism but not under intersection with a regular set.

The closure result will help us to establish the relations of SOL to other known families of languages. It is easy to show that SOL $\supseteq$ TOL [81] and then, using the closure results, that SOL $\supsetneq$ ETOL [89]. The fact that the later inclusion and therefore, of course, also the former is proper follows from the result that SOL is incomparable with the family of context-sensitive languages. Actually it will be shown that any recursively enumerable set over T with an end marker can be expressed as an intersection of an SOL language over an extended alphabet with the set of all the terminal strings with the endmarker.

2. Preliminaries.

We assume the knowledge of the basic notions and notation of formal language theory, see e.g. [HU^{+},1o2]. We start with a slightly modified, but equivalent, definition of extended table OL-systems [89], involving as special cases OL-systems [61] EOL-systems [35] and TOL-systems [81].

Definition: An extended table L-system without interaction (ETOL system) is a 4-tuple $G = (V,T,\mathcal{P},\sigma)$ where

(i) V is a finite nonempty set, the alphabet of G,

(ii) $T \subseteq V$, the terminal alphabet of G,

(iii) $\mathcal{P}$ is a finite set of tables. $\mathcal{P} = \{P_1,\ldots,P_n\}$ for some $n \geq 1$, where each $P_i \subseteq V \times V^*$. Element (u,v) of P_i, $1 \leq i \leq n$, is called a production and is usually written in the form $u \to v$. Every P_i, $1 \leq i \leq n$, satisfies the following (completness) condition: For each $a \in V$ there is $w \in V^*$ so that $(a,w) \in P_i$,

(iv) $\sigma \in V^+$, the axiom of G.

Definition: An ETOL-system $G = (V,T,\mathcal{P},\sigma)$ is called

(i) a TOL-system if $V = T$;

(ii) an EOL-system if $\mathcal{P} = \{P_1\}$;

(iii) an OL-system if $V = T$ and $\mathcal{P} = \{P_1\}$.

Definition: Given an ETOL-system $G = (V,T,P,\sigma)$ we write $x \underset{G}{\Longrightarrow} y$ if there exist $a_1,\ldots,a_k \in V$ and $y_1,\ldots,y_k \in V^*$ so that, $x = a_1\ldots a_k$, $y = y_1\ldots y_k$ and for some $P_i \in \mathcal{P}$, $a_j \to y_j \in P_i$, $j = 1,\ldots,k$.

The transitive and reflexive closure of binary relation $\underset{G}{\Longrightarrow}$ is denoted by $\underset{G}{\Longrightarrow}^*$.

Definition: Let $G = (V,T,\mathcal{P},\sigma)$ be an ETOL system. The language generated by G is denoted by $L(G)$ and defined as $L(G) = \{w \in T^* : \sigma \underset{G}{\Longrightarrow}^* w\}$.

Notation: A language generated by an XYZ system, for any type XYZ will be called an XYZ-language. The family of all the XYZ languages is denoted by XYZ.

---

† |HU|: J.E. Hopcroft and J.D. Ullman: Formal Languages and their Relation to Automata, Addison-Wesley, 1969.

Before we can define SOL-systems we need to introduce a notation for labelled trees (forests). We will recursively define labelled rooted ordered forests and expressions denoting them. We are not interested in names of particular nodes in a forest, i.e. we actually consider the equivalence classes of isomorphic forests. We consider forests with labels of leaves from one alphabet and labels of branch nodes (nonleaves) from another distinct alphabet.

Definition: Let T,N be two alphabets, $T \cap N = \emptyset$, and let $[\ ,\ ]$ and λ be reserved symbols not in $T \cup N$.

(i) λ is a forest expression and denotes the empty tree (forest), i.e. the tree with no nodes.

(ii) For $a \in T$, a is a forest expression and denotes the tree with a single node (root) labelled by a.

(iii) If e_1, e_2 are forest expressions denoting nonempty forests α, β consisting from trees $\alpha_1, \ldots, \alpha_m$ and $\beta_1, \ldots, \beta_n$, respectively, then $e_1 e_2$ is a forest expression and denotes the forest consisting from trees $\alpha_1, \ldots, \alpha_m, \beta_1, \ldots, \beta_n$.

(iv) If $A \in N$ and e is a forest expression denoting nonempty forest α consisting of trees $\alpha_1, \ldots, \alpha_n$ then $A[e]$ is a forest expression and denotes the tree with the root labelled by A and the sons of the root, from left to right, the the roots of subtrees $\alpha_1, \ldots, \alpha_n$.

Notation. The set of all the forest expressions (forests) over alphabets N (labels of branch nodes) and T (labels of leaves) is denoted by $(N,T)_*$. Let $(N,T)_+ = (N,T)_* - \{\lambda\}$. In the following the elements of $(N,T)_*$ will be called structures (over N,T) and we will not distinguish between an expression and the forests denoted by it.

Notation. Let a be a particular occurence of symbol a in forest expression α. The label at the father of the node labelled by the considered occurence of a will be denoted by $\mathrm{Father}_\alpha(a)$. This notation will be used in such a way that there will be no confusion of which occurence of a is being considered.

Notation. Mapping Y (yield) maps λ to empty string (denoted by ε) and a forest in $(N,T)_+$ to the string of the labels of its leaves (from left to right).

3. Structered OL Systems.

Now we are ready to define formally structred OL systems.

Definition: A structured OL-schema (SOL-system) is a tuple $G = (N,T,P,\sigma)$ where

N is an alphabet of nonterminals (states of structural parts),

T is an alphabet of terminals,

P is a finite set of productions from $(N\cup(N\times N)) \times (N\cup\{\lambda\})\cup(T\cup(N\times T)) \times (N,T)_*$,

$\sigma \in (N,T)_+$, the initial structure.

The productions of an SOL-schema will be written in the following form (all possible types are given). $A \to C$, $A\cdot B \to C$, $a \to \alpha$ and $A\cdot a \to \alpha$ where $A,B \in N$, $C \in N\cup\{\lambda\}$, $a \in T$, $\alpha \in (N,T)_*$ and "$\to$", "$\cdot$" are special reserved delimiters.

Definition: We write $\alpha \Longrightarrow \beta$ for $\alpha \in (N,T)_+$ $\beta \in (N,T)_*$ where $\alpha = x_1\, x_2 \ldots x_n$ for $x_i \in N\cup T\cup\{[,]\}$, $1 \le i \le n$, if there exists $\beta' = w_1 w_2 \ldots w_n$ so that for $1 \le i \le n$:

(i) if $x_i \in \{|,|\}$ then $w_i = x_i$;

(ii) if $x_i \in T\cup N$ then either $x_i \to w_i \in P$ or $A\cdot x_i \to w_i \in P$ where $A_i = \text{father}_\alpha(x_i)$;

(iii) β is obtained from β' by repeated replacing of each subexpression of the form $X\lambda Y, \lambda[Z]$ or $A[\lambda]$ by XY, Z or λ, respectively, until either $\beta = \lambda$ or there is no occurence of λ in β.

Let $\Longrightarrow^*$ be the transitive and reflexive closure of relation $\Longrightarrow$.

Definition: The set of structures generated by G is denoted $T(G)$ and defined to be the set $T(G) = \{\alpha : \sigma \Longrightarrow^* \alpha\}$.

The language generated by G, denoted by $L(G)$, is the set of the yields of all the structures generated by G. Formally $L(G) = \{Y(\alpha) : \alpha \in T(G)\}$.

Definition: A structured OL-schema G is called a structured OL-system (SOL-system) if it satisfies the condition of completness: For every $\alpha \in T(G)$ there exists β such that $\alpha \underset{G}{\Longrightarrow} \beta$.

Our definition of completness requires that for every structure which can be developed from the starting structure there is a "next step" in development. After some definitions and auxiliary results it will be shown that the choice of a more restrictive definition of completness (strong completeness) requiring existence of a "next step" for every structure in $(N,T)_+$ does not change the families of sets of structures or languages generated by SOL-systems.

<u>Definition</u>: An SOL-system $G = (N,T,P,\sigma)$ is called <u>full</u> if

$P \subseteq \{S \to S\} \cup ((N\times\bar{N}) \times (\bar{N} \cup \{\lambda\})) \cup ((N\times T) \times (\bar{N},T)_*)$,

where $\bar{N} = N - \{S\}$, S being the root of σ, i.e. the father-context appears on the left side of every production with the exemption of the production which keeps unchanged the (reserved) label of the root.

<u>Definition</u>: SOL-systems G_1 and G_2 are called <u>equivalent</u> if $L(G_1) = L(G_2)$.

<u>Lemma 1</u>: For every SOL-system there exists an equivalent full SOL-system.

Proof. Given an SOL-system $G = (N,T,P,\sigma)$ we construct a full SOL-system $G' = (N',T,P',\sigma')$ where $N' = N \cup \{S\}$ for a new symbol S not in $N \cup T$, $\sigma' = S[\sigma]$, and $P' = \{A\cdot X\to w : A\cdot X\to w \in P\} \cup \{A\cdot X\to w : X\to w \in P$ and $A \in N'\} \cup \{S\to S\}$.

Clearly, $L(G') = L(G)$.

<u>Definition</u>: An SOL-system $G = (N,T,P,\sigma)$ is called <u>strongly complete</u> if for every $\alpha \in (N,T)_+$ there exists β such that $\alpha \underset{G}{\Longrightarrow} \beta$.

<u>Theorem 1</u>: For every SOL-system G there exists an equivalent strongly complete SOL system.

Proof. By Lemma 1 we may assume that $G = (N,T,P,\sigma)$ is full. We construct the SOL-system $G' = (N,T,P',\sigma)$ where $P' = P \cup \{A\cdot X\to X : A \in N, X \in N \cup T$ and there is no production of the form $A\cdot X\to W$ in P$\}$.

Clearly, G' is full and $L(G') = L(G)$.

Now we will study a special case of SOL-system, called simple SOL-system (SSOL-systems), in which essentially only terminal symbols are rewritten at every step of a derivation. We will show this subclass of SOL-systems generates exactly the same family of languages as several other types of systems known already to be equivalent, namely FMOL systems [9], EOL systems [35], and length preserving homomorphisms of OL languages [10,20]. This does not mean SSOL-systems are without interest, on the contrary they give an alternative mechanism for the description of languages from a very natural class with the advantage to exhibit explicitly the structure of generated objects. They also contribute another evidence to our opinion that the family of the length-preserving homomorphisms of OL-languages is a very natural class of languages.

Definition: AN SOL-system $G = (N,T,P,\sigma)$ is called simple (SSOL) if $P = \{A \to A : A \in N\} \cup P'$ where $P' \subseteq (N \times T \cup T) \times (N,T)_*$.

In the following we omit the "identity productions" of form $A \to A$ whenever an SSOL-system is exhibited.

Notation. Let COL = $\{h(L) : L \in OL$, h is a length-preserving homomorphism$\}$.

Lemma 2: COL $\subseteq$ SSOL.

Proof. Let $G = (\Sigma,P,\sigma)$ be an OL-system and h be a homomorphism from Σ^* to T^*. Clearly, we can assume withnout loss of generality that $\Sigma \cap T = \emptyset$.

Construct SSOL system $G' = (\Sigma \cup \{S\},T,P',\sigma')$ where

(i) S is a new symbol not in $\Sigma \cup T$.

(ii) Let $\sigma = a_1 \ldots a_n$, $a_i \in \Sigma$ for $i = 1,2,\ldots n$. Then $\sigma' = S[a_1[h(a_1)]a_2[h(a_2)] \;\ldots\; a_n[h(a_n)]]$.

(iii) $P' = \{a \cdot h(a) \to b_1[h(b_1)]b_2[h(b_2)] \;\ldots\; b_k[h(b_k)] :$ $: a,b_1,b_2,\ldots,b_k \in \Sigma$ and $a \to b_1 b_2 \ldots b_k \in P\}$.

Clearly, $h(L(G')) = L(G)$.

Lemma 3: SSOL $\subseteq$ COL.

Proof. Let $G = (N,T,P,\sigma)$ be an SSOL-system. By modification of Lemma 1 we can clearly assume that $P \subseteq (N \times T) \times (N,T)_*$ with "identity" productions omitted. Let $\Sigma = N \times T$ and let g be the mapping from $(N,T)_*$ into Σ^* which maps a structure $\alpha \in (N,T)_*$ to the string $(A_1,a_1) \ldots (A_n,a_n)$ such that $a_1 \ldots a_n = Y(\alpha)$ and $A_i = \text{father}_\alpha(a_i)$ for $1 \leq i \leq n$. In particular $g(\lambda) = \varepsilon$. We construct OL system $G' = (\Sigma,P',\sigma')$ where $\sigma' = g(\sigma)$ and $P' = \{(A,a) \to g(A|\beta|) : A \in N, a \in T$ and $A \cdot a \to \beta \in P\}$.

Note that if forest β does not include a tree consisting from a single node only, then $g(A|\beta|) = g(\beta)$. Let h be the homomorphism from Σ^* to T^* defined by $h((A,a)) = a$ for every $(A,a) \in \Sigma$.

It is easy to verify that $h(L(G')) = L(G)$.

Theorem 2: SSOL = COL = EOL = FMOL.

Proof. By Lemma 2 and 3 we have the first equation; the definitions of FMOL languages and other results are in [9,20]

4. Closure Properties of SOL.

To show the relation of SOL to other known families of languages we will need some closure results which will be shown first. The most interesting is the closure of SOL under ε-free homomorphisms which in particular means that codings (length-preserving homomorphisms) do not increase the descriptive power of SOL-systems.

Theorem 3: Family SOL is closed under ε-free homomorphisms.

Proof. Given an SOL language L over T and a homomorphism h from T^* to Σ^* we may assume by Lemma 1 that L is generated by full SOL system $G = (N,T,P,\sigma)$ and we construct SOL-system $G' = (N',\Sigma,P'\sigma')$ as follows.

Let $N' = N \cup T \cup (N\times T) \cup \{\bar{A} : A \in N\} \cup \{Q\}$ where Q is a new symbol not in $N \cup T$. Let f be the homomorphism from $(N,T)_*$ into $(N',\Sigma)_*$ defined as follows. The forest expression $f(\alpha)$ is obtained from expression α by replacing every terminal symbol from T, say a, by subexpression $a[a_1 Q[a_2] Q[a_3] \ldots Q[a_n]]$ where $h(a) = a_1 a_2 \ldots a_n$.

Let $\sigma' = f(\sigma)$ and productions P' be constructed as follows:

(i) $A \rightarrow \bar{A}$ is in P' for every A in N.

(ii) $A \cdot a \rightarrow (A,a)$ is in P' for all A in N and a in T.

(iii) $a \cdot t \rightarrow t$ is in P' for all a in T and t in Σ.

(iv) $\bar{S} \rightarrow S$ is in P'.

(v) If $A \cdot B \rightarrow X$ is in P then $\bar{A} \cdot \bar{B} \rightarrow X$ is in P' for all A,B in N and X in $N \cup \{\lambda\}$.

(vi) If $A \cdot a \rightarrow \alpha$ is in P and $h(a) = a_1 a_2 \ldots a_n$ then $(A,a) \cdot a_1 \rightarrow f(\alpha)$ is in P' for all A in N and a in T.

(vii) $(A,a) \rightarrow \lambda$ is in P' for all A in N and a in T.

(viii) $Q \rightarrow \lambda$ is in P'.

(ix) $Q \cdot t \rightarrow \lambda$ for every t in Σ.

Clearly, in any derivation in G' the productions (i)-(iii) and the productions (iv)-(ix) can be used only in alternative steps, namely, the former in odd steps and later in even steps of any derivation. Realizing this it is straigthforward to verify that $L(G') = h(L(G))$.

Theorem 4: The family SOL is closed under union, concatenation and star.

Proof. Let $G_1 = (N_1,T_1,P_1,\sigma_1)$ and $G_2 = (N_2,T_2,P_2,\sigma_2)$ be SOL-systems. Assume that $N_1 \cap N_2 = \emptyset$.

To show the closure under union we construct an SOL-system $(N_3, T_1 \cup T_2, P_3, \sigma_3)$ as follows. Let $N_3 = N_1 \cup N_2 \cup \{S,Q\}$ with S and Q new symbols not in $N_1 \cup N_2 \cup T_1 \cup T_2$. Assume $Y(\sigma_1) = a_1 \dots a_n$. Let $\sigma_3 = S[a_1 Q[a_2 \dots a_n]]$ and $P_3 = P_1 \cup P_2 \cup \{S \cdot a_1 \to \sigma_1, S \cdot a_1 \to \sigma_2, Q \cdot a_i \to \lambda$ for $i = 2,\dots,n\}$.

Clearly, $L(G_3) = L(G_1) \cup L(G_2)$.

To show the closure under concatenation we construct SOL-system $(N_4, T_1 \cup T_2, P_4, \sigma_4)$ as follows. $N_4 = N_1 \cup N_2 \cup \{S,A,B,C,D,E,F,H,Q\}$ where $S,A,\dots,Q$ are new symbols. Assume $Y(\sigma_1) = a_1 \dots a_n$ and $Y(\sigma_2) = b_1 \dots b_m$. Let $\sigma_4 = S[A[C[a_1]E[a_2 \dots a_n]]A[D[b_1]E[b_2 \dots b_m]]]$ and $P_4 = P_1 \cup P_2 \cup P_4'$ where P_4' consists of the following productions:

(I)		(II)	
	$A \to A$		$A \to B$
	$A \cdot C \to C$		$B \cdot C \to F$
	$A \cdot D \to D$		$B \cdot D \to H$
	$A \cdot E \to E$		$B \cdot E \to Q$
	$C \cdot a_1 \to a_1$		$F \cdot a_1 \to \sigma_1$
	$D \cdot b_1 \to b_1$		$Q \cdot a_i \to \lambda$ for $i=2,\dots,n$
	$E \cdot a_i \to a_i$ for $i=2,\dots,n$		$H \cdot b_1 \to \sigma_2$
	$E \cdot b_i \to b_i$ for $i=2,\dots,n$		$Q \cdot b_i \to \lambda$ for $i=2,\dots,m$.

Productions of group (I) allow to delay the start of the generation of strings in $L(G_1)$ or $L(G_2)$ to assure that even by parallel generation all strings in $L(G_1) \cdot L(G_2)$ are obtained. Once the production $A \to B$ is used the productions of group (II) assure the start of generation from σ_1 by productions P_1 or from σ_2 by productions P_2. It is straightforward to verify that $L(G_4) = L(G_1) \cdot L(G_2)$.

Finaly, to show the closure of SOL under star we construct SOL-system $(N_5, T_1, P_5, \sigma_5)$ as follows. Let $N_5 = N_1 \cup \{S,A,B,C,D,E\}$ where S,A,B,C,D,E are new symbols not in $N_1 \cup T_1$. Assume $\sigma_1 = a_1 a_2 \dots a_n$. Let $\sigma_5 = S[a_1 Q[a_2 a_3 \dots a_n]]$ and $\alpha = A[C[a_1]D[a_2 a_3 \dots a_n]]$. Let $P_5 = P_1 \cup P'$ where P' consists of the following productions:

$S \to S$	$A \cdot C \to C$
$S \cdot a_1 \to \alpha\sigma_5$	$A \cdot D \to D$
$S \cdot a_1 \to \lambda$	$B \cdot C \to E$
$Q \to \lambda$	$B \cdot D \to Q$
$Q \cdot a_i \to \lambda$ for $2 \leq i \leq n$	$C \cdot a_1 \to a_1$
$A \to A$	$D \cdot a_i \to a_i$ for $2 \leq i \leq n$
$A \to B$	$E \cdot a_1 \to \sigma_1$

It is straigthforward to verify that G_5 generates only strings in $L(G_1)^*$. To see that all such strings are generated we observe that $S \overset{*}{\underset{G_5}{\Longrightarrow}} S[\alpha S[\alpha S[\alpha \ldots S[\alpha]]\ldots]]$ and that $\alpha \Longrightarrow^k \alpha \Longrightarrow B[C[a_1]D[a_2a_3\ldots a_n]] \Longrightarrow B[E[a_1]Q[a_2a_3\ldots a_n]] \Longrightarrow B[E[\sigma_1]] \overset{*}{\Longrightarrow} B[E[\beta]]$ for all $k \geq 0$ and β in $T(G_1)$. Therefore for any $m \geq 1$ and $\beta_1,\ldots,\beta_m$ in $T(G_1)$ we have $\alpha \Longrightarrow^{k_i} \alpha \Longrightarrow^* B[E[\beta_i]]$ for $1 \leq i \leq m$ and by suitable choice of k_i, $1 \leq i \leq m$, we can "synchronized" derivation $S \Longrightarrow^* S[B[E[\beta_1]]\ S[B[E[\beta_2]]\ \ldots$
$\ldots\ S[B[E[\beta_m]]]]\ldots]]$.
Since $\sigma_5 \Longrightarrow \lambda$ also $\varepsilon \in L(G_5)$.

5. Relation of SOL to other Families of Languages.

First we show that SOL-systems can simulate TOL-systems and then using the closure of SOL under ε-free homomorphisms this result will be generalized to ETOL-systems. It is easy to see that these results can be further generalized to (E)TOL-systems with some restrictions on the sequences of productions which may be used in a derivation.

Lemma 4: TOL $\subseteq$ SOL.

Proof. Given TOL system $G = (T,\{P_1,\ldots,P_n\},\sigma)$ we construct SOL-system $G' = (T,N,P,\sigma')$ where $N = \{0,1,\ldots,n\}$, $\sigma' = 0[\sigma]$ and $P = \{i\cdot a\to w : a\to w \in P_i\} \cup \cup \{i\to j : i \in N,\ j \in N - \{0\}\} \cup \{0\cdot a\to a : a \in T\}$.

Clearly, $L(G') = L(G)$ and therefore TOL $\subseteq$ SOL.

The following lemma shows that in certain restricted manner every recursively enumerable set can be represented by an SOL-system.

Lemma 5: Let L be a recursively enumerable set over Σ and let $\$,\#$ be not in Σ. There exists an SOL language $L' \subseteq (\Sigma \cup \{\$\})^*\{\#\}$ such that $L\{\#\} = L' \cap \Sigma^*\{\#\}$.

Proof. It follows from results in [G,H,P][†], see for example Lemma 1 in [P][†] that L can be generated by a phrase-structure grammar $G = (N,T,P,S)$ with productions only of the form $A \to B$, $A \to BC$, $AB \to AC$, $A \to a$ or $A \to \varepsilon$ for $A,B,C \in N$ and $a \in T$, i.e. there are only context-free or "left-context-sensitive" productions in P. We can then construct SOL system $G' = (N',T',P',\sigma)$ where $T' = T \cup \{\$,\#\}$, $N' = N \cup N^2 \cup \{\bar{A} : A \in N\} \cup \{Q\}$ for Q not in $N \cup T \cup \{\$,\#\}$, $\sigma = S[\$ \#]$ and P' is defined as follows.

(i) For all A,B,C in N and a in $T \cup \{\$\}$ the following productions are in P'.

$A \cdot B \to B$	$(A,B) \cdot a \to \$$
$(A,B) \cdot C \to (B,C)$	$Q \to \lambda$
$(A,B) \cdot (C,D) \to (B,C)$	$Q \cdot a \to \lambda$
$A \cdot (B \cdot C) \to B$	$A \cdot \# \to \#$
$A \cdot \bar{B} \to B$	$\bar{A} \cdot \# \to \$\#$
$(A,B) \cdot \bar{C} \to (B,C)$	$(A,B) \cdot \# \to \bar{B}[\#]$
$A \cdot a \to \$$	

(ii) If $A \to a$, $B \to b$ are in P and d is in $T \cup \{\$\}$ then the following productions are in P'.

$A \cdot d \to a$

$(A,B) \cdot d \to a\, Q|b|$

$\bar{A} \cdot \# \to a\#$.

(iii) If $A \to \varepsilon$ is in P then $D \cdot A \to Q$ is in P' for every D in N.

If $A \to B$ is in P then $D \cdot A \to B$ is in P' for every D in N.

If $A \to BC$ is in P then $D \cdot A \to (B,C)$ is in P' for every D in N.

If $AB \to AC$ is in P then $A \cdot B \to C$ is in P'.

Let h be the homomorphism from $(N \cup N^2 \cup \{\bar{A} : A \in N\})^*$ into N^* defined by $h(A) = h(\bar{A}) = A$ for every A in N and $h(A,B) = AB$ for all A,B in N. It can be verified (by induction on the length of a derivation) that if $\sigma \overset{*}{\underset{G'}{\Longrightarrow}} \alpha$ then α must be of the

† |G|: A.V. Gladkij, Formal grammars and languages (in Russian) Mir, Moscow, 1973

|H|: L.H. Haines, A representation for context sensitive languages, Transaction of the Amer. Math. Society, to appear.

|P|: M. Penttonen, LCS = CS, to appear in Information and Control.

form $X_1[t_1X_2[t_2X_3[\ldots X_{k-1}[t_{k-1}X_k[t_k\#]]\ldots]]]$ where t_i is in $T\cup\{\$\}$ for $i = 1,\ldots,k$, X_i is in $N\cup N^2$ for $i = 1,\ldots,k-1$ and X_k is in $N\cup N^2\cup\{\bar{A} : A\in N\}$ and $h(X_1X_2\ldots X_k)$ is in L(G). Moreover, if $t_1t_2\ldots t_k$ is in T^* then also $t_1t_2\ldots t_k$ is in L(G). Thus $L(G')\subseteq L(G)\cap T^*\{\#\}$.

To show the reverse inclusion we observe that every string x in L(G) can be generated by a derivation $S \Longrightarrow^* w \Longrightarrow^* x$ such that $w\in N^*$ and we do not use the productions of the form $A\to a$ in the derivation $S\Longrightarrow^* w$ and on the other hand we use only such productions in $w\Longrightarrow^* x$. Further we can see that

(i) If $A_1A_2\ldots A_n \underset{G}{\Longrightarrow} B_1B_2\ldots B_m$ for A_i in N for $1\le i\le n$ and B_j in N for $1\le j\le m$ then there exist $t_1,\ldots,t_n$, $s_1,\ldots,s_m$ in $T\cup\{\$\}$ such that
$A_1[t_1A_2[t_2\ A_3[\ldots A_{n-1}[t_{n-1}\ A_n[t_n\#]]\ldots]]] \underset{G'}{\Longrightarrow}^* B_1[s_1B_2[s_2\ B_3[\ldots$
$\ldots\ B_{m-1}[s_{m-1}B_m[s_m\#]]\ldots]]]$.

(ii) If $A_i\to a_i\in P$ for $1\le i\le k$ then
$A_1[t_1A_2[t_2\ldots A_{k-1}[t_{k-1}A_k[t_k\#]]\ldots]] \underset{G'}{\Longrightarrow} A_1[a_1A_2[a_2\ldots A_{k-1}[a_{k-1}A_k[a_k\#]]\ldots]]$.

Therefore every derivation in G can be simulated by a derivation in G' and $L(G)\cap T^*\{\#\}\subseteq L(G')$.

<u>Theorem 5</u>. Family SOL is incomparable with the family of context sensitive languages (CSL).

Proof. Every SOL languages is clearly exponencially dense in the terminilogy of [CO]†, i.e. for every SOL language L there exist constants p,q such that for every string u in L of length n, $n\ge p$ there is string v in L of length m so that $\frac{n}{q}\le m < n$. There are context-sensitive languages not satisfying this property, e.g. the language $\{a^{2^{2^n}} : n\ge 0\}$ therefore CSL $\nsubseteq$ SOL.

CSL is closed under intersection with a regular set therefore for every context-sensitive language L' the language $L'\cap\Sigma^*\{\#\}$ is again context sensitive. Thus the assumption SOL $\subseteq$ CSL is in contradiction with Lemma 5.

Corollary: Family SOL is not closed under intersection with a regular set.

Proof. By Lemma 5 and Theorem 5.

<u>Theorem 6</u>. ETOL $\subsetneq$ SOL $\cup$ $\{\{\varepsilon\}\}$.

---

† |CO| K. Culik II and J. Opatrny, Context in parallel rewriting, in this volume.

Proof. In [27] it is shown that ETOL $-\{\{\varepsilon\}\}$ is equal to the closure of TOL under length-preserving homomorphisms (codings). Therefore it follows by Lemma 4 and Theorem 3 that ETOL $\subseteq$ SOL $\cup \{\{\varepsilon\}\}$. In [7] it is shown that ETOL is included in the family of indexed languages [A]†. Thus our inclusion is proper by Theorem 5.

From Lemma 4 and results in [CO]* it follows that SOL is included neither in the family of languages generated by L-systems with interaction [88] nor in the family of predictive context languages [CO]*. We conjecture that both these families are incomparable with SOL.

---

† |A|: A.V. Aho, Indexed grammars - an extention of context-free grammars, JACM 15, (1968), 647 - 671.

* |CO| K. Čulik II and J. Opatrný, Context in parallel rewriting, in this volume.

CONTEXT IN PARALLEL REWRITING*

K. Čulik II and J. Opatrný
Department of Applied Analysis and Computer Science
University of Waterloo
Waterloo, Ontario, Canada

Abstract

Three new types of context sensitive parallel rewriting systems, called global context L-systems, rule context L-systems and predictive context L-systems are introduced in this paper. We investigate the generative power of these new types of context sensitive parallel rewriting systems and we compare it to the generative power of TOL-systems [81], L-systems with interaction [92], regular grammars and context sensitive grammars.

1. Introduction

Parallel rewriting systems were introduced in [59, 60] as a mathematical model for biological developmental systems. Most of the papers related to parallel rewriting have dealt with rewriting systems of context free type, e.g. OL-systems [61], TOL-systems [81], and their generalisations [9], [89].

A generalisation of context sensitive grammars with parallel rewriting known as L-systems with interactions has been studied in [92]. L-systems with interactions have the same basic rules (productions) for rewriting as OL-systems, but with restriction on their use given by right and left "context". A rule may be applied only in the given context.

However, in the case of parallel rewriting it is quite natural to consider different forms of "context". Since we are replacing all symbols at once, we may restrict the use of a rule, $a \to \alpha$ say, by the context adjacent to α after simultaneously replacing all the symbols in a string rather than by the context adjacent to a before the rule was applied. We will call this kind of context, predictive context.

Even more generally, the restriction on the use of a rule may concern rules used on adjacent symbols. We will call this type of restriction rule context.

Clearly, all these generalisations make sense only in the case of parallel rewriting.

We can also consider restrictions on the use of rules, which in distinction to the above are of a global rather than a local character. In a global

* The research was supported by the National Research Council of Canada, Grant No. A7403.

context L-system, in addition to the set of labeled rules, a control set over their labels is given. We can only rewrite a string with a sequence of rules with labels from the control set.

The new types of context sensitive L-systems introduced in this paper also have a natural biological motivation. The development of a cell might be completely independent of the other cells, i.e. in OL-systems, or it might depend on the configuration around the cell before the development takes place i.e. in L-systems with interactions, or it might be restricted in such a way that only compatible cells can occur adjacently, i.e. in predictive context L-systems, or only compatible developments can occur adjacently, i.e. in rule-context L-systems, or even the development of an organism as a whole is restricted by certain patterns, e.g. the development can be different in certain parts of the organisms, i.e. in global context L-systems.

In this paper we investigate the generative power of these new types of L-systems. Among other results it is shown that global context L-systems with regular control sets (regular global context L-systems) are equivalent to rule context L-systems. We also show that the family of regular global context L-languages properly contains the family of languages generated by L-systems with interactions and the family of TOL-languages.

2. Preliminaries

We shall assume that the reader is familiar with the basic formal languages theory, e.g. [102].

Now, we will review the definitions of OL and TOL-systems [91], [81], and L-systems with interactions [92], and we will introduce some notation used throughout the paper.

Definition 1. A table OL-system (TOL-system) is a 3-tuple $G = (\Sigma, P, \sigma)$, where:

(i) Σ is a finite, nonempty set, called the alphabet.

(ii) P is a finite set of tables, $P = \{P_1, P_2, \ldots, P_n\}$ for some $n \geq 1$, where each P_i, $i = 1,2,\ldots,n$ is a finite subset of $\Sigma \times \Sigma^*$. Element (a,α) of P_i, $1 \leq i \leq n$, is called a rule and is usually written in the form $a \to \alpha$. P must satisfy the following condition of completeness. For each $a \in \Sigma$ and i, $1 \leq i \leq n$, there exists $\alpha \in \Sigma^*$ so that $(a,\alpha) \in P_i$.

(iii) $\sigma \in \Sigma^+$, the initial string of G.

Given a TOL-system $G = (\Sigma, P, \sigma)$, we write $\alpha \underset{G}{\Rightarrow} \beta$, where $\alpha \in \Sigma^+$, $\beta \in \Sigma^*$, if there exist $k \geq 1$, $a_1, a_2, \ldots, a_k \in \Sigma$, and $\beta_1, \beta_2, \ldots, \beta_k \in \Sigma^*$ so that $\alpha = a_1 a_2 \ldots a_k$, $\beta = \beta_1 \beta_2 \ldots \beta_k$ and for some table $P_i \in P$, $a_j \to \beta_j \in P_i$ for $1 \leq j \leq k$.

The transitive and reflexive closure of the binary relation $\underset{G}{\Rightarrow}$ is denoted by $\underset{G}{\Rightarrow}^*$.

The language generated by a TOL-system G is denoted by L(G) and is defined to be the set $\{\alpha \in \Sigma^*: \sigma \underset{G}{\Rightarrow}^* \alpha\}$.

Definition 2. A TOL-system $G = (\Sigma, P, \sigma)$ is called an OL-system if P consists of exactly one table of rules, i.e. $P = \{P_1\}$.

Notation. Throughout the paper if r is any binary relation, then r^* denotes the reflexive and transitive closure of r, without repeating it specifically in every case.

Notation. The empty string is denoted by ε. The length of a string α is denoted by $|\alpha|$. For any string α and $k \geq 1$, we define $\mathrm{First}_k(\alpha)$ and $\mathrm{Last}_k(\alpha)$ as follows.

$$\mathrm{First}_k(\alpha) = \underline{\text{if}}\ |\alpha| \geq k\ \underline{\text{then}}\ \text{first } k \text{ symbols of } \alpha\ \underline{\text{else}}\ \alpha.$$

$$\mathrm{Last}_k(\alpha) = \underline{\text{if}}\ |\alpha| \geq k\ \underline{\text{then}}\ \text{last } k \text{ symbols of } \alpha\ \underline{\text{else}}\ \alpha.$$

For any string α, we define

$$\mathrm{First}_0(\alpha) = \varepsilon,\ \mathrm{First}(\alpha) = \bigcup_{k=1}^{|\alpha|} \{\mathrm{First}_k(\alpha)\},$$

$$\mathrm{Last}_0(\alpha) = \varepsilon,\ \mathrm{Last}(\alpha) = \bigcup_{k=1}^{|\alpha|} \{\mathrm{Last}_k(\alpha)\}.$$

Definition 3. A context L-system is a 3-tuple $G = (\Sigma, P, \sigma)$, where

(i) Σ is a finite, nonempty set of symbols, called the alphabet.

(ii) P is a finite subset of $\{\#,\varepsilon\}\cdot\Sigma^* \times \Sigma \times \Sigma^*\cdot\{\#,\varepsilon\} \times \Sigma^*$, called the set of rules, where # is a symbol not in Σ called the endmarker. A rule $(\alpha, a, \beta, \gamma) \in P$ is usually written as $\langle\alpha, a, \beta\rangle \rightarrow \gamma$.

(iii) $\sigma \in \Sigma^+$, the initial string.

Given a context L-system $G = (\Sigma, P, \sigma)$ we write $\alpha \underset{G}{\Rightarrow} \beta$ for $\alpha \in \Sigma^+$, $\beta \in \Sigma^*$, if there exist $k \geq 0$, $a_1, a_2, \ldots, a_k \in \Sigma$ and $\beta_1, \beta_2, \ldots, \beta_k \in \Sigma^*$ so that $\alpha = a_1 a_2 \ldots a_k$, $\beta = \beta_1 \beta_2 \ldots \beta_k$ and for every i, $1 \leq i \leq k$, there exist $m, n \geq 0$ such that $(\mathrm{Last}_m(\# a_1 a_2 \ldots a_{i-1}), a_i, \mathrm{First}_n(a_{i+1} a_{i+2} \ldots a_k \#), \beta_i) \in P$.

Context L-system G must be strongly complete, i.e. for any $\alpha \in \Sigma^+$ there exists $\beta \in \Sigma^*$ such that $\alpha \underset{G}{\Rightarrow} \beta$.

The language generated by a context L-system G is denoted by L(G) and is defined to be the set $\{\alpha \in \Sigma^*: \sigma \underset{G}{\Rightarrow}^* \alpha\}$.

Note. The definition of a context L-system given above is a simplification and an unessential generalisation of the definition of an L-system with interaction from [92]. It is obvious that both types of systems have the same generative power.

Notation. We say that a language L is a λ-language (where λ may be OL, TOL, context L, etc.) if there exists a λ-system G such that $L = L(G)$.

The family of context L-languages will be denoted by Ω.

If f is a mapping from Σ to subsets of Δ^*, then f can be extended to strings and languages over Σ as follows.

(i) $f(\varepsilon) = \{\varepsilon\}$.

(ii) for $a \in \Sigma$, $\alpha \in \Sigma^*$, $f(\alpha a) = f(\alpha)\cdot f(a)$, where "$\cdot$" is the operation of set concatenation.

(iii) for $L \subseteq \Sigma^*$, $f(L) = \{\alpha : \alpha \in f(\beta) \text{ for } \beta \in L\}$.

We will use these extended mappings later on without repeating the process of extension in every single case.

3. Context sensitive parallel rewriting systems

Now, we will define three different types of context sensitive parallel rewriting systems. All of them are using only one type of symbols, i.e. we are not considering any nonterminals.

First we will give the definition of global context L-systems. A global context L-system has, similarly as an OL-system, a finite set of context free rules, however, each rule has a finite number of labels. The use of rules in a global context L-system is restricted by a language over labels, called the control set.

Definition 4. A global context L-system is a 5-tuple $G = (\Sigma,\Gamma,P,C,\sigma)$, where:

(i) Σ is a finite, nonempty set of symbols, called the alphabet.

(ii) Γ is a finite, nonempty set of symbols, called the labels.

(iii) P is a finite, nonempty subset of $p(\Gamma) \times \Sigma \times \Sigma^*$, where $p(\Gamma)$ denotes the family of nonempty subsets of Γ. Element $(B,a,\alpha) \in P$ is called a rule and is usually written in the form $B{:}a \to \alpha$.

(iv) $C \subseteq \Gamma^*$, called the control set.

(v) $\sigma \in \Sigma^+$, the initial string.

Given a global context L-system $G = (\Sigma,\Gamma,P,C,\sigma)$, we write $\alpha \underset{G}{\Rightarrow} \beta$ for $\alpha \in \Sigma^+$, $\beta \in \Sigma^*$, if there exist $k \geq 1$, $a_1,a_2,\ldots,a_k \in \Sigma$, $\beta_1,\beta_2,\ldots,\beta_k \in \Sigma^*$ and $B_1,B_2,\ldots,B_k \in p(\Gamma)$ so that $\alpha = a_1a_2\ldots a_k$, $\beta = \beta_1\beta_2\ldots\beta_k$, $(B_j,a_j,\beta_j) \in P$, for $j = 1,2,\ldots,k$ and $B_1B_2\ldots B_k \cap C \neq \phi$.[1]

The language generated by a global context L-system G is denoted by L(G) and is defined to be the set $\{\alpha \in \Sigma^* : \sigma \Rightarrow^* \alpha\}$.

---

[1] $B_1B_2\ldots B_k$ is the concatenation of sets $B_1,B_2,\ldots,B_k$.

A global context L-system G is said to be a λ global context L-system if its control set is of the type λ. In this paper only regular global context L-systems will be studied and their control sets will be denoted by regular expressions.

The family of regular global L-languages will be denoted by Ψ.

Example 1 Let G_1 be a regular global context L-system, $G_1 = \{\{a\},\{S_1,S_2\},P,C,a\}$, where $P = \{\{s_1\}:a \to aa_1\{s_2\}:a \to aaa\}$ and C is denoted by regular expression $s_1^*+s_2^*$.

Clearly, at any step in a derivation, we can apply either the production $a \to aa$ to all symbols in a string, or the production $a \to aaa$ is used throughout the string. Therefore $L(G_1) = \{a^{2^i3^j} : i \geq 0, j \geq 0\}$.

Since we may consider an L-system as a model of the development of a filamentous organism, it is natural to require that for any stage of the development there exists a next stage of the development. Therefore, a condition of "completeness" is usually included in definitions of all versions of L-systems.

Now, we will give the formal definitions of the completeness and strong completeness for regular global context L-systems.

Definition 5. Let G be a regular global L-system with an alphabet Σ. G is complete if for any $\alpha \in L(G)$, $\alpha \neq \varepsilon$, there exists $\beta \in \Sigma^*$ so that $\alpha \underset{G}{\Rightarrow} \beta$.

Definition 6. Let G be a regular global L-system with an alphabet Σ. G is strongly complete if for any $\alpha \in \Sigma^+$ there exists $\beta \in \Sigma^*$ so that $\alpha \underset{G}{\Rightarrow} \beta$.

Note that in [92] only strongly complete systems were considered (and called complete). However, this is unnecessarily restrictive, there is no biological motivation to require that a next stage of the development is defined also for configurations of cells which can never occur in the development. Moreover, it follows from the next lemma that every complete regular global context L-system can be modified to an equivalent strongly complete regular global context L-system.

Lemma 1. For any regular global context L-system G, there effectively exists an equivalent regular global context L-system G' which is strongly complete.

Proof. Let $G = (\Sigma,\Gamma,P,C,\sigma)$ be a regular global context L-system. Let f be a finite substitution on Γ^* defined by $a \in f(k)$ if and only if there exists a rule $(B,a,\alpha) \in P$ so that $k \in B$. Let $R = f(C)$, let $R_1 = \Sigma^*-R$. Since regular languages are closed under finite substitution and complement, R and R_1 are regular languages. If $\alpha \in R$, then there exists $\beta \in \Sigma^*$ such that $\alpha \underset{G}{\Rightarrow} \beta$. If $R_1 = \phi$ then G is strongly complete.

Suppose that $R_1 \neq \phi$. Let s be a new symbol not in Γ. Let h be a homomorphism defined by $h(a) = s$ for any a in Σ. Let $G' = (\Sigma,\Gamma',P',C',\sigma)$, where $\Gamma' = \Gamma \cup \{s\}$, $C' = C \cup h(R_1)$, and $P' = P \cup \{(\{s\},a,a):a \in \Sigma\}$. From the construction of G' follows that G' is strongly complete and if $\alpha \in R$, and $\alpha \underset{G}{\Rightarrow} \beta$ for some $\beta \in \Sigma^*$, then $\alpha \underset{G'}{\Rightarrow} \beta$, and if $\alpha \in R_1$ then $\alpha \underset{G'}{\Rightarrow} \alpha$. Therefore $L(G') = L(G)$. □

<u>Lemma 2</u>. It is undecidable whether a regular global context L-system is complete.

<u>Proof.</u> We will show that for any instance of Post's Correspondence Problem [102] there exists a regular global context L-system which is complete if and only if the instance of Post's Correspondence Problem (PCP) does not have a solution.

Let $\Sigma = \{a_1,a_2,\ldots,a_n\}$ be a finite alphabet, and let A and B be two lists of strings in Σ^+ with the same number of strings in each list. Say $A = \alpha_1,\alpha_2,\ldots,\alpha_k$ and $B = \beta_1,\beta_2,\ldots,\beta_k$. Let $G = (\Sigma',\Gamma,P,C,\$)$ be a regular global L-system, where $\Sigma' = \Sigma \cup \{\$,\text{¢}\}$, $\Gamma = \{s_1,s_2,s_3,s_4\} \cup \{r_i:i = 1,2,\ldots,n\}$, $P = \{(\{s_1\},\$,\alpha_i\ \$\ \beta_i^r):i = 1,2,\ldots,n\} \cup \{(\{r_i\},a_i,\varepsilon):i = 1,2,\ldots,n\} \cup$ $\cup \{(\{s_3\},a_i,a_i):i = 1,2,\ldots,n\} \cup \{(\{s_2\},\$,\text{¢})\} \cup \{(\{s_4\},\text{¢},\text{¢})\}$, where β_i^r denotes the reverse of β_i, and C is denoted by $s_3^*s_1s_3^* + s_3^+s_2s_3^+ + s_3^+s_4 + s_4s_3^+ + s_3^+s_4s_3^+ +$

$+ s_3^*r_1s_4r_1s_3^* + s_3^*r_2s_4r_2s_3^* + \ldots + s_3^*r_ns_4r_ns_3^*$.

Clearly, $\$ \underset{G}{\Rightarrow}^* \alpha_{i_1}\alpha_{i_2}\ldots\alpha_{i_j}\$\beta_{i_j}^r\beta_{i_{j-1}}^r\ldots\beta_{i_1}^r \underset{G}{\Rightarrow} \alpha_{i_1}\alpha_{i_2}\ldots\alpha_{i_j}\text{¢}$ $\beta_{i_j}^r\beta_{i_{j-1}}^r\ldots\beta_{i_1}^r$ for $j \geq 1$, $i_1,i_2,\ldots,i_j$ being integers smaller or equal to k.

If $\alpha a\ \text{¢}\ a\beta \in L(G)$, where $\alpha,\beta \in \Sigma^*$, $a \in \Sigma$, then $\alpha a\ \text{¢}\ a\beta \underset{G}{\Rightarrow} \alpha\ \text{¢}\ \beta$. If $\alpha a\ \text{¢}\ b\beta \in L(G)$, where $\alpha,\beta \in \Sigma^*$, $a,b \in \Sigma$ and $a \neq b$ then $\alpha a\ \text{¢}\ b\beta \underset{G}{\Rightarrow} \alpha a\ \text{¢}\ b\beta$ is the only possible derivation in G from $\alpha a\ \text{¢}\ b\beta$. Therefore $\$ \underset{G}{\Rightarrow}^* \text{¢}$ if and only if the instance of PCP has a solution. Since $s_4 \notin C$, G is complete if and only if the instance of PCP does not have a solution. Thus it is not decidable whether G is complete. □

Now we will give the definition of a rule context L-system. A rule context L-system has a finite set of context free rules, each rule having a finite number of labels. For each rule p there are restrictions on what rules might be used on the symbols adjacent to the symbol on which p is used. These restrictions are specified by a finite number of triples.

<u>Definition 7</u>. A rule context L-system is a 5-tuple $G = (\Sigma,\Gamma,P,C,\sigma)$, where:

(i) Σ is a finite, nonempty set of symbols, called the <u>alphabet</u>.

(ii) Γ is a finite, nonempty set of symbols, called the <u>labels</u>.

(iii) P is a finite subset of $p(\Gamma) \times \Sigma \times \Sigma^*$, called the set of <u>rules</u>. Rule (B,a,α) in P is usually written in the form $B:a \rightarrow \alpha$.

(iv) C is a finite subset of $\{\#,\varepsilon\}\Gamma^* \times \Gamma \times \Gamma^* \{\#,\varepsilon\}$, called the context set, where # is a special symbol not in Γ, called the endmarker.

(v) $\sigma \in \Sigma^+$, the initial string.

Given a rule context L-system $G = (\Sigma,\Gamma,P,C,\sigma)$, we write $\alpha \underset{G}{\Rightarrow} \beta$ for $\alpha \in \Sigma^+$, $\beta \in \Sigma^*$ if there exist $k \geq 1$, $a_1,a_2,\ldots,a_k \in \Sigma$ $\beta_1,\beta_2,\ldots,\beta_k \in \Sigma^*$ and $s_1,s_2,\ldots,s_k \in \Gamma$ so that $\alpha = a_1a_2\ldots a_k$, $\beta = \beta_1\beta_2\ldots\beta_k$ and for every i, $1 \leq i \leq k$, there exist $(B_i,a_i,\beta_i) \in P$ and $m,n \geq 0$ so that $s_i \in B_i$ and $(\mathrm{Last}_m(\#s_1s_2\ldots s_{i-1})s_i, \mathrm{First}_n(s_{i+1}s_{i+2}\ldots s_k\#)) \in C$.

The language generated by a rule context L-system G is denoted by L(G) and is defined to be the set $\{\alpha \in \Sigma\ \sigma \underset{G}{\Rightarrow}^* \alpha\}$.

The family of rule context L-languages will be denoted by Φ.

Example 2. Let G_2 be a rule context L-system, $G_2 = (\{a\},\{s_1,s_2,s_3,s_4\},P,C,a\}$, where $P = \{\{s_1\}:a \to a^3,\{s_2\}:a \to a,\{s_3\}:a \to a^4,\{s_4\}:a \to a^2\}$ and $C = \{(\#,s_1,\#),(\#,s_4,\#),(\#,s_1,s_2),(s_1,s_2,\#),(s_2,s_1,s_2),(s_1,s_2,s_1),(\#,s_4,s_3),(s_3,s_1,\#),(s_1,s_4,s_3),(s_4,s_3,s_1),(s_3,s_1,s_4)\}$. Let α be a string in a^*. If the length of string α is divisible by 3, then according to control set C we can apply on α only rules with labels s_1,s_3,s_4 and the only string we can derive in G from α is the string $\alpha\alpha\alpha$. If the length of α is even then we can derive in G from α only the string $\alpha\alpha$. From the initial string of G_2 we can derive strings aa and aaa. Therefore $L(G_2) = \{a^{2^n}:n \geq 0\} \cup \{a^{3^n}:n \geq 0\}$.

Now, we will show that the family of rule context L-languages is equal to the family of regular global context L-systems.

Theorem 1. $\Psi = \Phi$.

Proof. Let $G_1 = (\Sigma,\Gamma,P,C,\sigma)$ be a rule context L-system. Let k,m be positive integers such that if $(\alpha,a,\beta) \in C$, then $|\alpha| < k$ and $|\beta| < m$. Let $L = \mathrm{First}(\#\Gamma^{k-1}) \cup \Gamma^k$, $R = \mathrm{Last}(\Gamma^{m-1}\#) \cup \Gamma^m$. Let A be a finite automaton, $A = (K,\Gamma,\delta,q_0,F)$, where $K = (L \times \Gamma \times R) \cup \{q_0\}$, $F = K \cap ((\Gamma \cup \{\#\})^* \times \Gamma \times \{\#\})$, and δ is defined as follows.

(i) If $(\#,p,\beta\#) \in C$, where $\beta \in \Gamma^*$ then $(\#,p,\beta\#) \in \delta(q_0,p)$.

(ii) If $(\#,p,\beta) \in C$ where $\beta \in \Gamma^*$, then $(\#,p,\beta\gamma_1\#) \in \delta(q_0,p)$ and $(\#,p,\beta\gamma_2) \in \delta(q_0,p)$, for every $\gamma_1,\gamma_2 \in \Gamma^*$ such that $\beta\gamma_1\#$, $\beta\gamma_2 \in R$.

(iii) If $(\alpha s,p,\beta) \in C$, where $\alpha \in \Gamma^* \cup \{\#\}\Gamma^*$, $\beta \in \Gamma^*$, $s,p \in \Gamma$ then $(\mathrm{Last}_k(\gamma_1\alpha s),p,\beta\gamma_2 q) \in \delta((\gamma_1\alpha,s,p\beta\gamma_2),p)$, and $(\mathrm{Last}_k(\gamma_1\alpha s),p,\beta\gamma_3\#) \in \delta((\gamma_1\alpha,s,p\beta\gamma_3\#),p)$ for any $q \in \Gamma \cup \{\#\},\gamma_2,\gamma_3 \in \Gamma^*$, $\gamma_1 \in \#\Gamma^* \cup \Gamma^+$ such that $\beta\gamma_2 q,\beta\gamma_3\# \in R$ and $\gamma_1\alpha \in L$.

(iv) If $(\varepsilon,p,\beta) \in C$, where $p \in \Gamma$, $\beta \in \Gamma^*$, then
$(\text{Last}_k(\gamma_1 s),p,\beta\gamma_2 q) \in \delta((\gamma_1,s,p\beta\gamma_2),p)$ and
$(\text{Last}_k(\gamma_1 s),p,\beta\gamma_3\#) \in \delta((\gamma_1,s,p\beta\gamma_3\#),p)$ for any
$s \in \Gamma$, $q \in \Gamma \cup \{\#\}$, $\gamma_1 \in L$, γ_2, $\gamma_3 \in \Gamma^*$ such that $\beta\gamma_2 q, \beta\gamma_3\# \in R$.

(v) If $(\alpha s,p,\beta\#) \in C$, where $\alpha \in \Gamma^* \cup \{\#\}\Gamma^*$, $\beta \in \Gamma^*$, $s,p \in \Gamma$ then
$(\text{Last}_k(\gamma_1\alpha s),p,\beta\#) \in \delta((\gamma_1\alpha,s,p\beta\#),p)$ for any $\gamma_1 \in \#\Gamma^* \cup \Gamma^+$ such that $\gamma_1\alpha \in L$.

(vi) If $(\varepsilon,p,\beta\#) \in C$, where $\beta \in \Gamma^*$, $p \in \Gamma$, then
$(\text{Last}_k(\gamma_1 s),p,\beta\#) \in \delta((\gamma_1,s,p\beta\#),p)$ for any $\gamma_1 \in L$.

$L(A)$ is a regular language and, clearly, α is in $L(A)$ if and only if α is a string of labels of rules which can be simultaneously applied to a string in Σ^* according to context set C. Therefore, the regular global context L-system $G_2 = (\Sigma,\Gamma,P,L(A),\sigma)$ will also generate language $L(G_1)$ and thus $\Phi \subseteq \Psi$.

Now, we will show the other inclusion. Let $G = (\Sigma,\Gamma,P,Q,\sigma)$ be a regular global context L-system. Let $A = (K,\Gamma,\delta,q_0,F)$ be a finite automaton such that $\delta(q,\varepsilon) = \phi$ for any $q \in K$ and $L(A) = Q$. Let G_3 be a rule context L-system, $G_3 = (\Sigma,\Gamma_3,P_3,C_3,\sigma)$, where $\Gamma_3 = \Gamma \times K$, $P_3 = \{(A \times K,a,\alpha):(A,a,\alpha) \in P\}$, and C_3 is defined as follows.

(i) If $\delta(q_0,a) \neq \phi$, where $a \in \Gamma$, then $(\#,(a,q_0),\varepsilon) \in C_3$.

(ii) If $r \in \delta(q,a)$ and $\delta(r,b) \neq \phi$ where $a,b \in \Gamma$ and $q,r \in K$, then $((a,q),(b,r),\varepsilon) \in C_3$.

(iii) If $r \in \delta(q,a)$ and $r \in F$, where $q \in K$, $a \in \Gamma$, then $(\varepsilon,(q,a),\#) \in C_3$.

It can be easily verified that $\alpha \underset{G_3}{\Rightarrow} \beta$ if and only if $\alpha \underset{G}{\Rightarrow} \beta$. Therefore $L(G_3) = L(G)$. □

Let the completeness and strong completeness is defined for rule context L-systems in the same way as for regular global context L-systems. Since rule context L-systems are effectively equivalent to regular global context L-systems, Lemma 1 and Lemma 2 also hold when replacing in them a regular global context L-system by a rule context L-system.

Since any triple in the context set in a rule context L-system implicitly includes also a restriction on the adjacent symbols, it is quite obvious that the family of rule context L-languages includes context L-languages. We will show in the next theorem that this inclusion is proper.

Theorem 2. $\Omega \subsetneq \Phi$.

Proof. Let $G = (\Sigma,P,\sigma)$ be a context L-system. We construct a rule context L-system $G' = (\Sigma,\Sigma,P',C,\sigma)$, where $P' = \{(\{a\},a,\beta):(\alpha_1,a,\alpha_2,\beta) \in P,\ a \in \Sigma,\ \beta \in \Sigma^*,\ \alpha_1 \in \{\#,\varepsilon\}\Sigma^*, \alpha_2 \in \Sigma^*\{\#,\varepsilon\}\}$, and $C = \{(\alpha,a,\beta):(\alpha,a,\beta,\gamma) \in P$ for some $\gamma \in \Sigma^*\}$. We have constructed the rule context L-system so that all rules for a symbol a in Σ have the same label a, and the context set of G' allows to obtain in G' exactly the same derivations as in G. Therefore $L(G) = L(G')$. Thus we have shown that $\Omega \subseteq \Phi$ and it remains to show that the inclusion is proper. In Example 2 the language $L = \{a^{2^n}:n \geq 0\} \cup \{a^{3^n}:n \geq 0\}$ is generated by a rule contex L-system. It has been shown in [92], that L is not in Ω. □

Now, we will give the definition of a predictive context L-system. In a predictive context L-system the use of a rule is restricted by the context of the right hand side of the rule after the simultaneous replacement of all the symbols in a string.

Definition 8. A predictive context L-system G is a 3-tuple (Σ,P,σ), where

(i) Σ is a finite, nonempty set of symbols, called the alphabet.

(ii) P is a finite subset of $\Sigma \times \{\#,\varepsilon\}\Sigma^* \times \Sigma^* \times \Sigma^* \{\#,\varepsilon\}$, called the set of rules, where # is a special symbol not in Σ, called the endmarker. A rule $(a,\beta_1,\alpha,\beta_2)$ in P is usually written in the form $a \rightarrow <\beta_1,\alpha,\beta_2>$. (We assume that "$<$" and "$>$" are symbols not in Σ.)

(iii) $\sigma \in \Sigma^+$, the initial string.

Given a predictive context L-system $G = (\Sigma,P,\sigma)$, we write $\alpha \Rightarrow \beta$ for $\alpha \in \Sigma^+$, $\beta \in \Sigma^*$ if there exist $k \geq 1$, $a_1,a_2,\ldots,a_k \in \Sigma$ and $\beta_1,\beta_2,\ldots,\beta_k \in \Sigma^*$ so that $\alpha = a_1a_2\ldots a_k$, $\beta = \beta_1\beta_2\ldots\beta_k$ and for every i, $1 \leq i \leq k$ there exist $m,n \geq 0$ such that

$$(a_i,\mathrm{Last}_m(\#\beta_1\beta_2\ldots\beta_{i-1}),\beta_i,\mathrm{First}_n(\beta_{i+1}\beta_{i+2}\ldots\beta_k\#)) \in P.$$

The language generated by a predictive context L-system G is denoted by L(G) and is defined to be the set $\{\alpha \in \Sigma^*:\sigma \underset{G}{\overset{*}{\Rightarrow}} \alpha\}$.

The family of predictive context L-languages is denoted by Π.

Example 3. Let G be the predictive context L-system $(\{a,b,c\},P,abc)$, where $P = \{a \rightarrow <\varepsilon,a,bc>,\ b \rightarrow <a,b,c>,\ c \rightarrow <b,c,a>,\ c \rightarrow <ab,cabc,\#>,\ a \rightarrow <\varepsilon,aa,bb>,$ $b \rightarrow <aa,bb,\varepsilon>,\ c \rightarrow <bb,cc,\varepsilon>,\ a \rightarrow <\varepsilon,a,a>,\ b \rightarrow <b,b,\varepsilon>,\ c \rightarrow <c,c,\varepsilon>$.

Using the first four rules in P we can generate from the string abc the string $(abc)^m$, $m \geq 1$. If we decide to use a rule which would double a symbol, then, clearly, we have to double each symbol throughout the whole string $(abc)^m$.

Therefore, $(abc)^m \underset{G}{\Rightarrow} (a^2b^2c^2)^m$ and from any string of the form $(a^ib^ic^i)^m$, where $i > 1$, $m \geq 1$ only the string $(a^{i+1}b^{i+1}c^{i+1})^m$ can be generated. Thus $L(G) = \{(a^ib^ic^i)^m: i \geq 1, m \geq 1\}$.

We can define the completeness and strong completeness for predictive context L-systems in the same way as for regular global context L-systems. We can prove that it is undecidable whether a predictive context L-system is complete. However, in this case we cannot show that for every predictive context L-system it is possible to construct an equivalent strongly complete predictive context L-system. We can only show that every complete predictive context L-system can be made strongly complete.

Lemma 3. The language $L = \{a^{3^i 2^j} : i \geq 0, j \geq 0\}$ is not a predictive context L-language.

Proof: Since the proof of this lemma is very tedious, we will present it only informally.

Suppose that there exists a predictive context L-system $G = (\Sigma, P, \sigma)$ such that $L(G) = \{a^{3^i 2^j} : i \geq 0, j \geq 0\}$. Then there exists exactly one integer j, $j \geq 0$ such that $a \to \langle a^i, a^j, a^h \rangle \in P$ for some integers i,h. Since L is infinite, $j \geq 1$. To be able to generate all string a^{3^i} for $i \geq 1$, j has to be a power of three, i.e. $j = 3^p$, $p \geq 1$. But then we cannot generate in G all strings a^{2^i} for $i \geq 1$. □

Theorem 3. $\Pi \subsetneq \Psi$.

Proof: Let $G = (\Sigma, P, \sigma)$ be a predictive context L-system. Let k, m be natural numbers such that $|\alpha| < k$, $|\gamma| < m$ for any $(a, \alpha, \beta, \gamma) \in P$. Let A be a finite automaton, $A = (K, P, \delta, q_0, F)$, where $K = (\mathrm{First}(\#\Sigma^{k-1}) \cup \Sigma^k) \times (\mathrm{Last}(\Sigma^{m-1}\#) \cup \Sigma^m) \cup \{q_0\}$, $F = K \cap (\Sigma \cup \{\#\})^* \times (\#)$, and δ is defined as follows.

(i) If $p = (a, \#, \beta, \gamma\#) \in P$ where $a \in \Sigma$, and $\beta, \gamma \in \Sigma^*$, then $(\mathrm{Last}_k(\#\beta), \gamma\#) \in \delta(q_0, p)$.

(ii) If $p = (a, \#, \beta, \gamma) \in P$, where $a \in \Sigma$, and $\beta, \gamma \in \Sigma^*$, then $(\mathrm{Last}_k(\#\beta), \gamma\delta_1\#) \in \delta(q_0, p)$ for any $\delta_1 \in \Sigma^*$ such that $|\delta_1| \leq m - |\gamma| - 1$, and $(\mathrm{Last}(\#\beta), \gamma\delta_2) \in \delta(q_0, p)$ for any $\delta_2 \in \Sigma^*$ such that $|\delta_2| = m - |\gamma|$.

(iii) If $p = (a, \alpha, \beta, \gamma) \in P$, where $\alpha \in \Sigma^* \cup \#\Sigma^+$ and $\beta, \gamma \in \Sigma^*$, then $(\mathrm{Last}_k(\gamma_1\alpha\beta), \gamma\gamma_2\delta) \in \delta((\gamma_1\alpha, \beta\gamma\gamma_2), p)$ for any $\gamma_1 \in \Sigma^* \cup \#\Sigma^*$, $\gamma_2 \in \Sigma^*$, $\delta \in \Sigma^* \cup \Sigma^*\#$ such that $(\gamma_1\alpha, \beta\gamma_2) \in K$ and $|\delta| = |\beta|$, and also $(\mathrm{Last}_k(\gamma_1\alpha\beta), \gamma\gamma_2\#) \in \delta((\gamma_1\alpha, \beta\gamma\gamma_2\#), p)$ for any $\gamma_1 \in \Sigma^* \cup \#\Sigma^*$, and $\gamma_2 \in \Sigma^*$ such that $(\gamma_1\alpha, \beta\gamma\gamma_2\#) \in K$.

(iv) If $p = (a,\alpha,\beta,\gamma\#) \in P$, where $\alpha \in \Sigma^* \cup \#\Sigma^+$ and $\beta,\gamma \in \Sigma^*$, then $(Last_k(\gamma_1\alpha\beta),\gamma\#) \in \delta((\gamma_1\alpha,\beta\gamma\#),p)$ for any $\gamma_1 \in \Sigma \cup \#\Sigma^*$ such that $(\gamma_1\alpha,\beta\gamma\#) \in K$.

It follows from the construction of automaton A that if $p_1p_2\ldots p_n \in L(A)$, where $p_i \in P$, $p_i = (a_i,\alpha_i,\beta_i,\gamma_i)$ for $1 \le i \le n$, then $a_1a_2\ldots a_n \underset{G}{\Rightarrow} \beta_1\beta_2\ldots\beta_n$ and vice versa. Therefore, the regular global context L-system $G' = (\Sigma,P,P',L(A),\sigma)$, where $P' = \{(\{a,\beta,\alpha,\gamma\},a,\alpha):(a,\beta,\alpha,\gamma) \in P\}$, generates also the language L(G). Thus $\Pi \subseteq \Psi$.

In Example 1 we have shown that the language $L = \{a^{3^i2^j} : i \ge 0, j \ge 0\}$ is a regular global context L-language. However, by Lemma 3, L is not a predictive context L-language. Thus, the inclusion is proper. □

It has been shown in [92] that the family of regular languages is included in the family of context L-systems. It is easy to modify this proof to show that all regular languages containing a nonempty string are also included in the family of predictive context L-languages.

Let the family of regular languages be denoted by REGULAR.

<u>Theorem 4</u>. $REGULAR-\{\{\varepsilon\},\phi\} \subsetneq \Pi$.

<u>Proof</u>. Similar to the proof that $REGULAR-\{\{\varepsilon\},\phi\}$ is included in Ω in [92]. □

Now, we will compare the generative power of TOL-systems with that of context sensitive L-systems. The family of TOL-languages will be denoted by TOL.

<u>Theorem 5.</u> $TOL \not\subseteq \Pi$.

<u>Proof</u>. TOL does not include all finite sets as shown in [81]. Therefore, it follows from Theorem 4 that $\Pi \not\subseteq TOL$. We have shown in Lemma 3 that the language $L = \{a^{3^i2^j} : i \ge 0, j \ge 0\}$ is not a predictive context L-language. However, L is generated by TOL-system $G = (\{a\},\{\{a \to aa\},\{a \to aaa\}\},a)$. Therefore, $TOL \not\subseteq \Pi$. □

<u>Theorem 6</u>. $TOL \subsetneq \Psi$.

<u>Proof</u>. Let $G = (\Sigma,P,\sigma)$ be a TOL-system, where $P = \{P_1,P_2,\ldots,P_n\}$. Let $G' = (\Sigma,\Gamma,P',Q,\sigma)$ be a regular global context L-system, where $\Gamma = \{s_1,s_2,\ldots,s_n\}$, Q is denoted by $s_1^+ + s_2^+ + \ldots + s_n^+$, and P' is defined as follows.

$P' = \{(A,a,\alpha):a \in \Sigma,\ \alpha \in \Sigma^*,\ (a,\alpha) \in P_i$ for some i, $1 \le i \le n$ and $A = \{s_j \in \Gamma:(a,\alpha) \in P_j\}\}$, i.e. a rule p has label s_j if and only if p is in the table P_j. Since the control set Q allows to use at one step in a derivation only rules which all are from the same table of P we have $L(G) = L(G')$. Thus $TOL \subseteq \Psi$.

It follows from Theorem 3 and Theorem 5 that the inclusion is proper. □

Lemma 4. The language $L = \{(a^n b^n c^n)^m : n,m \geq 1\}$ is not a context L-language.

Proof. We will give here only an informal proof to keep the paper short.

Suppose that there exists a context L-system $G = (\Sigma, P, \sigma)$ generating the language $L = \{(a^n b^n c^n)^m : n,m \geq 1\}$. Since G can generate all strings $a^n b^n c^n$ for $n \geq 0$, there exists exactly one integer i, $i \geq 1$ such that $\langle a^k, a, a^j \rangle \rightarrow a^i$ is in P for some integer k,j. Similarly, for rules involving only symbol b and only symbol c. Therefore, there exists a constant c such that for any $n \geq c$, if $(a^n b^n c^n)^m \underset{G}{\Rightarrow}^* \alpha$ then $\alpha = (a^k b^k c^k)^m$ for some integer $k \geq n$. Thus there exists an integer $j \geq 1$ such that the following holds. There exist infinitely many strings in L of type $(a^j b^j c^j)^m$ for some integer m and $(a^j b^j c^j)^m \underset{G}{\Rightarrow} (a^{j_1} b^{j_2} c^{j_2})^{n_1}$, $(a^j b^j c^j)^m \underset{G}{\Rightarrow} (a^{j_2} b^{j_2} c^{j_2})^{m_2}$ and $m_1 \neq m_2$, $j_1 \neq j_2$. Then we can generate in G also strings not in L, which is a contradiction to $L = L(G)$. □

Since we have shown in Example 3 that the language $L = \{(a^n b^n c^n)^m : n,m \geq 1\}$ is a predictive context L-language, it is clear that context L-languages do not include all predictive context L-languages.

Theorem 7. $\Pi \not\subseteq \Omega$.

Proof. It follows directly from Lemma 4 and Example 3. □

Now, we will compare the generative power of context sensitive grammars with that of predictive context L-systems and regular global context L-systems.

Theorem 8. For each type 0 language L over alphabet T, there exists a predictive context L-system G such that $L = L(G) \cap T^*$.

Proof. Let L be generated by a type 0 grammar $G_1 = (N,T,P,S)$. Let $G = (\Sigma, P', S)$ be a predictive context L-system, where $\Sigma = T \cup N \cup \{(p,p) : P \in P\} \cup \{(p,A) : p \in P \text{ and } A \in N \cup T\}$, and P' is constructed as follows.

(i) If $A \rightarrow \alpha \in P$, where $A \in N$, $\alpha \in (N \cup T)^*$, then $A \rightarrow \alpha \in P'$.

(ii) If $p = A_1 A_2 \ldots A_n \rightarrow B_1 B_2 \ldots B_m \in P$, where $A_1, A_2, \ldots, A_n, B_1, B_2, \ldots, B_m \in N \cup T$, $m \geq n$, then $A_i \rightarrow \langle (p,A_1)B_1(p,A_2)B_2 \ldots (p,A_{i-1})B_{i-1}, (p,A_i)B_i, (p,A_{i+1})B_{i+1}(p,A_{i+2})B_{i+2} \ldots (p,A_{n-1})B_{n-1}(p,A_n)B_n B_{n+1} \ldots B_m(p,p) \rangle \in P'$ for $1 \leq i \leq n-1$, and $A_n \rightarrow \langle (p,A_1)B_1(p,A_2)B_2 \ldots (p,A_{n-1})B_{n-1}, (p,A_n)B_n B_{n+1} \ldots B_m(p,p), \varepsilon \rangle \in P'$.

(iii) If $p = A_1A_2\ldots A_n \to B_1B_2\ldots B_m \in P$, where $A_1,A_2,\ldots,A_n$, $B_1,B_2,\ldots,B_m \in N \cup T$, $1 \le m < n$. Then $A_i \to \langle(p,A_1)B_1(p,A_2)B_2\ldots(p,A_{i-1})B_{i-1},(p,A_i)B_i,(p,A_{i+1})B_{i+1}$ $(p,A_{i+2})B_{i+2}\ldots(p,A_m)B_m(p,A_{m+1})(p,A_{m+2})\ldots(p,A_n)\rangle \in P'$ for $1 \le i \le m$, and $A_i \to \langle(p,A_1)B_1(p,A_2)B_2\ldots(p,A_m)B_m(p,A_{m+1})$ $(p,A_{m+2})\ldots(p,A_{i-1}),(p,A_i),(p,A_{i+1})(p,A_{i+2})\ldots(p,A_n)\rangle \in P'$ for $m+1 \le i \le n$.

(iv) If $p = A_1A_2\ldots A_n \to \varepsilon$, where $A_1,A_2,\ldots,A_n \in N \cup T$, $n > 1$, then $A_i \to \langle(p,A_1)(p,A_2)\ldots(p,A_{i-1}),(p,A_i),(p,A_{i+1})(p,A_{i+2})\ldots(p,A_n)\rangle \in P'$ for $1 \le i \le n$.

(v) $(p,A) \to \varepsilon \in P'$, and $(p,p) \to \varepsilon \in P'$ for any $p \in P$, $A \in N \cup T$.

(vi) $A \to A \in P'$ for any $A \in N \cup T$.

It follows from the construction that if $\alpha A_1A_2\ldots A_n\beta \underset{G_1}{\Rightarrow} \alpha B_1B_2\ldots B_m\beta$, where $A_1,A_2,\ldots,A_n,B_1,B_2,\ldots B_n \in N \cup T, \alpha,\beta \in (N \cup T)^*$ using the rule $A_1A_2\ldots A_n \to B_1B_2\ldots B_m, m \ge n$, then $\alpha A_1A_2\ldots A_n\beta \underset{G}{\Rightarrow} \alpha(p,A_1)B_1(p,A_2)B_2\ldots$ $(p,A_n)B_nB_{n+1}\ldots B_m(p,p)\beta \underset{G}{\Rightarrow} \alpha B_1B_2\ldots B_m\beta$, and if $\alpha\gamma\beta \underset{G}{\Rightarrow} \alpha(p,A_1)B_1(p,A_2)B_2\ldots$ $(p,A_n)B_nB_{n+1}\ldots B_n(p,p)$, then $\gamma = A_1A_2\ldots A_n$. The same can be shown if other types of rules of G_1 are used. Therefore $S \underset{G}{\Rightarrow}^* \alpha$, where $\alpha \in (N \cup T)^*$ if and only if $S \underset{G_1}{\Rightarrow}^* \alpha$. Thus $L(G_1) = L(G) \cap T^*$. □

Let the family of context-sensitive languages be denoted by CS.

Theorem 9. $\Pi \not\lessgtr$ CS.

Proof. Suppose that $\Pi \subseteq$ CS. Since context sensitive languages are included in recursive languages and recursive languages are closed under intersection, $L \cap T^*$ is a recursive language for any L in Π and any alphabet T. This is a contradiction to Theorem 8. Therefore, $\Pi \not\subseteq$ CS.

We have shown in Lemma 3 that the language $L = \{a^{3^i 2^j} : i \ge 0, j \ge 0\}$ is not in Π. However, L is clearly a context sensitive language. Therefore, CS $\not\subseteq \Pi$. □

Now, we would like to compare the family of context sensitive languages to the family of regular global context L-languages. It is clear from the previous theorem and from Theorem 3 that the family of regular global context L-languages is not included in the family of context sensitive languages. To prove that the family of regular global context L-languages does not contain all context-sensitive languages we introduce the concept of exponentially dense languages.

<u>Definition 9</u>. Language L is called <u>exponentially dense</u> if there exist constants c_1 and c_2 having the following property: For any $n \geq 0$ there exists a string α in L such that $c_1 e^{(n-1)c_2} \leq |\alpha| < c_1 e^{nc_2}$.

<u>Lemma 5</u>. Any regular global context L-language which is infinite is exponentially dense.

<u>Proof</u>. Let L be an infinite, regular context L-language. Let $G = (\Sigma,\Gamma,P,C,\sigma)$ be a regular global context L-system generating L. Let $c_1 = |\sigma|$, $d_2 = \max \{|\gamma|:(A,a,\gamma) \in P$ for some $A \subset \Gamma$, $a \in \Sigma$ and $\gamma \in \Sigma^*\}$. Let $c_2 = \log d_2$. Since L is infinite, $d_2 > 1$. If $n = 0$ then, clearly, $c_1 \leq |\sigma| < c_1 e^{c_2}$. Let n be an arbitrary fixed integer, $n > 0$. Since L is infinite, there exists $\alpha \in L$ such that $|\alpha| \geq c_1 e^{nc_2}$. As $\alpha \in L$ and $|\alpha| > |\sigma|$ there exist $k > 1$ and $\beta_1,\beta_2,\ldots,\beta_k \in L$ so that $\beta_i \Rightarrow \beta_{i+1}$ for $1 \leq i \leq k-1$, $\beta_1 = \sigma$ and $\beta_k = \alpha$. Let j be an integer, $1 \leq j < k$ such that $|\beta_j| < c_1 e^{nc_2}$ and $|\beta_{j+1}| \geq c_1 e^{nc_2}$. Clearly, such integer j exists. Now we have $|\beta_j| \geq |\beta_{j+1}|/d_2 \geq c_1 e^{nc_2}/d_2 = c_1 e^{(n-1)c_2}$. □

<u>Lemma 6.</u> The language $\{a^{2^{2^n}} : n \geq 0\}$ is not a regular global context L-language.

<u>Proof.</u> The language $\{a^{2^{2^n}} : n \geq 0\}$ is not exponentially dense and therefore by Lemma 6 is not a regular global context L-language. □

<u>Theorem 10</u>. $CS \nsubseteq \Psi$.

<u>Proof</u>. By Theorems 3 and 9, Ψ is not included in CS. The language $L = \{a^{2^{2^n}} : n \geq 0\}$ is a context sensitive language, however, L is not in Ψ by Lemma 6. □

NONTERMINALS AND CODINGS IN DEFINING VARIATIONS OF OL-SYSTEMS

Sven Skyum
Department of Computer Science
University of Aarhus
Aarhus, Denmark

Summary

The use of nonterminals versus the use of codings in variations of OL-systems is studied. It is shown that the use of nonterminals produces a comparatively low generative capacity in deterministic systems while it produces a comparatively high generative capacity in nondeterministic systems.

Finally it is proved that the family of context-free languages is contained in the family generated by codings on propagating OL-systems with a finite set of axioms, which was one of the open problems in [10]. All the results in this paper can be found in [71] and [72].

1. Definitions

By definition, an EOL-system is a quadruple $G = \langle \Sigma, P, \omega, \Delta \rangle$, where Σ and Δ are alphabets with $\Delta \subseteq \Sigma$, P is a finite set of context-free productions containing at least one production for every letter of Σ, and $\omega \in \Sigma^+$. The direct yield relation $\Rightarrow$ on the set Σ^* is defined as follows: $x \Rightarrow y$ holds iff there is an integer $k \geqq 1$, letters a_i and words α_1, $1 \leqq i \leqq n$, such that

$$x = a_1 \ldots a_n, \; y = \alpha_1 \ldots \alpha_n,$$

and $a_i \to \alpha_i$ is a production in P, for each $i = 1, \ldots, n$. The relation $\stackrel{*}{\Rightarrow}$ is the reflexive transitive closure of $\Rightarrow$. The language L(G) generated by G is defined by

$$L(G) = \{ w \in \Delta^* \mid \omega \stackrel{*}{\Rightarrow} w \}.$$

The EOL-system is an OL-system iff $\Delta = \Sigma$. It is <u>deterministic</u> (abbreviated: D) iff there is exactly one production for every letter of Σ. It is propagating (abbreviated: P) iff the right side of every productions is distinct from the empty word λ. We may also combine these notions and speak, for instance, of PDOL- or EPOL-systems.

We also consider generalizations of the systems defined above obtained by replacing the axiom ω by a finite set Ω of axioms. The language generated by such a system consists of the (finite) union of the languages generated by the systems obtained by choosing each element $\omega \in \Omega$ to be the axiom. This generalization is denoted by the letter F. Thus, we may speak of EPDFOL-systems.

For any class of systems, we use the same notation for the family of languages generated by these systems. E.g., EPDOL denotes the family of languages generated by EPDOL-systems.

By a coding we mean a length-preserving homomorphism (often also called a literal homomorphism). The prefix C attached to the name of a language family indicates that we are considering codings of the languages in the family.

2. Deterministic systems

We start by examining the relation between the use of nonterminals and codings in deterministic systems.

Theorem 2.1

EDOL $\subsetneq$ CDOL and EPDOL $\subsetneq$ CPDOL.

Proof

We will only prove the first inclusion. The second one is proved in the same way.

Now let $G = <\Sigma, P, \omega, \Delta>$ be an EDOL-system. The following describes the construction of a DOL-system $G = <\Sigma', P', \omega', \Sigma'>$ and a coding h from Σ' into Δ such that $L(G) = h(L(G'))$. For a word x, $\min(x)$ denotes the set of letters occurring in x.

Consider the sequence of words from Σ^* generated by $G, \omega = \omega_1, \omega_2, \omega_3, \ldots$. There exist natural numbers n and m such that $\min(\omega_m) = \min(\omega_{m+n})$, which implies that for any $i \geq 0$ and any j, $0 \leq j < n$:

$$(1) \qquad \min(\omega_{m+j}) = \min(\omega_{m+ni+j}).$$

Let d_k denote the cardinality of $\min(\omega_k)$, $1 \leq k < m+n$. Define

$$N_\Delta = \{k \in N \mid 1 \leq k < m+n,\ \min(\omega_k) \subseteq \Delta\}.$$

For any $k \in N_\Delta$ introduce new symbols not in Σ

$$\Sigma_k = \{ a_{kj} \mid 1 \leq j \leq d_k\},$$

and define isomorphism f_k mapping $\min(\omega_k)$ onto Σ_k, where

$$f_k(a) = a_{kj} \text{ iff } a \text{ is the j'th symbol of } \min(\omega_k),\ k \in N_\Delta$$

Note that the f_k's are defined for some fixed enumerations of the sets $\min(\omega_k)$. Σ' is going to be the union of the above defined Σ_k's:

$$\Sigma' = \bigcup_{k \in N_\Delta} \Sigma_k \quad .$$

Define k_1 and k_2 as the minimal and maximal elements of N_Δ.

For any of the letters a_{kj} where $k \neq k_2$ define production in P':

$$a_{kj} \rightarrow f_{k'}(\alpha)$$

where k' is the smallest element in N_Δ greater than k and α is the string derived from $f_k^{-1}(a_{kj})$ in $(k'-k)$ steps in G.

It follows from (1) that L(G) is finite if $k_2 < m$. If this is the case then define for any j, $1 \leq j \leq d_{k_2}$ production in P':

$$a_{k_2 j} \rightarrow a_{k_2 j}.$$

Otherwise, let k_3 denote the minimal element in N_Δ greater than or equal to m, and define productions in P' for any j, $1 \leq j \leq d_{k_2}$, for which $f_{k_2}^{-1}(a_{k_2 j})$ derives some string $\alpha \in \Delta^*$ in $(n-k_2+k_3)$ steps in G:

$$a_{k_2} j \rightarrow f_{k_3}(\alpha) \; .$$

Note that the use of f_{k_3} is well defined since $\min(\omega_{k_2+(n-k_2+k_3)}) = \min(\omega_{k_3})$ (from the fact that $k_3 \geq m$ and (1) above). Finally define the coding h from Σ' into Δ in the way that for every $a_{kj} \in \Sigma'$: $h(a_{kj}) = f_k^{-1}(a_{kj})$. Then

$$L(G) = h(L(G'))$$

where $G' = \langle \Sigma', P', f_{k_1}, (\omega_{k_1}), \Sigma' \rangle$, and this proves the inclusion of the theorem. The inclusion is proper because $\{a^n \mid n \geq 1\} \in$ CDOL\EDOL.

We have the following theorem as an immediate consequence of theorem 2.1.

Theorem 2.2

EDFOL $\subsetneq$ CDFOL and EPDFOL $\subsetneq$ CPDFOL.

3. Nondeterministic systems

We will now examine the relations between the nondeterministic families, corresponding to those occurring in Theorems 2.1 and 2.2.

The following two theorems correspond to Theorem 2.1. The proof of the first one can be found in [20].

Theorem 3.1

COL = EOL.

Theorem 3.2

CPOL $\subsetneq$ EPOL.

Proof

The inclusion is easily checked. The inclusion is proper because the language $L = \{a^n b^n c^n \mid n \geq 1\} \cup \{d^{3^n} \mid n \geq 1\}$ belongs to EPOL, but is does not belong to CPOL. The proof for the later statement can be found in [10].

Notice here that while the generating capacity due to the use of nonterminals was weaker than the generating capacity due to codings in deterministic propagating OL-systems, the converse is true if you are dealing with nondeterministic propagating OL-systems.

The following theorem corresponds to Theorem 2.2. The proof can be found in [72].

Theorem 3.3

CFOL = EFOL and CPFOL $\subseteq$ EPFOL.

It is an open problem whether or not the inclusion CPFOL $\subseteq$ EPFOL is proper.

A somewhat related problem is whether or not the family of context-free languages is included in the family CPFOL. Indeed we have the following theorem.

Theorem 3.4

The family of context-free languages is properly included in the family CPFOL.

Proof

Let $G = \langle V, \Sigma, P, S \rangle$ be a cf-grammar of a language not containing λ in Greibach-normal form (i.e., the productions are of the form $A \to a$ or $A \to aA_1 \dots A_n$). Suppose there are no useless symbols in V.

For each $A \in V$ we choose

$$w_A \in \{w \in \Sigma^* \mid A \overset{*}{\Rightarrow} w, \ |w| \text{ minimal}\}.$$

w_A will, in the rest of the proof, be fixed for every letter $A \in V$.

Define $k : V \to N$ by $k(A) = |w_A|$, and furthermore

$$s(A) = \{xw_x \in \Sigma^{k(A)}V^* \mid A \underset{left}{\overset{*}{\Rightarrow}} xw_x, |x| = k(A)\} \text{ and}$$

$$m(A) = \{x \in \Sigma^{k(A)} \mid \exists\, w \in V^* : xw \in s(A)\}$$

Since the grammar was in Greibach normal form, $s(A)$ and $m(A)$ are finite sets of strings.

Let $n : V \to N$ be defined as $n(A) = \{\text{number of strings in } m(A)\}$.

We will use $m(A)$ as an ordered set.

Now we can construct a PFOL-system H and a coding h such that $h(L(G)) = L(G)$:

$$H : \langle \Sigma \cup \bigcup_{\substack{A \in V \\ 1 \le i \le k(A) \\ 1 \le j \le n(A)}} A_i^j,\ P',\ \{S_1^1 S_2^1 \ldots S_{k(S)}^1, S_1^2 S_2^2 \ldots S_{k(S)}^2, \ldots, S_1^{n(S)} S_2^{n(S)} \ldots S_{k(S)}^{n(S)}\} \rangle$$

P' is defined **as** follows:

1) For all $a \in \Sigma$, $a \to a$ is in P'.
2) For all $A \in V$, $1 \le j \le n(A)$, and $1 \le i \le k(A)-1$, $A_i^j \to a_i^j$ is in P', where a_i^j is the i'th terminal in the j'th string in $m(A)$.
3) For all $A \in V$ and $1 \le j \le n(A)$

$$A_{k(A)}^j \to a_{k(A)}^j B_{11}^{k_1} B_{12}^{k_1} \ldots B_{1k(B_1)}^{k_1} B_{21}^{k_2} B_{22}^{k_2} \ldots B_{2k(B_2)}^{k_2} \ldots$$

$$\ldots B_{q1}^{k_q} B_{q2}^{k_q} \ldots B_{qk(B_q)}^{k_q}$$

is in P' for all $B_1, B_2, \ldots, B_q$ and $1 \le k_i \le n(B_i)$ where $xB_1 B_2 \ldots B_q \in S(A)$ and x is the j'th string in $m(A)$.

The coding h is defined by $h(a) = a$ for all $a \in \Sigma$, and $h(A_1^j A_2^j \ldots A_{k(A)}^j) = w_A$, for all $A \in V$ and $1 \le j \le n(A)$.

We prove that $L(G) \subseteq h(L(H))$. The other inclusion is shown in the same way.

Let $w \in L(G)$.
There exists a derivation of w in G such that

$$S = A_1 \overset{*}{\underset{left}{\Rightarrow}} x_1' A_2 A_3 \ldots A_n$$

$$\overset{*}{\Rightarrow} x_1' x_2' B_{21} \ldots B_{2q_2} x_3' B_{31} \ldots B_{3q_3} \ldots x_n' B_{n1} \ldots B_{nq_n}$$

$$\overset{*}{\Rightarrow} x_1' x_2' x_{21}'' \ldots x_{2q_2} x_3' x_{31}'' \ldots x_{3q_3}'' \ldots x_n' x_{n1}'' \ldots x_{nq_n}'' = w$$

where $x_i' \in m(A_i)$ for all $1 \leq i \leq n(A)$ and $B_{ij} \overset{*}{\Rightarrow} x_{ij}''$ for $2 \leq i \leq n$ and $1 \leq j \leq q_i$.

It suffices then to show that there exists an axiom $S_1^I S_2^I \ldots S_{k(S)}^I$ in H such that:

$$S_1^I S_2^I \ldots S_{k(S)}^I \underset{H}{\Rightarrow}$$

$$x_1' A_{21}^{k_2} A_{22}^{k_2} \ldots A_{2k(A_2)}^{k_2} A_{31}^{k_3} A_{32}^{k_3} \ldots A_{3k(A_3)}^{k_3} \ldots A_{n1}^{k_n} A_{n2}^{k_n} \ldots A_{nk(A_n)}^{k_n}$$

and

$A_{j1}^{k_j} A_{j2}^{k_j} \ldots A_{jk(A_j)}^{k_j} \underset{H}{\Rightarrow} x_j' w_j$ for all $2 \leq j \leq n$ but that is exactly how H is constructed.

LOOKING FOR A GENERAL FRAMEWORK

ITERATION GRAMMARS AND LINDENMAYER AFL'S

Arto Salomaa
Department of Computer Science
University of Aarhus
Aarhus, Denmark

One of the first observations concerning L-systems was that the corresponding language families have very weak closure properties, in fact, many of the families are anti-AFL's, i.e., closed under none of the AFL operations. However, this phenomenon is due to the lack of a terminal alphabet rather than to parallelism which is the essential feature concerning L-systems. E.g., the family TOL of all TOL-languages is an anti-AFL, whereas the family ETOL is a full AFL. Later on we will see how L-systems can be used to convert language families with weak closure properties into full AFL's in a rather natural way.

The basic notion in this paper, K-iteration grammar, is a slight generalization of the notion introduced by van Leeuwen [57]. The motivation for such a notion is three-fold:

i) It provides a uniform framework for discussing OL-systems and all of their context-free generalizations.

ii) It shows the relation between OL-systems and (iterated) substitutions.

iii) It associates with each family K of languages (having certain mild closure properties) some full AFL's, obtained from K in the "Lindenmayer way".

We make the following conventions, valid throughout this paper. All language families discussed are non-trivial, i.e., they contain at least one language containing a non-empty word. (A language family is understood as in [102].) Two generative devices are termed equivalent if they generate the same language or else the language generated by one device differs from the language generated by the other through the empty word λ. (Thus in this sense, for any context-free grammar, there is an equivalent context-free grammar with no λ-rules.)

We introduce first some standard terminology and notations. Let K be a family of languages. A K-substitution is a mapping σ from some alphabet V into K. The mapping σ is extended to languages over V in the usual fashion. For language families K_1 and K_2, we define

(1) $\mathrm{Sub}(K_1, K_2) = \{\sigma(L) \mid L \in K_2 \text{ and } \sigma \text{ is a } K_1\text{-substitution}\}$.

If K_2 = OL or K_2 = TOL, families (1) are called macro-OL and macro-TOL families, respectively, and denoted by K_1MOL and K_1MTOL. Macros were introduced in [7] and [9], where especially the cases K_1 = F (the family of finite languages) and K_1 = R (the family of regular languages) were investigated. Using the fact (cf. [55]) that the family of EOL-languages is closed under arbitrary homomorphism, it is easy to show that

$$\mathrm{FMOL} = \mathrm{EOL}.$$

(There seems to be no short direct proof for the inclusion FMOL $\subseteq$ EOL.) Similarly, one can prove that

$$\mathrm{FMTOL} = \mathrm{RMTOL} = \mathrm{ETOL}.$$

On the other hand, FMOL is properly included in RMOL because Herman's language

$$h^{-1}\{a^{2^n} \mid n \geqq 0\} \text{ with } h(a) = a,\ h(b) = \lambda,$$

is in the difference RMOL-FMOL, cf. [35]. The family RMOL is the smallest full AFL (and the smallest AFL) including the family OL, cf. [9] or [55]. It is also the closure of FMOL under inverse homomorphism.

We will now present the basic definition. Let K be a family of languages. A <u>K-iteration grammar</u> is a quadruple $G = (V_N, V_T, S, U)$, where V_N and V_T are disjoint alphabets (of nonterminals and terminals), $S \in V^+$ with $V = V_N \cup V_T$ (initial word) and $U = \{\sigma_1, \ldots, \sigma_n\}$ is a finite set of K-substitutions defined on V and with the property that, for each i and each $a \in V$, $\sigma_i(a)$ is a language over V. The language generated by such a grammar is defined by

$$\text{(2)} \quad L(G) = \cup\, \sigma_{i_1} \cdots \sigma_{i_k}(S) \cap V_T{}^*,$$

where the union is taken over all integers $k \geqq 1$ and over all ordered k-tuples $(i_1, \ldots, i_k)$ with $1 \leqq i_j \leqq n$. The family of languages generated by K-iteration grammars is denoted by K_{iter}. By $K_{iter}^{(t)}$ we denote the subfamily of K_{iter}, generated by such grammars, where U consists of at most t elements, for some $t \geqq 1$.

The different OL-families can now be easily characterized within this framework. Consider the special case K = F. Then

$$K_{iter}^{(1)} = F_{iter}^{(1)} = \mathrm{EOL} = \mathrm{FMOL}.$$

(Note that it suffices to choose, for each $a \in V$, $\sigma(a)$ to be the language consisting of the right sides of the productions with a on the left side.) Similarly,

$$F_{iter} = \mathrm{ETOL}\ (= \mathrm{FMTOL} = \mathrm{RMTOL}).$$

The families with D and/or P are characterized as follows. D means that the σ's are homomorphisms, P means that the σ's are λ-free. Thus, EPDTOL is the subfamily of F_{iter}, obtained by such grammars where all substitutions σ are λ-free homomorphisms.

If one wants to consider families without E (OL, TOL, etc.), then one simply assumes that V_N is empty (which means that the intersection with V_T^* in (2) is superfluous). Note that in the general case the generative capacity is not affected by assuming that $S \in V_N$. Finally, the macro-families KMOL and KMTOL are obtained by K-iteration grammars satisfying the following condition. There is a sub-alphabet V_I of V_N such that, for each i and each $a \in V_I$, $\sigma_i(a)$ is a finite language over V_N. Furthermore, for each i and each $a \in V_T$, $\sigma_i(a)$ is empty and, for each i and each $a \in V_N - V_I$, $\sigma_i(a)$ is a language (in K) over the alphabet V_T. (Here it is assumed that K contains all finite languages.)

Thus, all context-free L-systems find their counterpart in this formalism. Note, however, that so far (apart from regular macros) one has not considered in the theory of L-systems cases more general than K = F.

The basic tool needed in proofs for closure results is the following Theorem 1. We say that a K-iteration grammar is λ-free iff each of the substitutions σ_i is λ-free.

<u>Theorem 1.</u> ([55], [57], [103]) Assume that K is a language family closed under finite substitution and intersection with regular languages. Then for each K-iteration grammar, there is an equivalent λ-free K-iteration grammar.

Applying standard AFL-theory and the technique used to prove Medvedev's Theorem for finite automata, one can establish the following results:

<u>Theorem 2.</u> Assume that K satisfies the hypothesis of Theorem 1 and, furthermore, contains all regular languages. Then all of the families K_{iter}, $K_{iter}^{(t)}$, for any $t \geq 1$, KMOL and KMTOL are full AFL's.

Thus, Theorem 2 can be applied whenever K is a cone (also called a full trio). Since the full AFL's associated with K are obtained by parallel rewriting, they are naturally called <u>Lindenmayer AFL's.</u> Apart from the obvious inclusions

$$\text{KMOL} \subseteq \text{KMTOL} \subseteq K_{iter}\,,\quad \text{KMOL} \subseteq K_{iter}^{(1)} \subseteq K_{iter}^{(2)} \subseteq \ldots \subseteq K_{iter}\,,$$

very little is known about these AFL's, e.g., about the strictness of the inclusions.

It is shown by van Leeuwen ("Notes on pre-set pushdown automata", this volume) that $R_{iter}^{(1)}$ equals the family of languages accepted by pre-set pushdown automata. (In van Leeuwen's terminology, R_{iter} could be called "hyper-algebraic multi-extension of regular languages".)

A natural notion from the point of view of L-systems in AFL-theory is that of a <u>hyper-AFL</u>. By definition, a family K satisfying the hypothesis of Theorem 2 is a hyper-AFL iff $K_{iter} = K$. Hyper-AFL's are discussed in the paper by P.A. Christensen (this volume). This approach shows that, among the L-families, the family ETOL has a very interesting mathematical property.

Iteration grammars have been generalized by Derick Wood ("A note on Lindenmayer systems, spectra and equivalence", McMaster University Computer Science Technical Report No. 74/1) to cover L-languages with interactions. He also gives an example of how the uniform framework of iteration grammars can be used to generalize specific results. The example concerns the ultimate periodicity of spectra in EOL- and ETOL-systems, [20], [27]. Wood's result shows that the specific results mentioned depend only on the method of iterated substitution and not at all on the finiteness of the substitutions.

HYPER-AFL'S AND ETOL SYSTEMS

P. A. Christensen
Department of Computer Science
University of Aarhus
Aarhus, Denmark

The notions of K-iteration grammars and of hyper-AFL's are introduced in [57] and [103]. The notation follows that of [103].

Theorem

$$\mathrm{ETOL} = \mathrm{ETOL}^{(1)}_{\mathrm{iter}} = \mathrm{ETOL}_{\mathrm{iter}},$$ i.e. ETOL is a hyper-AFL.

Sketch of a proof

It is obvious from the definition of an iteration grammar that

$\mathrm{ETOL} \subseteq \mathrm{ETOL}^{(1)}_{\mathrm{iter}} \subseteq \mathrm{ETOL}_{\mathrm{iter}}$.

To prove $\mathrm{ETOL}_{\mathrm{iter}} \subseteq \mathrm{ETOL}$, let $G = (V_N, V_T, S, U)$ be an ETOL-iteration grammar with $U = \{\mathcal{T}_1, \ldots, \mathcal{T}_n\}$, where each $\mathcal{T}_j$ is an ETOL-substitution.

Assume that $\mathcal{T}_j(a_i) = L(G_{i,j})$, where $G_{i,j} = (V_N^{i,j}, V_T \cup V_N, T_{i,j}, S_{i,j})$ are synchronized versions of ETOL-systems and the alphabets $V_N^{i,j}$ are pairwise disjoint.

We define a new ETOL-system: $G' = (V_N', V_T', T', \bar{\bar{S}})$, where

$V_N' = \{\$\} \bigcup_{i,j} (V_N^{i,j} \cup \{\bar{S}_{i,j}\}) \cup \bar{V}_T \cup \bar{V}_N \cup \bar{\bar{V}}_T \cup \bar{\bar{V}}_N$ where \$ and all $\bar{S}_{i,j}$ are new symbols.

$\bar{V}_X = \{\bar{a} \mid a \in V_X\}$ and $\bar{\bar{V}}_X = \{\bar{\bar{a}} \mid a \in V_X\}$ for $X = N$ and $X = T$ are sets of new symbols.

If X is a string of symbols $X = b_1 \ldots b_k$, then $\bar{X} = \bar{b}_1 \ldots \bar{b}_k$ and $\bar{\bar{X}} = \bar{\bar{b}}_1 \ldots \bar{\bar{b}}_m$. The axiom of G' is defined as $\bar{\bar{S}}$ in exactly the same way.

Finally T' consists of the tables:

t_0:

$\bar{\bar{a}}_i \to \bar{S}_{i,j}$ for each i and each j

$A \to \$$ for any other symbol A.

For $1 \leq j \leq n$ there is the table:

t_j:

$\overline{S}_{i,j} \rightarrow \overline{S}_{i,j}$; $\overline{S}_{i,j} \rightarrow S_{i,j}$ for each i

$\bar{a} \rightarrow \bar{\bar{a}}$; $\bar{\bar{a}} \rightarrow \bar{\bar{a}}$ for each $a \in V_N \cup V_T$

$A \rightarrow \$$ for any other symbol A.

For $1 \leq j \leq n$ and $1 \leq i \leq |V_N \cup V_T|$ there is the set of tables:

$\tilde{T}_{i,j}$: which consists of all tables from $T_{i,j}$ where the table with the terminal productions ($G_{i,j}$ is synchronized) is changed to produce barred terminals instead. In all these tables we add the productions:

$\bar{\bar{a}} \rightarrow \bar{\bar{a}}$ for each $a \in V_N \cup V_T$

$\overline{S}_{k,j} \rightarrow \overline{S}_{k,j}$ for each k

$A \rightarrow \$$ for any other new symbol.

Finally there is the table with the terminal productions:

$\bar{\bar{a}} \rightarrow a$ for each $a \in V_T$

$A \rightarrow \$$ for any other symbol A.

The claim is now that $L(G) = L(G')$.

The reason for this is that rewriting a double- barred word via t_0's productions $\bar{\bar{a}}_i \rightarrow \overline{S}_{i,j}$ is the same as choosing the substitution $\mathcal{T}_j$ to be used. The substitution is then performed via the tables t_j and $\tilde{T}_{k,j}$, and when the substitution is performed, the word is again double-barred. We can choose a new substitution and so forth until we finally use the terminal table to reach a terminal word. If the tables to be used in the line of derivation are not chosen according to this scheme, a \$-symbol is introduced in the string, and from this it is impossible to reach a terminal word.

Therefore $\mathrm{ETOL} = \mathrm{ETOL}^{(1)}_{iter} = \mathrm{ETOL}_{iter}$, and since it is well-known that ETOL is a full AFL, we conclude that ETOL is a hyper-AFL.

Corollary 1

If K is a family of languages such that $F \subseteq K \subseteq ETOL$ then $K_{iter} = ETOL$.

Proof

$$ETOL = F_{iter} \subseteq K_{iter} \subseteq ETOL_{iter} = ETOL.$$

Thus we have for instance proved that:

$$ETOL = F_{iter} = R_{iter} = CF_{iter} = EOL_{iter} = ETOL_{iter} .$$

Since each hyper-AFL is a full AFL and since $ETOL = R_{iter}$, we conclude:

Corollary 2

ETOL is the smallest hyper-AFL.

In [56] it is stated that the family $R^{(1)}_{iter}$ is exactly the family of languages accepted by pre-set-pushdown automata, and we are now able to prove:

Corollary 3

$$R^{(1)}_{iter} \subsetneq R_{iter} = ETOL .$$

Proof

By definition $R^{(1)}_{iter} \subseteq R_{iter}$ and we know that $R_{iter} = ETOL$. Furthermore, hyper-AFL's are easily seen to be closed under substitution; in order to prove the corollary, it suffices to prove that $R^{(1)}_{iter}$ is not closed under substitution:

Let $L_1 = \{a^{2^n} \mid n \geq 0\}$ and $L_2 = \{ab^{2^m} \mid m \geq 0\}$, then obviously $L_1, L_2 \in OL \subseteq EOL = F^{(1)}_{iter} \subseteq R^{(1)}_{iter}$.

Define the substitution $\mathcal{T}$ by $\mathcal{T}(a) = L_2$. Then $\mathcal{T}(L_1)$ is the set of all words $ab^{2^{n_1}} ab^{2^{n_2}} \ldots ab^{2^{n_k}}$, where each $n_i \geq 0$ and there exists $l \geq 0$ such that $k = 2^l$. Define the finite substitution t by $t(a) = \{a\}$ and $t(b) = \{\lambda, b\}$ then the proof in [35] of the non-closure of EOL under inverse homomorphism shows that $t(\mathcal{T}(L_1)) \notin EOL = F^{(1)}_{iter}$. It is furthermore well-known that EOL is closed under finite substitution, therefore $\mathcal{T}(L_1) \notin F^{(1)}_{iter}$. But since infinite regular sets fulfil a pumping lemma, it is obvious that $\mathcal{T}(L_1) \notin R^{(1)}_{iter}$ and the corollary is proved.

Finally we mention that we have proved the existence of full AFL's K and $\overline{K}$ such that:

$$K_{iter}^{(1)} \subsetneq K_{iter} = \overline{K}_{iter}^{(1)} = \overline{K}iter$$

and $K \subsetneq K_{iter}$ but $(K_{iter})_{iter} = K_{iter}$ namely $K = R$ and $\overline{K} = ETOL$.

Ω-OL SYSTEMS*

Andrew L. Szilard
Department of Computer Science
University of Western Ontario

Definition 1.1.1

An operator domain is a set Ω with a mapping $a : \Omega \rightarrow N$; the elements of Ω are called operators, and if $\omega \varepsilon \Omega$, then $a(\omega)$ is called the arity of ω. If $a(\omega) = n$, we say that ω is an n-ary operator. We write $\Omega(n) = \{\omega \varepsilon \Omega | a(\omega) = n\}$.

Definition 1.1.2

Let A be a set and Ω an operator domain, then an Ω-algebra structure on A is a family of mappings $\Omega(n) \rightarrow A^{A^n}$, $n \varepsilon N$. Thus with each $\omega \varepsilon \Omega(n)$ we associate an n-ary operation on A.

$$\omega : A^n \rightarrow A$$

Definition 1.1.3

The set A with an Ω-algebra structure on A is called an Ω-algebra and is denoted by (A,Ω) or A_Ω.
A is called the carrier of A_Ω.

Definition 1.1.4

For any Ω-algebra A_Ω and any $\omega \varepsilon \Omega(n)$, the application of ω to an n tupple $(a_1, a_2, \ldots, a_n)$ from A gives an element of A. We write this element in postfix Polish notation $a_1 \; a_2 \ldots a_n\omega$. If n=0, then this means that $\omega \varepsilon A$. These ω's are called constant operators.

*An extract from the author's thesis:
"ON THE ALGEBRAIC FOUNDATIONS OF DEVELOPMENTAL SYSTEMS".

In what follows, we assume a fixed Ω structure throughout, and will omit sometimes the subscript Ω.

Definition 1.1.5

Given Ω-algebras A_Ω and B_Ω, a mapping $f : A \to B$ and $\omega \in \Omega(n)$, we say f is compatible with ω, if for all $a_1, \ldots, a_n \in A$

$$f(a_1)f(a_2)\ldots f(a_n)\omega = f(a_1 a_2 \ldots a_n \omega).$$

If f is compatible with each $\omega \in \Omega$, then f is said to be a homomorphism from A to B.

Definition 1.1.6

Given any two Ω-algebras A_Ω and B_Ω, we say that B_Ω is a sub-algebra of A_Ω if $B \subset A$ i.e., if the carrier of B_Ω is a subset of the carrier of A_Ω.

Definition 1.1.7

Given a family $(A_{i\Omega})i\epsilon I$ of Ω-algebras, $\prod_{i \epsilon I} A_{i\Omega}$, the associated direct product is defined as follows.

Let P be the Cartesian product of the A_i's with projections $\Pi_i : P \to A_i$, then any element $p \epsilon P$ is uniquely determined by its components $\Pi_i(p)$ and any choice of elements $(a_i \epsilon A_i)_{i \epsilon I}$ defines uniquely an element $p \epsilon P$ by $\Pi_i(p) = a_i$ for all $i \epsilon I$. Consequently if $p_1, p_2, \ldots, p_n \epsilon P$ and $\omega \epsilon \Omega(n)$, we can define $p_1 p_2 \ldots p_n \omega$ by the formuli

$$\Pi_i(p_1p_2\cdots p_n\omega) = \Pi_i(p_1)\Pi_i(p_2)\cdots\Pi_i(p_n)\omega \text{ for all } i \in I$$

This procedure defines an Ω structure on P simply by doing all operations componentwise. Consequently we have

Theorem 1.1.7

Direct product of Ω-algebras is an Ω-algebra. We note that the A_i's need not be distinct and that the projections are homomorphisms.

Definition 1.1.8

Let Ω be an operator domain and let $\overline{\Omega}$ be a shadow alphabet representing the operations of Ω, let X be an auxiliary alphabet disjoint from $\overline{\Omega}$. X is called the alphabet of free variables. We define the language of the Ω-words, $W_\Omega(X)$, as the following subset of $(X \cup \overline{\Omega})^*$

1. If $\omega \in \Omega(0)$, then $\overline{\omega} \in W_\Omega(X)$.

2. If $x \in X$, then $x \in W_\Omega(X)$.

3. If $a_1, a_2, \ldots, a_n \in W_\Omega(X)$ and $\omega \in \Omega(n)$, then $a_1a_2\ldots a_n\overline{\omega} \in W_\Omega(X)$.

4. Nothing else belongs to $W_\Omega(X)$ unless its being so follows from a finite number of applications of the set of rules 1,2 and 3.

Definition 1.1.9

Let X and $\overline{\Omega}$ be given as in Definition 1.1.8, then we define an Ω-algebra $(\Omega, (X \cup \overline{\Omega})^*)$ as follows for any $a_1, a_2, \ldots, a_n \in (X \cup \overline{\Omega})^*$ and any $\omega \in \Omega(n)$ $\omega(a_1, a_2, \ldots, a_n) = a_1 a_2 \ldots a_n \overline{\omega}$.

Theorem 1.1.10

The Ω-words $W_\Omega(X)$ for a given set X, form an Ω-algebra the subalgebra of $(\Omega, (X \cup \overline{\Omega})^*)$ generated by X.

Proof:

By Definition 1.1.8, the language of Ω-words is closed under the Ω operations and is generated by X. Consistent with this theorem, we have the following.

Definition 1.1.11

The Ω-algebra of the set of Ω-words $W_\Omega(X)$ is called an Ω-word algebra.

Definition 1.1.12

Given the set of Ω-words $W_\Omega(X)$, we define the following relation $<\Omega<$ over $W_\Omega(X)$, called the Ω-subword relation,

1) For all $n \in N$ and all $a_i \in W(X)$, $1 \leq i \leq n$, if $\omega \in \Omega(n)$, then $a_i <\Omega< b$ iff $a_1 a_2 \ldots a_n \omega = b$.

Furthermore, 2) for all $a,b,c \in W_\Omega(X)$

$a <\Omega< a$ and

3) if $a <\Omega< b$ and $b <\Omega< c$, then $a <\Omega< c$.

i.e., $<\Omega<$ is the reflexive transitive closure of the relation defined by 1).

If $a <\Omega< b$, then we say that a is an Ω-subword of b.

<u>Definition 1.1.12.1</u>

We define a mapping $h : W_\Omega(X) \to N$ as follows

$h(\omega) = 0$ for each $\omega \in \Omega(0)$

$h(x) = 0$ for each $x \in X$

$h(a_1 a_2 \ldots a_n \omega) = 1 + \max \{h(a_i) \mid 1 \leq i \leq n\}$

where $\omega \in \Omega(n)$ and $a \in W_\Omega(X)$.

We call h(a) the <u>height</u> of the Ω-word a.

These definitions allow us to represent Ω-words as ordered, labelled rooted trees, the free variables and nullary operators are the leaves of the tree, the other Ω-operators are the labels of the internal nodes. If $\omega \in \Omega(n)$, then n branches are eminating from the node labelled by ω. The right-most operator labels the root of the tree, and the distinction between free variables and nullary operators is only nominal. The reader is encouraged to draw Ω-words as trees in the examples.

Definition 1.1.12.2

Let v be an Ω-word of $W_\Omega(X)$, then we define a correspondence ℓ_v from the Ω-subwords of v into the non-negative integers as follows

$\ell_v(v) = 0$, and for any Ω-subwords b and a_i; $b, a_i < \Omega < v$, $\ell_v(a_i) = 1 + \ell_v(b)$ if $a_1 a_2 .. a_n \omega = b$, for all i, $1 \le i \le n$, and all $\omega \in \Omega(n)$.

We note that ℓ_v is not necessarily functional, since different occurrences of the same Ω-subword may have different values. We say that a certain occurrence of an Ω-subword u of v is on level n if $\ell_v(u) = n$.

The following standard theorems are stated without proof.

The reader is encouraged to consult any of the following excellent introductory reference texts:

A.G. KUROSH, Lectures on General Algebra, Chelsea (1963, 1965).

P.M. COHN, Universal Algebra, Harper-Row (1965).

Our notational conventions are chosen in attempt to parallel Cohn's symbolism, whose work is remarkably impressive for clarity and consistency.

Theorem 1.1.13

For any X and Y the corresponding Ω-algebras are isomorphic, $W_\Omega(X) \cong W_\Omega(Y)$, iff the cardinalities of X and Y are the same.

Theorem 1.1.14

The composition of homomorphisms Ω-algebras $f : A_\Omega \to B_\Omega$ and $g : B_\Omega \to C_\Omega$ is a homomorphism $f \circ g : A_\Omega \to C_\Omega$.

Theory 1.1.15

The image of a homomorphism $f : A_\Omega \to B_\Omega$ is a Ω-subalgebra of B_Ω.

Definition 1.1.16

An equivalence relation on an Ω-algebra A_Ω which is also a subalgebra of $A_\Omega \times A_\Omega$ is called a congruence relation on A_Ω.

Theorem 1.1.17

Let A be an Ω-algebra and ρ a congruence relation on A_Ω, then there is a homomorphism $\mathrm{nat}\rho : A_\Omega \to (A/\rho, \Omega)$.

Definition 1.1.18

The Ω-algebra $(A/\rho, \Omega)$ is called the quotient algebra of A_Ω by ρ.

Theorem 1.1.19

For any Ω-algebras A,B and any generating set X of A, a homomorphism h of A into B is uniquely determined by its restriction $h|X$.

Theorem 1.1.20

Let A_Ω be any Ω-algebra and X any set, then any mapping $\theta : X \to A$ may be uniquely extended to a homomorphism $\overline{\theta} : W_\Omega(X) \to A_\Omega$.

Theorem 1.1.21

Any Ω-algebra A is a homomorphic image of an Ω-word algebra $W_\Omega(X)$ for some set X.

Definition 1.1.22

Γ, a symmetric set of designated pairs of Ω-words in the Ω-word algebra $W_\Omega(Y)$, is called a set of identical relations that hold in $W_\Omega(X)$.

$\Gamma \subset W_\Omega(Y) \times W_\Omega(Y)$, $(w_1,w_2) \in \Gamma$ is written as $w_1=w_2$.

Two Ω-words v and u in $W_\Omega(X)$ are called equivalent with respect to Γ, $v =\Gamma= u$, iff there is a finite sequence of transformations $v_i \to v_{i+1}$ $i=1,\ldots,n-1$: $v=v_1$ and $u=v$ such that there are Ω-words p_i and q_i, Ω-subwords of v_i and v_{i+1} respectively, $p_i <\Omega< v_i$ and $q_i <\Omega< v_{i+1}$, and v_{i+1} is obtained from v_i by replacing p_i by q_i, furthermore, p_i and q_i are the homomorphic images of w_1 and w_2 respectively under an arbitrary map $h_i : Y \to W_\Omega(X)$ extended to a homorphism, where $(w_1,w_2) \in \Gamma$.

Theorem 1.1.23

For any Ω-word algebra $W_\Omega(X)$ and any set of identical relations $\Gamma \subset W_\Omega(X) \times W_\Omega(X)$, the relation $=\Gamma=$ is a congruence relation on $W_\Omega(X)$.

Proof:

Obviously $=\Gamma=$ is an equivalence relation, but since the relation $<\Omega<$ is transitive and since subwords may be replaced by equivalent subwords, it is also a congruence relation. In fact, let $a_i =\Gamma= b_i$ for all i, $1 \leq i \leq n$, then to show that for any $\omega \in \Omega(n)$, $a_1 \ldots a_n\omega =\Gamma= b_1 \ldots b_n\omega$, we are required to show that there is a finite sequence of transformations from $a_1 \ldots a_n\omega$ to $b_1 \ldots b_n\omega$. Suppose the length of the sequence of transformation from a_i to b_i is m_i, then the length of the required sequence of transformations is at most $\sum_{i=1}^{n} m_i$.

Definition 1.1.24

$W(\Omega,X,\Gamma)$ which denotes the factor algebra $(W_\Omega(X)/=\Gamma=,\Omega)$ (or any algebra isomorphic to it), is called the free Ω-algebra of the variety Γ generated by X.

Note the generators of this algebra are the sets of $=\Gamma=$ equivalent words, equivalent to the elements of X.

In practice, when Γ is understood, $=\Gamma=$ is written simply as $=$.

Example 1.1.25

Consider the following free Ω-algebra Gd_1, $Gd_1=W(\Omega,X,\Gamma)$, where

$$\Omega(i) = \phi \quad \text{for all } i \neq 2$$
$$\Omega(2) = \{o\}$$
$$X = \{a\} \quad \text{and } \Gamma=\phi$$

Gd_1 is called the free groupoid generated by a singleton.

The following are the first few elements of Gd_1 ordered lexicographically, within length and height.

a

aao

aaoao

aaaoo

aaoaaoo

aaoaoao

aaaoaoo

aaaaooo

Example 1.1.26

Consider the following free Ω-algebra Sg_1.

$Sg_1 = W(\Omega,X,\Gamma)$,

where

$$\Omega(i) = \phi \quad \text{for all } i \neq 2$$

$$\Omega(2) = \{o\}$$

$$X = \{a\} \text{ and } \Gamma = \{xyozo = xyzoo\} \quad .$$

Sg_1 is called the free semigroup generated by a singleton. The following are the first few elements of Sg_1 in normal form ordered by length. By normal form we mean here the highest form in the lexicographical order among equivalent Ω-words representing an element of Sg_1.

a

aao

aaaoo

aaaaooo

We may note that aaaoo = aaoao are equivalent forms and so are

aaaaooo = aaaoaoo = aaoaoao = aaoaaoo.

To show the equivalence of the first and last elements in the chain, we use the map h, h(x) = a, h(y) = a, h(z) = aao.

Example 1.1.27

Consider the following free Ω-algebra G_{p_2}.

$G_{p_2} = W(\Omega,X,\Gamma)$, where

$\Omega(0) = \{1\}$

$\Omega(1) = \{^{-1}\}$

$\Omega(2) = \{o\}$

$\Omega(i) = \phi \qquad i>2$

$X = \{a,b\}$

$$\Gamma = \{xyozo = xyzoo,\ xx^{-1}o = 1,\ x^{-1}xo = 1,\ x1o = x,\ 1xo = x,\ x^{-1}y^{-1}o = yxo^{-1},\ x^{-1-1} = x\}$$

G_{P_2} is the free group generated by two elements. Γ is not minimal, but a convenient set of identical relations for a free group.

The following are the first few elements of G_{P_2} in normal form ordered lexicographically within length.

$1, a, b, a^{-1}, b^{-1},$

$aao, abo, bao, bbo,$

$ab^{-1}o, a^{-1}bo, ba^{-1}o, b^{-1}ao,$

$a^{-1}a^{-1}o, a^{-1}b^{-1}o, b^{-1}a^{-1}o, b^{-1}b^{-1}o,$

$aaaoo,\ aaboo, \ldots.$

By normal form we mean here the highest form in the lexicographical order among equivalent Ω-words of minimal length.

Definition 1.2.1

Given a set A, we consider the set of all finitary operations on A, denoted by $\alpha(A)$,

$$\alpha(A) = \bigcup_{n\varepsilon N} A^{A^n} = \bigcup_{n\varepsilon N} \alpha_n(A)$$

where the set of n-ary operations on A is denoted by

$$\alpha_n(A) \text{ , } \alpha_n(A) = A^{A^n}.$$

We define the composition of $\omega_1,\omega_2,\ldots,\omega_m$ with ω as an n-ary operation, δ, for each $\omega_1,\omega_2,\ldots,\omega_m \in \alpha_n(A)$ and $\omega \in \alpha_m(A)$ as follows

$$\delta : A^n \to A$$

$$\delta(x) = (x\omega_1)(x\omega_2)\ldots(x\omega_m)\omega \quad \text{for each } x \in A^n.$$

Any ordered set of operations, whose arities obey the requirement for composition is said to be conforming. We define for all $n > 0$, n n-ary operations in $\alpha_n(A)$, namely

$\Pi_{n1},\Pi_{n2},\ldots,\Pi_{nn}$, where for any given i, $1 \leq i \leq n$

$$\Pi_{ni} : A^n \to A$$

$$\Pi_{ni}(a_1,a_2,\ldots,a_i,\ldots a_n) = a_i \qquad \text{for all } a_j \in A, \quad 1 \leq j \leq n.$$

Π_{ni} selects the i-th element in an n-tuple of elements of A.

Π_{ni} is called the <u>i-th component projection of an n-tuple</u>.

$\{\Pi_{ni} \mid 1 \leq i \leq n\}$ is called the set of n-ary projection operators.

A set β of operations on A is called a <u>closed set of operations on A</u>, or a <u>clone on A</u> in short, if and only if β contains the projection operators and the conforming ordered subsets of β are closed under composition.

<u>Example 1.2.2</u>

$\alpha(A)$ is a clone, $\alpha_n(A)$ is a clone.

<u>Definition 1.2.3</u>

Let A be an Ω-algebra, then the clone generated by the Ω-operators on A is called the <u>clone of action</u> of Ω on A.

<u>Theorem 1.2.4</u>

Let A be an Ω-algebra and β the clone of action of Ω on A, let $x \in A^n$ and β_n the set of n-ary operators in β, then

$(\{x\omega \mid \omega \in \beta_n\}, \beta_n)$ is the Ω-subalgebra generated by the entries of x.

<u>Proof</u>:

The n-ary projection operators will provide the generators and the operations in β will provide the Ω-algebra structure, the composition of the n-ary projection operators with elements of β are the set of all n-ary operators in β.

We may see this in a different form in the following.

Theorem 1.2.5

Let Ω be an operator domain, let $n \varepsilon N^+$, let $W_\Omega(X)$ be an Ω-word algebra generated by $X = \{x_1,x_2,\ldots,x_n\}$, let β be the clone of action of Ω on X, let Π_n be the vector of n-ary projection operators on X, namely

$$\Pi_n = (\Pi_{n1},\Pi_{n2},\ldots,\Pi_{nn}). \qquad \beta(\Pi_n) \text{ then}$$

denotes the set of n-ary operations that can be obtained from Π_n by repeated compositions of the projections and the operations in Ω, furthermore, there is an isomorphism between the elements of $W_\Omega(X)$ and $\beta(\Pi_n)$.

Proof:

Let us define a mapping ϕ from the elements of $W_\Omega(X)$ to the operations in $\beta(\Pi_n)$, and show that this mapping is an isomorphism.

1) $\phi(x_i) = \Pi_{ni} = \Pi_{ni}(\Pi_n)$.

Since the arity requirement for composition of operators in Ω are the same as the arity requirement for forming Ω-words, we may proceed inductively on the height of Ω-words as follows:

Suppose ϕ is defined for Y_k, the Ω-words of height less than k, so that $\phi(y) \in \beta(\Pi_n)$ for each $y \in Y_k$. Consider an Ω-word x of height equal to k such as $x = y_1 y_2 \cdots y_m \omega$, where $\omega \in \Omega(m)$. The y_i's are of height less than k, therefore, by hypothesis, each $\phi(y_i) \in \beta(\Pi_n)$ and $\phi(y_1), \phi(y_2), \ldots, \phi(y_m)$ with ω form a conforming ordered subset of operations, therefore we may define in Π_n

2) $\phi(x) - \omega(\phi(y_1), \phi(y_2), \ldots, \phi(y_m))$.

Since 1) defines ϕ for Ω-words of height 0, the induction is complete.

From 1) and 2) it is clear that ϕ is a homomorphism. Clearly every Ω operation can uniquely be so simulated and the composition of functions with a projection operator will not produce an additional function therefore ϕ is an isomorphism.

The following example is included simply to show an instance of the isomorphism and to make the notation more familiar.

Example 1.2.5

Let an Ω-word algebra $W_\Omega(X)$ be given as follows:

$X = \{a,b\}$

$\Omega(0) = \phi$

$\Omega(1) = \{*, ^{-1}\}$

$\Omega(2) = \{o\}$

$\Omega(i) = \phi$ for $i>2$

Let $\Pi_{21}(a,b) = a$ and $\Pi_{22}(a,b) = b$.

Consider the Ω-word

$x = abo^{-1}a{*}o$.

$$\phi(x) = \phi(abo^{-1}a{*}o) = o(\phi(abo^{-1}), \phi(a*)) =$$

$$= o(^{-1}(\phi(abo)), *(\phi(a))) =$$

$$= o(^{-1}(o(\phi(a), \phi(b)), *(\Pi_{21}(a,b))) =$$

$$= o(^{-1}(o(\Pi_{21}(a,b), \Pi_{22}(a,b)), *(\Pi_{21}(a,b)))$$

A few remarks at this point are in order. First of all, in Theorem 1.2.5 the concept of an isomorphism is used in the relaxed sense that the parsing tree of the Ω-word x is graph theoretically isomorphic to the composition tree of the operators in $\phi(x)$, as labeled ordered rooted trees.

Secondly, the operation $\phi(x)$ is an n-ary operation from $(X \cup \Omega)^{*n} \to (X \cup \Omega)^*$, where $X = \{x_1, x_2, \ldots, x_n\}$.

Thirdly, Theorem 1.2.5 is simply the formal notion of the operation of substitution for the free variables in a given Ω-word.

On the basis of these remarks, we adopt the following:

<u>Definition 1.2.6</u>

Let x be an Ω-word in the Ω-word algebra $W_\Omega(X)$, where $X = \{x_1, x_2, \ldots, x_n\}$. We denote the value of the n-ary operation $\phi(x)$, $\phi(x) : (X \cup \Omega)^{*n} \to (X \cup \Omega)^*$, given in the proof of Theorem 1.2.5 as

$x(y_1, y_2, \ldots, y_n)$ for any n-tuple $(y_1, \ldots, y_n)$ of strings in $(X \cup \Omega)^*$ and any $x \in W_\Omega(X)$. This convention identifies the word x with the operation it represents as a substitution formula.

Example 1.2.6

Following Example 1.2.5, we obtain

$$x = abo^{-1}a*o$$

$x(a,b) = abo^{-1}a*o$

$x(a,a^{-1}) = aa^{-1}o^{-1}a*o$

$x(a^{-1},abo) = a^{-1}aboo^{-1}a^{-1}*o$

$x(b,oa) = boao^{-1}b*o$

$abo^{-1}a*o(b,a) = bao^{-1}b*o$

We now introduce operations that are homomorphic images of compositions of operations in an Ω-word algebra.

To define operations of arbitrary arity, we will need a potentially infinite alphabet for the free substitutional variables. To specialize an operation, we use the scheme of explicit transformations, i.e., we permute or identify variables, put constants for variables and add new variables, all this may be accomplished by composition with the projection operators and substitution. Formally the development is given as follows:

Definition 1.2.7

Given an infinite set $X = \{x_1,x_2,x_3,\ldots\}$, consider the sequence of ordered subsets of S.

$X_1 = (x_1)$, $X_2 = (x_1,x_2),\ldots,X_n = (x_1,x_2,\ldots,x_n)$, ...

let Ω be a operator domain, let the corresponding Ω-word algebras be the sequence

$W_\Omega(X_1)$, $W_\Omega(X_2),\ldots,W_\Omega(X_n),\ldots$

let x be a given Ω-word in $W_\Omega(X_n)$ with the correspondingly denoted operation $x(x_1,x_2,\ldots,x_n) = x$, which is a homomorphism

$$x : W_\Omega(X_n)^n \to W_\Omega(X)$$

let Ω' be an operator domain and let d be a given arity preserving mapping, i.e.

$$d : \Omega \to \Omega'$$

such that

$$d[\omega] = \omega' \quad \text{implies} \quad a(\omega) = a(\omega') ,$$

let $A_{\Omega'}$ be an Ω'-algebra, and for any

$$a_1,a_2,\ldots,a_n \in A_{\Omega'} ,$$

let h be the homomorphic extension of the map $h(x_i) = a_i$, then we define the operation $\tilde{x}$ as follows

$$\tilde{x} : A^n \to A$$

$\tilde{x}(a_1,a_2,\ldots,a_n) = d[x](h(x_1),h(x_2),\ldots,h(x_n))$

(In practice d is bijective and Ω and Ω' may be identified). The definition of $\tilde{x}$ may be exhibited by the following commuting diagram of homomorphisms.

$$\begin{array}{ccc} W_\Omega(X_n)^n & \xrightarrow{\ h\ } & A^n \\ x \downarrow & & \downarrow \tilde{x} \\ W_\Omega(X_n) & \xrightarrow[\ h\ ]{} & A \end{array}$$

$\tilde{x}$ is called a <u>principal derived n-ary operation</u> on $A_{\Omega'}$, and is denoted by the expression $\tilde{x}(x_1,x_2,\ldots,x_n)$.

For any integer $k \leq n$ and any set of elements $b_1,b_2,\ldots,b_k \in A$, the operation $\tilde{x}(x_1,x_2,\ldots,x_m,b_1,b_2,\ldots,b_k)$, where $m=n-k$, is called a derived n-ary operation on $A_{\Omega'}$. In this definition we chose to specialize the last k arguments for notational convenience only.

<u>Example 1.2.7</u>

Consider the Ω_1-algebra given by

$A_{\Omega_1} = (\{1,a,b\}\ ,\ \{o,1,{}^{-1}\})$, where $a(o) = 2$, $a(1) = 0$, $a({}^{-1}) = 1$

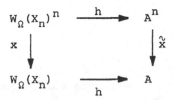

o	1	a	b
1	1	a	b
a	a	b	1
b	b	1	a

	1	a	b
$^{-1}$	1	b	a

It is easy to see that A_{Ω_1} is the cyclic group on $\{1,a,b\}$. Consider the subgroup closure operator

$$\kappa(x,y) = x^{-1}yo(x,y) = o(^{-1}(\Pi_x(x,y)),\Pi_x(x,y)),$$

where

$$\Pi_x(x,y) = x \quad \text{and} \quad \Pi_y(x,y) = y.$$

The operator κ is a principal derived binary operator on A_{Ω_1}.

Example 1.2.8

On the other hand, consider the Ω_2-algebra, given by $A_{\Omega_2} = (\{1,a,b\}, \{\kappa\})$, where $a(\kappa) = 2$ and the multiplication table for κ is given as derived in the previous example, then consider the operations $\underline{o}$, $\underline{1}$, and $^{-1}$, where

$$\underline{1}(x,y) = \kappa(\Pi_x(x,y), \Pi_x(x,y))$$

$$\underline{^{-1}}(x,y) = \kappa(\Pi_x(x,y), \underline{1}(x,y)) \quad \text{and}$$

$$\underline{o}(x,y) = \kappa(^{-1}(x,y), \Pi_y(x,y)).$$

The operations $\underline{1}(x,y)$, $\underline{\ }^{-1}(x,y)$ and $\underline{o}(x,y)$ are principal derived binary operations on A_{Ω_2}.

$\underline{1}$	1	a	b
1	1	1	1
a	1	1	1
b	1	1	1

$\underline{\ }^{-1}$	1	a	b
1	1	1	1
a	b	b	b
b	a	a	a

$\underline{o}$	1	a	b
1	1	a	b
a	a	b	1
b	b	1	a

and clearly they are respectively equivalent to the operations 1, $^{-1}$ and o in A_Ω in the previous example, in fact, they are given as the following derived operations:

$$1 = \kappa(1,1)\ ,\quad {}^{-1}(x) = \kappa(x,1) \quad \text{and} \quad o(x,y) = \underline{o}(x,y).$$

<u>Definition 1.2.9</u>

For an Ω-algebra A_Ω, the derived unary operations are called <u>derived translations on A_Ω</u>. If a derived unary operation $\underline{f}$ is principal, then $\underline{f}$ is called a <u>principal derived translation on A_Ω</u>. A subset S of A such that $S = \{a, f(a)\ ,\ f(f(a))\ ,\ f(f(f(a))),\dots\}$ is called a <u>splinter in A_Ω</u> or an <u>Ω-algebraic splinter in A</u> for any derived translation $\underline{f}$ and any element $\underline{a}$ in A. Splinters play an important role in the fundations of mathematics, and were studied by Ullian, Myhill, Young and Rogers; they consider $\underline{f}$ to be any recursive function. Splinters also turn up in disguise in the study of autonomous automata, in the study of cyclic submonoids of the monoid of endomorphisms of

Ω-algebras and in the study of fixed point theorems in general.

<u>Definition 1.2.10</u>

Let A_Ω be an Ω-algebra, we define the Ω'-algebra $\mathcal{B}(A)_{\Omega'}$, as follows. For any $\omega \in \Omega(n)$, we define ω' as follows

$$\omega' : \mathcal{B}(A)^n \to \mathcal{B}(A)$$

$$\omega'(X_1, X_2, \ldots, X_n) = \{\omega(x_1, x_2, \ldots, x_n) \mid x_i \in X_i \text{ for all } i,\ 1 \leq i \leq n\} .$$

We identify Ω and Ω'.

$\mathcal{B}(A)_\Omega$ is called the <u>Ω-set algebra on A</u>. In $\mathcal{B}(A)_\Omega$ the presence of the binary operator $\cup$ is tacitly assumed. As an immediate consequence of the definition, we have the following:

<u>Theorem 1.2.11</u>

For any Ω-set algebra $\mathcal{B}(A)_\Omega$ and any $\omega \in \Omega(n)$

$$\omega(X_1, X_2, \ldots, X_i, \ldots, X_n) \cup \omega(X_1, X_2, \ldots, X_i', \ldots, X_n) =$$

$$\omega(X_1, X_2, \ldots, X_i \cup X_i', \ldots, X_n)$$ where the X_i and X_i' are subsets of A.

<u>Proof:</u>

The left-hand side and the right-hand side are same as sets.

Example 1.2.11

Consider the free monoid generated by a doubleton

$\mathfrak{W}_2 = W(\Omega, Y, \Gamma)$, where $\Omega = \{\lambda, o\}$, $Y = \{a,b\}$

$a(\lambda) = 0$ and $a(o) = 2$, $\Gamma = \{xyozo = xyzoo,\ \lambda xo = x\lambda o\}$.

The first few normalized elements of $\mathfrak{W}_2$ in lexicographical order within length are

λ,a,b,aao,abo,bao,bbo,aaaoo,aaboo,abaoo,abboo,...

Here the binary operation $\underline{o}$ is called the string catenation and the following is an instance of that

$$o(aao,b) = aaobo = aaboo.$$

The operation symbol may be omitted in the forms. Consider the Ω-set algebra $\mathfrak{B}(\mathfrak{W}_2)_\Omega$ corresponding to $\mathfrak{W}_2$, namely the algebra of languages over the binary alphabet with operation set-catenation or set-product. The following is an instance of this operation:

$$o(\{a,aa\}, \{b,ab,aab\}) = \{ab,aab,aaab,aaaab\}.$$

Because of the previous theorem, we have the following identity for any set A,B,C,D in $\mathfrak{B}(\mathfrak{W}_2)_\Omega$

$$o(A \cup B,\ C \cup D) = o(A,C) \cup o(B,C) \cup o(A,D) \cup o(B,D).$$

A set valued set mapping f is called <u>monotonic</u> if it preserves the inclusion relation, i.e. $X \subset Y$ implies $f(X) \subset f(Y)$. Using this terminology, we can state Theorem 1.2.11 equivalently as follows:

Corollary 1.2.11

For any Ω-set algebra $\mathcal{B}(A)_\Omega$ any derived translation is monotonic.

Proof: Let $X \subset Y \subset A$ and without loss of generality assume that the derived translation f is given as follows

$f(V) = \omega(V,A_1,A_2,\ldots,A_{n-1})$ for all $V \subset A$, where $A_i \subseteq A$, $o<i<n$, and ω is in the clone of action of Ω such that $a(\omega) = n>o$, then $X \subset Y$ implies that $Y = X \cup Z$, where $Z \subset A$, furthermore by Theorem 1.2.11

$$f(Y) = f(X \cup Z) = \omega(X \cup Z,A_1,A_2,\ldots,A_{n-1}) =$$

$$\omega(X,A_1,A_2,\ldots,A_{n-1}) \cup \omega(Z,A_1,A_2,\ldots,A_{n-1}) = f(X) \cup f(Z),$$

therefore

$$f(X) \cup f(Y).$$

Corollary 1.2.12

For any Ω-set algebra $\mathcal{B}(A)_\Omega$ and any $\omega \in \Omega(n)$, the following inclusion holds:

$$\omega(X_1,X_2,\ldots,X_i,\ldots,X_n) \cap \omega(X_1,X_2,\ldots,X_i',\ldots,X_n) \supset$$

$$\omega(X_1,X_2,\ldots,X_i \cap X_i',\ldots,X_n) ,$$

where the X_i's and X_i' are subsets of A.

Proof:

The right-hand side is included in each term of the intersection on the left, by the previous theorem, consequently it is included in their intersection. We note that the inclusion is proper in general and that $\omega(X_1,\ldots,\phi,\ldots,X_n) = \phi$.

Furthermore, if $X \subset Y$, then the splinter $(Y,f(Y),f(f(Y)),\ldots)$ dominates the splinter $(X,f(X),f(f(X)),\ldots)$ as a set sequence.

Definition 1.2.13

Let f be a derived translation on A_Ω, let a be an element of A, then the mapping $S[f,a,A_\Omega]$ is called an f-splinter sequence on A_Ω generated by a.

$$S[f,a,A_\Omega] : N \to A_\Omega$$

$$S[f,a,A_\Omega](o) = a$$

$$S[f,a,A_\Omega](n) = f(S[f,a,A_\Omega](n-1))$$

In what follows, we generalize the concept of the splinter to direct powers of Ω-algebras. By <u>direct power</u> we mean a direct product in which all factors are identical. Thus

$$A^n_\Omega = \overset{1}{\underset{\sim}{A}}_\Omega \times \overset{2}{\underset{\sim}{A}}_\Omega \times \dots \times \overset{n}{\underset{\sim}{A}}_\Omega$$

<u>Definition 1.2.14</u>

τ, an n-tuple of derived n-ary operations on an Ω-algebra A_Ω is called a <u>derived transformation</u> on A^n_Ω. If all the derived n-ary operations are principal, then it is called a <u>principal derived transformation</u> on A^n_Ω.

Let $\tau = (t_1, t_2, \dots, t_n)$ and $t_i : A^n \to A$, $1 \le i \le n$, then

$\tau : A^n \to A^n$.

<u>Definition 1.2.15</u>

Let τ be a derived transformation on A^m_Ω and $a \in A^m_\Omega$, then we define an <u>m-ary splinter</u> as the following set of elements of A^m

$\{a, \tau(a), \tau(\tau(a)), \tau(\tau(\tau(a))), \dots\}$

$S[A^m_\Omega, \tau, a]$ will denote the following mapping:

$S[A_{\Omega}^{m},\tau,a] : N \rightarrow A_{\Omega}^{m}$

$S[A_{\Omega}^{m},\tau,a](o) = a$

$S[A_{\Omega}^{m},\tau,a](n) = \tau(S[A_{\Omega}^{m},\tau,a](n-1))$ for $n>0$.

Let τ be a derived transformation on A_{Ω}^{m}, then the following set of transformations is called a splinter of transformations on A_{Ω}^{m}.

$\{\Pi_m,\tau,\tau^2,\ldots\}$, where τ^n is defined as follows:

$\tau^n : A^m \rightarrow A^m$

$\tau^n(a) = S[A_{\Omega}^{n},\tau,a](n)$.

Because of the associativity of composition and the identity action of the projection operations, we obtain the following:

Theorem 1.2.16

Given an Ω-algebra A_{Ω} and let $S = \{\Pi_m,\tau,\tau^2,\ldots\}$ be a splinter of transformation on A_{Ω}^{m}, then S with the operation composition forms a cyclic monoid generated by τ.

Proof:

Clearly, from what we said $\tau^{a+b} = \tau^a \circ \tau^b$ and

$\Pi_m \circ \tau^a = \tau^a \circ \Pi_m = \tau^a$

For consistency we have the following:

Definition 1.2.17

For any splinter transformation τ on A_{Ω}^{m}

$$\Pi_m = \tau^0$$

Definition 1.2.18

Let $W_{\Omega}(X)$ be an Ω-word algebra, where $X = \{x_1,\ldots,x_n\}$ and let $y = (y_1,y_2,\ldots,y_n)$ be an n-tuple of Ω-words in $W_{\Omega}(X)$, let

$\tau = (\phi(y_1), \phi(y_2),\ldots,\phi(y_n))$ be the corresponding n-tuple of n-ary operations, where for each i, $1 \leq i \leq n$, $\phi(y_i)$ is given

$$\phi(y_i) : (X \cup \Omega)^{*n} \to (X \cup \Omega)^*,$$

as defined by

Definition 1.2.6, then

τ is called an n-ary Ω-word transformation, and the set $\{\tau^0,\tau^1,\tau^2,\ldots\}$ is called an n-ary Ω-word transformation splinter.

Definition 1.2.19

Let $W_{\Omega}(X)$ be an Ω-word algebra with the finite ordered set of generators $X = (x_1,\ldots,x_n)$, let τ be an n-ary Ω-word transformation, let x be an Ω-word, then the triple $H_{\Omega}=(W_{\Omega}(X),\tau,x)$ is called an OL Ω-word system.

$L[H_\Omega]$, the language of the Ω-OL word system, is defined as the following set:

$$L[H_\Omega] = \{x(\tau^m(X)) \mid m \geq 0\}$$

$WS[H_\Omega]$, the Ω-word sequence defined by H_Ω is the following mapping:

$$WS[H_\Omega] : N \to W_\Omega(X)$$

$$WS[H_\Omega](m) = x(\tau^m(X)) \quad .$$

Theorem 1.2.20

Given an OL Ω-word system $H_\Omega = (W_\Omega(X), \tau, x)$, where X is any (non-empty) finite ordered alphabet, then for any non-negative integers such that $i+j = m$, the following equality holds:

$$WS[H_\Omega](m) = x(\tau^i(X)(\tau^j(X))) \quad .$$

Proof:

Let n be the cardinality of X, then for any n-tuple $a \in (X \cup \Omega)^{*n}$ and for any n-ary transformation χ, $\chi(X)(a) = \chi(a)$, therefore

$$\tau^i(X)(\tau^j(X)) = \tau^i(\tau^j(X)) = \tau^{i+j}(X) = \tau^m(X)$$

hence

$$x(\tau^i(X)(\tau^j(X))) = x(\tau^m(X)) = S[H_\Omega](m) \quad .$$

Corollary 1.2.20

$$WS[H_\Omega](m) = x(\tau^{m-1}(X)(\tau(X))$$

$$WS[H_\Omega](m) = x(\tau(X)(\tau^{m-1}(X)) \qquad \text{if } m>0.$$

Corollary 1.2.21

Let $X = (x_1,x_2,\ldots,x_n)$, and let $H_{k\Omega} = (W_\Omega(X),\tau,x_k)$ for all k, $1\le k\le n$, let

$$V_i = (WS[H_{1\Omega}](j),\ WS[H_{2\Omega}](j),\ldots,WS[H_{n\Omega}](j))$$

then

$$WS[H_\Omega](m) = x(\tau^i(V_j)) \text{ for each } i,j \text{ and } m$$

such that $i+j=n$.

In particular,

$$WS[H_\Omega](m) = x(\tau(V_{m-1})) = x(\tau^{m-1}(V_1))$$

if $m>0$.

Proof:

$$V_j = \tau^j(X).$$

Example 1.2.22

Let $X = (a,b)$, $\Omega = \{0\}$, $a(o) = 2$,

$$\tau(\alpha,\beta) = (\Pi_b(\alpha,\beta) , o(\Pi_b(\alpha,\beta) , \Pi_a(\alpha,\beta)))$$

where

$$\Pi_a(\alpha,\beta) = \alpha \quad \text{and} \quad \Pi_b(\alpha,\beta) = \beta \quad \text{for all } \alpha,\beta \text{ in } (X \cup \Omega)^*$$

Let $H = (W_\Omega(X),\tau,x)$, where $x = abo$.

From this we obtain the following:

$$\tau^2(\alpha,\beta) = (o(\Pi_b(\alpha,\beta),\Pi_a(\alpha,\beta)),o(o(\Pi_b(\alpha,\beta),\Pi_a(\alpha,\beta)),\Pi_b(\alpha,\beta)))$$

$$\tau^3(\alpha,\beta) = (o(o(\Pi_b(\alpha,\beta),\Pi_a(\alpha,\beta)),\Pi_b(\alpha,\beta)),$$

$$o(o(o(\Pi_b(\alpha,\beta),\Pi_a(\alpha,\beta)),\Pi_b(\alpha,\beta),o(\Pi_b(\alpha,\beta),\Pi_a(\alpha,\beta))))$$

$$\tau(X) = (b,o(b,a)) = (b,bao)$$

$$\tau^2(X) = (o(b,a),o(o(b,a),b)) = (bao,o(bao,b)) = (bao,baobo)$$

$$\tau^3(X) = (o(o(b,a),b),o(o(o(b,a),b),o(b,a))) =$$

$$= (o(bao,b),o(o(bao,b),bao)) =$$

$$= (baobo,o(baobo,bao)) = (baobo,baobobaoo)$$

$$\tau^2(\tau(X)) = \tau^2(b,bao) = (baobo,baobobaoo)$$

$$\tau(\tau^2(X)) = \tau(bao,baobo) = (baobo,baobobaoo)$$

WS[H](3) = x(baobo,baobobaoo) = baobobaobobaooo

$x(\tau(X)(\tau^2(X)))$ = abo((b,bao)((bao,baobo))) =

= abo(b(bao,baobo),bao(bao,baobo))

= abo(baobo,baobobaoo) =

= baobobaobobaooo

$x(\tau^2(X)(\tau(X)))$ = abo((bao,baobo)((b,bao))) =

= abo((bao(b,bao),baobo(b,bao))) =

= abo(baobo,baobobaoo) =

= baobobaobobaooo.

The image of an OL Ω-word system under a homomorphism h, is called Ω-OL system. It is clear that a statement similar to Theorem 1.2.20 may be phrased about the image, since we may commute h and τ. One way we may interpret Corollary 1.2.20 is as follows:

In a developmental system without interaction, the global pattern on the highest level is identical with the pattern of the first stage of the development, or in cosmic terms: The macro-cosmos reflects the microcosmos.

BOUNDED PARALLELISM AND REGULAR LANGUAGES

D. WOOD

Department of Applied Mathematics, McMaster University

CONTENTS

Section 1: Introduction and Overview.

If we examine the rewriting systems of Ibarra[(1)], the so called Simple Matrix Grammars (SMG), we see that rewriting has the following three facets, namely

(1) rewriting occurs in PARALLEL,

(2) the parallelism is, a priori, BOUNDED, and

(3) the rewriting is, a priori, CONTROLLED.

Secondly, if we examine the rewriting systems of Lindenmayer [61], the so called E0L systems, and compare and contrast with the

(1) Ibarra, O. H., Simple matrix languages, Information and Control 17 (1970), 359-394.

SMG's we find:

(1) rewriting again occurs in PARALLEL,

(2) the parallelism is, a priori, UNBOUNDED and EXHAUSTIVE, and

(3) the rewriting is, a priori, UNCONTROLLED.

Later extensions to E0L systems have lead to two kinds of CONTROL

(a) 'RULE-CONTEXT-FREE' CONTROL - Rozenberg's Tabled Systems [81]; rules are applied EXHAUSTIVELY from one table of rules from a given set of tables. However, within this restriction a particular rule is applied independently of the other rules that are applied at the same time.

(b) 'RULE-CONTEXT' CONTROL - [11]. The application of a particular rule is dependent upon its context within the sequence of rules applied at a particular time.

In the light of these developments in E0L systems, simple matrix grammars can be considered to have either 'RULE-CONTEXT' or 'RULE-CONTEXT-FREE' CONTROL. In the following we present a survey of results on the effect of changing facet (3) for SMG to:

(3) the rewriting is UNCONTROLLED.

This is the investigation of E0L-like systems where the parallelism is bounded, and can be considered to be the investigation of the development of filamentous organisms under an environment which deprives the cells of "food". We consider two different kind of generating systems, finite state generators and right linear grammars, which we generalise to give n-parallel finite state generators and n-parallel right linear grammars.

Section 2: n-parallel finite state generators.

Definition

A *finite state generator* (FSG) G, is a quintuple (N,T,E,S,F) where

N is a finite set of *points*,

T is a terminal *alphabet*,

E is a set of *edges*, E VxT*xV,

S N is a set of *entry* points, and

F N is a set of *exit* points.

Example 1

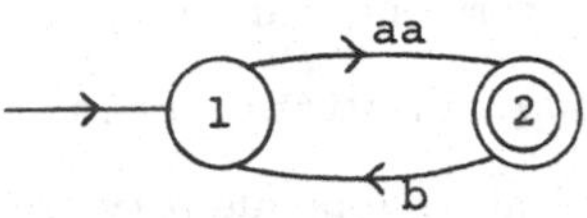

N = {1,2}, T = {a,b},

E = {(1,aa,2), (2,b,1)}

S = {1} and F = {2}.

Definition

Given G, an FSG, then we write $u \to vx$ if u,v in N, x in T* and (u,x,v) in E.

Similarly, we write $u \to^{i} vx$, $i>0$ if there exist sequences $u_0, \dots, u_i$ and $x_1, \dots, x_i$ such that

$u_j \to u_{j+1} x_{j+1}$, $0 \leq j < i$,

$x = x_1 \dots x_i$, $u = u_0$ and $v = u_i$.

We write $u \to^{+} vx$ if there exists $i>0$ such that $u \to^{i} vx$, and we write $u \to^{*} vx$ if either $u \to^{+} vx$ or $u = v$ and $x = \varepsilon$. The *language* generated by an FSG G is

$L(G) = \{x: \ u \to^{*} vx, \ u \text{ in } S, \ v \text{ in } F\}$.

We say $L \subseteq T^{*}$ is a *finite state language* (FSL) iff there exists an FSG G such that L = L(G). We usually say L is a *regular set*, so we denote the family of FSL's by $\mathcal{R}$.

Example 1 (cont.)

$L(G) = \{aa, aabaa, aabaabaa, \dots\}$

$= \{aa(baa)^{i}: \ i \geq 0\}$.

We can now consider n-parallel FSGs. The basic idea is to have n FSG's operating synchronously and in parallel. Rather than repeating a generalised form of the notation above, we develop the model informally.

Consider a 2-PFSG (2-parallel FSG) G:

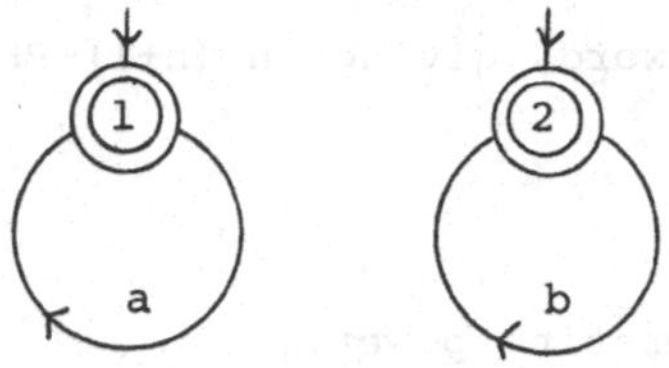

Initially these two processors (or generators) (G_1 and G_2) are both *alive* and *idle*. We start them up simultaneously and synchronously (by which we mean we move along edges at the same time).

Thus we have:

<u>point reached and word generated so far:</u>

	G_1	G_2
time = 0	1	2
= 1	1a	2b
= 2	1aa	2bb
= 3	1aaa	2bbb
...	...	...

If the two processors each reach an exit point at the same time, then we catenate the two words generated so far. Here we have, since both points 1 and 2 are exit points that:

<u>word generated by G so far</u>

time = 0	ε
1	ab
2	a^2b^2
3	a^3b^3
...	...

Thus, we say $L(G) = \{a^ib^i: i \geq 0\}$.

In a similar way we can generate languages given by an n-PFSG, $n \geq 1$, called n-PFSL's. Let $\mathcal{F}_n$ denote the family of n-PFSL's.

We have:

<u>Result 1</u>: $\mathcal{R} = \mathcal{F}_1$, trivially.

<u>Result 2</u>: For $n \geq 1$, $\mathcal{F}_n \subseteq \mathcal{F}_{n+1}$.

Proof: Simply add an extra processor G_{n+1} to G, which generates nothing but the empty word, giving an (n+1)-PFSG, i.e.

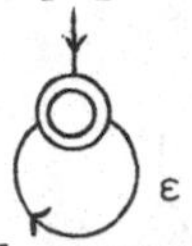

Result 3: ε-edges do add generating power.

Proof: Consider $L = \{a^i b^j : 0 \leq i \leq j\}$, L cannot be generated without an ε-edge occurring in at least one processor.

Result 4: For $n \geq 2$, $L_n = \{a_1^{\ i} \ldots a_n^{\ i} : i \geq 0\}$ is in $\mathcal{F}_n$ but not in $\mathcal{F}_{n-1}$.

Corollary: For $n \geq 1$, $\mathcal{F}_n \subsetneqq \mathcal{F}_{n+1}$: an infinite hierarchy of languages.

Result 5: $\mathcal{F}_2 \subsetneqq$ family of one-counter languages.

Result 6: For $n \geq 1$, $\mathcal{F}_n \subsetneqq$ family of context-sensitive languages.

Result 7: For $n \geq 3$, $\mathcal{F}_n$ and the family of context-free languages are incomparable.

These results will be found in Wood[(2)].

Section 3: Variations on the basic model of n-PFSG's.

In the previous section, the terminology *alive* and *idle* with respect to n-PFSG's was introduced. If we say that an FSG *dies* when it reaches an exit point, then a word is output by an n-PFSG whenever all n processors die at the same time. We also say a processor is *active* when it is alive and not idle.

Variation 1: Given m FSGs, $m>0$ and n, $0<n<m$ then allow n live processors (at most) to be active at one time, and no longer require that n processors die together. A word is generated by $G_1, \ldots, G_m$ if initially, they become alive simultaneously and n of them become active for one time step, then another n become active for the next

---

(2) Wood, D., Properties of n-parallel finite state languages, Utilitas Mathematica 4 (1973), 103-113.

time step, and so on until all m processors are dead. Then we catenate the m words together left to right, to give a word generated by $G_1,\ldots,G_m$. Let $\mathcal{F}_{(m,n)}$ be the family of languages defined by this model. Then we have:

Result 8: $\mathcal{R} = \mathcal{F}_{(m,n)}$ for all m,n, 0<n<m. That is the model degenerates.

Variation 2: Let the m processors proceeding from left to right become active n at a time (if there are less than n, then the remaining number of processors), and all n die simultaneously. Let $\mathcal{F}_{m,n}$ denote the corresponding family of languages.

Result 9: For m>0, $0<n\leq m$, where m = np+q, $0\leq q<n$, then $\mathcal{F}_{m,n} = (\mathcal{F}_n)^p \mathcal{F}_q$.

Result 10: $\mathcal{F}_{m,n} \subsetneqq \mathcal{F}_{m+1,n}$, for all m,n, $0<n\leq m$.

Result 11: $\mathcal{F}_{m,n}$ and $\mathcal{F}_{m,n+1}$ are incomparable, for all m,n, $0<n\leq m$.

Note that $\mathcal{F}_{m,m} = \mathcal{F}_m$ and $\mathcal{F}_{m,1} = \mathcal{R}$, for all m>0.

Variation 3: We can impose more structure on the n-PFSG by introducing a traffic cop, who by making use of a book of regulations determines which edges are allowable edges for the n FSG's at this time instant.

Example 2

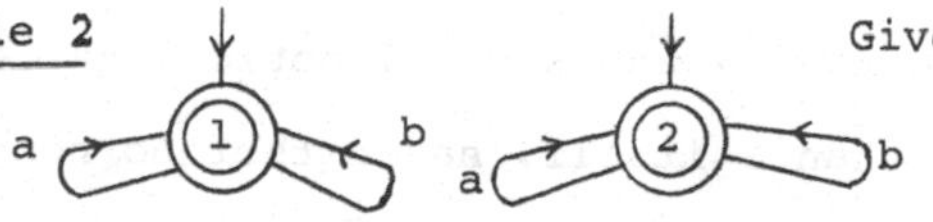

Given the 2-PFSG G:

with the rule book {<(1,a,1),(2,a,2)>, <(1,b,1),(2,b,2)>} then processor G_1 can only traverse the a-edge whenever processor G_2 traverses an a-edge, thus L(G) = {ww: w in {a,b}*}. The rule book is usually called a *control set*, the corresponding family of languages is denoted $\mathcal{F}_n^C$.

Result 12: $\mathcal{F}_n \subsetneqq \mathcal{F}_n^C$, for all n>1.

Result 13: $\mathcal{F}_n^C = \mathcal{R}_{[n]}$, the family of *n-right linear SML*(3).

---

(3) see footnote 1.

These results can be found in Wood[4]

Section 4: An alternative formulation, n-PRLG's and closure properties.

Definition

For $n\geq 1$, let $G = (N_1,\ldots,N_n,T,S,P)$ where N_i, $1\leq i\leq n$, are disjoint nonterminal alphabets,

T is a terminal alphabet,

S is a sentence symbol, S not in $\bigcup_{i=1}^{n} N_i = N$,

P is a finite set of rules of the form:

(i) $S\rightarrow X_1\ldots X_n$, X_i in N_i,

(ii) $X\rightarrow aY$, X,Y in N_i, some i, a in T*, and

(iii) $X\rightarrow a$, X in N_i, some i, a in T*.

G is an *n-parallel right linear grammar, n-PRLG.*

We write $x \Rightarrow y$ iff

either x = S and $S\rightarrow y$ in P,

or $x = y_1X_1\ldots y_nX_n$, $y = y_1x_1\ldots y_nx_n$, y_i in T*, X_i in N_i, x_i in $T^*\cup T^*N_i$ and $X_i\rightarrow x_i$ in P, $1\leq i\leq n$.

In the usual way we obtain $x \overset{+}{\Rightarrow} y$ and $x \overset{*}{\Rightarrow} y$, notice that either a valid sentential form, other than S itself, has either no nonterminals or exactly n nonterminals. $L(G) = \{x\colon\ S \overset{+}{\Rightarrow} x,\ x \text{ in } T^*\}$, and $L\subseteq T^*$ is an n-PRLL iff there exists an n-PRLG G such that L = L(G). Let the family of n-PRLL's be $\mathcal{R}_n$.

Result 14: $\mathcal{R}_1 = \mathcal{R}$.

Result 15: $\mathcal{F}_n \subsetneq \mathcal{R}_n$, for all n>1.

Result 16: Closure and non-closure results for $\mathcal{F}_n$ and $\mathcal{R}_n$, n>1.

---

(4) Wood, D., Two variations on n-parallel finite state generators, McMaster University CS TR 73/3 (1973).

operation	$\mathcal{F}_n$	$\mathcal{R}_n$
union	No	Yes
homomorphism	No	Yes
finite substitution	No	Yes
substitution	No	No
catenation	No	No
intersection	No	No
complementation	No	No
intersection with regular set	No	Yes
a-NGSM maps (accepting states)	No	Yes

These results are detailed in Rosebrugh and Wood[5] and Wood[6].

Section 5: <u>Characterisation Theorems for</u> $\mathcal{F}_{||}$ <u>and</u> $\mathcal{R}_{||}$.

<u>Definition</u>

Let $\mathcal{F}_{||} = \bigcup_{i=1}^{\infty} \mathcal{F}_i$ and $\mathcal{R}_{||} = \bigcup_{i=1}^{\infty} \mathcal{R}_i$ and $\langle M\rangle$ denote an *infinite sequence* $M_1, M_2, \ldots$ where $M_i \subseteq T^*$. Define $L(M) = \{x:\ x \text{ in } M_i,$ some $i \geq 1\}$. A sequence $\langle M\rangle$ is a *regular sequence* iff there exists an FSG G such that $L(M) = L(G)$ and $M_i = \{x:\ u \to^i vx,\ u \text{ in } S,\ v \text{ in } F\}$.

Given two sequences $\langle M_1\rangle$ and $\langle M_2\rangle$ define $\langle M_1\rangle \odot \langle M_2\rangle$, the *synchronised product* of $\langle M_1\rangle$ with $\langle M_2\rangle$, as the sequence $M_{11}M_{21}, M_{12}M_{22}, \ldots$. Define $\langle M_1\rangle \oplus \langle M_2\rangle$, the *synchronised union* of $\langle M_1\rangle$ with $\langle M_2\rangle$, as the sequence, $M_{11} \cup M_{21}, M_{12} \cup M_{22}, \ldots$

<u>Result 17</u>: For $n>0$, L in $\mathcal{R}_n$ iff there exist $m \times n$ regular sequences $\langle M_{ij}\rangle$, $1 \leq i \leq m$, $1 \leq j \leq n$ for some $m \geq 1$ such that

(5) Rosebrugh, R. D., and Wood, D., Restricted parallelism and right linear grammars, McMaster University CS TR 72/6 (1972).
(6) See footnote 2.

$$L = L(M) \text{ where } \langle M\rangle = \langle M_{11}\rangle \odot \langle M_{12}\rangle \odot \ldots \langle M_{1n}\rangle$$
$$\oplus \langle M_{21}\rangle \ldots.$$
$$\vdots$$
$$\oplus \langle M_{m1}\rangle \odot \ldots \odot \langle M_{mn}\rangle$$

<u>Result 18:</u> For $n>0$, L in $\mathcal{F}_n$ iff there exist n regular sequences $\langle M_i\rangle$ such that $L = L(M)$ where $\langle M\rangle = \langle M_1\rangle \odot \ldots \odot \langle M_n\rangle$.

<u>Definition</u>

Let $\mathcal{S}$ be the smallest family of sequences containing the regular sequences and closed under $\odot$ and $\oplus$ and let $L(\mathcal{S}) = \{L(M): \langle M\rangle \text{ in } \mathcal{S}\}$.

<u>Result 19:</u> <u>Sequence Characterisation of</u> $\mathcal{R}_{||}$.

$\mathcal{R}_{||} = L(\mathcal{S})$.

<u>Definition</u>

Let $\mathcal{J}$ be the smallest family of sequences containing the regular sequences and closed under $\odot$.

<u>Result 20:</u> <u>Sequence Characterisation of</u> $\mathcal{F}_{||}$.

$L(\mathcal{J}) = \mathcal{F}_{||}$

<u>Definition</u>

An a-NGSM is a *nondeterministic generalised sequential machine with accepting states.* Let $L_n = \{a_1^{\,i}\ldots a_n^{\,i}: i \geq 0\}$.

<u>Result 21:</u> <u>Image Theorem for $\mathcal{R}_n$ and $\mathcal{F}_n$</u>

For all L in $\mathcal{R}_n$, $n>0$ there exists an a-NGSM M such that $L = M(L_n)$. Since $\mathcal{F}_n \subsetneq \mathcal{R}_n$ the result holds for $\mathcal{F}_n$.

<u>Result 22:</u> <u>Language Characterisation of</u> $\mathcal{R}_n$.

For $n>0$, $\mathcal{R}_n$ is the smallest family of languages containing L_n and closed under union and a-NGSM maps.

For further details see Wood[7] and Rosebrugh and Wood[8].

---

(7) See footnote 2.

(8) Rosebrugh, R. D., and Wood, D., A characterization theorem for n-parallel right linear languages, Journal of Computer and System Sciences <u>7</u> (1973), 579-582.

Section 6: Concluding Remarks.

We close by first posing two open problems and secondly introducing some possibilities for future research.

Open problem 1: Is the equivalence of two n-PRLG's decidable or undecidable?

Open problem 2: Prove $\mathcal{R}_{||}$ is not closed under intersection. It is easy to construct examples of languages which are formed by the intersection of two n-PRLL, which intuitively are not in $\mathcal{R}_{||}$. But some new (or adapted) proof techniques are needed.

Future research possibilities

(1) Can generalise n-PRLG (or n-RLSMG) in the same way that Salomaa [103] has generalised E0L systems.

(2) Rewriting in E0L systems has been considered as a one-state NGSM map, Salomaa [103] has considered one extension of this notion, however it can be extended in another way by allowing more than one state in the NGSM. This extension can then be applied to n-PRLG (n-PFSG and n-RLSMG).

MULTIDIMENSIONAL LINDENMAYER ORGANISMS

Brian H. Mayoh
Department of Computer Science
University of Aarhus
Aarhus, Denmark

Summary

Most cellular organisms in the real world are not one-dimensional. How can we model the global development of such organisms by rules that are local to each cell? It is not unreasonable to suppose that the development of an individual cell depends on the cell state and the cell context, the state and position of the neighbours of the cell. In this paper we present models in which this cell information and the attendant local developmental rules can be represented discretely. The precise mathematical description of the models is left to an appendix.

von Neumann models

The first class of models we shall discuss have been much studied (e.g., Cellular automata, ed. E.F. Codd, Academic Press, 1968; Essays on cellular automata, ed. A.W. Burks, 1970). The distinguishing feature of models in this class is that the positions of the cells in an organism are fixed once and for all. As an organism develops the states of the neighbours of a cell may change, but the number and positions of its neighbours may not. The local developmental rules need only specify a new cell state for each of the finitely many possible cell contexts.

In figure 1 we compare a von Neumann model for the development of the red algae Callithamnion Roseum with the corresponding OL-system. We suppose that the cells of the organism lie on the points with integer coordinates in 2-dimensional Euclidean space so each cell has 8 neighbours. The seed, the initial configuration of the organism, has the cell at the origin in state a and all other cells in the "vacuous" state. The context independent local developmental rules are:

$$a \to b,\ b \to b,\ c \to b,\ d \to e,\ e \to f,\ f \to g,\ h \to h,\ h' \to h' .$$

The context dependent rules are given in figure 2. If the reader continues the development of the algae in figure 1, he will appreciate the following disadvantages of the von Neumann model:

- growth and cell division can only occur when there are cells in the vacuous state;

- unwanted interaction because of the severe restrictions on growth direction;
- the inflexibility caused by having a fixed global limit on the number of neighbours a cell can have.

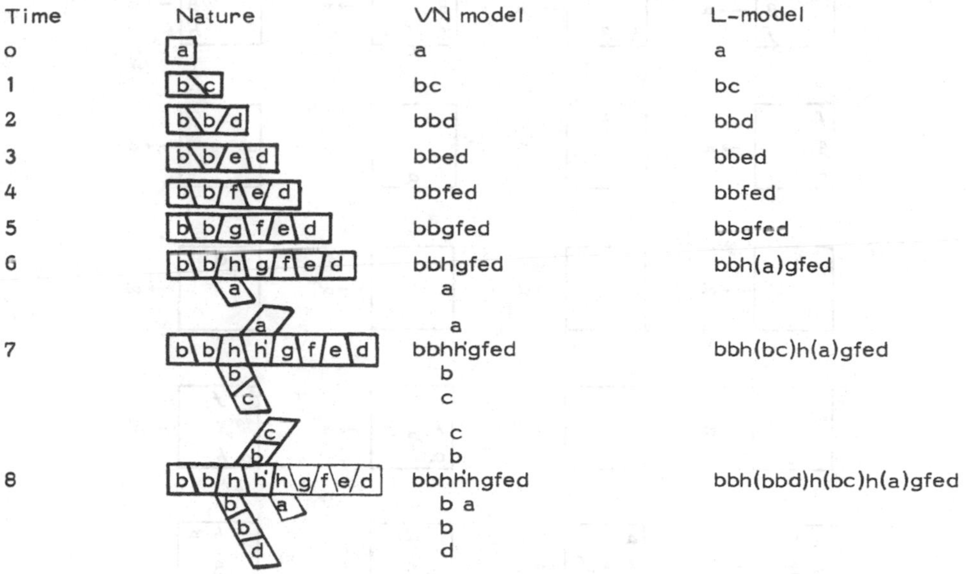

Figure 1. The development of Callithamnion Roseum

Papers by Szilard (this volume) and Lindenmayer [in 45] have indicated how the von Neumann model can be modified so that these disadvantages are somewhat mitigated.

Web models

Our second class of models was invented by J.L. Pfaltz and A. Rosenfeld (Web grammars, Proc. Joint Int. Conf. on Artificial Intelligence, Washington, 1969) for other purposes. The distinguishing feature of models in this class is that the positions of the cells in an organism can be represented by an unordered graph, where there is an edge between two vertices if and only if the corresponding cells are neighbours. The price we pay for removing the restriction on the possible number of neighbours is that cell contexts give no indication of the relative positions of cell neighbours.

Suppose we can apply a local developmental rule to a particular cell with a particular context. What should it give us? The natural answer is a latent organ-

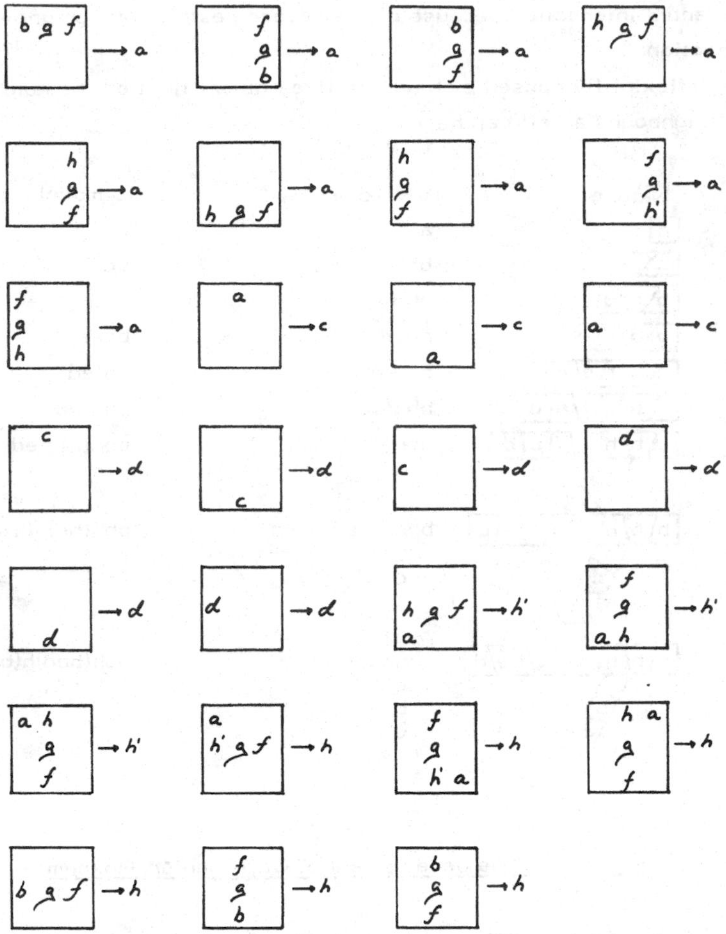

A problem at time 12.

```
       d
       e
       f  d
       g  e
       b  b  c
       b  b  b
  bbhhhhhhhgfed
     b  b  b  a
     b  b  b
    ah  f  d
     g?e
     f  d
     e
     d
```

Figure 2. Details of the VN model in figure 1.

ism, a labelled graph just like that which represents the whole organism. In this way every vertex of the labelled graph for the whole organism produces its own labelled graph and these must be joined by some embedding algorithm.

Let us look at figure 3 which shows the web model for our red algae. The seed, is represented by the graph consisting of a single vertex labelled by a. All the local developmental rules are context independent, and to be found in the tableau:

State	a	b	c	d	e	f	g	h
Latent organism	b-c	b	b-d	e-d	f	g	h-a	h

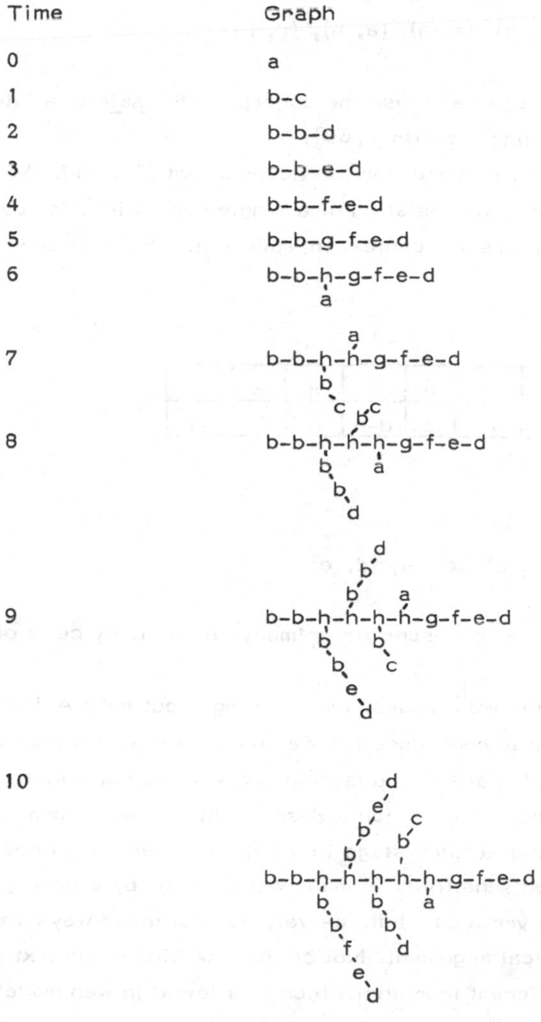

Figure 3. The web model for Callithamnion Roseum.

But what is the embedding algorithm? The literature on web grammars shows the choice of embedding algorithm may influence greatly the expressive power of our class of web models. Experimenting with various possibilities has shown that the following embedding algorithm is a reasonably simple and powerful choice. For a particular web model we have a forbidden list of state pairs. Using this and a collection of latent organisms, one for each vertex in a labelled graph, we build a new graph by 1) replacing the vertices by the corresponding latent organisms; 2) for each edge (v, v') in the original graph, joining each vertex in the latent organism for v with each vertex in the latent organism for v'; 3) dropping the edges added at step 2 which would give a state pair in the forbidden list. For our red algae the forbidden list is:

(b, d), (f, d), (a, b), (a, g), (a, h), (c, h)

In this particular example we can also use the concept of the skin of a latent organism to give a simpler embedding algorithm [69].

Figure 4 illustrates a web model for the development of a leaf. Again the seed is represented by the graph consisting of a single vertex labelled by a. Again all the local developmental rules are context independent. This time the rule tableau is:

State	a	b	c	d	e	f
Latent organism	b–a	c	d–e	d	f	c–c

and the forbidden list is:

(a, d), (a, e), (b, e), (c, e), (d, e).

We notice, that states a and d represent the primary and tertiary cells of Nägeli [61].

Web models have their weaknesses. On learning about them Aristid Lindenmayer challenged the author to reproduce the way nature creates a closed surface. It so happens that web models have no zip mechanism – if two cells in an organism are disconnected, then there is no way for a descendant of one of them to be linked to a descendant of the other at a later stage in the development. It is possible to introduce the needed context sensitivity in many ways – e.g. by allowing rules to apply to subgraphs not just vertices – but, as yet, none of these ways can be justified by a convincing biological argument. Notice that the kind of context sensitivity needed to make a box is different from that which is allowed in web models. To see the allowable kind of context sensitivity consider the fictive organism, the IMIAD,

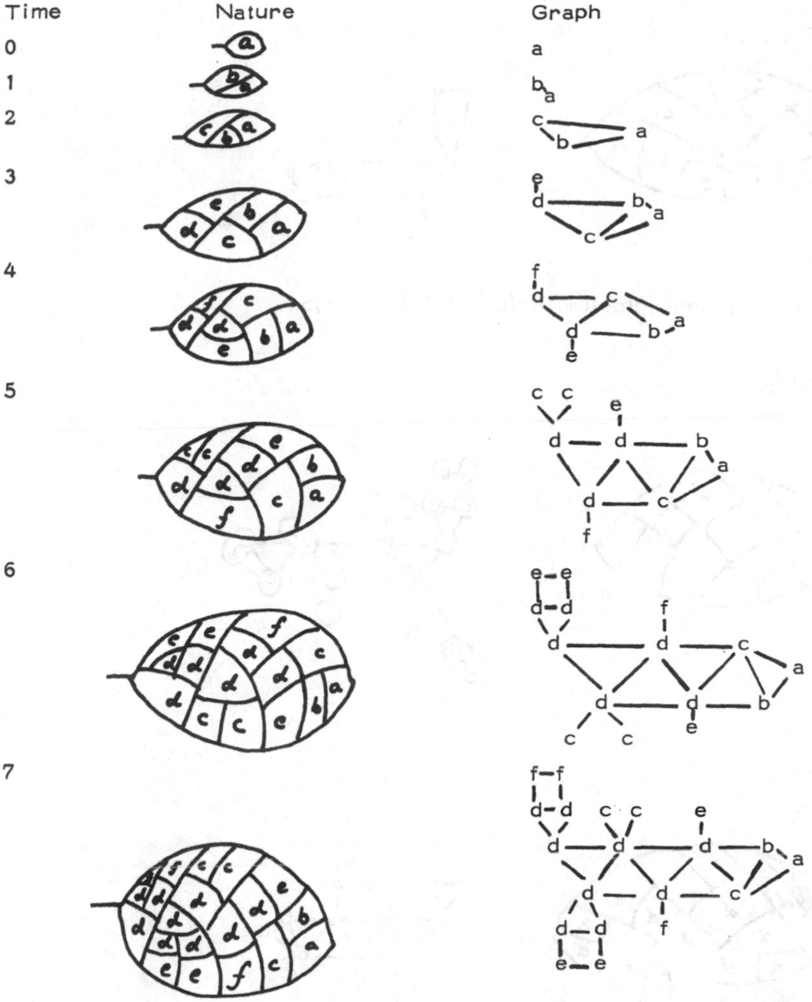

Figure 4. The web model for Phascum Cuspidatum.

Time 6.

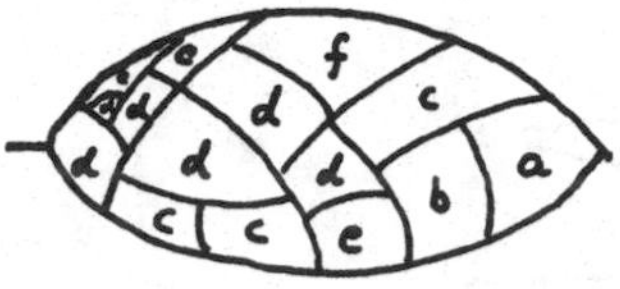

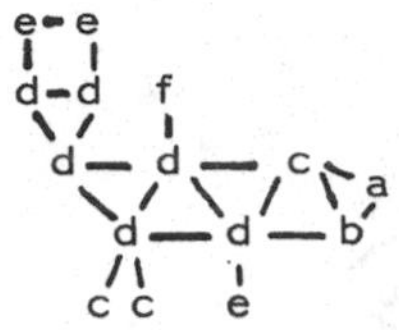

OL-representation: (d(de)(de))(d(c)(c))(d(f))(de)(c)ba

Time 6 1/2.

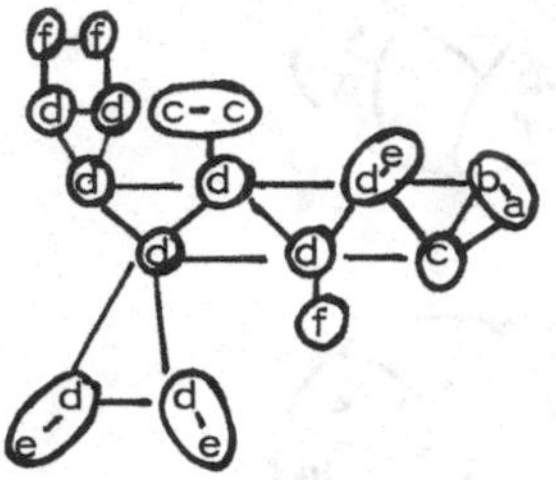

Time 7.

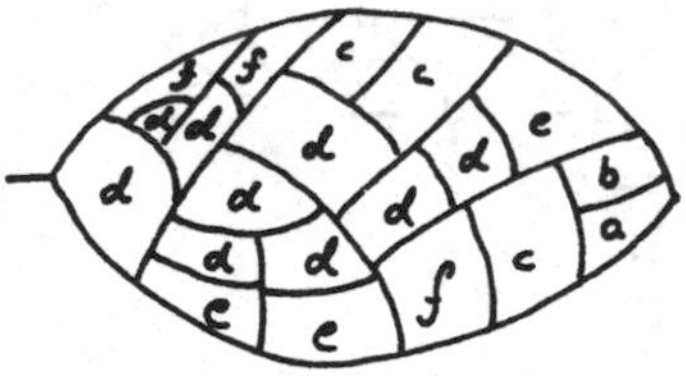

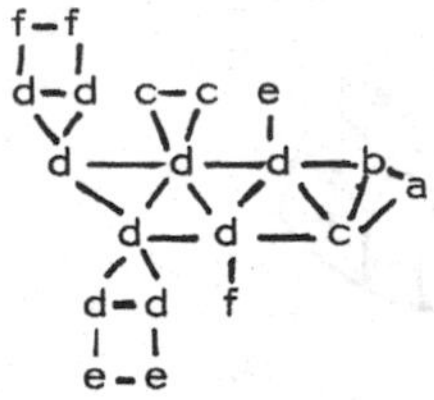

Figure 5. An epoch in the life of Phascum Cuspidatum.

of figure 6. Its development is not monotonous, even although it is only a two cell state fish.

Local development rules.

	state	●	gives latent organism ●--o
if 1 or 3 neighbours	state	o	gives latent organism o--o
otherwise	state	o	gives latent organism ●--●

Forbidden list. (●, o) (●, ●)

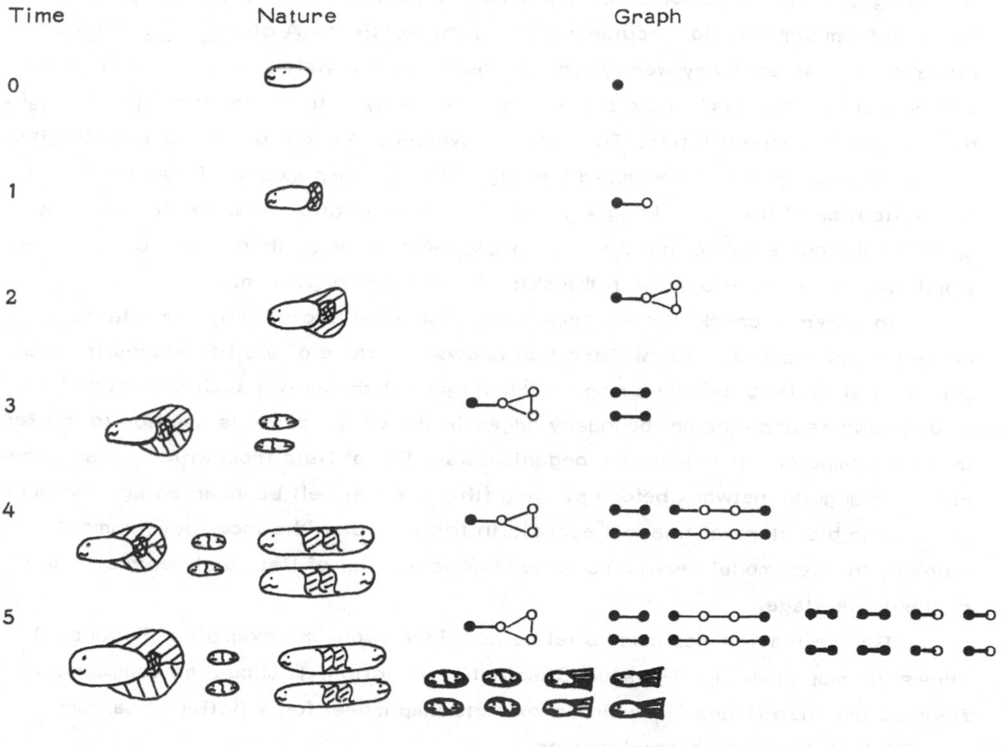

Figure 6. The development of an IMIAD.

Map models

For all their virtues web models cannot represent the relative positions of the neighbours of a cell. Following Rosenfeld and Strong (A grammar for maps, Software Engineering v. 2, ed. J. Tou, Academic Press 1971) we can improve the models by allowing the edges of the underlying graph to be ordered. This influences the model in two ways:

- the ordering in the context can be used to restrict the choice of applicable local developmental rules;
- the ordering in the graph influences the interconnection of the latent organisms produced by the local developmental rules.

Figure 7 illustrates the second of these. The point to note is that any subregion of France that touches Sp, It, Be must also touch H. This restriction cannot be expressed if the underlying graph is unordered.

It is very difficult to give a precise rule for connecting several ordered graphs into one large ordered graph. Furthermore, we shall later want to consider cells which touch one another in several places and even cells which enclose other cells. Ordered graphs cannot express this, and we have a problem. The way out was suggested to the author by J. Thatcher: to consider an ordered graph as a function from vertices to circular words on the vertices. A circular word on an alphabet A is an ordinary word A on A except that it consists of one or more subwords that are "cycles" in the sense: the first (last) letter is the right (left) neighbour of the last (first) letter. The circular words are used in the appendix to give a precise description of the embedding algorithm for map models. Figure 8 shows an application of this embedding algorithm. The restriction on the rule is met by splitting the context of 4 into the two words, 56 ∞ and ∞ 5, then substituting these words for ∞ in the two cells in the skin of the latent organism.

In order to check that the embedding algorithm is correctly formulated, a computer program has been written that draws a picture of the life stages in an organism that is described by a map model. Figure 9 shows two such pictures. The smooth curves and straight boundary edges in the computer plots are due to the fact that the computer represents the organism as a list of lists from which it can generate a triangular network before plotting (the internal cell boundaries are the perpendicular bisectors of triangle edges). In the computer the local developmental rules of the web model become rules to change the list of lists that represent the current life stage.

Before leaving map models let us consider two more examples. Figure 10 shows the map model for Phascum Cuspidatum in action. It should be compared with figure 5 and also figure 11, which shows the map model for a fictive organism UACER that develops internal organs.

Query: Can France divide so that one part has only ṁ neighbours and the other has only + neighbours?

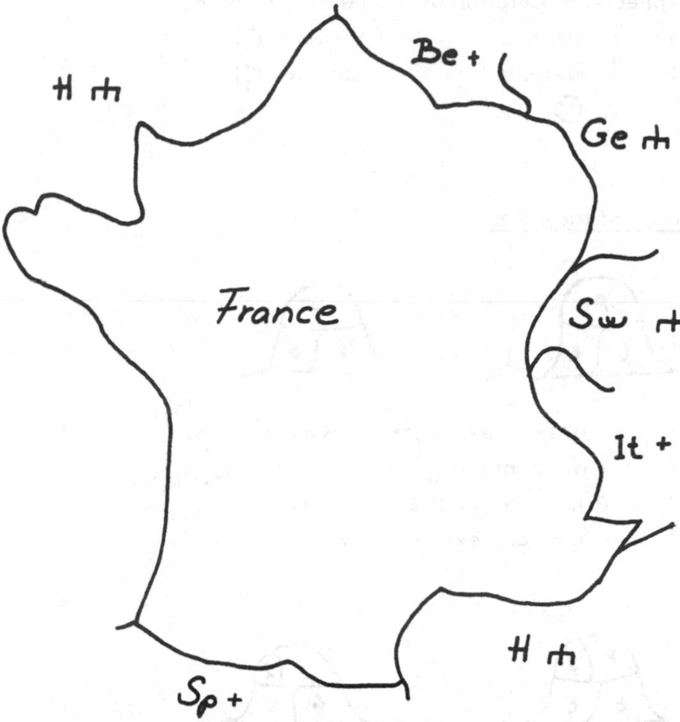

In answering this problem it helps to consider the context of France as the "circular" word.

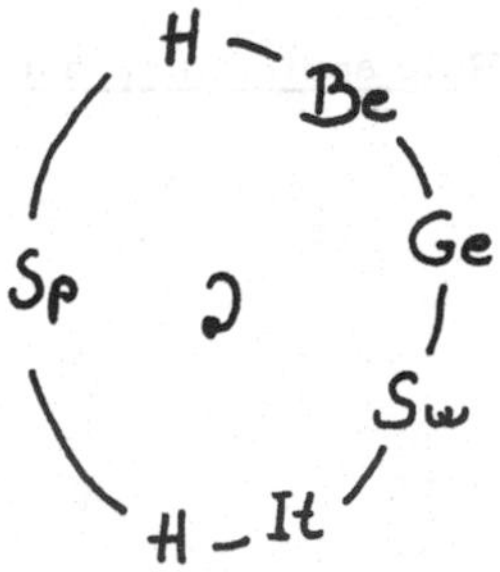

Figure 7. The religious war problem.

Rule

Name	Condition	Latent Organism	Restriction
BUD	state p	(p / s)	Split touchs ∞

More precise decription of the latent organism.

cell 1	state: p	context: (∞ 2)
cell 2	state: s	context: (∞ 1)
skin	1 2	

An application of the rule.

Before:

cell 5	old context: 6 4 ∞	new context: 6 1 2 ∞
cell 6	old context: ∞ 4 5	new context: ∞ 1 5 6
cell 1	l. o. context: 2 ∞	new context: 5 6 2 ∞
cell 2	l. o. context: 1 ∞	new context: 1 ∞ 5

After:

Figure 8. Rule application in map models.

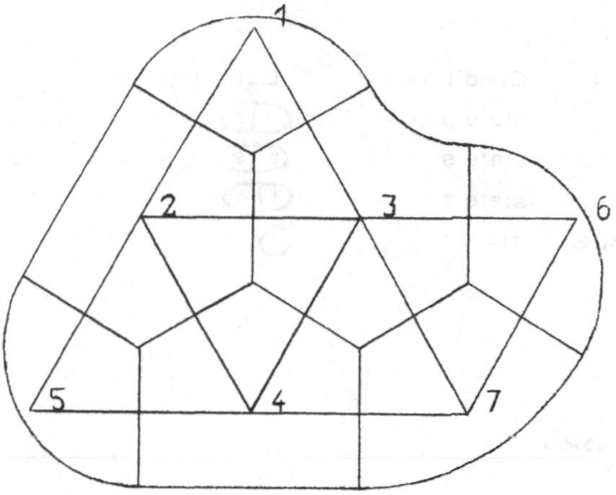

Splitting of cell 4 produces cell 8
Splitting of cell 7 produces cell 9
Splitting of cell 6 produces cell 10

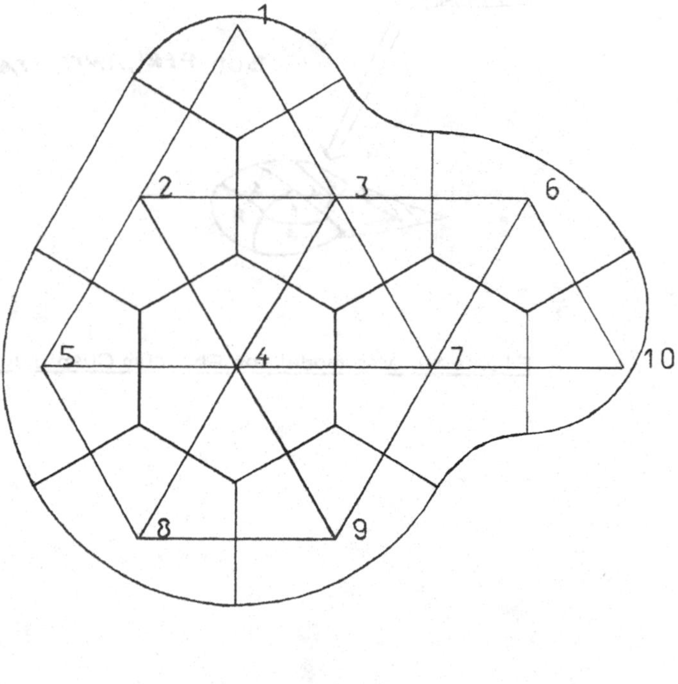

Figure 9. An epoch in the life of a leaf.

Rules:

Name	Condition	Lat. org.	Restriction
BUD	state p	(p|s)	split touchs ∞ once
ANTI	state s	(s|s)	split touchs ∞ once
PERI	state s	(t|s)	s but not split touchs ∞
STABLE	state t	(t)	NONE

Life history.

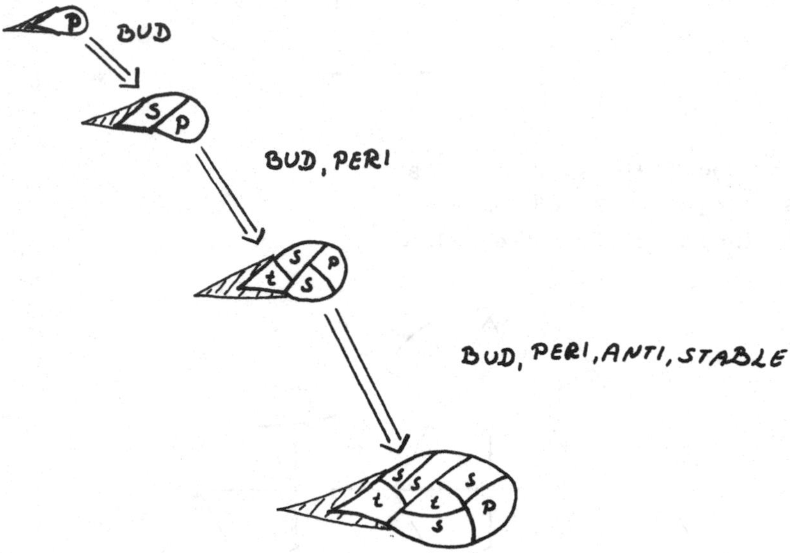

Figure 10. Map model for Phascum Cuspidatum

Rules

Name	Condition	Lat. org.	Restriction
BABY	state p	s p	none
SPLIT	state s	s s	none
HOLE	state s	t s	none
STABLE	state t	t	none

Life history

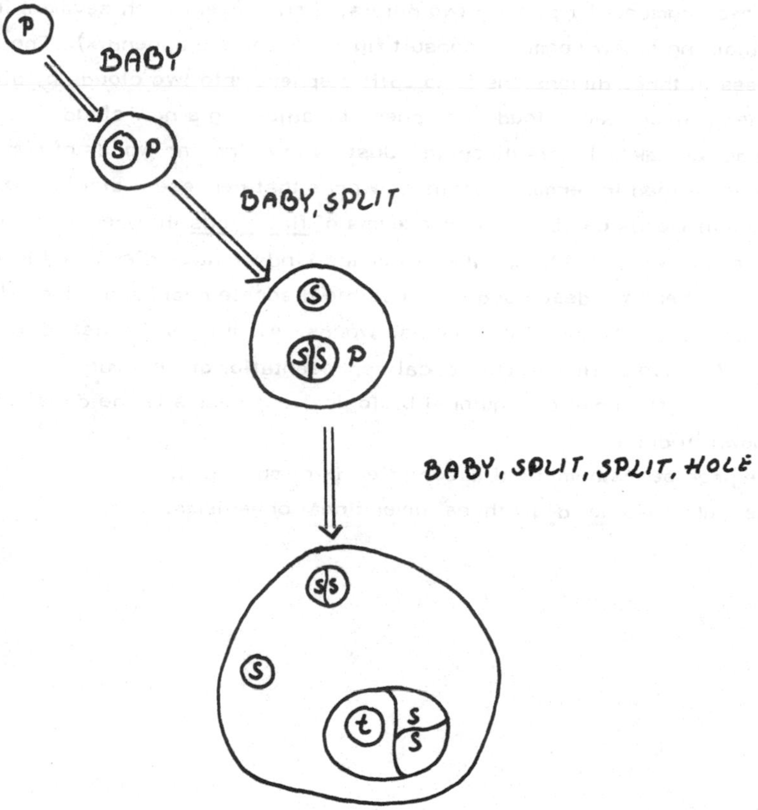

Figure 11. Internal organs: growth of a UACER

Globe models

At last we can indicate how to model three dimensional organisms. Imagine a demon inside one of the cells of a two dimensional organism. It would see the outside world as a circle, divided into segments by the neighbouring cells, and it could model this world as a circular word. Now imagine a demon inside one of the cells of a three dimensional organism. It would see the outside world as a sphere, divided into clouds (regions, contact areas) by the neighbouring cells. It could model this world using spherical words if only we had a suitable definition of spherical words. Revive the two-dimensional demon for a moment. It could split a circle into two segments by picking two points, then convert each segment into a circle by adjoining a new segment (consult figure 8 and the appendix). The analogous process in three dimensions is to split a sphere into two clouds by picking a circle, then convert each cloud to a sphere by adjoining a new cloud.

How do we make all this discrete? Just as the circular words of our map models can be defined in terms of ordinary words that represent circle segments, so the spherical words can be defined in terms of flat words that represent clouds. But what is a flat word. Nothing but a map of the kind we have discussed in the previous section. There we described two possible discrete representations: labelled ordered graphs and functions into circular words. All this is discussed in more detail in [69]. We favour a more schematical representation of the model here because:

- for very few three dimensional biological organisms is the development known in detail;
- the precise mathematical description is complicated;
- the author cannot draw three dimensional organisms.

Appendix

The mathematical description of the models

We define a model class to be a triple consisting of:

1) a set of configuration spaces;
2) a set of rule repertoires;
3) an algorithm Ψ which, given a rule repertoire R and a configuration space Γ, provides a binary relation on Γ.

A model in such a class is (Γ, R, y_0) where Γ is a configuration space, R is a rule repertoire, and y_0 is an element of Γ called the seed of the model. If y and y' are configurations in Γ, we write:

$y \to y'$ for $\Psi(R, \Gamma)$ holds on (y, y') ;
$y \Rightarrow y'$ for the transitive closure of $\to$.

We define the language of the model to be the set of configurations y such that $y_0 \Rightarrow y$.

In all our models we will have sets:

Structure, State, Context, Latent Organism

and these sets will be such that:

4) State is finite;
5) the configuration space Γ of the model is the set of linear words on State x Structure;
6) the rule repertoire R of the model is a finite subset of

$$\text{State} \times 2^{\text{Context}} \times \text{Latent Organism}.$$

The configurations are denoted by (B, L x D), and the rules are denoted by (S, P, I). For this to make sense B must be a subset of integers, L must be a function from B to State, D must be a function from B to Structure, S must be in State, P must be a property of contexts, and I must be a latent organism.

Before we fill in this general frame work, let us introduce a few concepts we shall need. A circular word on a set X is a triple (B, π, F), where B is a finite set of integers, π is a permutation of B, and F is a function from B into X. We denote the empty circular word on X by Φ. Suppose $C = (B, \pi, F)$ is a circular word on X. If π is the identity permutation, we call C a linear word on X. If G is a function from X to Y, then we write $G * C$ for $(B, \pi, G \cdot F)$, a circular word on Y. Now we can compare the four model classes discussed in the paper:

model class	von Neumann	Web	Map	Globe
Structure	Integer^m	subset of Integer	circular words on Integer	circular words on circular words on Integer
Context	State^m	multiset on State	circular words on State	circular words on circular words on State
Latent Organism	State	Configuration Space	Configuration Space X Restriction	Configuration Space X Restriction

<u>The von Neumann model class</u>

In a model of this class we have an integer m, and a finite set State with a designated element s_0 such that: Structure = Integer^m, Context = State^m, Latent organism = State. In addition we have designated functions $\delta_1, \delta_2 \ldots \delta_m$ from Integer to Integer. Contrary to what one might expect, m is the number of elements in the context and this is totally unrelated to the spatial dimensionality of the organism that we are trying to model. Another unusual feature of our formulation of a von Neumann model is the definition of $(B, L \times D) \to (B', L' \times D')$. For this we require

1) $B' = B \cup [y \mid x = \delta_i(y) \text{ for some } x \in B \text{ and some } i]$;
2) $D'(y) = (\delta_1(y), \delta_2(y), \ldots, \delta_m(y)$ for $y \in B'$;
3) for each $y \in B'$ there is a rule $(L''(y), P(y), L'(y))$ such that P(y) holds of the context

$$(L'' \circ \delta_1(y), L'' \circ \delta_2(y), \ldots, L'' \circ \delta_m(y))$$

where $L''(y) = \underline{\text{if}}\ y \in B\ \underline{\text{then}}\ L(y)\ \underline{\text{else}}\ s_0$.

<u>Example 1</u>

$m = 1, \ \delta_1(n) = n-1.$

There are three states: a, b, s_0.

The seed is $[[17], L_0 \times D_0]$ where $L_0(17) = a$, $D_0(17) = 16$. The Rule repertoire is: (a, true, b), (b, true, b), (s_0, true, a), (s_0, true, s_0). There are two configurations y such that seed $\to$ y:

$[[17, 18], L_1 \times D_1]$ where $L_1(17) = b$, $L_1(18) = a$, $D_1(17)=(16)$, $D_1(18)=(17)$;
$[[17, 18], L_2 \times D_2]$ where $L_2(17) = b$, $L_1(18) = s_0$, $D_1(17)=(16)$, $D_1(18)=(17)$.

<u>Example 2</u> (Conway's life)

Suppose the points with integer coefficients in two-dimensional Euclidean space are numbered in some way. Then we have a 1:1 function J from such points onto Integer, and we can define $\delta_1, \delta_2, \ldots, \delta_8$ as <u>the</u> functions from Integer to Integer given by:

$$\delta_1(J(x,y)) = J(x-1,y) \quad , \quad \delta_2(J(x,y)) = J(x+1,y)$$
$$\delta_3(J(x,y)) = J(x-1,y-1) \, , \quad \delta_4(J(x,y)) = J(x+1,y-1)$$
$$\delta_5(J(x,y)) = J(x-1,y+1) \, , \quad \delta_6(J(x,y)) = J(x+1,y+1)$$
$$\delta_7(J(x,y)) = J(x,y+1) \quad , \quad \delta_8(J(x,y)) = J(x,y-1)$$

Suppose there are two states: s_1, s_0. Suppose that the rule repertoire is: (s_0, BORN, s_1), $(s_0, \neg\,\text{BORN}, s_1)$, (s_1, LIVE, s_1), $(s_1, \neg\,\text{LIVE}, s_0)$ where BORN (LIVE) is true of contexts containing 3 (2 or 3) occurrences of the state s_1. Let us define the seed as $(B_0, L_0 \times D_0)$ where

$$B_0 \quad = [J(0,0),\ J(0,1),\ J(0,2),\ J(1,0),\ J(1,1),\ J(1,2),\ J(2,1)].$$
$$L_0(x) = s_1 \quad \text{for} \quad x \in B_0;$$
$$D_0(x) = (\delta_1(x),\ \delta_2(x), \ldots, \delta_8(x)) \quad \text{for } x \in B_0.$$

This time there is only one y such that Seed → y.
It is $(B_1, L_1 \times D_1)$ where:

$$B_1 \quad = [J(i,j) \mid -1 \le i,j \le 3] - [J(3,-1),\ J(3,3)];$$
$$L_1(x) = \underline{\text{if}}\ x = J(0,0) \vee x = J(0,2) \vee x = J(-1,1)$$
$$\vee\ x = J(2,0) \vee x = J(2,1) \vee x = J(2,2)\ \ \underline{\text{then}}\ s_1\ \underline{\text{else}}\ s_0;$$
$$D_1(x) = (\delta_1(x),\ \delta_2(x), \ldots, \delta_8(x) \quad \text{for } x \in B_1.$$

<u>The Web model class.</u>

In a model of this class we have a finite set S t a t e such that: S t r u c t u r e = a subset of I n t e g e r, C o n t e x t = a set of functions from S t a t e to I n t e g e r, Latent Organism = C o n f i g u r a t i o n S p a c e. In addition we have a finite subset of S t a t e^2 called the <u>forbidden set</u>. By definition we have:

$$(B,\ L \times D) \rightarrow (B',\ L' \times D')$$

if and only if there is a function ρ from B to Latent Organism and a function τ from B to subsets of I n t e g e r such that:

1) if $x, y \in B$, then $y \notin \tau(x)$ and $\tau(y)$ is disjoint from $\tau(x)$;

2) for each $x \in B$ there is a rule $(L(x), P(x), \rho(x))$ such that $P(x)$ holds of the context $C(x)$ given by:

$$C(x)(s) = \text{number of } y \in D(x) \text{ such that } L(y) = s;$$

3) $\tau(x)$ has the same cardinality as the first component of $\rho(x)$;

4) $(B', L' \times D') = \mathcal{W}(B, D, \rho, \tau, \text{forbidden set})$.
Clearly we must define the function $\mathcal{W}$. For each $x \in B$ we have a latent organism $\rho(x) = (B_x, L_x \times D_x)$. By condition (3) there is a uniquely defined order preserving function h from $\tau(x)$ onto B_x. We define:

$$\begin{aligned} B'' &= \text{union of } \tau(x) \text{ for } x \in B \\ L''(y) &= L_x \circ h_x(y) \text{ for } y \in \tau(x) \\ D''(y) &= h_x^{-1} \circ D_x \circ h_x(y) \text{ for } y \in \tau(x) \\ D'''(y) &= [y' \mid (\exists x')(x' \in D(x) \wedge y' \in \tau(x') \\ &\qquad \wedge (L''(y), L''(y')) \notin \text{forbidden set})] \end{aligned}$$

$$\mathcal{W}(B, D, \rho, \tau, \text{forbidden set}) = (B'', L'' \times (D'' \cup D''')).$$

<u>Example 3</u>

There are two states: a, b. The forbidden set consists of: (a, b), (b, a). The Seed is $([1], L_0 \times D_0)$ where $L_0(1) = a$, $D_0(1) = \emptyset$. We shall need two other configurations:

$$\alpha = ([2,3], L_\alpha \times D_\alpha) \text{ where } L_\alpha(2) = b,\ D_\alpha(2) = [3]$$
$$L_\alpha(3) = a,\ D_\alpha(3) = [2];$$
$$\beta = ([4], L_\beta \times D_\beta) \quad \text{where } L_\beta(4) = b,\ D_\beta(4) = \emptyset.$$

Now we can give the Rule repertoire: (a, true, α), (b, true, β). To find a new member of the language, we choose ρ and τ such that $\rho(1) = \alpha$, $\tau(1) = [7,9]$. Our function h_1 becomes: $h_1(7) = 2$, $h_1(9) = 3$, and we get

$$\begin{aligned} B'' &= [7,9] \\ L''(7) &= L_\alpha(2) = b,\ L''(9) = L_\alpha(3) = a \\ D''(7) &= h_1^{-1} \circ D_\alpha(2) = [9],\ D''(9) = h_1^{-1} \circ D_\alpha(3) = [7] \\ \text{Seed} &\to (B'', L'' \times D''). \end{aligned}$$

<u>Example 4</u>

There are three states: a, b, e. The forbidden set consists of (a, b), (b, a). The Seed is $([1,2,3,4], L_0 \times D_0)$ where:

$$L_0(1) = b,\quad L_0(2) = b,\quad L_0(3) = e,\quad L_0(4) = a$$
$$D_0(1) = [2,3],\ D_0(2) = [1,3],\ D_0(3) = [1,2,4],\ D_0(4) = [3].$$

We shall need three other configurations:

$\alpha = ([1], L_\alpha \times D_\alpha)$ where $L_\alpha(1) = a$, $D_\alpha(1) = \emptyset$

$\beta = ([1], L_\beta \times D_\beta)$ where $L_\beta(1) = b$, $D_\beta(1) = \emptyset$

$\epsilon = ([1,2], L_\epsilon \times D_\epsilon)$ where $L_\epsilon(1) = L_\epsilon(2) = b$, $D_\epsilon(1) = [2]$, $D_\epsilon(2) = [1]$.

Now we can give the Rule repertoire: (a, true, α), (b, true, β), (e, true, ϵ). To find a new member of the language, we choose ρ and τ such that:

$\rho(1) = \beta \quad \rho(2) = \beta \quad \rho(3) = \epsilon \quad \rho(4) = \alpha$

$\tau(1) = [5] \quad \tau(2) = [6] \quad \tau(3) = [7,8] \quad \tau(4) = [9]$.

Our functions h_1, h_2, h_3, h_4 become: $h_1(5) = 1 = h_2(6)$, $h_3(7) = 1$, $h_3(8) = 2$, $h_4(9) = 1$, and we get:

$$B'' = [5,6,7,8,9]$$

$L''(5) = L_\beta(1) = b$	$D''(5) = \emptyset$	$D'''(5) = [6,7,8]$
$L''(6) = L_\beta(1) = b$	$D''(6) = \emptyset$	$D'''(6) = [5,7,8]$
$L''(7) = L_\epsilon(1) = b$	$D''(7) = [8]$	$D'''(7) = [5,6]$
$L''(8) = L_\epsilon(2) = b$	$D''(8) = [7]$	$D'''(8) = [5,6]$
$L''(9) = L_\alpha(1) = a$	$D''(9) = \emptyset$	$D'''(9) = \emptyset$

Seed $\rightarrow$ ($[5,6,7,8,9]$, $L'' \times (D'' \cup D''')$).

The Map model class

In a model of this class we have a finite set State such that: Structure = circular words on Integer, Context = circular words on State, Latent Organism = Configuration space x Restriction where

Restriction = subsets of $\text{Integer}^2 \times$ State.

By definition we have $(B \cup \{0\}, L \times D) \rightarrow (B' \cup \{0\}, L' \times D')$ if and only if there is a function ρ from B to Latent Organism, a function σ from Integer^2 to (Integer*)* , and a function τ from B to subsets of Integer such that:

1) if $x, y \in B$, then $0, y \notin \tau(x)$ and $\tau(x)$ is disjoint from $\tau(x)$;

2) for each $x \in B$ there is a rule $(L(x), P(x), \rho(x))$ such that $P(x)$ holds of the context $L * D(x)$;

3) $\tau(x) \cup \{0\}$ has the same cardinality as the first component of the first component of $\rho(x)$;

4) σ is consistent with respect to (B, L, D, ρ, τ) (see note below);

5) $(B' \cup \{0\}, L' \times D') = \mathfrak{M}(B, L, D, \rho, \sigma, \tau)$.

Clearly we must define the function $\mathcal{M}$. For each $x \in B$ we have a latent organism $\rho(x) = ((B_x, L_x \times D_x), r_x)$. By condition (3) there is a uniquely defined 1:1 order-preserving function h_x from $\tau(x) \cup \{0\}$ onto B_x. We define:

$$B'' = \text{union of } \tau(x) \qquad \text{for } x \in B$$
$$L''(y) = L_x \circ h_x(y) \qquad \text{for } y \in \tau(x)$$
$$D''(y) = h_x^{-1} * (D_x \circ h_x(y)) \text{ for } y \in \tau(x).$$

Now we have to define the patching together of a number of configurations. For each $x \in B$, $y \in \tau(x)$ we define (see note below):

$$w(y) = \text{Flatten } (\sigma_y * D(x)) \text{ where } \sigma_y(x') = \sigma(y, x')$$
$$D'''(y) = \text{Substitute } (w(y), D''(y))$$

If we set $D'''(0) = \Phi$ and $L''(0) = L(0)$, then we can define $\mathcal{M}(B, L, D, \rho, \sigma, \tau)$ to be $(B'' \cup \{0\}, L'', D''')$.

Note

After a careful study of the two examples we are about to give, the eager reader should be able to give a precise definition of:Flatten, Substitute, σ is consistent with respect to (B, L, D, ρ, τ). Here we will only mention:

- the most interesting consistency requirement on σ is that we may not have $(h_x^{-1}(i), h_x^{-1}(j), L(y))$ in r_x when we have $i, j \in \tau(x) \wedge \sigma(i,j) = y$ for $x, y \in B$;
- Flatten reads around a circular word, and it produces linear words as it proceeds;
- Substitute (w, c) replaces occurrences of 0 in the circular word c by linear words from w.

Example 5 is the discrete version of figure 8. Let us begin by inviting the reader to draw the following circular words on Integer:

$D_0(0) = D'''(0) = \Phi$

$D_0(4) = ([0,1,2], \pi_0, v_4)$
where $\pi_0(0) = 1$, $\pi_0(1) = 2$, $\pi_0(2) = 0$
$v_4(0) = 0$, $v_4(1) = 5$, $v_4(2) = 6$

$D_0(5) = ([0,1,2], \pi_0, v_5)$ where $v_5(0) = 0$, $v_5(1) = 5$, $v_5(2) = 4$

$D_0(6) = ([0,1,2], \pi_0, v_6)$ where $v_6(0) = 0$, $v_6(1) = 4$, $v_6(2) = 5$

$D_\alpha(0) = ([0,1], \pi_\alpha, v_0)$
where $\pi_\alpha(0) = 1$, $\pi_\alpha(1) = 0$, $v_0(0) = 1$, $v_0(1) = 2$

$D_\alpha(1) = ([0,1], \pi_\alpha, v_1)$ where $v_1(0) = 0$, $v_1(1) = 2$

$D_\alpha(2) = ([0,1], \pi_\alpha, v_2)$ where $v_2(0) = 0$, $v_2(1) = 1$

$D_\beta(0) = ([1],\ \text{identity},\ \text{identity})$

$D_\beta(1) = ([0],\ \text{identity},\ \text{identity})$

$D'''(1) = ([0,1,2],\ \pi_0,\ v_1')$ where $v_1'(0) = 0,\ v_1'(1) = 2,\ v_1'(2) = 8$

$D'''(7) = ([0,1,2],\ \pi_0,\ v_7')$ where $v_7'(0) = 0,\ v_7'(1) = 8,\ v_7'(2) = 2$

$D'''(2) = ([0,1,2,3],\ \pi',\ v_2')$
where $\pi'(0) = 1,\ \pi'(1) = 2,\ \pi'(2) = 3,\ \pi'(3) = 0$
$v_2'(0) = 0,\ v_2'(1) = 7,\ v_2'(2) = 8,\ v_2'(3) = 1$

$D'''(8) = ([0,1,2,3],\ \pi',\ v_8')$
where $v_8'(0) = 0,\ v_8'(1) = 1,\ v_8'(2) = 2,\ v_8'(3) = 7.$

Now we can give the model. There are four states: p, s, t, s_0. The Seed is $([0,4,5,6],\ L_0 \times D_0)$ where $L_0(0) = s_0,\ L_0(4) = p,\ L_0(5) = t,\ L_0(6) = t$. We shall need two other configurations:

$\alpha = ([0,1,2],\ L_\alpha \times D_\alpha)$ where $L_\alpha(0) = s_0,\ L_\alpha(1) = p,\ L_\alpha(2) = s$

$\beta = ([0,1]\ \ ,\ L_\beta \times D_\beta)$ where $L_\beta(0) = s_0,\ L_\beta(1) = t.$

The rule repertoire is: $(p,\ \text{true},\ (\alpha,\ [(2,1,s_0)]))$,
$(t,\ \text{true},\ (\beta,\ \emptyset))$.

To find a new member of the language, we can choose the functions ρ, τ given by: $\rho(4) = (\alpha,\ [(2,1,s_0)]),\ \rho(5) = \rho(6) = (\beta,\emptyset),\ \tau(4) = [1,2],\ \tau(5) = [7],\ \tau(6) = [8]$. Our functions h_4 h_5 h_6 become $h_4(1) = 1,\ h_4(2) = 2,\ h_5(7) = 1,\ h_6(8) = 1$, and we get:

$B'' = [1,2,7,8]$	$L''(0) = s_0$
$L''(1) = L_\alpha(1) = p$	$D''(1) = D_\alpha(1)$
$L''(2) = L_\alpha(2) = s$	$D''(2) = D_\alpha(2)$
$L''(7) = L_\beta(1) = t$	$D''(7) = h_5^{-1} * D_\beta(1) = ([0],\ \text{id},\ \text{id})$
$L''(8) = L_\beta(1) = t$	$D''(8) = h_6^{-1} * D_\beta(1) = ([0],\ \text{id},\ \text{id})$

Now we patch the structures together using a function σ satisfying: $\sigma(1,2) = 0$, $\sigma(2,1) = 6,\ \sigma(1,5) = \Lambda,\ \sigma(1,6) = 8,\ \sigma(2,5) = 7,\ \sigma(2,6) = 8,\ \sigma(7,6) = 8,\ \sigma(7,4) = 2$, $\sigma(8,4) = 12,\ \sigma(8,5) = 7$. We note that the only applied rule with a non-empty restriction is satisfied because $L(6) \neq s_0$, and continue by computing:

$$w(1) = 8,\ w(2) = 78,\ w(3) = 82,\ w(4) = 127.$$

Substituting these in D'' gives:

$$\text{Seed} \rightarrow ([0,1,2,7,8],\ L'',\ D''').$$

<u>Example 6</u> shows other features of map models. Again we begin by inviting the reader to draw the following circular words in integer:

$D_0(0)$	$= D'''(0) = \Phi$
$D_0(11)$	$= ([0,12,13,14], \pi_{11}, \text{identity})$
	where $\pi_{11}(0) = 14$, $\pi_{11}(14) = 12$, $\pi_{11}(12) = 13$, $\pi_{11}(13) = 0$
$D_0(12)$	$= ([11,13,14], \pi_{12}, \text{identity})$
	where $\pi_{12}(11) = 14$, $\pi_{12}(14) = 13$, $\pi_{12}(13) = 11$
$D_0(13)$	$= ([0,11,12,14], \pi_{13}, \text{identity})$
	where $\pi_{13}(0) = 11$, $\pi_{13}(11) = 12$, $\pi_{13}(12) = 14$, $\pi_{13}(14) = 0$
$D_0(14)$	$= ([0,11,12,13], \pi_{14}, \text{identity})$
$D_\alpha(0)$	$= ([4,5], \pi_{\alpha_0}, \text{identity})$ where $\pi_{\alpha_0}(4) = 5$, $\pi_{\alpha_0}(5) = 4$
$D_\alpha(4)$	$= ([0,5], \pi_{\alpha_4}, \text{identity})$ where $\pi_{\alpha_4}(0) = 5$, $\pi_{\alpha_4}(5) = 0$
$D_\alpha(5)$	$= ([0,4], \pi_{\alpha_5}, \text{identity})$ where $\pi_{\alpha_5}(0) = 4$, $\pi_{\alpha_5}(4) = 0$
$D_\beta(0)$	$= ([1,2,3], \pi_{\beta_0}, \text{identity})$
	where $\pi_{\beta_0}(1) = 2$, $\pi_{\beta_0}(2) = 3$, $\pi_{\beta_0}(3) = 1$
$D_\beta(1)$	$= ([0,2,3], \pi_{\beta_1}, \text{identity})$
	where $\pi_{\beta_1}(0) = 2$, $\pi_{\beta_1}(2) = 3$, $\pi_{\beta_1}(3) = 0$
$D_\beta(2)$	$= ([0,1,3], \pi_{\beta_2}, \text{identity})$
	where $\pi_{\beta_2}(0) = 3$, $\pi_{\beta_2}(3) = 1$, $\pi_{\beta_2}(1) = 0$
$D_\beta(3)$	$= ([0,1,2], \pi_{\beta_3}, \text{identity})$
	where $\pi_{\beta_3}(0) = 1$, $\pi_{\beta_3}(1) = 2$, $\pi_{\beta_3}(2) = 0$
$D_\epsilon(0)$	$= ([7,8], \pi_{\epsilon_0}, \text{identity})$ where $\pi_{\epsilon_0}(7) = 8$, $\pi_{\epsilon_0}(8) = 7$
$D_\epsilon(7)$	$= ([0,8], \pi_{\epsilon_7}, \text{identity})$ where $\pi_{\epsilon_7}(0) = 8$, $\pi_{\epsilon_7}(8) = 0$
$D_\epsilon(8)$	$= ([0,7], \pi_{\epsilon_8}, \text{identity})$ where $\pi_{\epsilon_8}(0) = 7$, $\pi_{\epsilon_8}(7) = 0$
$D_\delta(0)$	$= ([6,9], \pi_{\delta_0}, \text{identity})$ where $\pi_{\delta_0}(6) = 9$, $\pi_{\delta_0}(9) = 6$
$D_\delta(6)$	$= ([0,9], \pi_{\delta_6}, \text{identity})$ where $\pi_{\delta_6}(0) = 9$, $\pi_{\delta_6}(9) = 0$
$D_\delta(9)$	$= ([0,6], \pi_{\delta_9}, \text{identity})$ where $\pi_{\delta_9}(0) = 6$, $\pi_{\delta_9}(6) = 0$
$D'''(1)$	$= ([2,3,4,5,7,8], \pi_1', \text{identity})$
	where $\pi_1'(8)=7$, $\pi_1'(7)=4$, $\pi_1'(4)=5$, $\pi_1'(5)=2$, $\pi_1'(2)=3$, $\pi_1'(3)=8$
$D'''(2)$	$= ([1,3,5], \pi_2', \text{identity})$
	where $\pi_2'(5)=3$, $\pi_2'(3)=1$, $\pi_2'(1)=5$
$D'''(3)$	$= ([1,2,5,6,7,8], \pi_3', \text{identity})$
	where $\pi_3'(5)=6$, $\pi_3'(6)=7$, $\pi_3'(7)=8$, $\pi_3'(8)=1$, $\pi_3'(1)=2$, $\pi_3'(2)=5$
$D'''(4)$	$= ([0,1,5,7], \pi_4', \text{identity})$
	where $\pi_4'(0)=5$, $\pi_4'(5)=1$, $\pi_4'(1)=7$, $\pi_4'(7)=0$
$D'''(5)$	$= ([0,1,2,3,4,6], \pi_5', \text{identity})$
	where $\pi_5'(0)=6$, $\pi_5'(6)=3$, $\pi_5'(3)=2$, $\pi_5'(2)=1$, $\pi_5'(1)=4$, $\pi_5'(4)=0$
$D'''(6)$	$= ([0,3,5,7,9,10], \pi_6'$, <u>if</u> i=10 <u>then</u> 0 <u>else</u> i)
	where $\pi_6'(0)=7$, $\pi_6'(7)=3$, $\pi_6'(3)=5$, $\pi_6'(5)=10$, $\pi_6'(10)=9$, $\pi_6'(9)=0$
$D'''(7)$	$= ([0,1,3,4,6,8], \pi_7', \text{identity})$
	where $\pi_7'(0)=4$, $\pi_7'(4)=1$, $\pi_7'(1)=8$, $\pi_7'(8)=3$, $\pi_7'(3)=6$, $\pi_7'(6)=0$
$D'''(8)$	$= ([1,3,7], \pi_8', \text{identity})$
	where $\pi_8'(3)=7$, $\pi_8'(7)=1$, $\pi_8'(1)=3$

$D'''(9) \quad = D_\delta(9)$.

Now we can give the model. There are five states: a, b, c, d, s_0. The Seed is ($[0,11,12,13,14]$, $L_0 \times D_0$) where $L_0(0) = s_0$, $L_0(11) = a$, $L_0(12) = b$, $L_0(13) = c$, $L_0(14) = d$. We shall need four other configurations:

$\alpha = ([0,4,5], L_\alpha \times D_\alpha)$ where $L_\alpha(0) = s_0$, $L_\alpha(4) = L_\alpha(5) = a$

$\beta = ([0,1,2,3], L_\beta \times D_\beta)$ where $L_\beta(0) = s_0$, $L_\beta(1) = L_\beta(2) = L_\beta(3) = b$

$\epsilon = ([0,7,8], L_\epsilon \times D_\epsilon)$ where $L_\epsilon(0) = s_0$, $L_\epsilon(7) = L_\epsilon(8) = c$

$\delta = ([0,6,9], L_\delta \times D_\delta)$ where $L_\delta(0) = s_0$, $L_\delta(6) = L_\delta(9) = d$.

The rule repertoire is: (A, true, $(\alpha,\emptyset)$), (b, true, $(\beta,\emptyset)$), (c, true, $(\epsilon,\emptyset)$), (d, true, $(\delta,\emptyset)$). To find a new member of the language, we can choose the functions ρ and τ given by:

$$\rho(11) = (\alpha,\emptyset) \quad \rho(12) = (\beta,\emptyset) \quad \rho(13) = (\epsilon,\emptyset) \quad \rho(14) = (\delta,\emptyset)$$
$$\tau(11) = [4,5] \quad \tau(12) = [1,2,3] \quad \tau(13) = [7,8] \quad \tau(14) = [6,9].$$

With this choice h_{11}, h_{12}, h_{13}, h_{14} are identity mappings and we get:

$B'' = [1,2,3,4,5,6,7,8,9]$	$L''(0) = s_0$
$L''(1) = L_\beta(1) = b$	$D''(1) = D_\beta(1)$
$L''(2) = L_\beta(2) = b$	$D''(2) = D_\beta(2)$
$L''(3) = L_\beta(3) = b$	$D''(3) = D_\beta(3)$
$L''(4) = L_\alpha(4) = a$	$D''(4) = D_\alpha(4)$
$L''(5) = L_\alpha(5) = a$	$D''(5) = D_\alpha(5)$
$L''(6) = L_\delta(6) = d$	$D''(6) = D_\delta(6)$
$L''(7) = L_\epsilon(7) = c$	$D''(7) = D_\epsilon(7)$
$L''(8) = L_\epsilon(8) = c$	$D''(8) = D_\epsilon(8)$
$L''(9) = L_\delta(9) = d$	$D''(9) = D_\delta(9)$

Now we patch the structures together using a function σ satisfying: $\sigma(1,2) = 11$, $\sigma(2,3) = 11$, $\sigma(1,3) = 13$, $\sigma(4,5) = 0$, $\sigma(5,4) = 12$, $\sigma(6,9) = 0$, $\sigma(9,6) = 0$, $\sigma(7,8) = 12$, $\sigma(8,7) = 12$, $\sigma(1,11) = 45$, $\sigma(1,14) = \Lambda$, $\sigma(1,13) = 87$, $\sigma(2,11) = 5$, $\sigma(2,14) = \Lambda$, $\sigma(2,13) = \Lambda$, $\sigma(3,11) = 5$, $\sigma(3,14) = 6$, $\sigma(3,13) = 78$, $\sigma(4,14) = \Lambda$, $\sigma(4,12) = 1$, $\sigma(4,13) = 7$, $\sigma(5,14) = 6$, $\sigma(5,12) = 321$, $\sigma(5,13) = \Lambda$, $\sigma(6,13) = 7$, $\sigma(6,12) = 3$, $\sigma(6,11) = 5$, $\sigma(7,11) = 4$, $\sigma(7,12) = 1, 3$, $\sigma(7,14) = 6$, $\sigma(8,11) = \Lambda$, $\sigma(8,12) = 13$, $\sigma(8,14) = \Lambda$, $\sigma(9,13) = \Lambda$, $\sigma(9,12) = \Lambda$, $\sigma(9,11) = \Lambda$. We note that all rules have empty restricitons and continue by computing:

$w(1) = 8745$, $w(2) = 5$, $w(3) = 5678$
$w(4) = 17$, $w(5) = 6321$
$w(6) = 735$, $w(9) = \Lambda$
$w(7) = 41, 36$, $w(8) = 31$.

Substituting these in D'' gives:

$$\text{Seed} \rightarrow ([0,1,2,3,4,5,6,7,8,9], L'', D''').$$

BIBLIOGRAPHY

BIBLIOGRAPHY ON L SYSTEMS

prepared by

K. P. LEE

Department of Computer Science
State University of New York at Buffalo
4226 Ridge Lea Road
Amherst, New York 14226
U.S.A.

G. ROZENBERG

Mathematical Institute
Utrecht University
Utrecht - De Uithof
The Netherlands

and

Department of Mathematics
Antwerp University, UIA
Universiteitsplein 1
2610 Wilrijk, Belgium

[1] R. Baker and G.T. Herman, CELIA - a cellular linear iterative array simulator, _Proceedings of the Fourth Conference on Applications of Simulation_, 1970, 64-73.

[2] R. Baker and G.T. Herman, Simulation of organisms using a developmental model, Part I: Basic description, _International Journal of Bio-Medical Computing_, 1972, v.3, 201-215.

[3] R. Baker and G.T. Herman, Simulation of organisms using a developmental model, Part II: The heterocyst formation problem in blue-green algae, _International Journal of Bio-Medical Computing_, 1972, v.3, 251-267.

[4] J. Berstel, Une remarque sur certains langages de Lindenmayer, unpublished manuscript.

[5] M. Blattner, The unsolvability of the equality problem for sentential forms of context-free grammars, _Journal of Computer and System Sciences_, 1973, v.7, 463-468.

[6] P.A. Christensen, Hyper AFL's and ET0L systems, Masters' thesis, University of Aarhus, 1974.

[7] K. Čulik II, On some families of languages related to developmental systems, to appear in International Journal of Computer Mathematics.

[8] K. Čulik II and T.S.E. Maibaum, Parallel rewriting on terms, to appear in Proceedings of the Second Colloquium on Automata, Languages and Programming, Saarbrücken, July, 1974.

[9] K. Čulik II and J. Opatrný, Macro 0L systems, submitted for publication.

[10] K. Čulik II and J. Opatrný, Literal homomorphisms of 0L languages, to appear in International Journal of Computer Mathematics.

[11] K. Čulik II and J. Opatrný, Context in parallel rewriting, submitted for publication.

[12] D. van Dalen, A note on some systems of Lindenmayer, Mathematical Systems Theory, 1971, v.5, 128-140.

[13] P. Doucet, Some results on 0L-languages, in Abstracts of the IV International Congres for Logic, Methodology and Philosophy of Science, Bucarest, 1971.

[14] P. Doucet, On the membership question in some Lindenmayer systems, Indagationes Mathematicae, 1972, v.34, 45-52.

[15] P. Doucet, The growth of word length in D0L systems, University of Aarhus, Computer Science Department, technical report No.15, 1973, 83-94.

[16] P.J. Downey, 0L systems, Developmental systems and recursion schemes, extended abstract.

[17] A. Ehrenfeucht and G. Rozenberg, A limit theorem for sets of subwords in deterministic T0L systems, Information Processing Letters, 1973, v.2, 70-73.

[18] A. Ehrenfeucht, K.P. Lee and G. Rozenberg, Subword complexities of various classes of deterministic developmental languages without interactions, submitted for publication.

[19] A. Ehrenfeucht and G. Rozenberg, Some ET0L languages which are not deterministic, Technical Report CU-CS-018-73, Department of Computer Science, University of Colorado.

[20] A. Ehrenfeucht and G. Rozenberg, The equality of E0L languages and codings of 0L languages, to appear in International Journal of Computer Mathematics.

[21] A. Ehrenfeucht and G. Rozenberg, A note on the structure of polynomially bounded D0L systems, submitted for publication.

[22] A. Ehrenfeucht and G. Rozenberg, A characterization theorem for a subclass of ET0L languages, submitted for publication.

[23] A. Ehrenfeucht and G. Rozenberg, Three useful results concerning L-languages without interactions.

[24] A. Ehrenfeucht and G. Rozenberg, The number of occurrences of letters versus their distribution in some E0L languages, to appear in Information and Control.

[25] A. Ehrenfeucht and G. Rozenberg, Trade-off between the use of nonterminals, codings and homomorphisms in defining languages for some classes of rewriting systems, to appear in Proceedings of the Second Colloquium on Automata, Languages and Programming, Saarbrücken, July, 1974.

[26] A. Ehrenfeucht, K.P. Lee and G. Rozenberg, Generatively deterministic L languages. Subword point of view.

[27] A. Ehrenfeucht and G. Rozenberg, Nonterminals versus homomorphisms

in defining languages for some classes of rewriting systems, submitted for publication.

[28] H. Feliciangeli and G.T. Herman, Algorithms for producing grammars from sample derivations: A common problem of formal language theory and developmental biology, Journal of Computer and System Sciences, 1973, v.7, 97-118.

[29] D. Frijters, Growth and flowering of Aster: basically a T1L system, working report, Theoretical Biology Group, Utrecht University, The Netherlands.

[30] S. Ginsburg and B. Rovan, Word-length and D0L languages, submitted for publication.

[31] S. Ginsburg and G. Rozenberg, T0L systems and control sets, to appear in Information and Control.

[32] F.H. Hellendoorn and A. Lindenmayer, Experimental and computer studies on transitional phyllotaxis in Bryophyllum, manuscript.

[33] G.T. Herman, The computing ability of a developmental model for filamentous organisms, Journal of Theoretical Biology, 1969, v.25, 421-435.

[34] G.T. Herman, Role of environment in developmental models, Journal of Theoretical Biology, 1970, v.29, 329-341.

[35] G.T. Herman, Closure properties of some families of languages associated with biological systems, Information and Control, 1974, v.24, 101-121.

[36] G.T. Herman, Models for cellular interactions in development without polarity of individual cells. Part I: General discription and the problem of universal computing ability, International Journal

of Systems Sciences, 1971, v.2, 271-289.

[37] G.T. Herman, Models for cellular interactions in development without polarity of individual cells. Part II: Problems of synchronization and regulation, International Journal of Systems Sciences, 1972, v.3, 149-175.

[38] G.T. Herman, Polar organisms with apolar individual cells, in Logic, Methodology and Philosophy of Science IV, edited by P. Suppes et al, North-Holland, Amsterdam, 1973.

[39] G.T. Herman, A biologically motivated extension of Algol-like languages, Information and Control, 1973, v.22, 487-502.

[40] G.T. Herman, K.P. Lee, J. van Leeuwen and G. Rozenberg, Characterization of unary developmental languages, Discrete Mathematics, 1973, v.6, 235-247.

[41] G.T. Herman, K.P. Lee, J. van Leeuwen and G. Rozenberg, Unary developmental systems and languages, Departmental report 23-72, Department of Computer Science, State University of New York at Buffalo, 1972.

[42] G.T. Herman, A. Lindenmayer and G. Rozenberg, Description of developmental languages using recurrence systems, to appear in Mathematical Systems Theory.

[43] G.T. Herman and W.H. Liu, The daugther of CELIA, the French flag and the firing squad, abstract in Proceedings of the 1973 Winter Simulation Conference, Simulation, 1973, v.21, 33-41.

[44] G.T. Herman, W.H. Liu, S. Rowland and A. Walker, Synchronization of growing cellular arrays, Quarterly Bulletin of the Center for Theoretical Biology, State University of New York at Buffalo, 1972, v.5, No.2, 143-196, to appear in Information and Control.

[45] G.T. Herman and G. Rozenberg, Developmental systems and languages, to be published by North-Holland Publishing Company, (September 1974).

[46] G.T. Herman and A. Walker, The syntactic inference problem as applied to biological systems, in "Machine Intelligence 7", edited by B. Meltzer and D. Michie, Edinburgh University Press, 1972, 347-356.

[47] G.T. Herman and A. Walker, Context-free languages in biological systems, to appear in International Journal of Computer Mathematics.

[48] P. Hogeweg and B. Hesper, A model study of bio-morphological description, to appear in Pattern Recognition.

[49] A.K. Joshi and L.S. Levy, Developmental tree adjunct grammars, extended abstract.

[50] J. Karhumäki, An example of a PD2L system with the growth type $2\frac{1}{2}$, Information Processing Letters, 1974, v.2, 131-134.

[51] K.P. Lee, Inclusion properties of unary developmental languages, Masters' project, Department of Computer Science, State University of New York at Buffalo, 1972.

[52] K.P. Lee and G. Rozenberg, The length sets of DOL languages are uniformly bounded, to appear in Information Processing Letters.

[53] J. van Leeuwen, Canonical restrictions of Lindenmayer languages, in Abstracts of the IVth International Congress for Logic, Methodology and Philosophy of Science, Bucharest, 1971.

[54] J. van Leeuwen, A note on uniform Lindenmayer-languages, unpublished manuscript.

[55] J. van Leeuwen, Pre-set pushdown automata and 0L grammars, University of California, Berkeley, Computer Science Technical Report 10, 1973.

[56] J. van Leeuwen, Hyper AFL's and all preset PDA languages are indexed, memorandum, 1973,

[57] J. van Leeuwen, F-iteration languages, extended abstract, 1973.

[58] J. van Leeuwen, The complexity of developmental languages, extended abstract, 1973.

[59] A. Lindenmayer, Mathematical models for cellular interactions in development, Part I, Journal of Theoretical Biology, 1968, v.18, 280-299.

[60] A. Lindenmayer, Mathematical models for cellular interactions in development, Part II, Journal of Theoretical Biology, 1968, v.18, 300-315.

[61] A. Lindenmayer, Developmental systems without cellular interactions, their languages and grammars, Journal of Theoretical Biology, 1971, v.30, 455-484.

[62] A. Lindenmayer, Cellular automata, formal languages and developmental systems, in Logic, Methodology and Philosophy of Science IV, edited by P. Suppes et al, North-Holland, Amsterdam, 1973.

[63] A. Lindenmayer, Polarity, symmetry and development, manuscript.

[64] A. Lindenmayer, Growth functions of multicellular organisms and cellular programs, Abstracts of the 10th Symposium on Biomathematics and Computer Science in the Life Sciences, Houston, March, 1973.

[65] A. Lindenmayer, Development of multicellular organisms viewed as

parallel rewriting without nonterminal symbols, Workshop on Parallel Rewriting Systems, Hamilton, Canada, March, 1973.

[66] A. Lindenmayer and G. Rozenberg, Developmental systems and languages, Proceedings of the Fourth ACM Symposium on Theory of Computing, 1972, 214-221.

[67] W.H. Liu, CELIA user's manual, Department of Computer Science, State University of New York at Buffalo, 1972.

[68] H.B. Lück, Zellproduktion und Form, Acta Bot. Neerlandica, 1973, v.22, 251-252.

[69] B. Mayoh, Mathematical models for cellular organisms, University of Aarhus, Computer Science Department, technical report No. 12, 1973.

[70] M. Nielsen, On the decidability of some equivalence problems for D0L systems, to appear in Information and Control.

[71] M. Nielsen, G. Rozenberg, A. Salomaa and S. Skyum, Nonterminals, homomorphisms and codings in different variations of 0L systems. Part I. Deterministic systems, submitted for publication.

[72] M. Nielsen, G. Rozenberg, A. Salomaa and S. Skyum, Nonterminals, homomorphisms and codings in different variations of 0L systems. Part II. Nondeterministic systems, submitted for publication.

[73] M. Novotný, Operators reducing generalized 0L systems, manuscript.

[74] A. Paz, Similarity in DT0L and related problems, State University of New York at Stony Brook, Department of Computer Science, technical report No.15, 1973.

[75] A. Paz and A Salomaa, Integral sequential word functions and growth equivalence of Lindenmayer systems, Information and Control,

1973, v.23, 313-343.

[76] W. Pollul and D. Schütt, Characterization of growth in deterministic Lindenmayer systems, submitted for publication.

[77] A. Reedy and W.J. Savitch, Ambiguity in developmental systems, extended abstract.

[78] G. Rozenberg, Some results on 0L-languages, Elektr. Rekencentr. Utrecht Publ., No.93, 1970.

[79] G. Rozenberg, On some properties of propagating D0L systems, Part I, Elektr. Rekencentr. Utrecht Publ., No.106, 1971.

[80] G. Rozenberg, The equivalence problem for deterministic T0L systems is undecidable, Information Processing Letters, 1972, v.1, 201-204; Errata, 252.

[81] G. Rozenberg, T0L systems and languages, Information and Control, 1973, v.23, 357-381.

[82] G. Rozenberg, D0L sequences, Discrete Mathematics, 1974, v.7, 323-347.

[83] G. Rozenberg, Circularities in D0L sequences, to appear in Revue Roum. de Math. Pures et Appl.

[84] G. Rozenberg, Direct proofs of the undecidability of the equivalence problem for sentential forms of linear context-free grammars and the equivalence problem for 0L systems, Information Processing Letters, 1972, v.1, 233-235.

[85] G. Rozenberg, On 0L-systems with restricted use of productions, to appear in Journal of Computer and System Sciences.

[86] G. Rozenberg, L-systems with interactions: the hierarchy, Depart-

mental report 28-72, Department of Computer Science, State University of New York at Buffalo, 1972.

[87] G. Rozenberg, Propagating L-systems with interactions, Departmental report 29-72, Department of Computer Science, State University of New York at Buffalo, 1972.

[88] G. Rozenberg, L-systems with interactions, to appear in Journal of Computer and System Sciences.

[89] G. Rozenberg, Extension of tabled OL-systems and languages, International Journal of Computer and Information Sciences, 1973, v.2, 311-334.

[90] G. Rozenberg, On a family of acceptors for some classes of developmental languages, to appear in International Journal of Computer Mathematics.

[91] G. Rozenberg and P. Doucet, On OL-languages, Information and Control, 1971, v.19, 302-318.

[92] G. Rozenberg and K.P. Lee, Some properties of the class of L-languages with interactions, submitted for publication, available as technical report.

[93] G. Rozenberg and K.P. Lee, Developmental systems with finite axiom sets, Part I. Systems without interactions, to appear in International Journal of Computer Mathematics.

[94] G. Rozenberg and K.P. Lee, Developmental systems with finite axiom sets, Part II. Systems with interactions, to appear in International Journal of Computer Mathematics.

[95] G. Rozenberg and A. Lindenmayer, Developmental systems with locally catenative formulas, Acta Informatica, 1973, v.2, 214-248.

[96] G. Rozenberg and D. Wood, Generative models for parallel processes, submitted for publication, available as technical report.

[97] K. Ruohonen, Some regenerative Lindenmayer models, Thesis, University of Turku, 1974.

[98] A. Salomaa, On exponential growth in Lindenmayer systems, Indagationes Mathematicae, 1973, v.35, 23-30.

[99] A. Salomaa, On sentential forms of context-free grammars, Acta Informatica, 1973, v.2, 40-49.

[100] A. Salomaa, Solution of a decision problem concerning unary Lindenmayer systems, to appear in Discrete Mathematics.

[101] A. Salomaa, Developmental languages - a new type of formal languages, Annals of the University of Turku, 1973, Ser.B 126, 183-189.

[102] A. Salomaa, "Lindenmayer systems: parallel rewriting without terminals", Paragraph 13 in Part II of "Formal Languages", Academic Press, May, 1973.

[103] A. Salomaa, Macros, iterated substitution and Lindenmayer AFL's, University of Aarhus, Computer Science Department, technical report No. 18, 1973.

[104] A. Salomaa, On some recent problems concerning developmental languages, Proceedings of the Conference on Automata and Formal Languages, Bonn, July, 1973, to appear.

[105] A. Salomaa, On some decidability problems concerning developmental languages, Proceedings of the Third Scandinavian Logic Symposium, North-Holland Publishing Company, to appear.

[106] A. Salomaa, Growth functions associated with some new types of grammars, Proceedings of the Conference on Algebraic Automata Theory, Szeged, August, 1973, to appear.

[107] A. Salomaa, L-systems: a device in biologically motivated automata theory, Proceedings of the Conference on Mathematical Foundations of Computer Science, High Tatras, September, 1973, 147-151.

[108] W.J. Savitch, Some characterizations of Lindenmayer systems in terms of Chomsky-type grammars and stack machines, submitted for publication.

[109] R. Siromoney and G. Siromoney, Parallel 0-Lindenmayer languages, manuscript.

[110] V. Surapipith and A. Lindenmayer, Thioguanine-dependent light sensivity of perithecial initiation in Sordaria fimicola, J.Gen. Microb., 1969, v.57, 227-237.

[111] A.L. Szilard, Growth functions of Lindenmayer systems, University of Western Ontario, Computer Science Department, Technical Report No.4, 1971.

[112] A.H. Veen and A. Lindenmayer, A computer model for phyllotaxis based on diffusion of an inhibitor on a cylindrical surface, manuscript, part of M.S. thesis of A.H. Veen, Moore School of Electrical Engineering, University of Pennsylvania, Philadelphia, 1973.

[113] P. Vitányi, Context-variable Lindenmayer systems and some simple regenerative structures, technical report No. NR 24/72, Mathematisch Centrum, Amsterdam, 1972.

[114] P. Vitányi, DOL-languages and a feasible solution for a word problem, technical report No. MR 138/72, Mathematisch Centrum, Amsterdam, 1972.

[115] P. Vitányi, Growth of strings in parallel rewriting systems, extended abstract.

[116] P. Vitányi, Structure of growth in Lindenmayer systems, Indagationes Mathematicae, 1973, v.35, 247-253.

[117] P. Vitányi, A note on nonrecursive and deterministic Lindenmayer languages, technical report No. IW 11/73, Mathematisch Centrum, Amsterdam, 1973.

[118] A. Walker, Dynamically stable strings in developmental systems and the Chomsky hierarchy, extended abstract.